한국 인권문제

민주화 관련 기타 자료 1

한국 인권문제

민주화 관련 기타 자료 1

한국학술정보

| 머리말

　일제 강점기 독립운동과 병행되었던 한국의 인권운동은 해방이 되었음에도 큰 결실을 보지 못했다. 1950년대 반공을 앞세운 이승만 정부와 한국전쟁, 역시 경제발전과 반공을 내세우다 유신 체제에 이르렀던 박정희 정권, 쿠데타로 집권한 1980년대 전두환 정권까지, 한국의 인권은 이를 보장해야 할 국가와 정부에 의해 도리어 억압받고 침해되었다. 이런 배경상 근대 한국의 인권운동은 반독재, 민주화운동과 결을 같이했고, 대체로 국외에 본부를 둔 인권 단체나 정치로부터 상대적으로 자유로운 종교 단체에 의해 주도되곤 했다. 이는 1980년 5·18광주민주화운동을 계기로 보다 근적인 변혁을 요구하는 형태로 조직화되었고, 그 활동 영역도 정치를 넘어 노동자, 농민, 빈민 등으로 확대되었다. 이들이 없었다면 한국은 1987년 군부 독재 종식하고 절차적 민주주의를 도입할 수 없었을 것이다. 민주화 이후에도 수많은 어려움이 있었지만, 한국의 인권운동은 점차 전문적이고 독립된 운동으로 분화되며 더 많은 이들의 참여를 이끌어냈고, 지금까지 많은 결실을 맺을 수 있었다.

　본 총서는 1980년대 중반부터 1990년대 초반까지, 외교부에서 작성하여 30여 년간 유지했던 한국 인권문제와 관련한 국내외 자료를 담고 있다. 6월 항쟁이 일어나고 민주화 선언이 이뤄지는 등 한국 인권운동에 많은 변화가 있었던 시기다. 당시 인권문제와 관련한 국내외 사안들, 각종 사건에 대한 미국과 우방국, 유엔의 반응, 최초의 한국 인권보고서 제출과 아동의 권리에 관한 협약 과정, 유엔인권위원회 활동, 기타 민주화 관련 자료 등 총 18권으로 구성되었다. 전체 분량은 약 9천여 쪽에 이른다.

2024년 3월

한국학술정보(주)

┃ 일러두기

· 본 총서에 실린 자료는 2022년 4월과 2023년 4월에 각각 공개한 외교문서 4,827권, 76만 여 쪽 가운데 일부를 발췌한 것이다.

· 각 권의 제목과 순서는 공개된 원본을 최대한 반영하였으나, 주제에 따라 일부는 적절히 변경하였다.

· 원본 자료는 A4 판형에 맞게 축소하거나 원본 비율을 유지한 채 A4 페이지 안에 삽입하였다. 또한 현재 시점에선 공개되지 않아 '공란'이란 표기만 있는 페이지 역시 그대로 실었다.

· 외교부가 공개한 문서 각 권의 첫 페이지에는 '정리 보존 문서 목록'이란 이름으로 기록물 종류, 일자, 명칭, 간단한 내용 등의 정보가 수록되어 있으며, 이를 기준으로 0001번부터 번호가 매겨져 있다. 이는 삭제하지 않고 총서에 그대로 수록하였다.

· 보고서 내용에 관한 더 자세한 정보가 필요하다면, 외교부가 온라인상에 제공하는 『대한민국 외교사료요약집』 1991년과 1992년 자료를 참조할 수 있다.

| 차례

기록물종류	문서-일반공문서철	등록번호	27520	등록일자	2007-04-24
분류번호	701	국가코드	CN	주제	
문서철명	한국 인권문제에 대한 카나다 관계기관의 문의, 1985-86				
생산과	북미과	생산년도	1985 - 1986	보존기간	영구
담당과(그룹)	외교정책	정책총괄		서가번호	--
참조분류					
권차명					
내용목차	* 강종헌, 이철, 서준식, 김근태, 카나다 기독단체 성명문 등 * 2016년 공개대상				

마/이/크/로/필/름/사/항

촬영연도	*롤 번호	화일 번호	후레임 번호	보관함 번호

0001

위
要341

협 조 문	응신기일 198 . .
분류기호 및 문서번호 감사 125.4-462	제목 민원서류 송부
수 신 미주국장	발신일자 : 198 5 . 8 . 6 .

85. 8. 1.자 당부에 접수된 별첨 민원서류는 「강종흔의 구속에 대한 재검토 요청」 내용으로 발신인의 주소가 없는 바, 귀국으로 송부하니 업무에 참고하시기 바랍니다.

첨부 : 민원서류 1부. 끝.

감   사   관

0002

1205 - 8 A
1981. 12. 1 승인

190mm×268mm(인쇄용지(2급)60g/m²)
가 33 - 41   1984. 10. 10.

His Excellency Lee Won-kyong
Ministry of Foreign Affairs
I Sejong-no
Chongno-gu
Seoul
Republic of Korea

Your Excellency:

May I urgently and respectfully request you to intervene on
behalf of Kang Jong-hon, presently serving a 20 year term in
Taejon Prison, Choongnam (prison number 3595).

Kang Jong-hon was arrested in Seoul in November, 1975 and
charged under the National Security Act. I am distressed to
hear reports that the conditions under which his confession
was obtained were in violation of Article II (2) of the
Constitution of the Republic of Korea, which states: "No
citizen shall be tortured or be compelled to testify against
himself in criminal cases".

I would humbly ask you to investigate this case in light of
my petition.

Yours respectfully and sincerely,

Alison Cude
Alison Cude

0003

기 안 용 지

분류기호 문서번호	미북 700-	(전화번호)	전결규정	조 항
				전결사항

처리기간	3일 요함	장 관
시행일자	1985. 9. 23.	
보존연한		

보 조 기 관	국 장 전결	심 의 관	협
	과 장		

| 기안책임자 | 위성락 | 북 미 과 |

경 유	
수 신	법무부장관
참 조	교정국장
제 목	수감자 관련자료 협조 요청

발송 No. 1985. 9. 24 외무부

검열 1985. 9. 24 통제관

본국 인권단체로 부터

주한카나다대사관은 하기 수감자에 대한 문의가 빈번히

제기되고 있다고 전제, 동인들의 범죄사실, 현황, 향후 전망등을

문의하여 왔으니 동 내용을 당부에 송부하여 주시기 바랍니다.

1. 강종헌 (Kang Jong-Hon)

　　ㅇ 1951.9.16 생

　　ㅇ 1975년 구속

　　ㅇ 대구교도소 복역중 (번호 3244)

　　ㅇ 재일교포

2. 이 철

　　ㅇ 1948.10.7 생

　　ㅇ 1975년 구속

　　ㅇ 대구교도소 복역중 (번호 3603)

　　ㅇ 재일교포

정서
관인
발송

0004

1205-25 (2-1) A (잡)
1981. 12. 18 승인

정 직 질 서 창 조

190mm × 268mm (인쇄용지 2급 60g/㎡)
가 33 - 41 1985. 2. 6

10   한국 인권문제 민주화 관련 기타 자료 1

3. 이강옹 (Lee Kwang Ung)

    ° 45세가량

    ° 1982.11 구속

    ° 광주고도소 복역중 (번호 2947)

    ° 오송회 사건 관련자.   끝.

0005

통 화 요 록
----

1. 일 시 : 1985.9.27(금) 11:40
2. 송 화 자 : 법무부 보안과 김규천 사무관
3. 수 화 자 : 북미과 워성락 사무관
4. 내 용

김사무관 : 주한카대사관의 수감자 현황자료 요청건에
대하여 해당자들이 재일교포 간첩단 사건
관련자이기 때문에 공안적 차원에서 사건
상세를 공개하지 않는 방침으로 임해왔음.
공개할 경우 안기부와 협조해야 함.
현재상태 및 전망도 특기할 사항이 없는바
문서로 회신을 하지않고 전화통보로 대체
하였으면 좋겠음.

워사무관 : 귀측에서 통보가능한 내용을 알려주기 바람.

김사무관 : 현재 동인들의 상태는 이상없으며 정상적인
복역생활을 하고있음. 향후 전망도 일반론
적으로 동인들의 복역성적에 달려있는 문제
이나 현재로서 이렇다할 전망이 없음.
법무부로서는 동인들의 현황이나 전망을 계속

공람	북미과	분석미제과일	담당	과장	심의관	국장	차관보	차관	장관
			51	차형					

85 10.2   09:40   Issac에게 관련통보

0006

문의함으로서 말썽의 소지를 만들려는
사례에 많이 접한바 있음.

워사무관 : 알겠음.   끝.

0007

면 담 요 록

1. 일   시 : 1985년 10 월 7 일(월 요일)16:00 시 ~ 17:00 시

2. 장   소 : 북미과

3. 면 담 자 : 이양 북미과장

       Sheppy 주한카나다대사관 참사관

       (위성락 사무관 배석)

4. 내   용 :

   참사관 : 금일 말씀드리고자 하는 사항은 본국의 훈령에 따른 것이
            아니고 순전히 비공식적으로 의견을 고환하고 협조를
            구하고자 하는 사항임.

            카나다는 전통적으로 인권문제에 관심을 가져왔으며
            유권자들의 관심도 큼. 본인은 지난 2년간 본부에서
            한국 담당을 하였는데 그동안 카나다는 이문제에 별로
            active 하지 않았음. 그런데 멀로니 수상 방한과 관련
            상황이 변화할 가능성이 있음.

공람	북미과	접수년월일	담 당	과 장	심의관	국 장	차관보	차 관	장 관
			이	서	虎	乙			

0008

즉 국내 인권단체나 종교 단체로 부터 제기되어온
압력이 명년초의 멀로니 수상 방한에 즈음하여
가중될 것으로 예상됨. 멀로니 수상은 이문제에 적극
적인(positive)사람임.

또 다른 이유로 클라크 외상이 인권문제에 많은 관심을
가지고 있다는 점을 들수 있음.

이러한 상황에서 근래 국내 인권단체등이 나름 대로의
정보를 기초로 unbalanced picture 를 제시하는
경우가 많은 데 카나다 정부가 보다 정확한 정보를 가지고
이에 대처할수 있다면 문제의 제기를 미리 막을수 있다고
보아 구속자의 현황등 정보제공에 가능한 협조를 요청
하고 자함.

즉 본인은 제기되지 않아야 할 시점에서 문제가 제기
되는 것을 막기위해 주 한대사관의 입장에서balanced picture
를   reporting back하려고 함.

과 장 : 우선 오늘은 주로 귀하의 설명을 듣겠음. 그런데 귀하는
         멀로니 수상 방한시 인권문제가 제기되리라고 보는지?

참사관 : 멀로니 수상 방한시기가 가까와지면 인권단체들의 로비
         활동이 극심해 질것을 우려하는 것임.

- 2 -

0009

과 장 :   개인적인 생각이지만 멀로니 수상이 방한시에 이 문제를
          제기하는 것은 diplomatic 하지 않다고 보며 이 문제를
          제기하기 보다 한·카 양국관계 강화 방안을 토의하고
          싶어 할 것으로 믿음. 귀하는 어떠한 점이 한국의 인권
          문제라고 보는지 ?

참사관 :   본인의 representation에 오해가 없기 바람. 본인 개인적으로
          한국의 인권문제에 이렇다할 의견이 없음. 여기온 목적은
          협조를 구하고자 하는 것임.

          수상 또한 이 문제를 제기하고 싶지 않을 것임.
          본인으로서는 사소한 문제라도 양국관계에 불필요한 문제의
          제기를 미연에 대처해 나가자는 데 취지가 있음.

과 장 :   알다시피 인권문제에 대한 정의와 perception 이 아주
          다양함. 공산주의에 대한 입장은 나라마다 다르지 않은가?
          귀측이 문의해온 사안은 공산주의 간첩단 사건이었으며
          인권 문제와는 무관한 것임. 본인이 귀측의 문의를 받고
          맨먼저 가진 우려는 카나다내 일부 친공 계열이 수감되어
          있는 공산주의자들에 관한 불필요한 문제 야기를 위해
          카나다 대사관을 이용하려 하지 않나 하는 것이었음.

- 3 -

0010

참사관 : 본인은 랑군 사태, 칼사건때 한국 담당이었으며 한국의
지정학적위치, 남·북 대치 상황들을 잘알고 있어 귀하의
견해에 동의함.

그러나 카나다내 인권단체들의 perception 을
바꿀수는 없는만큼 국내 압력이 올라감에 따라 이에
대처하여 주한대사관이 제시하는 사실도 보다 자세해져야
할것으로 생각하는 것임.

본인이 이문제를 제기하는 것이 아니고 협조 관계를
희망하는 것임.

과 장 : 귀하의 개인적 입장은 이해할수도 있으나, 주한카나다
대사관이 갑자기 이러한 문제를 제기하는데 대해 unhappy
하게 생각함.

귀하는 카나다내 인권단체가 북한의 인권에 대해 문제를
제기하는 것을 본 적이 있는지?

참사관 : 북한의 인권문제가 terrible 하다고 생각하며 카나다가
북한의 인권문제를 제기하지 않는것은 unfair 하다고
생각함.

과 장 : 그렇다면 그들은 한국에 대해 unfair 하게 대하는것이
아닌가? 그런점을 카나다 정부가 설명하면 되지 않겠는가?

- 4 -

0011

참사관 : 본인의 뜻을 절대 오해하지 말기 바람. 다른 뜻이
없으며 이 문제에 관하여 협조 하자는 뜻 뿐임.
귀하의 반응에 놀랐음.

과 장 : 본인도 귀하의 설명에 놀란것이 사실임. 한·카 양국
관계에 있어서 인권문제가 거론 되리라고는 전혀
예상치 못했음. 앞으로 사실 확인에 관한 문제는
가능한한 협조 하겠음.

참사관 : 내년초 수상 방한과 즈음하여 이문제가 크게 번질것을
우려하는 이외 다른뜻은 없음. 가능한한 협조 바람.

끝.

0012

통 화 요 록
----

1. 일   시 : 85.10.11(금), 16:20

2. 송 화 자 : 법무부 검찰 3과 이정섭 사무관

3. 수 화 자 : 위성락 사무관

4. 내   용 (김병곤, 황인하의 범죄사실 관련)

   이사무관 : 상부에 보고한 결과, 동인들의 범죄사실을
              외국인이 이해못할 면도 있어 이를 알리지
              않기로 하였음.

   위사무관 : 아국 실정법을 위반한 범죄사실을 비공개로
              한다는것은 불필요한 오해를 야기할수 있으므로
              범죄배경등은 제외한 범죄사실과 현재의 상태만
              알려주기 바람.

   이사무관 : 알겠음.

            (이하 이사무관 통보 내용)

가. 범죄사실

  ㅇ 김병곤 (EYC 총무부장), 황인하(민청년 상임위의장)

   : 85.6.27, 11:00-13:00간 서울 대학에서 전학련과
     연계하여 불법집회를 주동하는등 4회에 걸쳐
     집시법 위반   85. 10. 15 11:00 Issac 에게
                                   통보
                                 (Issac
                                  위선락과 의
                                  하번 사이이
                                  먹으러가 말습니다
                                  진사)

공 답	열 람 미 제	담 당	과 장	심의관	국 장	차관보	차 관	장 관
		이	화	鄭 김				

0013

　　　　　ｏ 김병곤 ： 85.2.5, 17:00 파고 다공원 앞, 반정부
　　　　　　　　　　　 구호를 외치고 유인물 살포

　　　　　ｏ 황인하 ： 85.2.22 기독교회관에서 반정부 유인물
　　　　　　　　　　　 작성 배포

　　나. 구속사유
　　　　ｏ 집시법 위반
　　　　ｏ 국가모독, 허위사실 유포

　　다. 법적상태
　　　　ｏ 김병곤 ： 85.7.15 구속
　　　　　　　　　　 85.8.9 기소
　　　　　　　　　　 85.10.7 1회 공판
　　　　ｏ 황인하 ： 85.7.15 구속
　　　　　　　　　　 85.8.9 기소
　　　　　　　　　　 85.10.4 1회 공판

0014

주 카 나 다 대 사 관

−51(村)

카나다(정) 700 − 68   1985. 10. 17.

수   신 : 장 관

참   조 : 미주국장

제   목 : 수감자 관련 건의

                대 : 미북 700 − 1402(85. 5. 10)

        대호 수감자 서준식과 관련, 당지 Amnesty International 지부,
종교단체, 개인명의등의 진정서한이 이따금씩 당관에 내도하고 있는 바, 이에대해
당관은 별첨(안) 설명자료를 작성, 송부함으로써 동 진정 단체 및 진정인에 대해
이해를 구하고저 건의 하오니 회시하여 주시기 바랍니다.

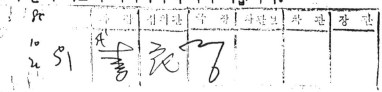

유   첨 : 설명서한(안) 1부.   끝.

일반문서로 재분류, 86. 12. 31)

주   카   나   다   대

0015

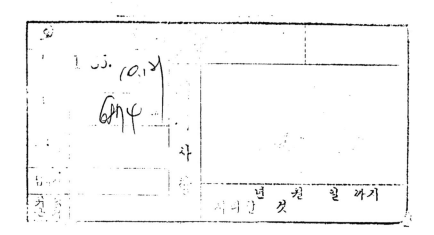

In reference to your letter dated   , regarding
the detention of Mr. Soh Joon-shik, I would like to offer an
explanation of the situation that led to his arrest.

Mr. Soh was recruited by his eldest brother, Mr. Soh Sun-
woong, a known agent of the North Korean government, in May,1970.
Acting on his brother's instructions, he was responsible not only
for putting together the underground student organization in the
Republic of Korea but also for supplying intelligence on the activities of students there.
Investigation showed Mr. Soh crossed into North Korea in August,
1970, and returned the following month later after further training.

As you are aware, the Republic and its people, believing in
the principles of democracy and liberalism, have been the focus
of continuous provocation by North Korea and its agents since the
Korea War.
We must be fully prepared to prevent any recurrence of theis aggr-
ession.
In doing so, however, we must draw a distinction between espionage
and the peaceful expression of political beliefs.
I don't think I need to point out that espionage is prohibited in
Canada also.

I regret to say that since Mr. Soh's detention at Chunju
Preventive Custody Centre, he has shown no remorse over his activities.
He even insists on encouraging and stimulating his pro-communist
ideology.
That leaves the authorities no choice, under the provisions of
the Social Safety Law, but to keep Mr. Soh isolated.

0017

I do not hesitate in the least to assure you that Mr. Soh
would be released immediately if he recanted his Communist stance
and showed appreciation of the values of democracy and freedom.

                              Yours Sincerely,

                              JUNG IL OH
                              Counsellor

기 안 용 지

분류기호 문서번호	미북 700- 2913	(전화번호)		전결규정	조 항
					전결사항

처리기간		장 관			
시행일자	1985.11.4.				
보존연한					

보 조 기 관	국 장	전 결		협	
	심의관				
	과 장	榷		조	
기 안 책 임 자	위성락	북 미 과		통	

경 유				
수 신	주 카나다 대사			
참 조				
제 목	수감자 관련 건의			

대 : 카나다 (정) 700-68 (85.10.17)

연 : 미북 700-1402 (85.5.9)

연호 송부 자료를 참조하여

서준식의 범죄사실과 해당죄명 및 현재의 법적지위등 객관적   정서

사실을 위주로 서한을 작성하여 조치하시기 바랍니다.   끝.

예 고 : 85년.원시 일반문서 (1985. 12 기)   관인

발송

V

0010

―――――"拷問·容共 造作 共同對策委"의―――――

虛構的 主張에 對한 實相

1985. 11. 8.

0020

虛構的　主張의　背景

最近　當局의　搜査結果

- 問題除籍生들의　集團인　「民靑聯」을　主導한
  金權泰가　李乙鎬（民靑聯　政策副室長）의
  〃民族・民主主議革命（ＮＤＲ）〃　理論支援을
  받아　〃民衆聯合政權〃　樹立目標로

- 〃3民鬪〃　〃깃발〃　〃서울大民推委〃
  〃僞裝就業勞鬪〃로　이어지는　學園騷擾　및
  各種　勞動紛爭　等　學・勞連帯鬪爭의　背後
  操縱者로　判明

0021

○ 金槿泰의 「民靑聯」을 背後에서 活動方向提示,
　　資金支援을 하면서 現政權打倒를 窮極的 目標로
　　活動中인 在野運動圈勢力들은

△ 前衛鬪爭戰列이 崩壞된데다

△ 自身들의 背後追窮에 對한 不安感을 느끼고
　　이를 謀免, 自身들의 企図를 隱弊, 合理化
　　시키기 爲해

△ 分明히 밝혀진 事實마저도 否認하고 〃拷問·
　　容共造作〃이라는 事實無根한 虛構的인
　　主張으로

　- 拘束者의 鬪爭意識을 鼓吹하는 한편

　- 對內外의 輿論喚起로 政府를 窮地에 몰아
　　넣으려는 發惡的인 自救行爲 恣行

0022

○ 또한 金大中·金泳三 等 「民推協」을 中心으로
   한 在野政治人들은 拷問이라는 政治外的인 人權
   問題를 잇슈로 在野運動圈団体와 連繫勢力을
   糾合, 場外 改憲鬪爭의 발판形成을 劃策

※ 所謂 〃拷問 및 容共造作沮止對策委〃라는
   不法団体를 任意的으로 結成, 11.8.19:00
   惠化洞 聖堂에서 報告大會를 開催코 世界人權
   団体에게 보내는 메시지採択 等을 企図하는
   等 事大主義的인 作態를 露骨化하고 있어 國威
   損傷 予防 및 社會安定的 次元에서 行事를
   放置할 수 없는 狀況

0023

發 足 經 緯

○ 前 民靑聯議長 金槿泰에 對한 拷問說을 契機로 民推協과 民統聯이 主軸이 되어 在野運動圈을 糾合, 對政府 鬪爭을 展開할 目的으로

△ 10.17 運動圈 代表 35名이 1次會合을 갖고 汎国民的인 共同對策委 構成에 合議

△ 準備委員 李吉載(教社協總務), 権皓景(NCC人権委 事務局長), 金炳午(民推協 副幹事長), 李富栄(民統聯 民生委員長) 等이 主軸이 되어 組織人選 作業

○ 이들 準備委員들은 當局에 依해 準備모임(10.24, 10.29)이 沮止되자 11.4 基督教會舘에서 奇襲的으로 發起文과 構成員 名單을 發表, 同團体 發起節次로 看做

△ 顧 問(9名): 金大中, 金泳三, 李敏雨, 文益煥, 洪南淳 等

△ 共同代表(14名): 桂勳悌, 楊淳稙, 金勝勳, 朴炯圭, 白基玩, 宋建鎬 等

0024

△ 對策委員 (241名) :

```
            <階 層 別   分 布>
 -  民  推  協 :   51名
 -  新  韓  黨 :   50名
 -  運動圈 団体 ( 18個 ) :  61名
 -  改  新  教 :   33名
 -  天  主  教 :   24名
 -  仏     教 :   10名
 -  拘束者 家族 :   12名
```

※ 組織規模를 誇示하기 위해 本人의 受諾도 없이 一方
　的으로 多數 包含

| 団 体 性 格 |

○ 人權問題 等 非政治的 잇슈로 出帆

△ 國內外 關心 喚起

△ 在野 宗教界 勢力의 同参 誘導

△ 直接的인 政治的 잇슈 隱蔽로 對國民 同調輿論 造成

△ 與圈 政界의 正面 對立을 回避하면서 在野運動圈 団体
　를 總結集

0025

령-20 83. 8. 1

-5-

○ 非政治性 團体를 標榜, 野圈의 改憲 鬪爭을 위한 場外
政治의 主体로 變貌 確実視

○ 場內政治의 制限性과 野黨內의 各系派間 利害相反 等을
克服하고 民推協 (共同議長 : 金大中 , 金泳三) 側에서 對与
鬪爭의 優位 先占을 위한 前衛 組織으로 活用 可能性
多分

活 動 戰 略

○ 隨時 人權 蹂躪 및 拷問事例集 發刊 配布로 國內外
輿論 喚起

○ 拷問 및 暴力根絕을 위한 汎國民的 署名 運動 展開

○ 拘束学生에 對한 國家保安法 適用 撤回要求 및 이른바
〃良心囚〃의 釋放運動 支援

○ 窮極的으로 民主化를 標榜한 汎國民的 改憲鬪爭으로
連絡 劃策

活 動 実 態

○ 11.4 基督敎會舘에서 內外信 記者들에게 〃發起文〃
과

0026

△ 〃國民에게 보내는 呼訴文〃(金槿泰 等 拷問主張)

△ 〃世界人權團体들에게 보내는 메시지〃 等 配布

※ 同 메시지는 世界人權團体에 送付

○ 11.8.19:00 惠化洞 聖堂에서 〃拷問 및 容共造作 沮止
위한 報告大會〃를 開催코자 企図

△ 〃報告大會〃 案內伝單 2万枚를 各 運動圈 團体, 駐韓
外國公館 等에 配布

○ 民推協에서는 11.11 ~ 11.13間 同 事務室에서 大規模
(500名予想)로 拷問 反對籠城을 展開하고자 隱密裡에
推進中

0027

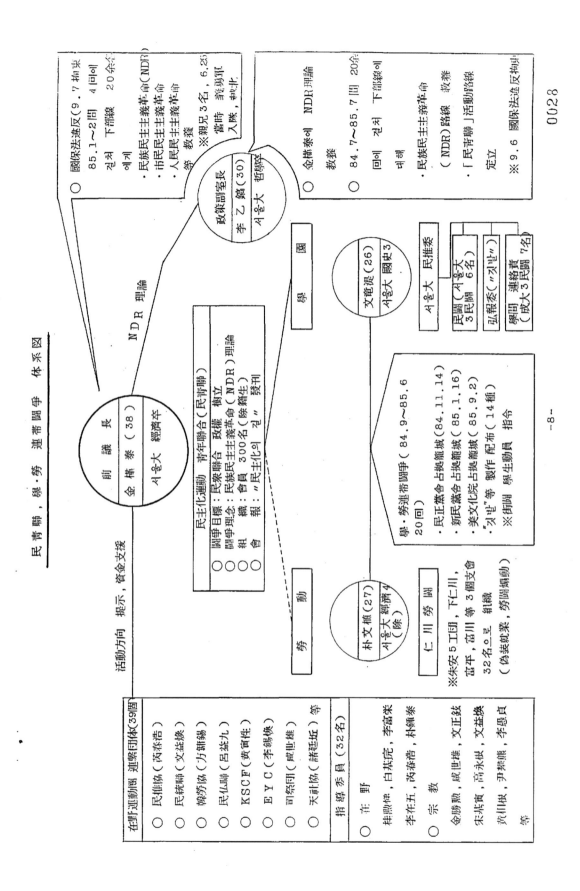

民靑聯 , 學·勞 連帶鬪爭 体系図

	主張內容別 實相

主 張 內 容	實 相
金槿泰 容共造作 및 拷問 前 民靑聯議長 金槿泰의 容共性 罵倒는 當局의 造作	○ 本名은 親兄 3名을 비롯 親姻戚 10名이 越北 또는 處刑된 家庭環境에서 成長 ○ 서울大 卒業後 就業抛棄, 所謂 自身의 一生 目標라고 主張하는 〃社會主義勞動運動〃을 위한 이른바 職業革命家 活動 恣行 ○ 83.9.30 除籍生糾合 民靑聯 結成, 北傀의 人民民主主義와 類似한 이른바 〃民族民主主義 革命〃主張, 構成員과 問題學生 深層意識化 ○ 그 實踐課業으로 學園街 不純背後組織인 서울大 民推委 背後操縱 △ 學勞連帶鬪爭(84.9〜85.9.22) △ 新韓黨舍 占拠籠城(85.1.16 서울大) △ 서울美文化院 占拠籠城(85.5.23 5個大 聯合) △ 〃깃발〃 等 不穩油印物 製作 配布(84.8 〜85.6 14種)等 示威 展開 使嗾

링-29 86. 6. 1　　　　　　　　　-9-　　　　　　　　0020

主 張 內 容	實　　　　　　相
事件調査 (9.4～ 9.20間)過程에서 拷問	○　金樺泰　拷問主張은 △　本名이　檢察로　送致될　當時　檢察 　　庁舎　複道에서　妻　印宰根　目擊時　突然 　　複道에　주저앉아　拷問을　當한것　처럼 　　四肢를　비틀며　엄살 △　이를　目擊한　妻　印宰根은　金樺泰가 　　甚한　拷問을　當한것으로　造作, 意図的 　　으로　國內外에　歪曲　傳播, 本名의　救命 　　과　鬪爭方法의　一環으로　悪用 △　本名은　拷問主張과는　달리　一切의　痕迹 　　이　없고　얼굴色도　健康, 步行　및　挙動 　　도　正常 △　担當辯護人団에서　拷問痕迹　証拠保全申請 　　(10.2)하였으나　同　事件　担當　김오수 　　判事는 　　-　國立医療院에　鑑定人推薦　依賴(10.4) 　　-　同院　整形外科　副科長　조덕연이　鑑定 　　　医師로　選定(10.8)까지　되었으나 　　"證拠保全　必要性을　認定할수　없다"고　判示

主張內容	實相
李乙鎬拷問 李乙鎬（30歲, 民靑聯研究室 副室長）가 繼續 된 拷問搜査로 精神錯亂 ※ 金槿泰에 NDR 理論 敎養, 서울大 ″民推委″ 事件 背後 操縱・ 國保法違反으로 拘束（9.6）	○ 過去 3차례에 걸쳐 精神分裂症勢로 入院 加療（75.3 東서울神經精神科, 77.11 市立精神病院, 81.6 서울大 附屬病院） ○ 搜査過程에서 食事,排泄,잠자리 等 健康狀態 細心한 配慮 ○ 生活環境의 変化 等으로 精神疾患 再發可能性 不無, 10.15~12.9間 서울市立精神病院에 鑑定留置中 ※ 調査過程의 拷問暴行主張과는 전혀 無關,本人도 拷問 等 苛酷行爲 當한 事實 없음을 陳述 ○ 国會 安東善（新民黨）議員이 病院을 訪問 11.7.11:00 家族과 同席,面談 한바 ″病院에서 잘해 주어 별일 없다″ 고 答弁,安東善議員도 ″실제와 보니 듣던 바와는 事實이 다르다″고 確認

主張內容	實 相
許仁會拷問 許仁會(前 高大 總學生會長,3民 鬪委全國委員長)는 調査過程(9.8 拘束)에서 拷問 으로 意識不明 狀態였다고 主張	○ 本名은 85.4.17 全學聯傘下 3民鬪 委員長으로 △ 美文化院占拠籠城支持 示威主導 △ 全南大 學生示威 背後操縦 △ 高大 汎國民 時局大討論會 主導 等 各種 學園 不法示威 40余回 主動 ○ 85.9.6 焚身自殺危脅用 석유통携帶, 高大에 潜入,學內示威主導와 檢擧된後 警察調査過程에서 犯行一切를 몇몇하게 陳述 ○ 特히 本名은 △ 拘束後 父母들이 거의 每日 面會, 拷問當했다는 말을 한 事實없고 △ 本名拷問說關聯,父母가 面會時 身体 異狀없음을 確認 面會은 父母,高大學生処長(金成福), 高大總學生會副會長(尹永喆,土木4) 等에게 ″拷問받은 事實없다,健康하다″고 強調

主張內容	實 相
禹宗元 死因 禹宗元 (서울大 , 社會福祉 4 , 民推委 事件關聯 手配者) 自殺事件을 拷問에 依한 他殺 , 死体 遺棄라고 主張 (85.10.12 10:35 忠北 永同郡 황간面 京釜線下行線 鉄路 辺에서 屍体로 發見)	○ 在學中 (85.1.12) 煉炭가스中毒으로 4日間 昏睡狀態 , 治療後 一部記憶喪失 等 脳機能障碍로 平素 悲観 ○ 屍体 捜索結果 , 本人親筆確認 〃어머니 , 兄 , 누나들 , 叔父님 罪悚합니다〃內容의 遺書發見 遺族들의 自殺確認下에 屍体引導 ○ 屍体検案醫師 (영창醫院 院長 조영호 , 50歲) 가 墜落에 依한 頭蓋骨骨切死亡으로 確認 ○ 屍体 墜落部分이 파여져 있고 革帯빠클이 떨어진 狀態로 屍体周辺 情況上 墜落死 確認 (大田 鉄道庁 미륵駅 線路長 윤석홍 , 35歲)

主張內容	實相
鄭鎮寬殴打 大邱矯導所에서 鄭鎮寬(仁荷大 除籍生)等 四人을 無差別 殴打, 치아와 턱뼈損傷 ※ 83.12 國保法 違反 拘束(懲役 3年 確定)	○ 85.7.31 저녁食事中 監房이 좁다는 트집으로 食器쟁반과 汚物을 내던지는 等 騒乱惹起 ○ 矯導官이 制止하자 意図的으로 高喊과 乱動을 부리면서 스스로 머리를 鉄窓에 부딪치는 等 自傷行爲 (2.5㎝ 裂傷) ※ 곧 醫務室에 移送 完治 ○ 矯導官의 殴打나 歯芽가 부러지고 턱뼈가 損傷되었다는 主張은 事實 無根

主張內容	實 相
東亞日報 編輯陣 苛酷行爲 編輯局長 이채주 等 3名을 8.29 中共機不時着事件 記事關聯 連行, 苛酷行爲 主張	○ 同事件이 國家安保와 對中共 外交關係 　等 重要事案으로 公式發表以外의 　報道自制 事前（ 5回 ） 協調要請 ○ 全言論機關이 趣旨를 理解하였으나 　東亞日報만이 方針을 無視 , 事前報道 , 　△ 中共과의 關係改善을 妨害하려는 　　北傀策動을 支援한 結果招來 ○ 事實 經緯確認을 爲해 任意同行調査 　過程에서 本人들이 스스로 잘못을 　순순히 是認 , 調査가 쉽게 終結 　△ 苛酷行爲는 事實無根

主張內容	實相
宋光永 焚身自殺 景園大 學生(法2) 宋光永이 85.9. 17.校庭에서 學園 安定法 反對 焚身 自殺,烈士로 追慕 (9.17 入院, 10.21 死亡)	○ 本名은 平素 不遇한 家庭環境(偏母 行商 極貧者)과 前科關係로 悲觀 ── ＜前 科 內 容＞ ── △ 84.11 强姦致傷罪로 懲役 2年6月 執猶 4年 ○ 成績不良으로 學事警告 2回, 特히 2學期 未登錄으로 9.18 除籍措置가 確實하자 하루前 焚身 ○ 平素에도 〃光化門4거리에서 죽어 버리겠다〃는 等 厭世自殺일 뿐인데 一部 運動圈人士들이 學園安定法 反對 焚身自殺로 美化

拷問 및 容共造作 沮止 共同對策委 構成員

区　分	構　　成　　員
顧　問 （9名）	金在俊（牧師，基長曾經総會長） 咸錫憲（牧師，퀘이커教　韓國代表）　　尹譽熊（牧師） 洪南淳（辯護士，光州拘束者協會長）　　李敏雨（新韓黨總裁） 文益煥（民統聯議長）　　　　　　　　池學淳（原州教區長） 金大中（民推協　共同議長）　　　　　金泳三（民推協　共同議長）
共同代表 （14名）	桂勳悌（民統聯副議長）　　　　　　　金勝勳（神父，民統聯副議長） 朴炯圭（基長曾經総會長）　　　　　　徐敬元（가農會長） 楊淳植（新韓黨副総裁）　　　　　　　李愚貞（教授，女神學者協會長） 趙南基（牧師，教社協會長）　　　　　金命潤（民推協副議長） 朴永禄（民推協副議長）　　　　　　　白基琓（民統聯서울支部議長） 宋建鎬（民言協議長）　　　　　　　　崔炳佑（新韓黨副総裁） 李小仙（서勞聯　顧問）　　　　　　　李貞淑（拘束者家族）

區分	세부	構成員
對策委員（241名）	改新教（33名）	姜瑗夏（春川人權委員長）　　　　　琴栄均（NCC 木曜礼拜委員長） 金東完（牧會者正平協議長）　　　　김재열（NCC 人權委員） 金僑永（基監宣教局総務）　　　　　金昌慶（忠北人權委員長） 朴尙奕（原州人權委員長）　　　　　朴鍾基（聖公會教務院長） 高永根（牧民宣教會長）　　　　　　김근상（牧會者正平協副議長） 金祥根（基長総務）　　　　　　　　金鍾五（城南人權委員長） 김진석（牧會者正平協副議長）　　　文貞植（全南 NCC 人權委員長） 朴永模（水原人權委総務）　　　　　朴鍾徳（大田人權委員　）

형－29　85. 8. 1

0038

区　分	構　　成　　員	
"	卞善奎（天安人權委員長）	辛三錫（全北NCC人權委総務）
	廉容沢（全州NCC人權委員長）	安基重（錦江人權委員長）
	吳忠一（KSCF理事長）	元亨洙（牧會者正平協代弁人）
	이명남（牧會者正平協副議長）	李正學（NCC都農宣教委員長）
	李海學（城南人權委員）	張基天（前KSCF理事長）
	張成竜（牧會者正平協副議長）	趙承赫（基督産業開發院長）
	崔聖黙（釜山NCC人權委総務）	최승렬（牧會者正平協副議長）
	許秉燮（基民研所長）	洪寿夏（大邱人權委総務）
	황규록（仁川人權委員長）	
" 天主教 (24名)	郭東哲（清州사직聖堂神父）	金秉相（仁川教区副主教）
	金炳宰（大田도마동聖堂神父）	金成鏞（JOC光州指導神父）
	金英信（全北完州上關聖堂神父）	金沢岩（竜山聖堂神父）
	文正鉉（全北장계聖堂神父）	朴鍾瑾（全北임실聖堂神父）
	孫德万（釜山은천聖堂神父）	申鉉奉（가農原州指導神父）
	楊　弘（화곡동聖堂神父）	吳盛栢（점촌聖堂神父）
	吳寿永（釜山초량聖堂神父）	吳泰淳（면목동聖堂神父）
	李啓暢（대사동聖堂神父）	李守鉉（全州正平委會長）
	鄭亨達（光州농성동聖堂神父）	鄭鎬庚（가農指導神父）
	趙喆鉉（大建神大教授）	崔基植（原州教区社會司牧局長）
	咸世雄（서울教区弘報局長）	許淵九（大邱東村聖堂神父）
	扈寅秀（富平聖堂神父）	黄相根（JOC指導神父）

형-29　83. 8. 1

0039

區分	構 成 員	
仏教 (10名)	境牛（僧侶），木牛（〃），碧牛（〃），性然（〃）， 月雲（〃），智善（〃），真寬（〃），真常（〃），玄基（〃）， 惠照（〃）	
拘束者家族 (12名)	김영희（깃발 박문식 母）	김왕수（大宇어패럴 김준용 父）
	金春玉（美文化院 金敏錫母）	南順子（三民 김봉환 母）
	이숙희（淸溪 김영대 妻）	李次德（三民 이성봉 父）
	李淸子（三民 李春 母）	민향숙（在日同胞 李哲 約婚女）
	印宰根（民靑聯 金横泰 妻）	崔貞順（民靑聯 이을호 妻）
	조아기（효성 김영미 母）	咸貞錫（美文化院 咸雲炅 父）
運動圏團体 (61名)	姜希南（民統聯 中央委員長）	劉雲弼（民統聯 指導委員）
	李斗洙（ 〃 指導委員）	全學碩（ 〃 ）
	李敦明（ 〃 ）	金炳傑（ 〃 ）
	高銀（ 〃 ）	李浩哲（ 〃 ）
	金芝河（ 〃 ）	李昌馥（民統聯 事務處長）
	林采正（民統聯 政策企劃室長）	李富栄（ 〃 民生委員長）
	郭泰栄（ 〃 人権委員長）	張琪杓（ 〃 事務次長）
	趙春九（ 〃 社會局長）	吳大栄（ 〃 會員）
	李在五（〃 서울支部副議長）	安承吉（ 〃 江原支部長）
	朴武學（〃 江原支部 事務局長）	朴炳琪（ 〃 慶北支部長）
	柳康夏（〃 慶北支部副議長）	柳淵昌（〃〃慶北支部 副議長）
	李應碩（〃 慶南支部長）	俞英式（〃 慶南支部 事務局長）

區　　分	構　　　　成　　　　員	
〃	金奎東（自實顧問）	申庚林（自實顧問）
	千勝世（　〃　　）	梁性佑（自實常任運營委員）
	朴泰洵（自實常任運營委員）	李文求（　　　〃　　　　）
	趙泰一（　　〃　　　）	黃晳暎（　　　〃　　　）
	金仁漢（民言協　代表委員）	崔長鶴（民言協　代表委員）
	金泰弘（　　〃　　　）	金承均（　　　〃　　　）
	金鍾澈（民文協　共同代表）	元東石（民文協　共同代表）
	趙鏞振（가農　副會長）	裵宗烈（基農　會長）
	李奉九（忠南基農總務）	金英源（基農　副會長）
	方鏞錫（韓勞協委員長）	李英順（韓勞協　幹事）
	朴順姬（韓勞協運營委員）	남상헌（　〃　　運營委員）
	李總角（　　〃　　　）	鄭鎭東（基勞協會長）
	李玉順（서勞聯　副委員長）	尹順女（天社協委員長）
	諸廷坵（天社協運營委員）	呂益九（民仏聯議長）
	韓慶南（民靑聯議長）	金永根（서울敎區　大學聯幹事）
	文圭鉉（全民協議長）	宣鎭栄（全民協議長）
	金順浩（忠南民協議長）	元亨洙（忠南民協議長）
	朴竜來（忠北民協議長）	宋基寅（釜民協會長）
	李浩雄（仁社聯議長）	
民推協 (50名)	金昌槿（副議長）	朴鍾泰（副議長）
	芮春浩（　〃　）	竜南眞（　〃　）
	洪英基（　〃　）	尹奕杓（　〃　）

행－29　83. 8. 1

0041

區　　分	構　　　成　　　員	
〃	太倫基（副議長）	李相敦（常任運營委員）
	金相賢（常任運營委員）	金德竜（　　〃　　）
	金道鉉（　　〃　　）	金炳午（副幹事長）
	金允植（副幹事長）	金忠變（常任運營委員）
	文富植（常任運營委員）	孫周恒（　　〃　　）
	辛相佑（　　〃　　）	安弼洙（　　〃　　）
	崔泳謹（　　〃　　）	韓光玉（代　辯　人）
	黃明秀（幹　事　長）	權大福（常任運營委員）
	權斗五（常任運營委員）	金光一（　　〃　　）
	金吉俊（　　〃　　）	金鍾完（　　〃　　）
	金昌煥（　　〃　　）	宋佐彬（　　〃　　）
	申鎭旭（　　〃　　）	李愚兌（　　〃　　）
	李鍾南（　　〃　　）	丁采權（　　〃　　）
	鄭東勳（　　〃　　）	鄭棧鎬（　　〃　　）
	李協（　　〃　　）	鄭憲柱（　　〃　　）
	金守（　　〃　　）	尹哲夏（　　〃　　）
	李官炯（　　〃　　）	李玩衡（　　〃　　）
	趙昇衡（　　〃　　）	金殷楫（　　〃　　）
	李興禄（　　〃　　）	李基洪（　　〃　　）
	崔鍾泰（總務局長）	朴熙富（組織局長）
	徐好錫（人權局長）	李珍求（國際局長）
	金壯坤（文教局長）	元聖喜（社會局長）

행-29　83. 8. 1

0042

區　分	構　　成　　員	
新韓黨 (51名)	姜三載（國會議員）	金東圭（國會議員）
	權五台（　〃　）	金東旭（　〃　）
	金東英（院內總務）	金奉旭（　〃　）
	金東周（國會議員）	金聖植（　〃　）
	金奉祚（　〃　）	金完泰（　〃　）
	金令培（　〃　）	金正秀（　〃　）
	金正吉（　〃　）	金鉉圭（　〃　）
	金漢洙（　〃　）	金炯暎（　〃　）
	金顯秀（　〃　）	明華燮（　〃　）
	金泰竜（　〃　）	文正秀（　〃　）
	睦堯相（　〃　）	朴旺植（　〃　）
	朴寬用（　〃　）	朴鍾律（　〃　）
	朴容万（中央常務委議長）	朴漢相（　〃　）
	朴燦鍾（人權擁護委員長）	徐錫宰（　〃　）
	潘亨植（　〃　）	辛基夏（　〃　）
	宋千永（　〃　）	安東善（　〃　）
	慎順範（　〃　）	尹栄卓（　〃　）
	柳成煥（　〃　）	李永權（　〃　）
	李尚玟（　〃　）	李哲（　〃　）
	李重載（副總裁）	張基旭（　〃　）
	李宅敦（國會議員）	趙舜衡（黨紀委員長）
	趙炳鳳（　〃　）	趙洪來（國會議員）
	趙永寿（　〃　）	崔薫（　〃　）
	崔洛道（　〃　）	許京万（　〃　）
	韓錫奉（　〃　）	黄珞周（　〃　）
	洪思德（代辯人）	

영－29　83. 8. 1

0043

기 안 용 지

분류기호 문서번호	미북 700-46	(전화번호)	전 결 규 정	조 항
처리기간		장 관	전결사항	
시행일자	1986. 1. 7.			
보존연한				

보 조 기 관	국 장		심 의 관	협	
	과 장				
기 안 책 임 자	위성락	북 미 과		조	

경 유		발 신		통 제	
수 신	주 카나다대사				
참 조					
제 목	자료송부				

대 : CNW-1572

1. 대호 송부요청한 김근 태등의 범죄사실에 대한 자료중
김근 태관련 자료를 별첨 송부합니다.

2. 기타자료는 관계부처에 요청중인바, 추후 송부할
예정입니다.

첨 부 : 상기 자료 1부.   끝.

	정서
	관인
	발송

0044

THE TRUTH BEHIND THE CONTROVERSY OVER INVESTIGATIONS INTO RECENT VIOLENT STUDENT DEMONSTRATIONS

NOVEMBER , 1985

SUPREME PROSECUTOR'S OFFICE

0045

CONTENTS

I.   THE TRUTH BEHIND THE CONTROVERSY OVER
      THE INVESTIGATION OF THE CASES

      1.   The Case of Kim Keun-Tae, Former Chairman of the
            Youth Federation for Democracy.

      A.   Summary of Case

      On September 30, 1983, Kim Keun-Tae formed an illegal
organization called the Youth Federation for Democracy (YFD)
with expelled college students as its principal members. Since
then he led the group as its chairman until August 1985. He
was arrested on September 7, 1985 on charges of violating the
National Security Law, etc., by the National Police Headquarters (Anti-State Investigation Team). After police
interrogation Kim was transferred to the prosecution on
September 26. On October 25, he was indicted to the court.

      B.   Truth

      When interrogated by the prosecutors, Kim Keun-Tae
refused to make any statement by exercising his right to keep
silence. This is in and of itself a powerful proof that he was
not manhandled or forced to give self-incriminating statement.
He was neither subjected to any form of physical abuse (such as
beating or electric shocks) during the police investigation as
there was no need to force a confession out of him. Under
Korean law a confession to the police cannot be used as evidence if the defendant denies it at the court.

.0047

The torture allegation appears to have arisen under the following circumstances:

When Kim was transferred from the National Police Headquarters to the Seoul District Prosecutor's Office on September 26, 1985 he saw his wife, In Chae-Kun, waiting on the fourth floor of the prosecution building. Thereupon, he abruptly dropped to the floor on his back and told her that he had been severely tortured. Observing this, In Chae-Kun decided to use the torture allegation in her campaign to get her husband acquitted and gave distorted information to religious, academic and labor circles and even to overseas Koreans. Learning of such allegations of torture, the prosecution conducted a series of investigations to confirm the truth of the matter. However, no trace of any torture was found. Kim's complexion appeared healthy and there was no sign of torture in his walk or other physical and mental movements.

Taken the fact that Kim refused to give any statement even before the prosecutors and instead alleged that he had been tortured by the police, it is believed that he falsely conducted before his wife with an intention of covering up his wrongdoing and getting himself acquitted. It is also highly expected that when he is met by his family and lawyers, he will continue to stick to his false allegation that he has been tortured by the investigative authorities.

Activist opposition groups which have guided and financed the YFD from behind the scenes with the ultimate goal of toppling the present government are making an issue out of this false allegation for the following reasons:

0048

(1)   They fear that if the YFD, the vanguard in their
      political struggle, crumbles and the criminal
      investigations continue, their link to the YFD will
      be uncovered. Accordingly, they want to find a pre-
      text to thwart such developments.

(2)   By drumming up the allegation of torture, the
      activist opposition groups are attempting to arouse
      the sympathy of religious, academic and labor
      circles and stir international opinion as well.
      They are distorting the actual facts of the case to
      drive the government into a corner and eventually to
      get Kim acquitted and save themselves.

(3)   They are also trying to use the case as a rallying
      point for antigovernment groups and to accelerate
      their political struggle.

2.   The Case of Huh In-Hoe, Chairman of the Sammintu.

      A.   Summary of Case

      Huh In-Hoe was elected chairman of the Sammintu (Struggle
Committee for Democracy, the Nation and People) on April 17,
1985 while he was president of the Korea University Student
Association. Since then, he has led or incited more than 40
illegal demonstrations on and off campus, including the seizure
of the USIS library in downtown Seoul. On September 6, he
presented himself at Korea University with a can of kerosene,
doused himself with the fuel and threatened to immolate
himself. In that way, he incited his fellow students to

.0040

demonstrate on campus and led the student demonstrators out
onto the street. Thereupon, he was arrested by the police.

Arrest warrant for Huh was executed on September 8,
1985. He was interrogated by the National Police Headquarters
(Anti-State Investigation Team) and transferred to the Seoul
District Prosecutor's Office on September 17. Huh was indicted
on October 5 to the court.

B.   Truth

During the police investigation, Huh behaved as if he
were a minor hero, candidly and with an apparent sense of
pride, voluntarily describing all the offenses that he had
committed.

On the day he was transferred to the prosecution, the
prosecutor in charge asked him about his health, whereupon he
replied that he was in excellent health. He added, "I was
uneasy while I was running away. Now I have gained peace of
mind and find it comfortable here." He actually looked healthy
and comfortable. The same day Huh was visited by his father at
the prosecutor's office. He told his father not to worry about
him because he was in good health, adding that he was well
treated by the police and had nothing to complain about. In
the evening of the same day, Huh had supper with the prosecutor
in charge. Before eating, he said, "Thank you for supper" and
otherwise behaved courteously. The prosecutor told him that
unlike most students these days, he had a good manner. Huh
replied that the police officers who interrogated him often
said the same thing, adding that the officers seemed to be well
impressed with him and treated him kindly.

0050

During the prosecutor's interrogation, he was visited
almost daily by his parent, sister, uncle, aunt and many other
relatives, and also by a professor who is the Director of
Student Affairs at Korea University and fellow students. He
invariably told the visitors not to worry about him since he
was well and comfortable. He never said to them that he had
been harshly interrogated. Since Huh's charges had already
been proved by his accomplices who had been arrested earlier,
there was no need for the investigating officers to sternly
interrogate him.

Upon learning of the allegations that Huh had been
tortured with electric shocks, the prosecutor in charge
summoned him to his office on October 21, 1985 to inquire of
the matter. Huh said that his blisters and peeling skin were
due to the kerosene with which he had doused himself, adding
that he did not understand how the groundless rumor of the
torture had originated. More recently, however, Huh confided
to the prosecutor that he said to his lawyer who visited him at
the detention house that he was once rather harshly interrogated at the National Police Headquarters. When the prosecutor asked Huh why he had never hinted at any such occur-
rence earlier, he replied he was only telling the truth. In
light of all relevant circumstances mentioned above, Huh's
allegation was not credible and no traces of torture have been
found. It is surmised that though initially Huh was quite
candid, behaving with apparent pride as a leader of student
activism, he later changed his mind fearing that he might be
accused by his fellow students of too readily submitting to the
investigation.

0051

Activist opposition groups are raising controversy over the manner of investigation into Huh's activities for much the same reasons as noted in the case of Kim Keun-Tae:

(1) They are attempting to make the Huh case appear as if it had been fabricated through torture. In that way, they hope to stir up domestic and international protest over the case and embarrass the government with the ultimate goal of having Huh acquitted.

(2) Furthermore, they hope to fan antigovernment sentiment among students and accelerate their political struggle in league with disaffected students.

3. The Case of Lee Ul-Ho, Policy Director of the Youth Federation for Democracy

A. Summary of Case

Late in June 1984, Lee Ul-Ho joined the Youth Federation for Democracy (YFD) and has held the position of its Policy Director since August 1985.

On September 6, 1985, Lee was arrested by the National Police Headquarters on charges of violating the National Security Law, etc., and was transferred to the prosecution on September 24. On October 15, 1985, while under the pro- secutor's investigation, Lee showed symptoms of schizophrenia. A writ of psychiatric examination was issued by Judge Kim Oh-Su of the Seoul District Criminal Court on the same day, which authorized Lee's hospitalization from October 15 to December 9. Currently, Lee is being examined at the expense of the state at the Seoul Municipal Mental Hospital.

B.   Truth

Lee has told the prosecution that he was never subjected to torture or any other form of cruelty. Lee's wife, Choe Chong-Sun, also stated to the prosecution on October 14 that although she mentioned torture when she learned that her husband had a mental relapse, she did not mean physical torture but simply wanted to emphasize that his protracted detention was tantamount to "mental torture." Choe is asking the Catholic Fathers Association to exercise their good offices to have her husband acquitted. In doing so, she is not alledging that he has been tortured.

Previously, Lee was hospitalized on three occasions for the treatment of schizophrenia: At Seoul National University Hospital from January 28, 1975 to February 21, 1975; at Seoul Municipal Mental Hospital from November 25, 1977 to January 17, 1978; and at the East Seoul Neuropsychiatric Clinic from June 15, 1981 to August 14, 1981.

The physicians who are now examining Lee state that so far they have not found any sign that the relapse of his mental illness has been caused by interrogations.

The opposition activists, however, are falsely asserting that Lee's mental condition is due to torture. The reasons for this allegation are as follows:

(1)   The activist opposition groups have been guiding and
      financially supporting the YFD with the ultimate
      goal of bringing down the present government. They
      now fear that the YFD, the vanguard in their
      political struggle, will collapse and that further
      investigations into the YFD will uncover their links
      with it. Accordingly, they want to find a pretext
      to prevent such a development.

(2)   By alleging that Lee has been tortured, the opposi-
      tion activists are attempting to arouse the sympathy
      of domestic religious, academic and labor circles
      and stir up international opinion. By disseminating
      distorted facts, they hope to put the government in
      a difficult position with the aim of getting Lee
      acquitted and saving themselves.

(3)   At the same time, they are trying to take advantage
      of the situation to rally antigovernment forces and
      strengthen their political struggle.

4.   The Case of Chung Chin-Kwan, President of the Paekpom's
     Thought Study Group

     A.   Summary of Case

     Since his expulsion from Inha University, Chung Chin-kwan
has led the Paekpom's Thought Study Group whose membership
consists largely of Inha students. In August 1983, Chung
produced and distributed subversive pamphlets. He also
regularly listened to North Korean broadcasts. For these

0054

offenses, he was arrested on December 26, 1983 on charges of violating the National Security Law. On March 14, 1984, he was sentenced to three years' imprisonment with a three-year suspension of civil rights. Currently, he is serving his term at the Tae-gu Penitentiary.

B.   Truth

While eating supper on the evening of July 31, 1985, Chung Chin-Kwan, together with 15 other inmates, went berserk, complaining that the cell was overcrowded. They threw table-ware, food trays and food. When the wardens tried to stop them, Chung shouted at them and wildly resisted. He struck his head against the bars, rolled over in the hall and deliberately hit his chin on the wall. He thus injured himself, causing lacerations. However, his injuries were promptly treated and soon healed.

The facts of the affair, however, were grossly distorted by Lee Chul, one of the inmates who participated in the above rampage. Lee, a former graduate course student of Korea University and a Korean resident in Japan, had been sentenced to death for having operated as a North Korean undercover agent. His sentence, however, was later commuted to life imprisonment and again reduced to 20 years. With a view to attracting public attention to himself and the other inmates to promote his campaign to be freed from prison, Lee told his wife, Min Hyang-Suk, and her mother, Cho Man-Jo, when they visited him on August 13, 1985, that he and the other inmates were beaten by the wardens, without mentioning the fact that they had caused a disturbance. Lee also told them that Chung Chin-Kwan's teeth were broken and his chin hurt because of beatings.

Thus, the allegation that Chung was beaten and injured by the wardens is groundless.

II.   THE TRUTH BEHIND THE CONTROVERSY OVER THE NATURE OF THE CASES

1.   The Case of the Sammintu

A.   What is Sammintu?

Sammintu is an abbreviation of the Korean name of the Struggle Committee for the People's Three Ideals -- that is, "unification of nation, liberation of the masses, and winning of democracy."

Analyses of pamphlets produced and distributed by members of the Sammintu (composed of university-level units and their national alliance) and statements they have made to the law-enforcement officers show that their "sammin ideals" including "democracy of the masses" closely paralleled North Korean ideology and propaganda.

B.   Definition of the masses

In defining "the masses" the Sammintu groups divide Korean society into five to seven classes in line with the Marxist class theory, as illustrated by their pamphlets, "The Kwangju Turmoil in the Context of the History of the Mass Movement" and "One Step Forward." They maintain that "the masses" comprise "laborers, farmers and the urban have-nots,"

0056

and exclude the so-called middle class, including small and
medium sized merchants, industrialists, and skilled workers.
Their division of classes and definition of the masses are
identical with North Korea's.

C.   Realization of Sammin ideals

To realize "the liberation of the masses" and "winning of
democracy" the Sammintu asserts that "the dictatorship that
only serves foreign economic interests must be destroyed
through a revolution led by the masses to achieve a society in
which the massses will be the masters." They hold that
students must first enhance the revolutionary capabilities of
the masses and enlist part of the middle class as auxiliary
forces to mount a massive and violent uprising of the masses
leading to a revolution to overthrow bourgeois democracy and
build "socialism" or "democracy of the masses." Such thinking,
as reflected in statements that two Seoul National University
students, Kim Tae-Ryong and Ha Tong-Hyop have made before the
investigation authorities, is again identical with North
Korea's "theory of people's democratic revolution."

D.   As to national unification

In discussing "national unification," the Sammintu groups
have branded the present Korean government as "a captive regime
dependent on the United States" and call the Republic of Korea
"a U.S. neocolony." The activist students assert that the
United States is perpetuating the division of Korea by turning
the South into an anti-Soviet outpost and a nuclear base. Such
assertions are contained, for example, in "One Step Forward" as
well as in "Breaking the Chain of Bondage," a pamphlet dated

0057

April 17, 1984, and distributed by the Union for the Defense of National Independence which is affiliated with the National Alliance of Student Associations.

A pamphlet distributed by Sogang University students entitled, "Bringing the Sammin Banner to Mt. Paektusan," maintains that to achieve national unification, the United States must be driven away and the present captive government must be overthrown.

Such Sammintu assertions are again in line with the North Korean propaganda that unification is possible only when the United States is kicked out of the Korean peninsula.

E.   Conclusion

In sum, the so-called "sammin ideals and democracy of the masses" that the leaders of the Sammintu pursue evidently represents a pro-communist ideology which benefits North Korea and is congruous with their routine assertions and their strategy and tactics for a revolution in the South. Accordingly, the Sammintu can be defined as a pro-communist organization which aids the enemy, as evidenced by the Sammintu member's own statements as well as the pamphlets they have authored. It is totally groundless to charge that the authorities have framed the Sammintu as pro-communist.

2.   The Case of the Council for the Promotion of Democracy

A.   The ideal of so-called NDR

The concept of "national democratic revolution" (NDR)

0058

advocated by the Council for the Promotion of Democracy (CPD) runs as follows:

(1) The dilemma of Korean society at present is due to a contradiction between a military dictatorship, monopolistic conglomerates serving foreign interests and the U.S. and Japanese imperialists on the one hand and the Korean people on the other.

(2) Laborers must be the leading force of change and students should play the spearheading role, especially by heightening the awareness of laborers. Farmers and the urban have-nots should be enlisted as auxiliary forces in a violent revolution led by the organized people to overthrow the present regime and establish a people's government.

B. The term, contents, and sources of NDR

The sources of information about the concept of "national democratic revolution" include the following:

A note for a seminar prepared by CPD member Kim Hui-Kap with guidance from the CPD leadership describes the idea of national democratic revolution with such English abbreviations as NDR (national democratic revolution), F (Fascism), Imp (imperialism), SM (student movement), and LM (labor movement). His note clearly shows that SR (socialism revolution) is the next stage to NDR.

While in hiding, Ahn Pyong-Yong, Yun Song-Ju and Hwang In-San wrote manuscripts entitled, "The Class Composition and

Class Diversification of Korean Society," "Student Movements in the 1980s," and "A General Theory of Student Movements." These papers give a detailed description of the concept of "national democratic revolution."

The first and second issues of the "Kkippal (Banner)", a magazine produced by Ahn Pyong-Yong, Yun Song-Ju and others also discuss in specific terms the concept of "national democratic revolution" and ways to implement it. The pro-communist nature of the magazine is now widely recognized.

Ahn, Yun, Hwang and others have translated such Communist books as "What to Do by Lenin", "The Basis for Leninism by Stalin", "Contradictions and Practices by Mao Tse-tung", and "A History of the Russian Revolution by Trotsky". (These translations are still in an initial draft stage.) In addition, over 400 kinds of Marxist books and pro-communist pamphlets have been impounded. All this proves their pro-communist inclinations.

Furthermore, their ideology of "national democratic revolution" is in the same vein as the so-called "theory of national liberation and people's democracy" described in such publications of the North Korean Social Sciences Publishing Company as "Dictionary of Politics", "Dictionary of Philosophy" and "The Theory of Revolution in South Korea and National Unification based on the Kim Il-Sung Ideology". (The North Korean theory of revolution is clearly described even in the national ethics textbook for high school use in the South.)

기 안 용 지

분류기호 문서번호	미북 700-	(전화번호)	전결규정	조 항
처리기간		장 관		전결사항
시행일자	1986. 1. 7.			
보존연한				

보 조 기 관	국 장	전결	심 의 관		협	
	과 장					
기 안 책 임 자	위성락	북 미 과		조	

경 유		발		통	
수 신	법무부장관	신		제	
참 조					

제 목	수감자 관련 자료요청

주 카나다대사는 카나다의 인권 및 종교 단체로부터 강종훈

(Kang Jong-Hon) 에 대한 문의와 진정이 빈번히 제기되고

있음을 보고하고 이에대한 이해를 제고 키 위하여 동인의 범죄

내용과 관련법규에 관한 자료를 요청하여 왔으니 이를 당부에

송부하여 주시기 바랍니다. 끝.

정서
관인
발송

0061

1205-25(2-1) A (갑)
1981. 12. 18승인

정직 질서 창조

190mm×268mm (인쇄용지 2급 60g./㎡)
가 40-41 1985. 8. 7.

기 안 용 지

분류기호 문서번호	미북 700- 41	(전화번호)	전결규정	조 항
			전결사항	

처리기간		장 관
시행일자	1986. 1. 8.	
보존연한		

보 조 기 관	국 장	심 의 관	협	
	과 장			
	기안책임자 윅성락	북 미 과	조	

경유 수신 참조	법무부장관	발 신	

제 목	기소자 관련 자료요청

　　　주카나다대사는 카나다내에서 하기 기소자에 대한 진정과

문의가 빈번히 제기되고 있는바, 동 진정과 문의에 대해 정확한

범죄사실을 알림으로써 이해를 제고할 필요가 있음을 보고하고

관련자료를 요청하여 왔으니 동인들의 범죄내용과 관련법규를

당부에 통보하여주시기 바랍니다.

　　　　　　　　　-　아　래　-

　　　° 안상군 (Ahn Sang-Gun)

　　　° 이진숙 (Lee Chin-Suk).　　　끝.

0062

1205-25(2-1) A (갑)
1981. 12. 18승인

190mm×268mm (인쇄용지 2급 60g./㎡)
가 40-41 1985. 8. 7.

주 국 련 대 표 부

주국련 731- **152**   1986. 2. 27.

수신 장관

참조 미주국장, 정보문화국장

제목 카나다 기독교 단체의 대북한 교류관계 서한

        연 : 주국련 731-007 (86.1.7)

    연호와 관련하여 Canada Asia Working Group   이 당관앞으로

송부한 대북한 교류관계 서한을 별첨과 같이 송부하오니 업무에 참고하시기

바랍니다.

    첨 부 : 동 서한 사본 1부. 끝.

        주 국 련 대

선 결			결재(공람)		
접수일시	1966 3. 3	번호			
처리과		14862			

0063

CANADA ASIA working group

11 Madison Avenue, Toronto
Ontario, Canada M5R 2S2

(416) 924-9351

A Canadian Inter-Church Coalition on Asian Concerns

February 13, 1986

His Excellency Dr. Kyung Won Kim
Ambassador Extraordinary and Plenipotentiary
Permanent Observer Mission of the Republic of Korea
  to the United Nations
866 United Nations Plaza, Suite 300
New York, N.Y. 10017
U.S.A.

Dear Mr. Ambassador:

You are aware of the long historic relationships which Canadian churches have with Korean churches. For some of us this relationship was primarily with Christian communities in what now is the Democratic People's Republic of Korea.

We have participated in ecumenical international consultations on Peace and Justice in Northeast Asia such as those held at Tozanso, Japan, and Stoney Point, N.Y. We seek to work within our Canadian church constituencies to understand better the realities of the division of the Korean peninsula and work toward reconciliation.

We share this statement for information and are always open to any response you might wish to share.

Yours sincerely,

The Reverend Terry Brown
Chair
Canada Asia Working Group

Encl.

TB:mdc

0064

CANADA ASIA working group

A Canadian Inter-Church Coalition on Asian Concerns

The Canada Asia Working Group (CAWG), an inter-church coalition whose supporters include the Anglican, Presbyterian and United Churches of Canada, the Canadian Catholic Organization on Development and Peace, and the Scarborough Foreign Mission Society, is mandated to work on human rights and justice issues that link Canada and Asia.

Over the last six years the Canada Asia Working Group has given considerable attention to concerns coming from the Korean peninsula. The appended Working Statement on North Korea has been in process for more than a year. It arose from the perception that the time was right for Canadian churches to work more deliberately to understand the tensions in the Korean peninsula and to do what we can to build a climate that facilitates a reconciliation which might lead to reunification.

The Statement was shared with Canadian church supporting bodies for comment at several stages. It is now issued as a working document of the Canada Asia Working Group in the hope it will be used by the churches as a basis for their own work on Korea questions and for educational processes among church members.

December, 1985

0065

CANADA ASIA WORKING GROUP WORKING STATEMENT ON NORTH KOREA

Introduction

In 1984-85 the Protestant churches celebrated the 100th anniversary of the beginning of Protestant mission in Korea as the Roman Catholic church celebrated the 200th anniversary of Catholic mission. The Canadian churches several of which have been partners with Korean churches for a significant part of that period welcomed the opportunity to rejoice with our Korean sisters and brothers and gave thanks for God's faithful guidance over many perilous decades.

Until 1945 the church served in a country that had been one and undivided for thirteen centuries, although for 35 years Koreans had been under harsh Japanese occupation. The deliverance from that occupation at the end of World War II gave rise to high hopes. These hopes were frustrated, however, when Korea was divided by Russia and the United States into North and South, corresponding to Russian and American spheres of influence, with the concurrence of other United Nations members.

Following this division, Canada continued to maintain relationships with the Republic of Korea (South). Any possibility of similar relationships with the Democratic People's Republic of Korea (North) were effectively eliminated by the Korean War.

In 1946 the Korean Christian Federation was created in the North as an ostensible vehicle for freedom of religion. Many Christians remained opposed to the Communist government, however, and, since Christianity was viewed by the government authorities as a foreign religion, were often regarded with suspicion as potential American agents. The movement of refugees to the South was greatly accelerated during the Korean War.

Following that war the borders became permanently closed and contact between the two parts of the country virtually ceased. As far as has been known, the church as an organized body ceased to exist in the North. Small groups of Christians have continued to meet in homes. Over the past couple of years there have been tentative feelers put out by the Korean Christian Federation to churches in other parts of the world, especially those in Europe, although we know little about the nature of the Federation and its present activities. At least two church-related groups of American Christians met with Federation officials and visited North Korean Christians in late 1984. In November, 1985, two World Council of Churches staff members visited North Korea at the invitation of the central committee of the Federation.

Among the people in South Korea there has remained, in spite of enforced division of their country, a deep sense of the oneness of the Korean people and a dedication to ultimate reunification. In the official statements of some Korean churches over the years this goal has been affirmed. In our solidarity with them, therefore, we are called to understand this longing. Despite seemingly insuperable political obstacles we seek a way to help ease tensions that stand in the way of bringing reunification into reality.

0066

As we examine this situation, we remember the positive role some churches in
Canada played in keeping relationships with the Chinese people during the
period of isolation. We recall, too, the contribution of the Canadian
government in according diplomatic recognition to China in advance of many of
the Western powers. Perhaps this says something to us in regard to future
relations with North Korea.

The Current Situation

In recent months there have been increasing numbers of people from the
Western world able to visit North Korea. We have benefited from their
observations. Other groups, both church and non-church, are making plans to
visit. While this kind of informal contact is increasing, Western
governments appear reluctant to open contacts on a more formal basis.

At the end of October, 1984, an Ecumenical Consultation on Peace and Justice
in North-East Asia under the auspices of the World Council of Churches was
held in Japan. The Consultation statement pointed out that since World War
II North-East Asia has been a region of continuing tension with problems of
reconciliation, political freedom, human rights and democratization finding a
common concern and response among the churches. The Korean peninsula is at
the heart of this tension. "This tension gravely endangers this region and
its peoples, making it one of the potentially greatest threats to world peace
and a possible trigger of a global nuclear war."

Recent initiatives were identified as giving reason for hope and a basis for
action: proposals for tripartite talks involving both Koreas on the
re-establishing of relationships; the giving of flood relief aid by North
Korea and its reception by the South; proposals for trade talks between the
two countries, the decision to resume the Red Cross talks and the September,
1985 limited visits of separated family members.

The emergence of such initiatives and the commitment of the world churches to
pursue policies that will contribute to the lessening of tensions in the
region, make it appropriate that churches in Canada seek ways of being a part
of this process. Recommendations of the Ecumenical Consultation are
reflected in the following affirmations.

Seeking New Directions

We seek to discover how in the providence of God we may recognize and respond
to the new realities in the Democratic People's Republic of Korea.

1. We recognize that God continues to be active among people in North
    Korea. We seek to discern signs of God's activity that we may
    respond appropriately.

2. We acknowledge that the way ahead is uncertain. We do not see
    clearly the steps to be taken. Nevertheless, in the conviction that
    we are on God's way, we remain open to the leading of the Holy
    Spirit.

3. We acknowledge the tragedy of the division of the Korean people and the complicity of the Western world in that division. We recognize the sorrow of our partners in the South because of the continuing separation from their compatriots in the North. We support the recommendation of the 1984 Ecumenical Consultation to help promote initiatives towards re-establishing contacts between separated families.

4. We are not called to be neutral bystanders but to join in the process of reconciliation and justice leading to the reunification of the Korean peninsula. We are called to overcome the stereotypes, prejudice and climate of hostility towards North Korea which militate against reconciliation.

5. We affirm the desirability of the Canadian church to know and understand better the situation of the people of North Korea. We need to seek and disseminate accurate information about both North and South Korea to correct the distortions often used for political purposes.

6. We believe it desirable to encourage groups of Canadian church members to make visits to North Korea where possible, to open up people-to-people contacts and to share their experiences on their return to Canada. In this connection, it will be essential to co-operate with the World Council of Churches and the Christian Conference of Asia as they develop relationships with the church in North Korea.

7. Since to date Canadian diplomats and government officials have not encouraged contacts with North Korea, we see value in sharing with them such reliable information as we obtain and the results of our own contacts. We urge their co-operation in facilitating people-to-people exchanges both through visits to North Korea and academic and cultural exchanges that bring North Koreans to Canada.

We make this statement not from assurance of ease in developing new directions but from a firm conviction that the time is right to move forward and that it is God's will that we do so.

November, 1985

0068

카나다 기독교단체 Canada Asia Working Group   의

대북한 고류관련 성명문

○ Canada Asia Working Group(CAWG) 는 카나다내 범교파
   연합체로서 아시아와 관련된 인권 및 정의문제를 다룸.

○ 본 단체는 한반도 분단현실 및 긴장상태에 대한 이해를 증진
   시키고 한반도 통일을 위한 화합을 촉진시키기 위해 카나다
   교회의 자체적인 노력을 추구하고 있음.

○ 성명문 요지
   - 카나다교회는 한반도 통일로 인도될 화해와 정의실현
     과정에 참여해야하며, 화합을 저해시키는 북한 에 대한
     편견, 적대적 분위기등을 극복해야함.
   - 정치적 목적을 위한 왜곡 시정을 위해 남·북한에 관한
     정확한 정보를 수득, 전파시켜야함.
   - 카나다 교회단체의 북한방문을 장려하고 북한과 주민대
     주민의 접촉을 개설해야 함.
   - 카나다교회의 대북한 고류증진에 있어 카나다 정부의
     협조를 촉구함.

                                                    0060

카나다 기독교 단체(Canada Asia Working Group) 의 대북한 교류관계 성명문

○ Terry Brown   동 단체회장은 86•2•13자 주유엔대사 앞으로
 서한송부• 동 단체소개서 및 대북한 교류관계 성명문을 첨부

 - 서한내용

   • 역사적으로 카나다교회중 일부는 현재북한 (DPRK) 이된
     지역의 교회와 주로 관계를 가지고 있었음•

   • 우리는 일본 '도잔소'와 뉴욕주 'Stoney Point' 에서
     개최된 '동북아에서의 평화와 정의에 대한 전기독교 국제
     협의회'에 참석하였으며 한반도의 분단현실에 대한 이해를
     증진시키고 화합을 추진하기 위해 카나다 교회의 자체적인
     노력을 추구하고 있음•

   • 별첨 성명문은 정보제공을 위해 제공하며 정보교환을 위한
     어떠한 회답도 환영함•

 - Canada Asia Working Group   소개서 내용

   • 카나다내 각종파 교회 및 선교 단체를 포함하는 연합체로서
     아시아와 관련된 인권 및 정의 (justice) 문제에 대한
     업무를 위임받고 있음•

   • 동 단체는 지난 6년간 한반도 문제에 관심을 가져왔으며•
     별첨 북한에 관한 Working Statement 는 카나다
     교회가 한반도의 긴장상태를 이해하고 통일을 위한 화해를
     촉진시키기 위한 분위기 조성을 위해 입할 적절한 시기라는
     인식에서 지난 1년간 추진해온 것임•

공람	북미과 86년 3월 7일 홍지인	담 당	과 장	심의관	국 장 전결	차관보	차 관	장 관

0070

- 동 성명문은 카나다 교회가 한국문제에 대한 자체적인
  입을 추진하는 근거로 삼고, 또한 교회 구성원들에게
  교육시키기 위한 동 단체의 자료(working document)
  로서 발행되었음.

○ 북한에 관한 성명문(Canada Asia Working Group

  Working Statement on North Korea)

  (서 론)

  - 2차대전이후 한국은 미국과 쏘련에 의해 남·북한으로 분단
    된후 카나다는 대한민국(남한)과 관계를 유지해오고 있음.
    DPRK (북한)과의 이와 유사한 관계의 가능성은 한국전쟁에
    의해 배제되었음.

  - 1946 북에서는 종교자유를 위해 한국교회연합 (Korean
    Christian Federation) 이 창설되었음. 많은 기독교
    인들은 공산주의 정부에 반대하였으며, 기독교인들은 수시로
    미국의 첩자들이라는 의심을 받기도 하였는 바, 한국전쟁중
    남한으로의 피난이 가속화됨.

  - 전쟁후 남·북간의 접촉은 단절되고 알려진 바로는 북한에는
    조직체로서의 교회는 더이상 존재하지 않고 소규모의 기독교
    인들이 가정에서 모임을 계속하고 있음. 우리는 한국교회
    연합(KCF) 의 성격과 현재활동에 대해서는 잘 모르나 지난
    수년간 KCF 는 주로 유럽에 있는 교회에 tentitive

0071

feeler 들을 파견하였음. 84년말 적어도 수개의 미국
기독교관련 그룹이 KCF 관계자들과 만났으며, 북한
기독교인들을 방문하였음. 85.11 두명의 세계교회협의회
(WCC) 회원이 KCF 중앙위원회 초청으로 북한을 방문하였음

- 남한의 사람들 사이에는 한국민의 단일성과 통일에의 염원이
  깊게 남아있음. 한국교회와의 연대속에서 우리도 이러한
  염원을 이해하고자 하며, 극복할수 없는 것처럼 보이는
  정치적 장애에도 불구하고 통일을 저해하는 긴장을 완화
  하는것을 도울수 있는 방안을 모색하고 있음.

- 이러한 상황을 고찰하면서 우리는 카나다의 일부교회가 중공이
  고립되었던 시절에 중공인들과의 관계를 유지함으로서 보여준
  긍정적인 역할을 기억하고 있으며, 또한 카나다 정부가 다른
  많은 서구국가들에 앞서 중공을 외교적으로 승인함으로써
  기여한 바도 기억하고 있음. 이것은 우리에게 장차 우리의
  북한과의 관계와 관련, 시사하는 바가 있음.

(현재 상황)
- 근래 서방으로부터 북한을 방문할수 있는 사람들이 증가되어
  왔으며, 그들의 북한에 대한 관찰은 참고가 되었음. 그밖에
  일부 교회단체 또는 비교회 단체들이 북한 방문계획을 세우고
  있음. 이러한 비공식 접촉이 증가하는데도 서방국가 정부
  들은 좀더 공식적인 접촉을 개시하는데 주저하고 있음.

0072

- 1984.10월말 WCC 주관으로 일본에서 '동북아에서의 평화、 정의에 대한 범교회 협의회'가 개최되었음. 동 협의회 성명서는 2차세계대전 이후 동북아지역은 화합、정치적자유、 인권、민주화등에 있어서의 문제와 함께 긴장이 계속 되어온 지역임을 지적하였음. 한반도는 세계 핵전쟁 까지 촉발 시킬수 있는 지역으로 이러한 긴장의 핵심지역임.

- 아래와같은 최근 움직임은 우리에게 희망을 주고、행동 근거를 제시해 주는 것으로 인식하고 있음.
  - 남북한을 포함한 3자회담 제의
  - 북한의 수해 구호물품 제공과 남한의 접수
  - 경제회담 제의
  - 적십자회담 재개 결정 및 소수이산가족의 상호 방문

- 이러한 움직임의 출현과 이지역에서의 긴장감소에 공헌할 정책을 추구하겠다는 세계교회의 Commitment 는 카나다 교회들이 이러한 Process 의 일부가 되고자 하는것이 적절하다는것을 말해줌. 범교회협의회의 건의는 아래 우리의 확인사항에 반영되었음.

(새로운 방향모색)
- 우리는 신의 섭리속에서 북한의 현실에 대해 인식하고 대응 할수있는 방법을 추구하고 있음.
  1. 우리는 북한주민들 사이에도 신이 활발히 존재함을 인식하고 있으며、우리의 적절한 대응이 가능한 신의 활동의 징표를 인식하고자 하고 있음.

0073

2. 우리는 앞길이 불확실하다는 것을 인정하며 우리가
   취해야하는 조치를 확실히 알지 못하지만 신의 도리를
   따르고 있다는 신념속에서 우리는 성령의 인도를 기꺼이
   받아들일것임.

3. 우리는 분단에 따른 한국민의 비극과 이에대한 서방
   세계의 복잡한 연루를 인식하고 있으며, 남한의 신도들이
   북한 동포로 부터 분리되어온 때문에 느끼는 슬픔을
   인정함. 우리는 남북 이산가족 접촉 재개 촉진을 돕자는
   1984년 벙고획협의회의 건의를 지지함.

4. 우리는 한반도 통일문제로 인도될 화해와 정의 실현
   과정에 있어 방관자가 될수 없으며, 이에 참여해야함.
   우리는 화합을 저해시키는, 북한에 대한 Stereotypes,
   편견 및 적대적 분위기를 극복해야함.

5. 우리는 카나다 고획들이 북한 주민의 실상에 관해 더
   잘알고 이해하고자 하는 희망을 수긍하며 정치적 목적을
   위한 왜곡을 시정하기 위해 남.북한에 관해 정확한 정보를
   추구하고 전파하는것을 요함.

6. 우리는 카나다 고획단체들이 북한의 가능한 지역을 방문
   하도록 고무시키고, 주민대 주민의 접촉을 개설하고,
   그들이 카나다에 돌아왔을 때 그들이 경험한 바를 함께
   나누는것이 바람직하다고 믿고있음. 북한고획와 관계를
   전개해 나감에 있어 WCC 및 CCA (Christian
   Conference of Asia) 와 협력하는것이 필수적일것임.

0074

7. 우리는 지금까지 카나다 외교관들과 정부관리들이
   북한과의 접촉을 장려해오지 않았기 때문에 우리
   스스로의 접촉결과 얻은 신빙성있는 정보들을 그들에게
   나누어 주는것이 가치있는 일이라고 보고 있으며,
   그들이 우리의 북한방문과 북한 사람들을 카나다로
   불러올수있는 학술, 문화적 교류를 통해 주민대 주민의
   교류를 촉진시키는데 협조해 주기를 촉구함.

- 우리는 새로운 방향으로 발전해 나가는 것이 용이하다는
  확신에서가 아니라 지금이 전진을 위한 적절한 시기이며
  우리가 그렇게하는 것은 신의 뜻이라는 신념에서 이성명을
  만들었음.

0075

외 무 부

번 호 : VCW-0593   일 시 : 60627 1800   종 별 :

수 신 : 장 관(영재,미북) 사본:주카나다대사-중계필

발 신 : 주 벤쿠버 총영사

제 목 :

1. 당지 벤쿠버 카나다 연합교회에서는 한국의 인권문제에 대해 종종 문제를 제기해 왔는바, 본직은 6.27. 최영사와 함께 동 교회의 목사 VASANT R. SAKLIKER(인권문제 책일자)에 대한 순화대책의 일환으로 동인을 오찬에 초대하고(장소: 엑소포내 한국 식당) 아울러 한국관 및 아국 민속무용 공연을 관람토록 하였음.

2. 동인에 의하면 카나다 연합교회 연차총회가 86.8.12-22간 카나다 온타리오주의 SU DBURY 시에서 개최되어 세계 인권문제도 취급할 예정이라하며, 이때 아국의 인권문제 에 관한 RESOLUTION을 체택할 계획이라고 하였음.

3. 앞으로 동인 및 동인 추종자들을 계속 접촉, 순화코자함.

(총영사 강신성-국장)

예고: 86.12.31.일반

일반문서로 재분류 (1986.12.기)

영교국   차관실   1차보   2차보   미주국   정문국   청와대   안 기

86.06.29 01:03
의신 2과 통제관

0076

기 안 용 지

분류기호 문서번호	미북 700-**22166** (전화:)		시 행 상 특별취급	
보존기간	영구·준영구. 10. 5. 3. 1.	장 관		
수 신 처 보존기간				
시행일자	1986.6.25.			

<table>
<tr><td rowspan="3">보
조
기
관</td><td>국 장</td><td>전 결</td><td rowspan="3">협
조
기
관</td><td></td><td>문 서 통 제</td><td></td></tr>
<tr><td>심의관</td><td>ν</td><td></td><td rowspan="2">허 인
'86.6. 27
문지관</td><td></td></tr>
<tr><td>과 장</td><td></td><td></td><td>발 송 인</td></tr>
<tr><td colspan="3">기안책임자   홍지인</td><td></td><td></td></tr>
</table>

경 유 수 신 참 조	주몬트리올 총영사	발신명의	발수송 1986. 6. 27 외무부	
제 목	청원서 송부			

    대 : 몬트리올(정) 720-130

    1. 대호 청원서한 관련, 강종헌 (Kang Jong-hon)   은

재일동포로서 1970.8경 북괴 공작지도원에게 포섭되어 월북, 간첩

교육을 받았으며 1971.4경 모국 유학생을 가장하여 국내에 잠입하여

국가 기밀을 탐지, 재일북괴 공작원에게 보고하는등 간첩활동을 한

범죄사실로 1977.3.15, 대법원에서 사형을 선고 받고, 그후 징역 20년

으로 감형되어 현재 복역중에 있읍니다.

                   / 계속 /   0077

1505-25(2-1) 일(1)갑
85. 9. 9. 승인

190mm×268mm 인쇄용지 2급 60g /㎡
가 40-41·1985. 10. 29.

2. 동 청원서한에 대하여 동인은 양심수가 아니라 간첩

죄를 범한 범죄자이며, 또한 대한민국 헌법은 고문을 절대 금지하고

있을 뿐만 아니라 고문으로 인한 자백은 증거 능력이 없는등 인권

침해 방지를 위한 제도적 장치를 두고 있으므로 동인이 고문에 의한

자백을 근거로 처벌되었다는 주장은 전혀 사실과 다르다는 요지로

적절히 회신하기 바랍니다.   끝.

0078

ㄷ : 속신 : 터5백 봉이라장는

An Interim Report of the Investigation

on Rep. Yoo Sung-hwan of the NKDP

October, 1986

1. Prior to his cabinet interpellation in a plenary
   Assembly session on October 14, 1986, Representative
   Yoo Sung-hwan distributed to the press a manuscript
   of his remarks supporting the Communist North Korean
   cause, thus corresponding to its strategy and tactics.

   The gist of his manuscript is as follows;

   - National policy should be reunification rather
     than anti-communism.

   - The Inchon incident was a public struggle for
     the survival against the exploitation and a
     spontaneous fighting against the policy of
     major powers to perpetuate the division of
     the Korean peninsula.

   - The authorities fabricated the Sam Min(People,
     Nation, Democracy) ideology as pro-communist.

   The Prosecution, which is undertaking investigation
   on lawmaker Yoo Sung-hwan's violation of the National
   Security Law, has brought following facts to light
   in the process of interrogation and the investigation
   is still underway.

2. It is almost certain that the manuscript of lawmaker
   Yoo was not written by himself but by the figures
   affiliated to the leftist circle. In particular,
   it was found through the investigation that a
   figure named "L", who once was a member of the
   radical leftist student circle, has been deeply
   involved in drafting the manuscript.

1

0080

The prosecution is conducting thorough investigation
on the possibility of Representative Yoo's connection
with the radical leftist groups, such as the United
People's Movement for Democracy and National Unification,
through Yang Soon-Suk, Yoo's secretary, who used to
collect and distribute the impure books and publications
issued by such groups.

3. Rep. Yoo promised to correct some parts of his
   manuscript when Speaker, Chairman of Internal
   Affairs Committee of the National Assembly and
   DJP Floor Leader pointed out in advance that
   those parts were likely to cause trouble.

   However, he breached the promise and made a speech
   without correcting any part of his manuscript.
   Such a behavior of Rep. Yoo evidences his criminal
   intent more clearly.

   The Prosecution interprets that the very contents
   of his speech as well as his act of distributing
   the manuscript in advance to reporters go beyond
   the scope of the Assemblyman's privilege of immunity.

   Originally, the privilege means that a lawmaker
   would not take the responsibility for his speech
   and vote made in the due course of discharging
   his duties in the National Assembly.

2

0081

It does not mean that a lawmaker can make any
remark in the National Assembly session when
one considers the fact that the privilege is
granted to enhance the effectiveness of lawmaker's
performance of duties.

The scope of immunity strictly confines to the
activities concerning the performance of duties
and thus the speech in the due process means the
one made according to the official precedure and
in connection with agenda.

Therefore, it would be difficult to interpret
Rep. Yoo's speech, which explicitly violated
the positive law and has nothing to do with
agenda, as an official activity, thus including
it into the scope of immunity.

This reasoning coincides with the logic that a
libelous or extremely insulting remark, even if
it was made in accordance with the official
procedure, cannot be protected by the privilege
of immunity because such a remark cannot be regarded
as a part of the performance of duties in any
sense.

3

0082

정 리 보 존 문 서 목 록

기록물종류	일반공문서철	등록번호	21462	등록일자	1995-01-11
분류번호	701	국가코드	US	보존기간	영구
명 칭	김대중 복권 및 한국의 민주화 촉구 결의안 (Kerry결의안) 제출 및 대책, 1985-86				
생 산 과	북미과	생산년도	1985~1986	담당그룹	북미국
내용목차	1. 기본문서 2. 자 료 * 1985.12.19 Kerry 상원의원, 공동결의안 상원 제출 1985.12.20 Feighan 하원의원, 하원측 결의안 제출 1986.1.3 주미국 대사, 국무성 의회 담당 차관보 면담 - 동결의안 문제해소 노력촉구 1986.1.16 주미국 대사, 대사명의 한국측입장 설명 서한 발송				

0001

1. 기본문서

0002

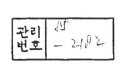

외 무 부 착 신 전 보

번 호 : USW-4287   일 시 : 509261744   종 별 :

수 신 : 장 관 (미북)

발 신 : 주 미 대사대리

제 목 : 상원동향

1. 국무성 제보에 의하면, JOHN F. KERRY 상원의원 (민주, 매서츄세츠, 외무위

소속) 은 김대중에 대한 정치활동 허용을 촉구하는 결의안을 명 9.27. 발의할 예정이

라함.

2. 당관은 본건 관련 상세사항을 탐문중인바 확인즉시 추보하겠음.

(공사 한탁채)

예 고 : 1985.12.31. 일반

예고문에의거 일반문서로
재분류 198 .   .   서립

0003

√ 미주국   차관실   1 차보   청와대   안 기

발 신 전 보

번 호: WUS-3251   일 시: PM7 P30   전보종별: ___지 급___

수 신: 주 미 대사·~~총영사~~ 대리

발 신: 장 관 대리 (미북)

제 목: Kerry 의원 결의안 발의

대 : USW-4287

대호 Kerry 의원 결의안 발의 움직임과 관련, 귀하는 동 의원을 직접 접촉하여 아래 내용으로 동 결의안 발의가 적절치 못함을 설명하고 동 결의안 발의를 철회토록 촉구 바람. ~~동 접촉~~
~~결과 보고바람.~~

- 아 래 -

1. 김대중은 80.7.9 내란음모 및 국가보안법등 위반으로 기소된후, 최종심에서 사형을 선고 받았으나 두 차례 특사조치에 따라 는바 있음. 그후 20년으로 감형을 받아 요던중 도미 신병치료와 국가안보 및 정치 안정을 해치는 행위를 하지 않겠다는 서약등 개전의 정을 참작하여 ~~도미신병치료허용 및 형집행 정지 처분중에 있음.~~ 앞으로 동인에 대해 그이상의 관용을 베푸는것은 ~~(동 관용을 베푼바)~~ 따라서 이러한 조치를 통하여 정부가 ~~전적으로 한국정부가~~ 판단 결정할 문제로서 이에 대해 미 의회가 ~~관 ~~실정법 ~~범법자를 복권시킨다는 것은 '법앞에 만인 평등의 원칙'과 명백한 내정간섭 임. ~~법치국 가로서의 법질서 유지를 파기하는 일임.~~ 거론

2. 제 5공화국 정부는 출범후부터 학원 자유화, 김대중, 김영삼, 김종필을 포함한 정치활동 피규제자 전원 해금, 민주적인

양고재	85년 3월 2일 미북과	기안자	과 장	심의관	국 장	제 차관보	차 관	장 관

발신시간:

외신과	접수자	과 장

0004

2.12총선등 파격적인 자유화 조치를 단행하여 88년의 평화적 정권교체 달성을 위한 민주적 기반을 성공적으로 조성하여 왔는 바, 이러한 중요한 시기에 미의회에서의 여사한 결의안 거론은 한•미관계 발전에 크게 역행하는 처사임.

3. 또한 한국은 '86 아시안게임과 '88 올림픽등 국제적인 행사개최를 앞두고 그 어느때 보다도 정치와 사회안정이 중요시되고 있음에 비추어 우방국 의회에서의 여사한 결의안의 거론은 자제 되어야 할것임.   (장관대리)

예고 : 85.12.31.일반.

예고문에 의거 일반문서로
재분류 1985.12. 기서명 [서명]

0005

외 무 부   착 신 전 보

번 호 : USW-4326   일 시 : 50927 1903   종 별 :

수 신 : 장 관 (미북)

발 신 : 주 미 대사대리

제 목 : KERRY 의원 결의안

대 : WUS-3251

1. 대호관련, KERRY 의원은 현재 선거구인 보스톤에 체재중이므로 우선 동의원의
외교문제 담당 보좌관인 RICHARD MCCALL 을 금 9.27 장재룡 참사관이 면담, 대호
견해를 전달하고 KERRY 의원이 표제 결의안 발의를 철회토록 건의해 줄것을 강력히
촉구함. 2. 이에 대해 동 보좌관은 KERRY 의원이 아시아의 민주발전에 개인적으
로 깊은 관심을 갖고 있을뿐 아니라 동의원의 출신주인 마사츄세츠주내에 외국의 반
정부 인사들이 다수 거주하는 관계로 외국 인권문제에 대한 선거구민들의 높은 관심
표명이 있어 왔으므로 표제결의안을 구상하게 된것이라고 설명함. 그러나 한국정부
의 꾸준한 민주화 노력에 대한 설명에 유의하고 또미의회가 공개적으로 외국정부에
압력을 행사하는 듯한 인상은 부작용만을 초래할것이라는 견해에 공감하므로 KERRY
의원이 10.1(화)워싱톤에 귀임하는대로 동결의안발의 보류를 건의 할것이지만 금번
결의안 발의에 대한 KERRY 의원의 결심이 거의 굳어져 있는것 같으므로 자신의
건의 결과에 대해서는 무어라 분명히 예측하기 어렵다고말함.

3. 한편 KERRY 의원이 현재까지 검토중에 있었던 긴의안은 한국의 민주발전 및
김대중의 민권과 자유회복을 희망하는 상원의 뜻(SENSE OF THE SENATE) 을 밝히기
위한 NON-BINDING RESOLUTION 으로서, 최종 문안 및 발의시기등은 동의원 귀임후
결정할 예정이었다 함

(공사 한탁채)

예고 : 85.12.31일반

0006

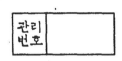

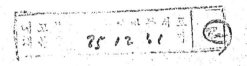

외 무 부 착 신 전 보

번 호 : USW-4399   입 시 : 510022224   종 별 :

수 신 : 장 관 (북미과 이양과장)

발 신 : 주 미 대사대리(장재룡)

제 목 : KERRY 의원 결의안

연 : USW-4326

1. KERRY 의원은 금 10.2. 현재 연호 결의안을 발의치 않은 것으로 파악됨.

2. 동의원은 워싱턴 귀임후 MCCALL 보좌관의 건의에 따라 발의 여부를 신중히 검토중인것으로 보이나, 본건에 관한 동의원의 견해가 상당히 강하다는 것이 주변의 이야기이므로 현상태가 철회 가능성을 의미하는것으로는 해석치 않고자 함.

3. 한공사와 KERRY 의원간 면담을 신청하였으나, 회보를 받지 못하고 있음. 끝.

예 고 : 1985.12.31. 까지

미주국

0007

외 무 부 착 전 전 보

번 호 : USW-5333   일 시 : 511271934   종 별 : 지급

수 신 : 장 관 (미북)

발 신 : 주 미 대사

제 목 : KEERY 의원등 결의안

연 : USW-4287, 4326

1. KERRY 상원의원은 SIMON 상원의원과 공동으로 김대중 복권 및 한국의 민주발전을 희망하는 내용의 결의안을 별첨과 같이 작성, 여타 의원들의 동조를 위하여 DEAR COLLEAGUE LETTER 로 회람중이라함.

2. 동 결의안은 상금 발의되지는 않았는바, 결의안 초안에 대한 상원내 반응 및 동조의원등 상세가 파악되는대로 추보하겠음.

3. 본직은 KERRY 의원 및 여타 상원의원들과 다각적으로 접촉하여 여사한 결의안의 부당성을 지적하고 저지를 위해 최선을 다하겠음.

(대사 류병현)

예 고 : 1986.6.30. 일반

첨부 :

1. 결의안 제안설명 서한

2. 결의안 초안

(첨부1)

OCTOBER 23, 1985

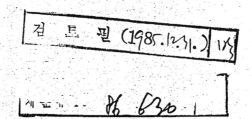

검 토 필 (1985.12.31.기) 15

86 630

DEAR COLLEAGUE:

AS WAS REPORTED IN THE OCTOBER 20,1985 EDITION OF THE NEW YORK TIMES, THE POLITICAL SITUATION IN SOUTH KOREA HAS TAKEN A TURN FOR THE WORSE IN RECENT MONTHS, PRECIPITATING EXPRESSIONS OF CONCERN ON THE PART OF THE ADMINISTRATION.

0008

√ 미주국 차관실 1 차보 청와대 안 기 3 분류

ACCORDING TO THE TIMES REPORT:

"IN RECENT MONTHS, THE AUTHORITARIAN GOVERNMENT OF PRESIDENT CHUN DOO HWAN HAS SWUNG AWAY FROM RELATIVELY TOLERANT POLICIES OF THE PREVIOUS TWO YEARS TOWARD A NEW CRACKDOWN ON DISSIDENTS. STUDENTS ACCUSED OF BEING PRO-COMMUNIST HAVE BEEN ARRESTED. TEACHERS HAVE BEEN DISMISSED FOR WRITING MAGAZINE ARTICLES LABELED AS SEDITIOUS. THREE JOURNALISTS WERE DETAINED AND BEATEN RECENTLY BY SECURITY AGENTS. JUDGES DEEMED OVERLY SYMPATHETIC TO ACTIVISTS HAVE BEEN REASSIGNED."

"PERHAPS THE MOST VIVID EXAMPLE OF THE GOVERNMENT'S HARD LINE WAS A PLAN TO CREATE 'REORIENTATION' CENTERS FOR STUDENTS REGARDED AS LEFT-WING RADICALS. THIS IDEA SMACKED OF 'RE-EDUCATION CAMPS' TO MANY PEOPLE, AND MR. CHUN WAS FORCED TO BACK DOWN BEFOREFIERCE POLITICAL OPPOSITION. AMONG THE CRITICS -- TACTFUL IN PUBLIC, MORE AGGRESSIVE IN PRIVATE -- WERE UNITED STATES DIPLOMATS AND STATE DEPARTMENT OFFICIALS IN WASHINGTON..."

"THIS CRACKDOWN COMES AT A TIME WHEN KOREAN DEMOCRATIC OPPOSITION LEADER, KIM DAE JUNG, CONTINUES TO BE DENIED HIS BASIC RIGHTS. KIM DAE JUNG IS A GREAT FRIEND OF THE UNITED STATES WHO IS STAUNCHLY ANTI-COMMUNIST AND ONE OF THE GREATEST FRIENDS OF DEMOCRACY WE HAVE IN THAT AREA OF THE WORLD.

이하계속

외 무 부　　　착 신 전 보
지급

번 호 : USW-5334　　　일 시 : 511272008　　　종 별 : 지급
수 신 : 장 관
발 신 : 주 미 대사
제 목 : USW-5333 의 계속

KIM RETURNED TO HIS HOMELAND IN FEBRUARY OF THIS YEAR TO REJOIN THE DEMOCRATIC

KOREAN LEADERSHIP AND TO HELP BUILD A NEW DEMOCRATIC OPPOSITION PARTY. SINCE HIS

RETURN, HE HAS INTERMITTENTLY BEEN UNDER HOUSE ARREST: HE CAN NEITHER BECOME A

MEMBER OF A POLITICAL PARTY NOR ENCOURAGE OTHERS TO DO SO: AND HE CANNOT VOTE, C

AMPAIGN NOR RUN FOR POLITICAL OFFICE. HE REMAINS UNDER A SUSPENDED SEVENTEEN AND

ONE-HALF YEAR SENTENCE ON CHARGES THAT THE STATE DEAPRTMENT MAINTAINS WERE FABRI

CATED IN 1980.

SEVERAL HUNDRED OTHER POLITICAL PRISONERS AND FORMER POLITICAL PRISONERS SUFFER

FROM THE SAME FUNDAMENTAL RESTRICTIONS WHICH HAVE BEEN IMPOSED ON KIM DAE JUNG

. UNTIL THEY ARE LIFTED, DEMOCRACY HAS NO GENUINE OPPORTUNITY IN THE REPUBLIC OF

KOREA.

THAT IS WHY WE ARE INTRODUCING THE ATTACHED SENATE CONCURRENT RESOLUTION WHICH

DETAILS OUR CONCERNS FOR DEMOCRACY IN A COUNTRY WHICH HAS BEEN A CLOSE ALLY OF T

HE UNITED STATES SINCE ITS FOUNDING IN 1984. WE BELIEVE IT IS IMPORTANT FOR THE

MILLIONS OF KOREANS STRIVING FOR DEMOCRACY TO HAVE A CLEAR MESSAGE FROM THE AMER

ICAN PEOPLE THAT WE SHARE THEIR CONVICTIONS AND THEIR ASPIRATIONS.

JUST AS IT IS IMPORTANT FOR U.S. CREDIBILITY AROUND THE WORLD THAT DEMOCRACY BE

RESTORED IN THE PHILIPPINES, WE BELIEVE THAT THE DEMOCRATIC FORCES IN THE REPUB

LIC OF KOREA DESERVE OUR SUPPORT AS WELL. AS IS THE CASE WITH THE PHILIPPINES, T

HE UNITEDSTATES HAS HAD A UNIQUE RELATIONSHIP WITH THE REPUBLIC OF KOREA. SOME 5

0010

4,346 AMERICAN SERVICEMEN GAVE THEIR LIVES IN THE KOREAN WAR TO PREVENT A COMICM UNIST TAKEOVER OF THAT COUNTRY AND 103,248 OF OUR COUNTRYMEN WERE WOUNDED IN THA T STRUGGLE. THE AMERICAN PEOPLE HAVE CONTRIBUTED MORE THAN $19 BILLION IN ECONOM IC AND MILITARY ASSISTANCE TO THE REPUBLIC OF KOREA SINCE 1948 AND WE CONTINUE T O PROVIDE FINANCIAL RESOURCES TO SUPPORT THE PRESENCE OF 40,000 AMERICAN SERVICE MEN ONKOREAN SOIL. OUR COMMITMENT TO THE SECURITY OF THE REPUBLIC OF KOREA HAS B EEN UNSWERVING.

BECAUSE OF THIS UNIQUE RELATIONSHIP, WE BELIEVE WE HAVE A PARTICULAR OBLIGATION TO SUPPORT THE DEMOCRATIC FORCES IN THE REPUBLIC OF KOREA, FORCES WHICH SHARE O UR OWN VALUES AND ASPIRATIONS. AND WE BELIEVE THE MOST IMPORTANT CONTRIBUTUIN TH E SENATE CAN MAKE AT THIS TIME IS TO CALL UPON THE GOVERNMENT OF THE REPUBLIC OF KOREA TO REINSTATE THE POLITICAL AND INDIVIDUAL RIGHTS OF KIM DAEJUNG.

THEREFORE, WE URGE THAT YOU JOIN US IN SPONSORING THIS RESOLUTION. IF YOU DESIR E TO DO SO, PLEASE CALL DICK MCCALL AT EXT. 4-2742.

SINCERELY

PAUL SIMON, JOHN F. KERRY END

이하계속

0011

PAGE 2

외 무 부 착 신 전 보

번 호 : USW-5335　　입 시 : 511272010　　종 별 :

수 신 : 장 관

발 신 : 주 미 대 사

제 목 : USW-5333 의 계속

CONCURRENT RESOLUTION

A RESOLUTION EXPRESSING THE SENSE OF THE SENATE THAT THE CIVIL AND POLITICAL RI
GHTS OF KIM DAE JUNG BE RESTORED AND THAT TRUE DEMOCRACY BE INSTITUTED IN THE RE
PUBLIC OF KOREA.

WHEREAS, THE SENATE FINDS THAT ONE OF THE PRIMARY PURPOSES OF THE FOREIGN ASSIS
TANCE PROGRAMS OF THE UNITED STATES SHALL BE THAT OF FOSTERING THE GROWTH OF DEM
OCRATIC INSTITUTIONS, THE HOLDING OF FREE, FAIR AND HONESTELECTIONS, THE RESPECT
FOR FREEDOM OF SPEECH AND FREEDOM OF THE PRESS, AND THE PROTECTION OF INDIVIDUA
L CIVIL RIGHTS AND LIBERTIES THROUGH THE FUNCTIONING OF AN INDEPENDENT JUDICIARY
:

WHEREAS, THE PEOPLE OF THE UNITED STATES HAVE BEEN MORE THAN GENEROUS IN THEIR
COMMITMENT TO THE SECURITY AND ECONOMIC WELL-BEING OF THE REPUBLIC OF KOREA SIN
CE ITS FOUNDING IN 1948:

WHEREAS, THIS COMMITMENT RESULTED IN THE LOSS OF THE LIVES OF 54,346 AMERICAN S
ERVICEMEN AND 103,248 AMERICANSWOUNDED DURING THE KOREAN WAR

WHEREAS, THE AMERICAN PEOPLE HAVE CONTRIBUTED MORE THAN $19 BILLION IN ECONOMIC
AND MILITARY ASSISTANCE TO THE REPUBLIC OF KOREA SINCE 1948 AND CONTINUE TO PRO
VIDE FINANCIAL RESOURCES TO SUPPORT THE PRESENCE OF 40,000 AMERICAN SERVICEMEN O
N KOREAN SOIL

WHEREAS, RECENT DEVELOPMENTS INCLUDING THE INDICTMENTS OF MEMBERS OF THE NATION

0012

AL ASSEMBLY AND A RESURGENCE IN THE USE OF TORTURE AGAINST PROMINENT JOURNALIST

S AND OTHER DEMOCRATIC LEADERSARE CAUSE FOR GRAVE CONCERN OVER THE GOVERNMENT'S

COMMITMENT TO BASIC DEMOCRATIC PRINCIPLES

WHEREAS, THE RIGHT TO DUE PROCESS FOR THE PEOPLE OF THE REPUBLIC OF KOREA IS VI

RTUALLY NON-EXISTENT AND AN INDEPENDENT AND IMPARTIAL JUDICIAL SYSTEM, FOR ALL

INTENTS AND PURPOSES, DOES NOT FUNCTION AND

이하계속

```
┌─────┐
│관리│
│번호│
└─────┘
```

외 무 부 　 착 신 전 보

번 호 : USW-5336　　　입 시 : 511272010　　　증 법 :

수 신 : 장 관

발 신 : 주 미 대사

제 목 : USW-5333 의 계속

WHEREAS, THE PROSPECTS FOR ANY RELAXATION IN TENSIONS BETWEEN THE NORTH AND SOU

TH IS UNDERMINED BY POLITICAL INSTABILITY IN THE REPUBLIC OF KOREA NOW, THEREFOR

E BE IT

RESOLVED BY THE SENATE (THE HOUSE OF REPRESENTATIVES CONCURRING) THAT CONGRESS

FINDS AND DECLARES THAT THE PRIMARY PURPOSE OF UNITED STATES ASSISTANCE TO THE R

EPUBLIC OF KOREA SHALL BE TO PROMOTE THE RETURN TO TRUE DEMOCRACY IN THE REPUBLI

C OF KOREAAND TO THAT END CONGRESS PLACES THE HIGHEST PRIORITY ON:

(1) REPLACING THE CURRENT CLIMATE OF INTIMIDATION, ABUSES OF BASIC HUMAN RIGHTS

AND CIVIL LIBERTIES, AND OTHER ANTI-DEMOCRATIC ACTIONS WITH AN ATMOSPHERE OF DI

ALOGUE AND TRUST BETWEEN THE GOVERNMENT OF THE REPUBLIC OF KOREA AND THE DEMOCRA

TIC OPPOSITION IN THAT COUNTRY IN AN EFFORT TO PLACE EVENTS OF 1980 BEHIND THE P

EOPLE OF THE REPUBLIC OF KOREA

(2) THE FULL RESTORATION OF THE POLITICAL AND INDIVIDUAL RIGHTSOF KIM DAE JUNG

AND ALL OTHERS WHOSE POLITICAL RIGHTS ARE BEING RESTRICTED AND

(3) THE PEACEFUL AND FULLY DEMOCRATIC TRANSFER OF PRESIDENTIAL POWER IN THE REP

UBLIC OF KOREA IN THE 1988 ELECTIONS SHOULD BE OPEN TO ALL WHO ARE COMMITTED TO

THE DEMOCRATIC PROCESS. END

0014

PAGE 1

85.11.28　15:01
외신 2과　통제관

외 무 부   착 신 전 보

번 호 : USW-5377   입 시 : 512031811   종 별 :

수 신 : 장 관 (미북)

발 신 : 주 미 대 사

제 목 : KERRY 의원 결의안

연 : USW-5333

1. 인호 결의안에 대하여 금 12.3. 현재 7 명의 민주당 진보계 상원의원들이 공동 발의를 동의한 것으로 알려진바, 그중 확인된 4 명의 명단은 아래와같음.

- EDWARD KENNEDY
- CLAIBORNE PELL
- ALAN CRANSTON
- CHRISTOPHER DODD

2. 본건 앞으로의 진전상황을 계속 파악 하면서 본직은 우선 연호 결의안 발의시 1차적 심의를 거치게될 상원 외교위원회의   LUGAR   위원장등을 대상으로 동 저지를 위해 노력코자함.

(대사 김경원)

예고 : 1986.6.30. 일반

검 토 필 (1985.12.31.)

예고문에 의거 일반문서로
재분류 19○○.6.30. 서명

0015

미주국   차관실   1 차보   청와대   안 기

PAGE 1   85.12.04 13:06
                                           외신 2과 통제관

발 신 전 보

번 호 : WUS-4155 일 시 : 120 / 1900   전보종별 : 지급

수 신 : 주   미   대사·총영사

발 신 : 장   관 (미북)

제 목 : Kerry 의원 결의안

대 : USW-5333, 5377

Simon등 주동

1. 대호 관련, ~~우선~~ Kerry 의원을 접촉하여 동 결의안이 김대중의 복권문제를 비롯한 아국의 정치발전에 도움이 되지 않을 것임을 아래요지로 설명, 동 결의안을 ~~상정~~ 받아들이지 말도록 설득 바람.

  - 아국정부는 김대중의 정치활동 금지 약속 파기 및 동인에 대한 형집행 정지 사유인 신병치료 종료에도 불구하고 관용을 베풀어 스스로 자숙할것을 기대하며 정치활동 이외의 행동에 자유를 부여하고 있음.

  - 김대중의 복권여부는 동인의 반성과 법질서 존중등 향후 동인의 행동 여하에 전적으로 달려있음.

  - 국회 및 학원문제등 현금의 아국 국내정세 ~~에 유동성~~ 에 비추어 여사한 결의안 상정은 ~~~~ 관용과 화합을 위한 아국정부의 노력과 김에대한 관용조치를 오히려 어렵게 할 가능성도 있음.

0016

앙고재	85년 12월 일	기안자		과 장	심의관	국 장		차 관	장 관		외신관	접수자	통제
	미주과	홍지인											

- 또한 아국정부는 확고한 평화적 정권교체 의지를 가지고 개방과 자율화정책을 견지하며 정치발전을 위한 노력을 계속하고 있음. 아국의 정치발전을 위해서는 정치사회적인 안정과 더불어 미국등 우방의 적극적인 ~~측각~~ 이해 와 지원이 요청되고 있는바, 여사한 결의안은 한국정치 발전 노력에 저해요인이 될수 있음.

- 미의획의 아국의 정치상황~~에 대한 이해와 아국~~ 및 ~~정부의~~ 정치발전 ~~노력~~ 에 대한 ~~이해와 지원이~~ 이해가 필요함.

2. 아울러, Lugar 위원장외에 대호 4명의 의원들도 접촉, ~~상기요지를 설명,~~ 이해를 촉구하고 접촉 결과 보고바람.

(차관 이 상 옥)

예고 : 86.6.30.일반.

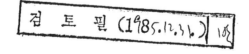

0017

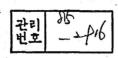

외 무 부 착 신 전 보

번 호 : USW-5514   일 시 : 512121911   종 별 :

수 신 : 장 관 (미북, 경동)

발 신 : 주 미 대 사

제 목 : KERRY 의원 결의안

언 : USW-5377

대 : WUS-4155

1. 본직은 12.11 SIMON 상원의원을 면담하고 표제건 관련 아국의 입장을 설명한 바는 내용을 아래 보고함. (MCDERMOTT 보좌관 및 장재룡 참사관 배석)

가. 본직은 아국정부가 국민 총화를 바탕으로 정치발전 및 민주화를 위한 부단한 노력을 계속중임을 설명하고, 이에 대한 우방의 이해와 지지를 촉구함. SIMON 의원은 자신이 한국의 인권문제에 관심을 갖는것은 한국을 아끼기 때문이라면서, 예컨대 김대중에 대한 자유활동 허용등은 한국정부의 이미지 고양에도 도움이 될것으로 본다고 말함.

나. 이에 대해 본직은 김대중이 언론 접촉등 자유로이 활동중임을 지적한바, 동 의원은 김이 가택 연금중인것으로 알고 있었다고 말하므로 여사한 소문은 사실과 다름을 분명히함. 본직은 이와함께 김이 정당한 법절차에 의하여 유죄 판결을 받은후 국민 화합적 차원에서 형 집행정지의 은전을 받고 있음을 상세히 설명한바, 동 의원은 미국이 김에 대한 재판결과를 인정하기 어렵다는 데 문제가 있음을 지적함. 본직은 김이 한국인으로서 한국법의 정당한 판정 결과에 승복하는것이 법치국가의 기본임을 재차 설명함.

다. 본직은 아국이 남북대치의 어려운 안보 상황하에서 88 년의 평화적 정권교체 실현, 경제발전의 지속, 남북 대화의 진행등 중요한 과제를 풀어나가고 있음을 설명하고, 이와같은 점진적 발전 과정에서 미의회의 결의안 제출 움직임등 공개적 압력은 오히려 부작용이 우려됨을 지적함. 이에 대해 동 의원은 한국의 현 국내 상황이 DE

∨ 미주국 차관실 1 차보 2 차보 경제국 청와대 안 기 김문주

PAGE 1

85.12.13 13:02
외신 2과 통제관

0018

LICATE 하다는것과 공개적 압력을 가하는 인상을줄 경우 부작용이 초래될수 있다는 것을 이해는 할수 있다는 반응을 보임.

타. 한편, 동 의원은 일리노이주내 한인사회의 발전에 언급한후 자신이 KAL 의 시카고 취항과 관련하여 적극적인 측면 지원을 다할 용의가 있음을 밝힘.

2. 표제 결의안은 12.11. 현재 발의되지 않았으며 여타 상원의원들에 대한 사전 호응획득 노력에 있어서도 진전이 없는것으로 파악된바, SIMON 의원과의 면담시 감측으로는 향후 아국 국내 정세와 관련한 특별한 사태발전이 없는한 동 의원이 적극 앞서서 추진할 생각은 없는것으로 보임. 그러나 KERRY 의원으로서는 상원 의 행이 내주까지 진행될 경우 기록을 위하여서도 자신의 결의안을 일단 발의할 계획인 것으로 탐문되고 있음. 본직은 KERRY 의원 및 여타 동조의원들과의 면담 실현을 위하여 노력중이나 년말 회기 종료를 앞둔 의회의 주요법안 심의 일정상 다소 어려움 이 있는바 계속 노력후 추보하겠음.

(대사 김경원)

예고 : 1986.12.31. 일반

검 토 필 (1985.12.31.기 [13]

예고문에 의거 일반문서로
재분류 1986.12.31 서명

0019

외 무 부 착신전보 지급

번 호 : USW-5621　　　일 시 : 512192050

수 신 : 장관 (미북)

발 신 : 주미 대사

제 목 : KERRY 의원 겸의안 밤의

언 : USW-5333(1), 5377(2)

1. KERRY 상원의원은 금 12.19. 오후 언호 겸의안을 상.하원 공동 겸의안 형식으로 밤의하였음. (S. CON. RES. 100).

등 겸의안 제안자로는 언호(2) 에 아래의원이 추가 되었음.

- ERNEST HOLLINGS (D-S)
- PAUL SARBANES (D-MD)
- DONALD RIEGLE (D-MI)
- TOM HARKIN (D-IA)

2. 상기 공동겸의안의 하원측 제안자는 EDWARD FEIGHAN (D-OH) 및 JULIAN DIXON (D-CA) 의원이며, 금일 제출된 겸의안은 언호(1) 에 약간의 자귀수정이 가해진바, 등 전문을 별첨 타전함.

3. 본직은 동 겸의안에 대한 상원외교위 및 하원외무위 심의과정에서의 저지를 위하여 이미 LUGAR 위원장, FASCELL 위원장등 외교위 소속 주요의원들과의 면담을 신청하여 놓고 있으나 금명간 회기 종료를 앞두고 의회의 폭주하는 일정관계상 지연되고 있는바, 내년도 회의가 시작되기전 다각적인 접촉을 통하여 적극 대처할 계획임.

별첨 : 영군

(대사 김경원)

예고 : 86.12.31. 일반

검 토 필 (1985.12.31)

0020

미주국　차관실　1차보　청와대　안 기

85.12.20 13:34
의신 2과 등제관

외 무 부   착 신 전 보

번 호 : USW-5622   일 시 : 512192004   종 별 :

수 신 :

발 신 :

제 목 : USW-5621 의 PART 2

CONCURRENT RESOLUTION

EXPRESSING THE SENSE OF THE CONGRESS THAT THE REPUBLIC OF KOREA SHOULD RESTORE

THE CIVIL AND POLITICAL RIGHTS OF KIM DAE JUNG AND THAT TRUE DEMOCRACY SHOULD BE

INSTITUTED IN THE REPUBLIC OF KOREA.

WEHREAS ONE OF THE PRIMARY PURPOSES OF UNITED STATES FOREIGN ASSISTANCE PROGRAM

S SHOULD BE TO FOSTER THE GROWTH OF DEMOCRATIC INSTITUTIONS, THE HOLDING OF FREE

, FAIR, AND HONEST ELECTIONS, RESPECT FORFREEDOM OF SPEECH AND FREEDOM OF THE PR

ESS, AND THE PROTECTION OF INDIVIDUAL CIVIL RIGHTS AND LIBERTIES THROUGH THE FUN

CTIONING OF AN INDEPENDENT JUDICIARY:

WHEREAS THE PEOPLE OF THE UNITED STATES HAVE BEEN MORE THAN GENEROUS IN THEIR C

OMMITMENT TO THE SECURITY AND ECONOMIC WELL-BEING OF THE REPUBLIC OF KOREA SINCE

ITS FOUNDING IN 1948

WHEREAS THIS COMMITMENT RESULTED IN THE LOSS OF THE LIVES OF 54,346 AMERICAN SE

RVICEMEN AND 103,248 AMERICANS WOUNDED DURING THE KOREAN CONFLICT

WHEREAS THE AMERICAN PEOPLE HAVE CONTRIBUTED MORE THAN $ 19 BILLION IN ECONOMIC

AND MILITARY ASSISTANCE TO TTHE REPUBLIC OF KOREA SINCE 1948 AND CONTINUE TO PR

OVIDE FINANCIAL RESOURCES TO SUPPORT THE PRESENCE OF 40,000 AMERICAN SERVICEMEN

ON KOREAN SOIL

WHEREAS RECENT DEVELOPMENTS, INCLUDING THE INDICTMENTS OF MEMBERS OF THE NATION

AL ASSEMBLY AND A RESURGENCE IN THE USE OF TORTURE AGAINST PROMINENT JOURNALIST

0021

PAGE   1

85.12.20 13:28
외신 2과 통제관

S AND OTHER DEMOCRATIC LEADERS, ARE CAUSE FOR GRAVECONCERN OVER THE COMMITMENT

OF THE GOVERNMENT OF THE REPUBLIC OF KOREA TO BASIC DEMOCRATIC PRINCIPLES

WHEREAS THE RIGHT TO DUE PROCES FOR THE PEOPLE OF THE REPUBLIC OF KOREA IS VIRT

UALLY NONEXISTENT, AND AN INDEPENDENT AND IMPARTIAL JUDICIAL SYSTEM, FOR ALL ITE

NTS AND PURPOSES, DOES NOT FUNCTION AND

WHEREAS THE PROSPECTS FOR ANY RELAXATION IN TENSIONS BETWEEN NORTH AND SOUTH IN

KOREA IS UNDERMINED BY POLITICAL INSTABILITY IN THE REPUBLIC OF KOREA: NOW, THE

REFORE BE IT

RESOLVED BY THE HOUSE OF REPRESENTATIVES (THE SENATE CONCURRING), THAT THE CO

NGRESS FINDS AND DECLARES THAT THE PRIMARY PURPOSES OF UNITED STATES ASSISTANCE

TO THE REPUBLIC OF KOREA SHALL BE TO PROMOTE THE RETURN TO TRUE DEMOCRACY IN THE

REPUBLIC OF KOREA. TO THAT END, THE CONGRESS PLACES THE HIGHEST PRIORITY ON—

(1) THE REPLACEMENT OF THE CURRENT CLIMATE OF INTIMIDATION, ABUSES OF BASIC HU

MAN RIGHTS AND CIVIL LIBERTIES, AND OTHER ANTIDEMOCRATIC ACTIONS, WITH AN ATMOSPH

ERE OF DIALOGUE AND TRUST BETWEEN THE GOVERNMENT OF THE REPUBLIC OF KOREA AND TH

E DEMOCRATIC OPPOSITION IN THAT COUNTRY

(2) THE FULL RESTORATION OF THE POLITICAL AND INDIVIDUAL RIGHTS OF KIM DAE JUNG

AND ALL OTHERS WHOSE POLITICAL RIGHTS ARE BEING RESTRICTED AND

(3) THE PEACEFUL AND FULLY DEMOCRATIC TRANSFER OF THE PRESIDENCY OF THE REPUBLI

C OF KOREA IN 1988 THROUGH GENUINE POPULAR ELECTIONS OPEN TO ALL WHO ARE COMMITT

ED TO THE DEMOCRATIC PROCESS. END

0022

발 신 전 보

번 호: WUS-1377 일 시: 12.21 15:00   전보종별: 긴 급

수 신: 주   미   대사·총영사

발 신: 장   관 (미북)

제 목: Kerry 의원 결의안 발의

       대 : USW-5621

       대호 결의안과 관련, 하기사항에 관해 조사하고 결과를
12·22(일) 12:00(서울시간)한 긴급 보고 바람.

       1· 대호 결의안에 대한 상세한 향후 심의절차

       2· 상기 심의절차가 외무(고)위원회와   관련소위원회의
청문회등을 거치는 일반적 절차를 취할것인지 여부와 약식절차를
거쳐 본회의에 바로 상정될 가능성 여부

       3· 제안 주도의원측의 결의안 통과를 위한 예상전략

       4· 의회일정에 비추어본 향후 심의일정

예고 : 86·12·31·일반·

| 예고문에 의거 일반문서로
재분류 19 86 12 31 서명 |

검 토 필 (1985.12.31.)

0023

앙 고 재	25 년 12 월 2 일	북 미 과	기안자	과 장	국 장	차 관	장 관	발신시간 :
					전결			외 신 과

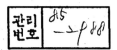

외 무 부

번 호 : USW-5655   일 시 : 51221 1800   종 별 : 긴급

수 신 : 장 관(미북)

발 신 : 주미대사

제 목 : KERRY 의원 결의안 발의

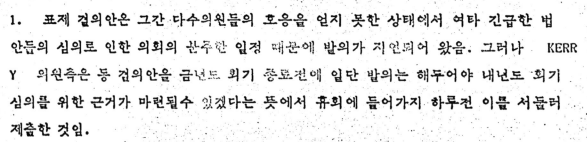

대 : WUS-4370

연 : USW-5621

1.   표제 결의안은 그간 다수의원들의 호응을 얻지 못한 상태에서 여타 긴급한 법
안들의 심의로 인한 의회의 산주한 일정 때문에 발의가 지연되어 왔음. 그러나   KERR
Y 의원측은 동 결의안을 금년도 회기 종료전에 일단 발의는 해두어야 내년도 회기
심의를 위한 근거가 마련될수 있겠다는 뜻에서 휴회에 들어가기 하루전 이를 서둘러
제출한 것임.

2. 동결의안에 대한 향후 심의절차 관련, 하원에서는 이를 외무위 아태소위 및 인권
소위에 동시 회부할 예정이라 하며, 상원에서도 외교위 동아태소위 심의를 먼저 거치
게될 것으로 보임. 현재로서는 약식 절차에 의한 본회의 직접상정은 예상되고 있지
않음.

3. 동 결의안이 내년도 개회후 외무(교)위에 회부된후 심의일정 관련, 현재로서는
비옵빈 경세등이 주요 관심사로 되어있고 또 외무(교)위측이 동 결의안을 굳이 서둘
러 처리할 의사는 없는것으로 보이므로 1.21. 이후 즉각적인 조치 가능성은 많지 않
온것으로 사료함. 오히려 동 결의안을 계류상태에 두고 아국내 정치적 발전추세를 관
망하는 TACTIC 을 취할 가능성이 있다는 견해도 있음.

4. 동 결의안 발의직후 외무(교)위 전문위원 등과 접촉한바에 의하면, 현재의 결의
안 문구가 너무 강경하여 외무(교)위가 이를 그대로 통과시킬 가능성은 적다는 것이
대체적 의견임. 따라서 주도의 원측은 결의안 문구를 약화시키는 등 타협적 자세를
보여 다수의원의 지지를 유도코자할 가능성이 있음.

0024

미주국   차관심   1차보   정문국   청와대   안기

PAGE 1   85.12.22 09:25
                                           외신 2과 통제관

5. 본직은 연호로 보고한바와 같이 내년도 개회건에 다수의 외무(교)위 소속 의원들과 접촉도록 계속 노력하겠음.

(대사김경원)

예고판: 1986.12.31. 일반

0025

발 신 전 보

번 호: WUS-4392 일 시: 12.24 1830   전보종별: 지급

수 신: 주　미　대사·총영사

발 신: 장　관 (미북)

제 목: Kerry 의원 결의안

연 : WUS-4370

대 : USW-5655

1. 연호 Kerry 의원 결의안과 관련 향후 동 결의안 처리 과정에서 예상될수 있는 ~~각항의원들의~~ 예상반응을 아래와같이 분류 상하선 선고(투)기 소속 하였을 경우 각항에 해당되는 의원을　　선정하여 지급 보고 바람.

　　가. 핵심 추진의원

　　나. 금번 제안에는 가담하지 않았으나 아국 국내 정치 문제에 대해 비판적 입장을 견지해온 의원으로서 동결의안 통과를 지지할 의원

　　다. 무의식적인 동조서명 또는 중립적 입장을 견지할 의원

　　라. 아국 입장을 지지 또는 심의과정에서 지지발언을 주도할 친한의원

2. 동 결의안 대책 수립을 위해 12.24. 소집된 관계관 회의 에서는 상기 1항 자료를 토대로 향후 다각적인 대처방안을 강구 키로 하였음을 참고 바람.

검 토 필 (1985.12.31.)

앙 고 재	85 년 12 월 31 일 미 과	기안자	과 장	국 장	제1차관보	차 관	장 관	발신시간 :
					전결			외 신 과

접수자	과 장

0026

3. 상기 회의에서는 동 결의안이 발의만된 상태에서 (소)위원회에서는 구체적인 action이 보류됨으로써 사실상 철회된 효과를 거두는 것을 최선의 목표로 삼기로 하였는 바, 이를 달성할수 있는 구체적 방안과 의견을 함께 보고 바람. (차 간)

예고 : 86.12.31.일반.

0027

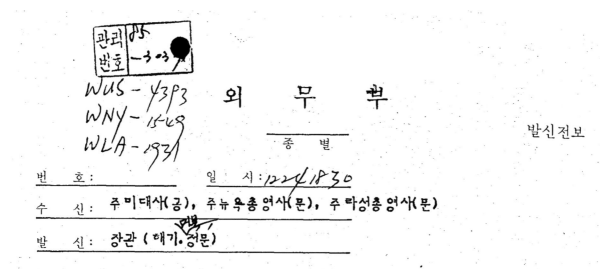

WUS - 4383
WNY - 1569
WLA - 1931

외 무 부

발신전보

종 별

번 호: 일 시:1224/1830

수   신: 주미대사(공), 주뉴욕총영사(문), 주라성총영사(문)

발   신: 장관 (해기.정문)

제   목: Kerry 의원 결의안

　　　표제 관련 귀지 김대중 동조 세력의 현지 언론, 교포매체 대상 활동을
중심으로 한 관련 동향 사전 파악 수시 보고 바람. (해긍관장- 유 태 완)

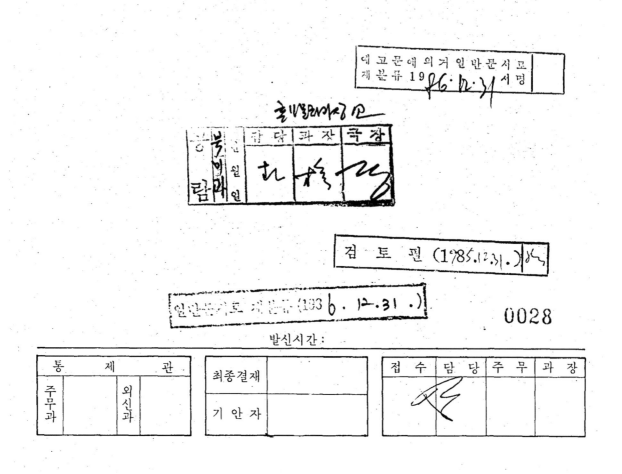

0028

발신시간 :

통	제		관	최종결재		접 수	담 당	주 무	과 장
주무과		외신과		기 안 자					

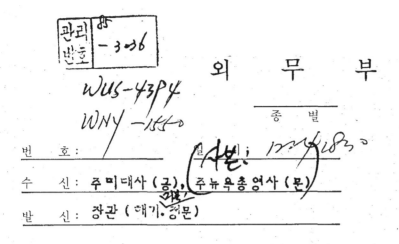

외 무 부

발신전보

관리
번호 85 - 306

WUS-43P4
WNY-155

종 별

번 호 :

일시 : 12 14 18 30

수 신 : 주미대사 (공), 주뉴육총영사 (문)

발 신 : 장관 (해기. 정문)

제 목 : Kerry 의원 결의안

1. Asian Studies Center 의 Backgrounder No. 22 ('85. 1. 25) 참조 바람.

2. '86. 1월초 방한예정인 H.F. 의 D. Plunk 와 접촉 다음 내용을 포함하는 반박논리 제시 Backgrounder 를 방한전 작성토록 협의하고 추진 사항 조속 보고 바람.

   o 김대중 자신의 한국판 "아퀴노" 화 (Aquinonize) 의도 및 일부 미의원 동조의 문제점

   o 외부세력을 이용 국내 정치 목적에 달성하려는 행위

   o 김대중 복권은 국내문제로 내정 간섭 우려 등 . (해궁관장 - 유 태 완)

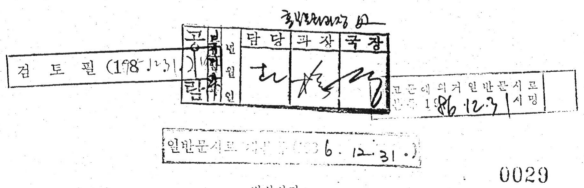

검 토 필 (198 .12.31)

	담 당	과 장	국 장

0029

발신시간 :

통	제	관
주무과		외신과

최종결재	
기 안 자	

접 수	담 당	주 무	과 장

발 신 전 보

번 호 : WUS-4430   일 시 : 51227 1830   전보종별 : __긴 급__

수 신 : 주   미   대사·총영사

발 신 : 장   관 (미북)

제 목 : Kerry 결의안

　　　　연 : WUS-4392

　　　1. 국회측은 연호 Kerry 결의안에 대한 반박자료를 작성하여
공동 제안의원 및 외교 (무)위원회 의원들에게 발송할것을 계획중인바,
이에대한 귀견과 함께 동자료 발송 대상, 방법 및 시기등에 관한
의견을 지급 보고 바람.

　　　2. 아울러 Kerry 의원을 비롯한 금번 결의안 공동 발의
의원에 대한 김대중등 재야인사 측근 세력의 배후 작용 여부도
가능한 파악 보고 바람. (북미)

예고 : 86.6.30.일반.

　　　　　　　　　검 토 필 (1986.12.31.)

　　　　예고문에 의거 일반문서로
　　　　재분류 19 86. 6. 30 서명

　　　　　　　　　　　　　　　　0030

앙 고 재	85년 12월 2일	북 미 과	기안자	과 장		국 장	제1차보실	차 관	장 관	발신시간 :			
							전결			외신과	접수자	과 장	

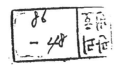

Kerry 결의안 관련 국회대책회의 결과보고
----

1. 일   시 : 1985.12.27. 08:00-10:00

2. 장   소 : Plaza Hotel

3. 참 석 자 : 봉두완, 이종찬, 현홍주, 김상구, 권정달, 지연태,
             나웅배, 이종율의원

4. 주요 협의내용

   가. 결의안제출 경위 및 전망보고 : 미주국장

   나. 협의내용

      ○ 결의안 분석

        - 아국 정치 현실에 대한 심한 왜곡과 더불어 국내
          문제에 대한 지나친 간섭을 담은 악의에찬 내용으로
          규정

      ○ 결의안 제출 배경

        - 진보계 의원들이 선거구민을 의식, 자신들의 image
          고양을 위해 제출
        - 김대중등 반체제인사 계열 및 반정부 교포들의 배후
          주동 가능성

      ○ 향후 추진방향

        - 동 결의안이 제반 심의단계(소위, 외교위, 본회의)
          에서 통과되지 않도록 전략 강구
        - 단, 과잉반응은 역효과를 초래할 우려가 있으므로
          신중히 추진

공람	박미과	담당	과 장	심의관	국 장	차관보	차 관	장 관

0031

- 동 결의안 제안이 공개될경우、야당측에 의해
  악용될 가능성에 대한 대비 필요

° 구체적 추진사항
  - 결의안에 대한 반박자료 작성후 각 의원에게 전달
  - 국회를 중심、정부、민간과의 완벽한 협조 체제 구축
  - 년초부터 의원들의 워싱톤 출장 최대활용
    (최비서관이 조정역할 수행)
  - 1월 방한예정인 Eagleton등 유관의원에 대한 대책
    강구
  - 소위원회 구성
    • 의원 : 현홍주의원
    • 실무작업지원 : 최창윤 비서관、도영심 전문위원、
                       미주국장

° 각부처 협조사항
  - 안기부 : 친 김대중계 배후세력 파악 및 대책수립
  - 해협위 : 주동의원들의 대아국 관계 파악、선거구의
             산업、무역등 제반 측면에서 아국과의
             관계 신속 파악 및 활용방안 강구
  - 외무부 : 1) 외무(고)위 소속 의원들의 관여도에
              따른 구룹별 분류
            2) 반박자료의 발송 대상、방법、시기등에
              관한 주미대사관 의견 파악

0032

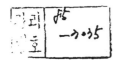

Kerry 상원의원 제출 결의안 관련 대책 회의
----

1. 일   시 : 1985.12.24, 10:30~11:25

2. 장   소 : 청와대 신관 3층 회의실

3. 참 석 자 : 정무 제1수석(주재)

    청와대 이정빈 비서관

    청와대 최창윤 비서관

    문공부 해외공보관장

    해외협력위 부단장

    외무부 미주국장

    안기부 3국부국장

    법무부 검찰국장

    상공부 통상진흥국장

4. 회의내용 :

가. Kerry 결의안의 파급효과 및 제출 배경

    정무수석 : 금번 결의안 제출 배경에 대한 파악이 우선

        선행되어야 할것인바, 안기부에서는 Kerry

        의원과 재미교포 및 김대중 측근 세력들 과의

        연계 여부를 잘 파악하기 바람.

0033

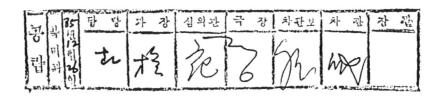

최비서관 : 미국 내에서는 크게 알려질 문제가 아닌데도
국내에서 이를 과대 인식하고 있음. 물론
미국 내의 교포신문에서 대대적인 보도를
할것임. 비율빈 결의안이 그러했듯이 이번
결의안 경우에도 미국 내에서 큰 관심을 끌지못할
것임. 문제는 일반국민들이 이를 과대하게 인식할
우려가 있기 때문인바 이에대한 대책이 수립
되어야 함.

이미 미의원들과 접촉 가능한 국회의원
들이 많으므로 청문회 개최 저지가 가능할
것으로 봄. 외무위원회 소속 의원수가
얼마되지 않으므로 적극 교섭에 임하면
성과를 거둘수 있을것임.

나. 추진목표

정무수석 : 금번 결의안과 관련, 아측이 취할수 있는
가장 최선의 방안은 어떤것인지 ?

미주국장 : 금년은 이미 회기가 종료 되었으므로 내년도
회의가 시작되는 1.21부터 재거론 될것임.
이상적인 방안으로는 내년 개회까지 Kerry
의원이 동 결의안을 철회하도록 노력하는
것이나 현실적으로 불가능한 것으로 보임.

0034

최비서관 : 차선책으로 동 결의안이 발의만되고 계류 된 상태에서
시간을 끌도록 하는 방안을 생각할수 있음.

정무수석 : 동 결의안의 계류 지연을 목표로 삼고 의원접촉
활동을 진행하되, 대상의원들을 몇몇 그룹으로
나누어 체계적인 대처가 필요할것임. 우선 핵심
추진의원, 금번 제안에는 가담하지 않았으나 한국
국내정치 문제에 대해 비판적 입장을 견지해온
의원, 무의식적인 동조 서명 또는 중립적 입장
표명의원, 아측입장 지지 및 심의과정에서 지지
발언을 주도할 친한의원으로 분류하여 각 그룹별로
대책을 수립토록 하는 것이 좋겠음. 우선 분류
작업은 주미대사관에서 현지 감각을 가지고 분류
하도록 조치바람.

다. 추진방안

(그룹별 대책수립)

정무수석 : 년내에 외무부 보고가 작성되는 대로 그룹별대책을
세우되 정무 1에서(최창윤 비서관) 국회의원의
파견여부를 검토하기 바람. 인선시 논리전개와
언어소통 능력등을 감안해야 할것임. 파견시기는
1월 10일 이후가 좋을 것 같음.

0035

최비서관 : 국회 '대미 특별반' 이 중심이 되어 미 상·하의원
들에 대해서 2 page 가량의 서한을 작성하여
발송하겠음.

(기본입장 자료 작성)
정무수석 : 미의원들에 대한 설득시에는 금번 결의안 내용의
부당성 지적과 함께 여사한 결의안 제출이 민주
발전과 평화적 정권교체에 방해가 됨을 설명할수
있어야 함.

통상국장 : 미의원들에게는 막연히 지지를 부탁하는것 보다는
아측 입장을 설득력있게 작성한 position paper
를 만들어 활용토록 해야 할것임. 친한의원들이
동료의원들을 설득할때도 도움이 될것임.

최비서관 : 영어로 작성된 3-4 page 의 position paper
를 비서실에서 작성한후 외무부와 안기부가 이를
검토토록 하겠음.

정무수석 : 아측 자료를 미의원에게 전달할때는 반드시 구두
설명과 자료수교를 병행하는것이 효과가 있는것
같음.

(Mr. Plunk 활용)

해공관장 : Heritage Foundation 의 Plunk 가
김대중문제에 관해 좋은글을 쓰고 있는데

0036

마침 1월초 방한 예정임. Mr. Plunk   에게
새로운 추이를 설명하고 반박자료를 작성하도록
하여 이를 활용하는 것이 좋을것 같음.

정무수석 : 사전에 필요한 information   을 주어 방한할때
아예 자료를 완성해서 오도록 하는것이 좋겠음.

(교포언론 동정 파악)

정무수석 : 아울러 해외공보관에서는 교포언론의 동정을 파악
토록 조치바람. 교포언론을 잘 활용하면 금번
결의안 제출 배경 파악에도 도움이 될것임.

(로비스트 활용)

정무수석 : 로비스트를 활용하는 방안에 대한 해협위측의
의견은 ?

부 단장 : Deaver 사와 Arnold & Porter   사가 통상
관계를 중심으로 일해왔기 때문에 큰 기대를 하기는
어려우나 기본 추진 방침이나 아측입장 논지개발은
가능하리라고 봄.

정무수석 : 이때문에 많은 돈을 들일 필요는 없다고 생각함.

3부국장 : 그렇기 때문에 미의회 문제만을 전담하는 로비스트
고용이 필요한것임.

0037

정무수석 : 동감임. 외무부와 안기부의 의견을 참조해서
청와대 비서실에서 잘 검토해 보기바람.

(지면인사 서신발송)

3부국장 : 우선 관계의원과 면식이 있는 정치인과 경제인의
서한발송을 유도해 보는것이 어떨런지 ?

정무수석 : 아측입장만 주장한 편지를 보내면 읽지도 않고
버릴 가능성이 많음. 갑자기 부담스런 편지를
보내는것 보다는 우선 간단한 인사편지를 보내고
구체적인 이야기는 만나서 하는것이 좋을 것임.

최비서관 : 연말에 2 page 정도의 서한을 송부할 예정임.
우리 국회의원들이 외무위원회 의원 과반수
이상과 전화로도 설득이 가능한 정도의 가까운
관계를 유지하고 있음.

(선거기반활용)

통상국장 : 대상의원들에 대한 결과가 나오면 선거구와 관련
있는 아국 업체등을 활용하여 간접적인 영향력
행사를 할수 있도록 가능한 방안을 강구하겠음.

정무수석 : 상공부와 해협위가 잘 검토해 주기 바람.

부단장 : Kerry 의원의 경우 선거구인 Massachusetts
주의 고 역량이 많지않아 소기의 성과를 거둘수

0038

있는지는 의문이지만 여타의원에 대해서는
가능한한 활용방안을 검토해 보겠음.

(결 론)

정무수석 : 금번 결의안을 계류 시킨다는 기본목표아래 우선
         금년내에 주미대사관의 대상의원 분류보고가 오면
         이를 토대로 대상의원의 성향과 배경세력(특히
         김대중 세력과의 연계관계)을 면밀히 연구하여
         1월 10일까지 구체적 대응책을 수립토록 하고
         그 시점에서 다시한번 회의를 개최토록 하는것이
         좋겠음.

검 토 필 (1985.12.31.) 내

0039

金大中 復権 등에 관한
美議会 決議案 対策会議

第1次會議

1. 일   시 : 1985.12.24.10:30~11:30

2. 장   소 : 비서실 3층 회의실

3. 회의주제 : 정무1수석

4. 참석자

〈 청와대 〉	〈 관계부처 〉
이정빈 비서관	문공부 해외공보관장
최창윤 비서관	해외협력위 부단장
	외무부 미주국장
	법무부 검찰국장
	상공부 통상진흥국장
	안기부 3국 부국장

5. 대책방안 토의결과

가. 결의안의 성격 및 문제점

o 결의안은 단순히 의회의 견해를 밝히는 것으로서
   미행정부로 하여금 어떤 조치를 취하도록 의무를 부과하는
   법적 구속력은 없음·

0040

o 그러나 동결의안이 미의회에 제출되었다는 사실 그 자체와
  향후 의회 심의과정에서 미의회 의원들의 아국 국내정세에
  대한 그릇된 인식 유발, 미국내 교포언론 보도확산 및
  국내 파급효과 우려

나. 심의전망

　　o 86년은 미의회 중간선거의 해로서 의회 회기는 8월중순의
　　　여름 휴회와 동시에 사실상 종료될 전망인 반면,
　　　결의안을 다루게 될 외무위원회의 86년중 주요 관심사는
　　　비율빈정세, 소관 예산심의 등으로서 결의안은 주요 심의
　　　안건이 되지 않을 것으로 예상

　　o 현재로서 외무위원회는 결의안을 계류상태에 두고 아국내
　　　정치발전 추세를 관망할 것으로 보이는 바,
　　　결국 심의여부는 아국 국내정세 발전상황과 주동의원들의
　　　적극성 여부에 많이 좌우될 것으로 관측됨.

　　* 다만 공동발의 의원의 수는 의회내 일반관례상 앞으로
　　　증가 예상

다. 대책방안

　　o 발의의원의 정치신념상 동 결의안을 철회토록 하는 것은
　　　불가능한 일임.

　　o 따라서 동결의안을 계류상태에서 99기 의회 종료와 함께
　　　사실상 폐기되도록 하는 것이 최선의 방책이 될 것인바,
　　　이를 위해 우선 각 관계부처는 다음사항을 준비 또는
　　　조사토록 함.

0041

1) 주동 배후세력 파악 (안기부·외무부)
 - 주동의원들의 선거구
 - 김대중 지지세력 등 반정부 교포활동

2) 의원성향별 그룹화 작업 (외무부·안기부)
 - 핵심 주동의원
 - 단순 공동제안 참여의원 및 무관심 의원
 - 아국에 대한 비판적인 의원
 - 아국 입장 대변 의원

3) 홍보관계 (문공부·외무부)
 - 현지 홍보활동 필요성 여부 및 방법
 - 교포신문 보도상황 파악 및 국내 보도관제

4) 반박논리 개발
 - 자체적으로 반박논리 개발 (청와대·외무부·안기부)
 - 헤리티지 파운데이션의 David Plunk 연구원
   활용 (문공부)

5) 개인의원별 대아국관계 기록조사 (안기부·상공부·외무부)

6) 아국 국회의원 활용방안 (최비서관)
 - 주요 아국의원의 서한발송 문제
 - 대 미의회의원 접촉 설득문제

第2次會議

관계부처별로 상기자료가 집약되면 가급적 1.10 이전
제2차회의를 개최토록 함.

0042

Kerry 決議案 關聯 動向

安企部

美議会　民主党　進步派議員, 金大中復権　및

韓国民主化　促求　共同決議案　提出

(1)　12.19　美議会　民主党　進步派　議員들은

○　上院에서　「케리」議員（마사츄세츠）이　金

大中　復権　및　韓国　民主発展을　促求하는

内容의　議案을　上・下院　共同決議案（CON-

CURRENT RESOLUTION）形態로　発議한

데　이어

※　決議案　共同提案者（7名）:「케네디」,「펠」,

「크랜스톤」,「도드」,「홀링스」,「사바

네스」,「리글」

○　下院에서도　「페이건」（오하이오）,「딕슨」

（캘리포니아）議員이　上院案과　同一한　内容

의　議案을　提案했음.

-1-

0044

⑵ 決議案 要旨

○ 美国의 対外 援助計劃의 基本目的은 民主
体制의 成長支援, 公正選挙, 言論의 自由 및
独立된 司法制度下의 個人의 権利와 自由
의 保障에 있음

○ 美国은 韓国戦 参戦, 190億弗 以上의 経
済・軍事援助 提供, 4万名의 美軍駐屯 등으
로 韓国의 安保와 経済成長에 寄与해 왔음

○ 그러나 最近 一部 国会議員의 起訴, 民主
指導者 및 言論人에 대한 拷問 등은 基
本的인 民主原則에 深刻한 憂慮를 惹起시
키고 있는바, 이러한 韓国의 政治的 不安
定은 南・北韓間 緊張緩和를 沮害할 것임

○ 美議会는 美国의 対韓 援助의 最優先的

-2-

0045

目標가 韓国에서의 真正한 民主制度를 回復
시키는데 있음을 認識, 다음 事項을 闡明함

△ 現在의 威脅, 基本權·自由의 抑圧 雰囲気
  및 非民主的 措置를 除去하고 政府와 民
  主 野党間 対話와 信頼의 雰囲気를 定着
  시킬 것

△ 金大中 및 모든 政治犯에 대한 政治的
  権利 및 市民的 自由를 回復시킬 것

△ 88 大統領 選挙는 民主的 節次를 承服
  하는 모든 사람에게 開放되어야 하며
  平和的이며 完全한 民主的 政権移護이
  되어야 함.

(3) 上記 決議案은

-3-

0046

○　単純한　両院의　見解를　表明하는　法的　拘
　　束力이　없는　것으로서

○　当初　9月末頃　「케리」上院議員　主導下에
　　作成, 上・下　両院議員들에　대한　事前　呼
　　応　獲得을　위해　回覧된　바　있으나, 特別
　　한　進展이　없자　一旦　民主党　進歩派의
　　見解를　밝힌다는　目的으로　同決議案을　発
　　議케　된　것인바

○　現在　大多数　議員들이　我国　国内情勢에
　　特別한　事態発展이　없는限　積極　推進을
　　躊躇하는　雰囲気인데다가

○　年末　会期　終了를　앞두고　있는　議会의
　　主要法案　審議日程에　비추어　年内　通過는
　　勿論　審議　自体도　어려운　実情임.

-4-

0047

⑷ 이번 上·下 両院議員의 対韓 関係 決議案 提出

움직임은

○ 80年 金大中 減刑 및 韓国民主化 促求

関聯, 美議会의 決議案 提案 以後 5年만에

最初로 提案된 것으로

※ 80·9·23 下院, 「봉커」議員 提案으로

外務委国際機構小委 通過, 本会議에서 否決

80·10·2 上院, 「케네디」議員 提案,

外交委 否決

○ 86年 美 中間選挙와 関聯 民主党 進歩派

를 中心으로 我国 政治発展問題에 대한

挙論이 美朝野에서 積極化될 兆朕으로 보

여져 이에 대한 対応策 講究가 要望됨.

-5-

0048

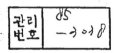

외 무 부 착신전보

번 호 : USW-5737   일 시 : 512271740   종 별 :

수 신 : 장 관 (미북)

발 신 : 주 미 대사

제 목 : KERRY 결의안

대 : WUS-4430

1. 표제 결의안 저지 대책의 일환으로 공동제안 의원들에 대한 면담추진과 함께 아국의 입장을 설명하는 본직 명의의 서한 발송을 계획중임 본직은 또한 상.하원 외교(부)위원회 심의 과정에서 동 결의안이 저지될수 있도록 하기 위하여 내년도 의회 개회가능한 다수 의원들과 접촉하여 아국 정부의 견해를 강력히 전달할 예정임

2. 한편 당관은 미국인 콘설턴트들과 동결의안 대책에 관하여 협의한바, 이들은 한결같이 당관의 저지 활동이 극히 조용하면서도 효과적인 방법으로 추진되어야만 부작용이 없을것이라는점을 강조하면서 당관의 상기 계획이 현 의회 분위기를 고려한 최선의 대책인것으로 본다는 견해를 표명하였음

3. 상기 당관의 계획과 미국인 콘설턴트들의 견해를 감안할때 현 상황하에서는 대호국회측 반박자료를 별도로 송부하기 보다 본직의 서한에 포함시켜 전달함이 좋을것으로 사료되는바 동 내용을 하시하여 주시기 건의함.

(대사 김경원)

예고 : 일반 86.6.30

검 토 필 (1985.12.31.)18

① 도위원에게 전달함 12/28. 11:30.

② 도위원 12/30. 연방법원의 동건 행위 예정

대고문에 의거 일반문서로
재분류 19 86. 6. 40 서명

외 무 부

착신전보

원 본

번 호 : USW-5765　　　일 시 : 512301847　　종 별 : 지급

수 신 : 장 관 (미북)

발 신 : 주 미 대사

제 목 : KERRY 결의안

대 : WUS-4392

연 : USW-5737

1. 연호로 보고한바와 같이 당관은 표제 결의안 공동발의 의원들에 대한 접촉으로 이들의 아국내 실정에 대한 이해를 제고하는 한편, 동 결의안 심의와 관련한 상.하원 외교(무) 위원회 중심인물 특히 LUGAR 상원 외교위원장, MURKOWSKI 동아태 소위원장, FASCELL 하원 외무위원장, SOLARZ 아태소위원장, YATRON 인권 소위원장등을 직접 만나 여사한 결의안의 부당성을 지적하고 표제 결의안에 대한 구체적 조치의 보류 또는 (소)위원회 심의과정에서의 저지를 강력히 요청할 예정임.

2. 동 결의안이 외교(무) 위원회에서 심의될 경우 각의원들의 예상 반응과 관련, 이들의 정치성향 및 인권문제에 관한 관심등을 감안하여 당관이 의회 콘설턴트들과의 협의를 거쳐 잠정적으로 분류한 내용은 아래와 같음. (동 결의안의 금년도 회기종료 직전 제출된 관계로 많은 의원들이 동 제출 사실조차 모르고 있으므로 현 단계에서 본건에 대한 각의원들의 예상 반응을 정확히 분류하기는 어려우며, 아래의 잠정 분류는 향후 수정될수 있음을 혜량바람. 또한 아프로의 심의과정에서 동 결의안 문안 수정등 상황 변동이 있을 경우에는 각의원들의 태도에도 변화가 예상됨)

가. 핵심 추진의원

1) 상원 : KERRY, PELL, SARBANES, CRANSTON, DODD

2) 하원 : FEIGHAN

나. 결의안 통과를 지지할 의원

1) 상원 : BIDEN, EAGLETON, MATHIAS, PRESSLER

✓ 미주국　　차관실　　1 차보　　청와대　　안 기　　　　　0050

2) JEKHTF : STUDDS, BARNES, CROCKETT, DYMALLY, TORRICELLI, WEISS, LEACH

다. 소극적 동조 또는 중립적 입장을 취할수 있는 의원

1) 상원 : BOSCHWITZ, TRIBLE, EVANS, ZORINSKY

2) 하원 : SOLARZ, WOLPE, GEJDENSON, LANTOS, BERMAN, LEVINE, GARCIA

라. 아국입장 지지예상 가능의원

1) 상원 : LUGAR, HELMS, KASSEBAUM, MURKOWSKI

2) 하원 : BROOMFIELD, LAGOMARSINO, MICA, GILMA , HYDE, SOLOMON, DORNAN.

(대사 김경원)

예 고 : 1986.12.31. 일반

검 토 필 (1985.12.31) 1/4

대 공관에 의거 일반문서로
재분류 19 86.12.31 서명

0051

외 무 부   착 신 전 보

번 호 : USW-5771   일 시 : 512311304   종 별 :

수 신 : 장 관(해기,미북,정문)

발 신 : 주 미 대 사

제 목 : KERRY 결의안

대 : WUS-4394

1. H.F. 의 PLUNK 는 연말 휴가중이며 86.1.9. 귀환즉시 BACKGROUNDER 작성건 협의예정임.

2. 85.12.31. 현재 동 결의안을 보도한 미디어는 없으며, 당관 CONSULTANT 들과 협의, 대외적이고 공개적인 반박보다는 제안의원들을 포함한 하원외교위 소속 의원들을 상대로한 조용한 접촉 설득을 전개해 나갈 계획임.(USW-5737, 5765 참조)

3. 단, 동 결의안의 공개토론과 언론 보도가능성에 대비, ASIAN STUDIES CENTER 의 BACKGROUNDER 등을 참조, 반박논리를 작성하겠음.

(대사 김경원)

예고 : 1986.6.30. 일반

예고문에 의거 일반문서로
재 분류 1986. 6.30 서명

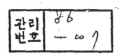

외 무 부   착신전보

번 호 : USW-0033   일 시 : 601031853   종 별 :

수 신 : 장 관(미북)

발 신 : 주 미 대사

제 목 : 국무성의회 담당 차관보 면담

연 : USW-5737

대 : WUS-4430

1. 본직은 금 1.3.(금) 오후 국무성의 의회 및 정부 부처간 업무 담당 차관보인 ....

LLI ... ... 를 신임 인사겸 예방, 대의회 활동 ... ... 의견을

... ... 참사관, ISOM 한국과장, RICK BOCK ... ... 관 배석)

2. 본직은 앞으로 대의회 있어서 아래 사항에 우선 중점을 둘계획임을 설명함.

가. 경제분야에서는 아국경제의 취약성 (무역적자, 외채, 국방비 부담, 구조적 문

제점등) 을 설명, 아국 현실에 대한 미국의 이해 촉구

나. 안보 분야에서협력의 중요성, 특히 88 서울 올림픽의 성공적 개최를 위한 한.미

간 협력 및 FMS 등

다. 아국에 대한 공개적 결의 (예컨데 KERRY 의원 결의안) 등이 아국에 미칠

영향을 고려 , 의회와의 접촉강화를 통해 이러한 문제점을 해소하는 방향으로 노력

3. 동 차관보는 본직의 설명에 공감과 지지를 표하면서 아래와 같이 언급함.

가. 무역문제에 대한 행정부의 입장은 확고하나, 금년이 선거의 해인만큼 각 지역

선거구 문제와 관련 미의회내에서 부본적으로 계속 논난이 예상됨.

나. 안보 문제와 관련, 재정적자 균형 법안이 국방 예산에 미칠 영향이 우려됨.

다. 법적 구속력이 없는 결의안은 한 의원이 발의하여 동료의원에게 요청하면 결의

안의 내용을 확인하거나 조사해 보지도 않고 동조 서명하는것이 미국 의회의 생리이

므로 이를 저지하기가 매우 어려운 실정일것임.

4. 본직은 KERRY 상원의원의 결의안 발의와 관련, KERRY 의원 및 공동 제안

√ 미주국   차관실   1차보   정문국   청와대   안기   0053

PAGE 1

85.01.04 10:45
의신 2과 통제관

의원들에게 이들의 주장을 반박하는 본직명의의 개별 서한을 발송예정임을 말하었던 바, 동인은 오랜동안 상원의원 보좌관등을 지낸 경험을 토대로 아래와 같이 말함.

가. 서한송부 자체가 해로울것은 없으나 <u>득별한기대는 하지않는것이 좋을것임</u>.

나. 편지를 보내는 경우에도 그들의 주장을 정면으로 공격하는것은 오히려 <u>역효과를</u> 초래할 (COUNTERPRODUCTIVE) 우려도 있음.

다. 서명을 한 의원들은 이미 COMMITT 를 한것으로 보아야 하므로 그들보다는 측면 지원인사, 예컨데 영향력이 있는 <u>위원장급 의원들과의</u> 면담등 접촉을 강화하는 것이 더욱 바람직하다고 생각함.

5. 금일 면담은, 본직과 평소 친분이 누터운 NICHOLAS PLATT 대사 (슐츠 국무 장관 비서실장) 와의 지난 12.30. 오찬시 대의회 활동 문제를 협의하는 가운데 동대 사가 의회문제에 경험이 많은 동 차관보와의 면담을 권장, 주선한데서 이루어진것임 을 첨언함.

(대사 김경원)

예고: 1986.12.31. 일반

0054

발 신 전 보

번 호: WUS-0087 일 시: 6010PZ46   전보종별: _____

수 신: 주   미   대사·총영사

발 신: 장   관 (미북)

제 목: Kerry 결의안

연 : WUS-4430

대 : USW-33,5737

1. 표제결의안에 대한 아측 입장 자료는 현재 국회측에서 작성중인바, 동 자료가 완성되면 본부 검토후 귀관에 송부 예정임.

2. 동 자료 접수시 이를 활용, 대호 건의대로 귀하명의 서한을 작성하여 귀하가 선정한 의원에게 발송하고 결과보고 바람.

3. 국회측에서는 아국 국회의원과 각별한 친분 관계를 유지하고 있는 관련 미의원을 소수 선정하여 대호 결의안중 특히 김대중 관계 부분의 왜곡된 점을 시정, 인식시키는 것을 내용으로 한 개인서한을 발송하는 것을 계속 검토중임. 동 서한은 본국에서 직접 발송할 예정인바, 발송시기등에 관한 귀견을 보고 바람. (차관)

예고 : 1986.12.31.일반.

예고문에 의거 일반문서로 재분류 19 86.12.31	서명

앙 고 재	36 년 1 월 일	북 미 과	기안자	과 장	심의관	국 장	제1차관보	차 관	장 관		발신시간 :

	접수자	과 장
외 신 과		

0055

국회 대미 특별위원회 (CSG) 정례 조찬회의 결과

1. 일   시 : 1986.1.8(수) 08:00 —

2. 장   소 :

3. 참 석 자 : CSG 소속의원, 김기환 해협위단장, 미주국장

4. 회의내용

가. Kerry 결의안 대책

소위원회보고 : Kerry 결의안에 대한 아측 입장자료가
곧 작성될 예정임. 동 자료는 김대중에
대한 왜곡된 견해 시정에 주안점을 두고
있음. 동 자료의 활용방법과 시기에 대해서는
주미대사관과 협의후 시행토록 하겠음.

미 주 국 장 :(85.12.28 주미대사 보고내용 및 86.1.4 Ball
차관보 면담 보고 설명후) 국회 작성자료를
주미대사관에 송부하여 일차적으로 공동제안
의원을 중심대상으로 한 주미대사 명의
서신작성에 활용할것을 희망함.

이종찬의원 : 원칙적으로 찬성함. 단지 금번 결의안중
김대중에 관한 부분이 심하게 왜곡되어
있어 개인적 친분을 바탕으로 극히 한정된
의원에 대한 서신발송은 필요한 것으로 봄.

공람	복미과 26년 1월 8일	담 당	과 장	심의관	국 장	차관보	차 관	장 관

0056

물론 동 서신발송 문제도 일단 주미대사의 의견을
청취한 이후에 실행하는것이 좋을것 같음.

봉두완의원 : 소위원회 활동에 대해서는 각하께도 상세히 보고
하였음. 각하께서는 '모범답안'을 잘 작성하여
이를 중심으로 소위원회가 계속 활동할 필요가
있다고 말씀하셨음. 2월초로 예정된 미 조찬
기도회 참석의원들도 방미시 소위 활동을 지원
하도록하되 현지에서의 부작용이 생기지 않도록
활동 대상 인원을 국한시키도록 하겠음.

김기환단장 : 관련의원에 대해 영향을 미칠수 있는 아국 관련
업체 명단을 작성중에 있으며 완성이 되는대로
보고할 예정임.

나. <u>Bush부통령 승계문제</u>

봉두완의원 : 최근 레이건대통령이 88년 대통령 선거시 공화당의
계속 집권과 Bush 부통령의 대통령 당선 가능성을
높이기 위해 대통령 임기만료 1년전에 사임하여
Bush 부통령이 승계토록 하는 방안을 모색중인
것으로 알려지고 있음. 물론 근거가 있는것은
아니나 일본 나까소네 내각도 민간업체를 중심으로
대책을 수립하고 있다함. 우리도 의원 각자가
관심을 가지고 필요시 대책을 수립해야 할것임.

0057

다. **주한미대사관과의 유대강화**

봉두완의원 : CSG 회원들과 주한미대사관 간부들과의 유기적
협조관계 유지를 위해   잠정적으로 1·21
워커대사 이하 참사관급 간부 7-8명과 서울근교의
적절한 장소에서 간담회를 가지기로 하였음·

라. **기타의원 활동**

봉두완의원 : 금번 방한한 Danforth 상원의원과 Fuqua
하원의원 일행에 대하여 본직 주최 만찬을 제공
하였음· 앞으로도 미의원 방한시에는   정부와
국회가 긴밀한 협조 체제를 유지해야 할것임·

한·카 친선협회 소속의원 5-6명이 3월중에
방한할 예정인데 CSG 가 카나다 의원들과도
적극적인 접촉을 하는것이 좋을것 같음· 끝·

0058

외 무 부   착 신 전 보

번 호 : USW-0130   일 시 : 601091832   종 별 :

수 신 : 장 관(해기,미북,정문)

발 신 : 주 미 대 사

제 목 : KERRY 결의안 대응

대 : WUS-4394

연 : USW-5771, 5572

1. 당관 공보관은 1.8. HERITAGE FOUNDATION 의 DARYL PLUNK 와 접촉, 동 결의안에 대한 대응 방안을 협의 반박 내용을 담은 BACKGROUNDER 를 준비하겠다는 약속을 받음.

2. 동인은 동건을 재단 연구원들과 협의, 한국 내정간섭적인 결의안 내용을 분석하고 한국내 정치현황에 대한 왜곡된 견해를 지적하는 이론 개발을 검토하겠다고 말함.

3. 동인은 1.11-2.1 방한 예정인바, 본부에서도 접촉 협의바라며, 앞서 건의한 정부 인사와의 면담 주선바람.

(대사김경원)

예고문 : 1986.6.30. 까지

0059

✓ 문공부   미주국   정문국   자료실 (한반 종합외대 연기)

PAGE 1   86.01.10 10:30
                                           외신 2과 등제관

발 신 전 보

번 호: WUS-0172   일 시: 60116 1130   전보종별: 지 급

수 신: 주   미   대사·총영사

발 신: 장   관 (미북)

제 목: Kerry 결의안

연 : WUS-97

    Kerry 결의안과 관련, 국회측에서 작성한 연호 1항자료를
금 파편 송부하였으니 동자료에 대한 귀하의 의견과 함께 발송시기
및 대상의원에 대한 검토결과를 보고 바람. (차관)

예고 : 86.12.31.일반.

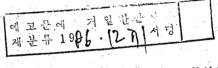

예고문에   거 일반관련
재분류 1986.12기 서명

0060

양고재	86년-1월-일	북미과	기안자	과 장	심의관	국 장	제1차관보	차 관	장 관	발신시간:
								전결		외신과 접수자 / 과 장

외 무 부 착 신 전 보

번 호 : USW-0241
일 시 : 601161808   종 별 : 지급

수 신 : 장관 (미북)

발 신 : 주미 대사

제 목 : KERRY 의원 결의안 대책

대: WUS-192(1), 미국700-99(2)

연: USW-5737

1.본직은 대호 자료 참조후 별첨과같이 본직명의 서한을 작성,의회 개회시기가 측박하였음에 비추어 금 1.16 이를 표제결의안 제안의원 12명에게 발송하고 LUGAR 상원외교위원장 및 FASCELL 하원외무위원장에게 각각 사본을 송부하였음.대호 서한안의 내용은 제안의원 면담 시 구두 설명할예정임.

2.아국 국회의원과 친분관계에 있는 미의원들에게 별도로 서한을 발송하는 문제에 관하여는,연호 보고와같이 현단계에서 아측이 과민한 반응을 보이는듯한 인상은 바람직하지 않은것으로 사료되므로 대상을 극히 제한하여 외교(무)위소속 의원중 개인적으로 각별한 친분관계에 있는 의 원들에게만 발송함이 적절할것으로 사료됨.서한내용은 대호(2)제3안의 내용으로 보다 간결하게 함이 효과적일것임.당관은 본부 지시에 따라   안 심의저지에 1차적 목표를 두고 2차적 목표로는 결의안 통과저지를 위해노력 - 동 서한 발송 시기는 1월말 또는 2월초 정도에 각의원들이 받아 볼수 있드록 함이 좋을것으로 보임.당관 활동에 참고코자하니 서한 발송 미측 대상의원 명단을 알려주시기 바람.

첨부: 본직서한

(대사 김경원)

예고:86.12.31 일반

첨부:서한

미주국   차관실   1차보   정문국   청와대   안 기   0061

THE HONORABLE JOHN KERRY

UNITED STATES SENATE

WASHINGTON,D.C. 20510

DEAR SENATOR KERRY:

I APPRECIATE YOUR INTEREST IN KOREAN POLITICAL DEVELOPMENTS AS EXPRESSED IN TH
E PROPOSED CONCURRENT RESOLUTION WHICH YOU RECENTLY INITIATED.IN THAT REGARD,I
WOULD LIKE TO DRAW YOUR ATTENTION TO THE FOLLOWINGFACTS AND EXPRESS MY OPENNESS
TO OUR DISCUSSING IN MORE DETAIL THE MATTERS ABOUT WHICH YOU,MY GOVERNMENT AND I
ARE CONCERNED.

MY GOVERNMENT IS COMMITTED TO A COURSE OF PROGRESSIVE EXPANSION OF POLITICAL AN
D CIVIL RIGHTS IN KOREA. INDEED,SINCE THE INAUGURATION OF THE FIFTH REPUBLIC IN
AUGUST OF 1980,KOREA HAS MADE SIGNIFICANT ADVANCES TOWARD BOTH POLITICAL DEMOCRA
TIZATION AND NATIONAL RECONCILIATION.THUS,FOR EXAMPLE,THE BAN ON POLITICALACTIVI
TIES WHICH HAD PREVIOUSLY BEEN IMPOSED ON CERTAIN POLITICIANS HAS NOW BEENLIFTED

.

이하 계속

PAGE 2

외 무 부   착 신 전 보

번 호 : USW-0243　　　일 시 : 601161817　　　종 별 :

수 신 :

발 신 :

제 목 : USW-0241 외　PART 2

MOREOVER,THE FREE AND FAIR ELECTIONS WHICH WERE HELD IN FEBRUARY 1985 ARE A DRA
MATIC INDICATION OF THE PROGRESS TOWARD DEMOCRATIZATION WHICH HAS ALREADY BEEN
MADE AND OF MY GOVERNMENT'S CONTINUING COMMITMENT TO THAT PROCESS. PRESIDENT CHU
N HIMSELF REMAINS COMMITTED TO LEAVING OFFICE IN 1988 AND TO A PEACEFUL TRANSFER
OF POWER AT THAT TIME. FINALLY, I CAN ASSURE YOU, AS WELL, THAT MY GOVERNMENT W
ILL CONTINUE TO GIVE CAREFUL CONSIDERATION TO ADDITIONAL STEPS IT MIGHT TAKE TO
FURTHER THIS PROCESS, INCLUDING POSSIBLE REVIEW OF MR. KIM DAE JUNG'S STATUS AS
CIRCUMSTANCES PERMIT. IN SUM,THE TREND TOWARD FURTHER DEMOCRATIZATION AND RECONC
ILIATION,TO WHICH BOTH THE KOREAN GOVERNMENT AND THE PEOPLE ARE STRONGLY COMMITT
ED,WILL CONTINUE TO PREVAIL.

AT THE SAME TIME, THE PACE OF OUR PROGRESS IS CONDITIONED BY OUR GEO-POLITICAL
REALITIES. AS THE U.S. STATE DEPARTMENT'S 1984 HUMAN RIGHTS REPORT NOTED,
BECAUSE OF THE THREAT FROM AN AGGRESSIVE COMMUNIST REGIME IN NORTH KOREA, ALL K
OREAN GOVERNMENTS SINCE THE REPUBLIC'S FOUNDING IN 1948 HAVE FELT IT NECESSARY
TO GIVE TOP PRIORITY TO MAINTAINING EXTERNAL AND INTERNAL SECURITY....
THIS THREAT IS VERY REAL,AND WE WOULD HOPE THAT THIS FACTOR WOULD BE FULLY TAKE
N INTO ACCOUNT BY KOREA'S FRIENDS AND ALLIES WHEN EVALUATING THE PACE OF OUR PRO
GRESS TOWARDS DEMOCRATIZATION.

I WOULD APPRECIATE AN OPPORTUNITY TO MEET WITH YOU IN PERSONTO EXCHANGE VIEWS O
N THIS MATTER AND OTHERS RELATING TO STRENGTHENING KOREA-U.S. FRIENDSHIP AND COO

0063

PERATION.

SINCERELY,

KYUNG-WON KIM

AMBASSADOR

PAGE 2

0064

외 무 부 착신전보

번 호 : USW-0249   일 시 : 601161905   종 별 :

수 신 : 장관 (미북,문공홍보정책)

발 신 : 주미대사

제 목 : KERRY 결의안 대책

표제결의안이 발의된후 시간이 경과됨에따라 동 내용이 당지 특파원들에게 알려지고
있으며 기사화될 가능성도 있는것으로 보이는바 적절한 대책을 강구바람

(대사 김경원)

예고:86.12.31일반

0065

√ 미주국   차관실   1차보   정문국   청와대   안 기   문공부

PAGE 1   86.01.17 10:43
                                                   외신 2과 통제관

1986. 1. 17.

외 　 　 무 　 　 부

공란	북미과	86년 1월 17일	담 당	과 장	심의관	국 장

0300

┌───┐
│ Kerry 의원 결의안 관련 주미대사 보고 │
└───┘

1. 주미대사명의 서한 발송

　가. 발송 일자

　　ㅇ 의회 개최시기가 촉박함에 따라 1.16 발송

　나. 발송 대상

　　ㅇ 원본 : 제안의원 12명

　　　- 상원 : Kerry, Simon, Kennedy,
　　　　　　　　Pell, Cranston, Dodd,
　　　　　　　　Hollings, Sarbanes, Riegle,
　　　　　　　　Harkin 의원

　　　- 하원 : Feighan, Dixon 의원

　　ㅇ 사본 : Lugar 상원외교위원장, Fascell
　　　　　　　　하원외무위원장

　다. 서한내용 : 별첨

2. 아국 국회의원 별도 서한 작성 문제

　가. 의 견

　　　현단계에서 아측이 과민한 반응을 보이는
　　　듯한 인상을 주지 않기 위해서 대상을 극히 제한

0067

하여 각별한 친분관계에 있는 의원들에게만 발송

나. 서한내용

　국회측 자료 제 III안 보다 간결한 서한이 효과적

다. 서한 발송 대상의원 명단 통보 요망

0068

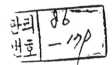

면 담 요 록

1. 일   시 : 1986년 1 월   17일(수요일)10:30-시~11:00 시

2. 장   소 : 미주국장실

3. 면 담 자 : 장선섭 미주국장

   Daryl Plunk 헤리티지재단 정책분석관

   (위성락 사무관 배석)

4. 내   용 :

   국 장 : Backgrounder   작성등을 통해 대아국 이해제고에
           노력해온 데 사의를 표함.

   Plunk : 사실 한국문제등에 관한 미국내 일반인의 느낌 (perception)
            은 무관심이며 상황에 대한 정확한 인식이 결여된 경우가
            많음.

            1980년에 한국으로부터 귀국했을때 한국이 받아야
            할 관심을 위해 일할 생각을 갖게되었으며 그 도구로서

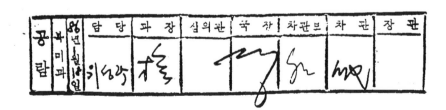

0069

헤리티지 재단 아시아 연구소를 선택하였음. 동
연구소는 미국 정부에 영향을 미칠 수 있는 두뇌
집단임.

예컨대 William Watts Association이 행한
여론조사에 의하면 조사대상의 80%가 한국이 미국의
원조를 대규모로 수령중인 것으로 인식하고 있음.
한미 무역문제도 이러한 오해 (misperception)와
관련이 있을 수 있는바 이는 불식되어야 할 오해임.

국　장 : 물론 각자의 느낌에 따라 국제정치를 보므로 오해가
있을 수 있는바, 그럼으로서 귀하와 같은 사람의 노력이
중요해지는 것임. 아주 올바른 일을 하고 계심.

Plunk : 남북 대화도 한예가 되는데 일부 미국인들은 대화전망을
너무 낙관적으로 보고 김일성의 대미접촉 제의에 순진
하게 응하려고 함. 미의원 방북이나 학자 교류등은
아직 시기상조이며 북한의 저의를 정확히 인식해야함.

국　장 : Dornan 의원의 방북시도때 귀하의 노력이 컸음.
남·북대화는 우선 실질적 성과가 거양되는지를 인내심을
갖고 지켜보아야 할 것임.

- ? -

Plunk : 미국은 강대국이므로 한국문제 해결에도 무엇인가를 해야
한다는 생각을 하는 경우가 있음. 그러나 북한은 미국을
이용하려 하고 있으며 미의원 방북은 북한에 이용당하는
것임.

이를 두고 북한은 레이건 대통령이 미·북한 관계
개선을 위해 의원을 파견하였다느니 미국의 한국정부에
대한 지지 약화의 표현이라는등 선전을 할것임.

국 장 : 김대중에 관한 Kerry 의원 결의안도 또하나의 오해
에서 비롯된 것인데 귀하의 협조를 기대함.

Plunk : 유사한 결의안이 매년 수백개씩 나오는데 대부분은
Personal Statement 에 그침

Kerry 결의안도 마찬가지로서 미국이 원조를
주므로 이래라 저래라 할수 있다는 Jingoistic 한
생각이 바탕에 있는 듯함.

국 장 : 본인의 견해로는 상기 결의안이 국내 정국 불안을 조장할
가능성도 있다고 생각함. 미국이 한국의 안정을 바라는
상황인데 불안정을 야기하는 결의안이 미의회에서 나온
다면 미국의 이익에도 합치되지 않을 것임.

- 3 -

0071

Plunk : 핵심을 지적하셨음. 미의회에 합리적인 의원도 많은
만큼 Personal Statement 에 그치기를 바람.

국 장 : 필요시 주미한국 대사관과 협조 바람.

Plunk : 계속 접촉하겠음. 대사관이 Kerry 결의안에 대해서
공식적으로 언급하지 말아야 함. 그렇지 않으면 여론의
관심을 끌게 되어 사태를 악화시킬 것임.

국 장 : 김대사가 잘 처리할 것으로 믿음. 국정연설에서 보듯이
평화적 정권교체등 민주화 의지는 강력함.

Plunk : 직선제의 일부 장점을 인정하고 그 단점을 지적한 것은
아주 훌륭한 주장이라고 봄.

(헤리티지 재단 관련 자료 수교후)
동봉한 자료중에는 제네바 미.쏘 정상회담 전망에
대한 자료가 있는바 동 자료를 그르바쵸프가 레이건
대통령에게 직접 인용, 전형적인 우익주장이라고 비판
한바 있음. 레이건 대통령은 "나도 보았는데 내용이
좋더라"고 응수하였음. 또한 그르바쵸프는 최고회의
연설에서 헤리티지 재단이 레이건 행정부의 이데올로
기적 본부라고 지칭하였음. 끝.

예 고 : 86.12.31. 일반

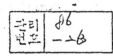

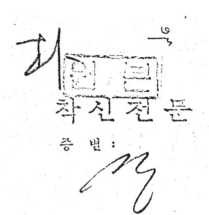

외 무 부 착신전문

번 호 : USW-0480　　　일 시 : 601301917　　　증 별 :

수 신 : 장 관 (미북)

발 신 : 주미대사

제 목 : KERRY 결의안 대책

1. 본직은 금 1.30. YATRON 하원 인권소위원장 및 SOLARZ 아태소위원장을 각각 면담, 프제 결의안과 관련한 아측입장을 전달하고 소위원회 심의 과정에서 동 결의안이 폐기되도록 협조하여 줄것을 강력히 요청한바 등인들의 반응을 아래 보고함.
(장재룡 참사관 배석)

가. YATRON 인권소위원장

1) 인권소위원장으로서의 직책상 한국내 인권문제에 관한 다수의 관심을 묵살하기는 어려움. 또히 김대중의 경우 체미 기간중 의회내 많은 인사들과 접촉이 있었던 관계 르 그의 장래 문제에 관심을 갖고있는 사람이 많은바 그의 약 20 년이나 되는 잔여 형기 기간중 일체의 정치활동이 허용될 전망이 없다면 이는 받아들이기 어려운 것으 로 생각되고 있음.

2) 대사께서 지적한대로 한국내 인권상황에 상당한 개선이 있다는 사실을 인정함. 그리고 미국이 70년대에서와 같이 공개적으로 외국의 인권문제를 거론할 경우 부작 이 더크다는 데도 알고 있음. 그러나 거듭말하지만 인권소위원장으로 인권 및 정치 권 문제에 대한 논의요구를 무조건 봉쇄할수 없는 본인의 사정도 이해바람. 본건 의 가 불가피하게 되더라도 한국에 대한 부당한 비난은 없도록 최선을 다할것임.

나. SOLARZ 아태 소위원장

1) 그간 필리핀 문제로 정신이 없어서 KERRY 결의안은 아직 들여다 볼 시간조차 없었으며 현시점에서 무어라 말하기 어려움. 본인이 원칙적으로 김대중의 복권을 지 지하고 있음은 주지의 사실인것으로 생각되나, 본인이 동 문제를 가지고 한국내 상황 을 더욱 어렵게 만들 의도는 없음.

√ 미주국　차관실　1차보　정문국　청와대　안 기　　　　0073

PAGE 1　　　　　　　　　　　　　　　　　　　　　86.01.31 13:07
　　　　　　　　　　　　　　　　　　　　　　　외신 2과 통제관

2) 이문제와 관련하여 본인은 최근 한국정부의 학생 및 반정부 인사들에 대한 고문 소식에 심각한 우려를 갖고 있음. 이러한 "조직적인 가혹행위" 에 대한 이야기가 계속 나온다면 이문제를 포함한 한국인권 문제 전반에 관하여 공청회가 개최될 가능성도 있음.

3) 대사께서 설명한대로 한국 인권상황에 진전이 있어 더이상 시끄러워지지 않는다면 다행이나, 그렇지 않다면 아태소위에서 이문제를 다루지 않을수 없을것임. 물론 현재로서는 아무런 구체적 계획이 없으며, 향후 논의가 있게될 경우에는 사전에 귀하와 접촉토록 하겠음.

2. 금일 면담시 감촉으로 보아 현재로서는 하원내 표제건에 대한 관심이 별로 크지 않은것으로 보이며, 동건 심의가 있게 되더라도 2 월말 이후가 될것으로 예상됨.(2.8 -18 간은 워싱턴 생인 기념 휴회임) 이경우에도 현 결의안이 그대로 통과될 전망은 희박한것으로 판단되는바, 이러한 상황하에서 동 결의안 추진측으로서는 본건 논의에 유리하게 작용할 한국내 정세변화가 있기를 기다리고자할 가능성도 있음. 본건 관련 진전상황을 주시하면서 주요의원 접촉 활동을 계속하고 결과 추보하겠음.

(대사 김경원)

예고 : 1986.12.31. 일반

예고문에 의거 일반문서로
재분류 19 86.12.31 서명

0074

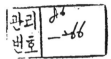

Kerry 결의안 관련 조찬회의 결과
----

1. 일   시 : 1986.1.30, 07:45-09:10

2. 장   소 : Plaza Hotel

3. 참 석 자 : 이상옥 외무 차관(주재)

　　　　　　　이정빈 청와대 비서관

　　　　　　　최창윤 청와대 비서관

　　　　　　　정주영 안기부 3국장

　　　　　　　장선섭 외무부 미주국장

　　　　　　　도영심 국회 외무위전문위원

4. 협의내용 :

가. 결의안 공동제안의원에 대한 주미대사관 접촉 강화 방안

　　ㅇ 주미대사의 해당의원 직접접촉을 원활하게 하기 위하여
　　　　친한 유력의원들의 중계역할 유도

　　　　- 하원 : Fascell 외무위원장, Gilman, Solomon
　　　　　　　　의원등

　　　　- 상원 : Murkowski 의원등

　　ㅇ 공동제안 의원의 보좌관 접촉강화를 통해 결의안 채택
　　　　저지 저변확대

　　　　- 주미대사관 정무공사및 의회담당 참사관 중점 활용

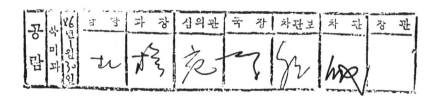

0075

나. 결의안 처리 전망에 관한 정보수집
  ○ 동 결의안의 구체적 심의과정 및 전망분석
  ○ 관련 청문회 개최 가능성 파악

다. 유력 교포를 통한 관련의원 순화
  ○ 친정부 교포 활용 문제는 계속 검토하기로 하되 제반
    여건을 감안, 신중을 기하도록 함.

라. 경제계인사 활용
  ○ 공동제안 또는 외무위소속 의원들과 개인적 친분을
    유지하고 있는 경제계 인사를 적의 활용
  ○ 우선 하기 인사명의 서한 발송후 결과에 따라 확대
    여부 검토
    - 삼성물산 박운서 부사장 : Torricelli 하원의원,
                              Murkowski 상원의원

    - 동방생명 이동복 사장 : Solarz 하원의원
  ○ 상기 서한발송이 효과적이라고 판단될 경우 구평회(럭키금성),
    허완구, 이명박씨(현대)등도 활용

마. 조찬기도회 참석의원 방미시 관련의원 접촉
  ○ 본건을 조용히 처리한다는 기본입장에 따라 참석의원중
    봉두완 외무위원장과 김현진 의원에 국한하여 접촉 추진
  ○ 접촉 대상의원은 국회측에서 선정

0076

바. 국회의장 방미시 결의안 관련의원 면담

    o 국회의장 방미시 Bush 상원의장, O'Neill 하원의장,

      Dole 원내총무등 의회지도자   접촉과 함께

      결의안 관련의원 면담 추진

      - 2.25   워싱턴 도착후 10일간은 입원

      - 3.5-7간   활동 가능

    o 수행원인 도영심 전문위원은 유력보좌관 접촉 추진

0077

미 의회의 김대중 복권 및 민주화 촉구 결의안 발의 관련 대책

86. 1.

국 가 안 전 기 획 부

1. 상황

   가. "존 케리" 상원의원(민주, 마세츄세츠)을 중심으로
      민주당 진보파 상.하 의원 12명이 85.12.19 "김대중 복권
      및 한국 민주화 촉구 공동 결의안"을 상원 외교위 및
      하원 외무위에 발의(결의안 내용 첨부 1 참조)

   나. 85.12.20-86.1.20간 미 의회가 휴회됨에 따라 동 결의안
      통과 추진 활동은 소강 상태 유지

2. 결의안 발의와 현지 불순 교민과의 연계 동향

   가. 한국 인권문제 연구소(소장 대리: 유종근)는 85.11월경
      의회 및 정부 요로에 김대중의 복권을 요망하는 서신 발송

   나.
      고포들과 이들의 활동을 동조하는
      마세츄세츠주 교포들은 85.11월경 "케리" 의원을 접촉,
      김대중 복권을 위해 노력해 줄 것을 당부

   다. "케리" 의원은 85년 11월경 "맥콜" 보좌관을 통해
      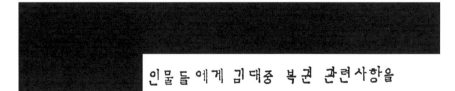
      인물들에게 김대중 복권 관련사항을

0079

1

문 의

(1) 동 반체제 인물들은 김대중 복권 및 한국 인권
    문제등을 왜곡, 과장 설명

(2) 이들은 상원 공동 발의자가 10명뿐임에 실망,
    상원 외교위 동아.태 소위(위원장: "프랭크
    머코우스키") 통과가 어려울 것으로 전망

3. 아측의 대책 추진 현황

가. 85.12.24 청와대 정무 제1수석 주재 관계부처 실무 대책
    회의에서 동 결의안의 상.하원 심의를 저지, 동 결의안이
    사실상 폐기되도록 유도하기로 결정

나. 미국 현지에서는 동 결의안 저지 활동을 공격적이며
    적극적인 방법(국내 인사의 미 의원 앞 서한 발송 및
    미국 의원 주장 정면 반대등)으로 추진할 경우, 물의 유발
    가능성이 있음을 감안, 조용히 저지 활동을 추진할
    것을 건의

    * 동 결의안 저지 활동에 대한 현지 의견

"윌리암 볼" 국무성 차관보 의견(86.1.3 주미대사와 면담시)	서한 송부의 성과를 기대하기는 곤란하며, 미국 의원들의 주장을 정면으로 반박할 경우 오히려 역효과 초래 가능성이 있음.
"프랭크" 헤리티지 재단 연구원 의견(86.1.17 외무부 미주국장 접촉시)	결의안에 대하여 공식적으로 언급할 경우 여론의 관심을 끌게 되어 사태를 악화시킬 우려가 있음.

0080

2

주미대사 (85.12.27 및 86.1.3 보고)	저지활동은 조용히 추진하여야 하며, 국회 반박 자료를 별도 발송하기 보다는 주미대사와 서한을 발송함이 바람직함.
주미 노정기 공사 (85.12.27 보고)	미국 일반인의 관심을 증대시켜서는 안되며, 주미 공관원들이 대상 의원들을 개별 설득해 나가는 것이 바람직함.

다. 주미대사는 결의안 발의 의원 12명에게 86.1.16 국내 인권
   상황을 설명하는 서한 발송 및 아국 국회의원이 별도
   서한을 발송할 경우 개인적으로 구별한 친분관계가 있는
   의원에게만 발송함이 효과적이라는 의견을 외무부에 보고

라. 주미대사는 동 결의안을 심의할 상원 외교위 "루가" 위원장
   (공화, 인디아나) 및 하원 외무위 "파셀" 위원장(민주,
   플로리다)를 주요 의원들을 접촉, 설득 활동을 전개 예정

마. 주미 아국 특파원들이 동건을 본국에 송고하여 국내 언론에
   보도될 가능성이 있음에 대비, 86.1.18 국내 보도 관제 조치

4. 결의안 관련 미 의회 동향 전망

   86.1.21 미 의회가 개회됨에 따라 재미 김대중 추종세력 및
   인권 단체들이 미 의원들에게 결의안 통과를 촉구할 경우,
   동 결의안에 대한 미 의회의 관심이 고조될 가능성이 있음.

0081

3

5. 향후 추진 대책

   가. 설득 논리

      주미대사가 86.1.16 결의안 발의 의원 12명에게 발송한
      서한에 포함된 하기 요지의 논리 활용

      (1) 한국 정부는 정치 및 인권의 점진적 발전을 위하여
          노력하고 있음.

      (2) 1980.8 제5공화국 출범이래 한국은 정치적 민주화에
          있어서 눈부신 발전을 이룩하였음.

          (가) 일부 정치인에 대한 정치 활동 규제조치 해제
          (나) 1985.2월 자유공명선거 실시
          (다) 평화적 정권 교체 천명

      (3) 상황이 허락할 경우 김대중의 법적지위 제고를 포함한
          추가적인 민주화 조치가 검토될 것임.

      (4) 한국 정부와 국민의 열망하는 민주화와 화합 추세는
          점차 강화될 것임.

      (5) 한국의 민주화 발전 속도를 평가할 때에는 호전적인
          북괴로 부터 위협받고 있는 특수 안보 상황을
          감안하여 주시기 바람.

   나. 설득 방법

      (1) 주미대사가 상원 외교위(17명) 및 하원 외무위(42명)
          소속 의원들에게 서한 발송 및 접촉활동 계속 추진

0082

4

(2) 방미 예정인 아국 국회의원들로 하여금 친분 있는
    관련 미 의원들을 설득

국회의장 방미 (2.11-13, 2.23-24)	이재형 의장, 봉두완 및 최명헌 의원	남미 순방시 경유
미 의회 조찬 기도회 참석 (1.31-2.10)	나석호, 정성만, 유흥수, 김재호, 홍우준 의원	

(3) 방미하는 국내 경제계 인사들로 하여금 친분있는
    관련 의원들을 설득 및 서한 발송

다. 재미 김대중 추종세력 및 인권단체들의 동견 관련 활동
   동향 및 견제 대책 수립, 추진

첨부: 1. "케리" 의원 결의안 국문 번역 내용 및 영문 결의안
      2. "케리" 의원 결의안 관련 일지
      3. 상원 외교위 및 하원 외무위 의원 성향 분류
      4. 주미대사 발송 서한 국문 번역 내용 및 영문 서한. 끝.

0083

5

첨부 1.

"케리" 외원 결의안 국문 번역 내용 및 영문 결의안

1. 미 의회는 김대중의 복권과 대한민국에서의 진정한 민주주의 확립을 촉구함.

2. 미국의 대외 원조 목적은 자유·공명선거의 실시, 언론·출판의 자유 존중, 개인의 권리와 자유의 보존등을 통해 민주주의 제도의 성장을 강화하는 것임.

3. 미국은 1948 한국정부 수립이래 한국의 안보와 경제적 번영을 위하여 다대한 기여를 해 왔으나, 국회의원에 대한 기소, 기자와 민주 인사들에 대한 고문재현 등을 비롯한 한국 내외 최근 사태 발전은 민주주의의 기본 원리에 심각한 우려를 낳게 하고 있음.

4. 남북한간의 긴장완화 전망은 현재 한국의 정치적 불안으로 인하여 위태로워지고 있는바, 미 상원은 하원과 함께 미국의 대한 원조가 한국의 진정한 민주주의 회복에 1차적 목적이 있으며, 동 목적 달성을 위해 다음 사항을 최우선으로 고려할 것을 결의함.

   가. 인권 및 시민 자유에 대한 침해와 여타의 비민주적 관행의 분위기를 한국 정부의 재야 민주세력간의 대화와 신뢰의 분위기로 전환시키도록 유도

   나. 김대중을 비롯한 정치적 권리가 제약받고 있는 모든 인사들에게 대한 정치적, 개인적 권리 회복

   다. 평화적이고 완전한 민주적 정권 이양을 위하여 1988년 한국 대통령 선거 절차의 민주화

0084

6

Concurrent Resolution

Expressing the sense of the Congress that the Republic of Korea should restore the civil and political rights of Kim Dae Jung and that true democracy should be instituted in the Republic of Korea.

Whereas one of the primary purposes of the United States Foreign Assistance Programs should be to foster the growth of democratic institutions, the holding of free, fair and honest elections, respect for freedom of speech and freedom of the press and the protection of individual civil rights and liberties through the functioning of an independent judiciary:

Whereas the people of the United States have been more than generous in their commitment to the security and economic well-being of the Republic of Korea since its founding in 1948.

Whereas this commitment resulted in the loss of the lives of 54,346 American servicemen and 103,248 Americans wounded during the Korean conflict whereas the American people have contributed more than $19 billion in economic and military assistance to the Republic of Korea since 1948 and continue to provide financial resources to support the presence of 40,000 American servicemen on Korean soil.

0085

Whereas recent developments, including the indictments of members of the national assembly and a

7

resurgence in the use of torture against prominent
journalists and other democratic leaders, are cause
for grave concern over the commitment of the Government of the Republic of Korea to basic democratic
principles.

Whereas the right to due process for the people
of the Republic of Korea is virtually nonexistent,
and an independent and impartial judicial system, for
all itents and purposes, does not function and

Whereas the prospects for any relaxation in
tensions between North and South in Korea is undermined
by political instability in the Republic of Korea.

: Now, therefore
be it resolved by the House of Representatives(the
Senate concurring), that the Congress finds and
declares that the primary purposes of United States
assistance to the Republic of Korea shall be to
promote the return to true democracy in the Republic
of Korea.   To that end, the Congress places the
highest priority on -

1) The replacement of the current climate of
   intimidation, abuses of basic human rights and
   civil liberties, and other antidemocratic actions,
   with an atmosphere of dialogue and trust between
   the Government of the Republic of Korea and the
   democratic opposition in that country

2) The full restoration of the political and individual
   rights of Kim Dae Jung and all others whose political
   rithts are being restricted and

0086

8

3) The peaceful and fully democratic transfer of the
   presidency of the Republic of Korea in 1988
   through genuine popular elections open to all
   who are committed to the democratic process.

첨부 2.

"케리" 의원 결의안 관련 일지

일 자	내 용
85.10.23	○ Kerry 및 Simon 상원의원 공동으로 김대중 복권 및 한국의 민주화 촉구 결의안을 작성, 동 제안 설명서를 상원내에 회람시킴.
12. 3	○ 민주당 진보계 상원의원 7명이 상기 결의안을 공동 발의키로 합의
12.11	○ 주미대사, "폴 사이먼" 상원의원 면담코 아측 입장 설명
12.19	○ 상원의원 10명, 하원의원 2명이 공동 제안자로 하여 상·하 양원 외무(외교) 위원회에 동 결의안 제출
12.24	○ 동 결의안 관련, 관계부처 대책 회의(정무 1 수석 주재)
86. 1. 3	○ 주미대사, 국무성 의회 담당 차관보를 방문, 의회와의 접촉 강화를 통한 동 결의안 문제 해소 노력 촉구
1.16	○ 주미대사, 동 결의안 제안 의원 12명에게 아국의 입장을 설명하는 서한 발송

0088

10

상원 외교위(17명) 및 하원 외무위(42명) 의원 성향 분류

구 분		인원수	상원의원	하원의원
결의안 지지의원	핵심추진 의원	6 명	Kerry, Pell, Sarbanes Cranston, Dodd	Feighan
	결의안 지지의원	11 명	Biden, Eagleton, Mathias, Pessler	Studds, Barnes, Crockett, Dymally, Torricelli, Weiss, Leach
중립적인 의원	결의안에 대한 소극적 동조의원	11 명	Boschwitz, Trible, Evans, Zorinsky	Solarz, Wolpe, Gejdenson, Lantos, Berman, Levine, Garcia
	중립적인 의원	20 명		Fascell, Yatron, Hamilton Kostmayer, Bonker, Mackay, Reid, L. Smith, Udall, Siljander, C. Smith, Snowe, Zschau, Ackerman, McCain, MackIII Roth, Bereuter, Burton, Dewine
아국입장 지지의원		11 명	Lugar, Helms, Kassebaum, Murkoski	Broomfield, Lagomarsino, Mica, Gilman, Hyde, Solomon, Dornan
계		59 명	17명	42명

* 상원 외교위 및 하원 외무위 소속이 아닌 결의안 공동 발의자
  - 상원(5명): Simon, Kennedy, Riegle, Hollings, Harkin
  - 하원(1명): Dixon

0089

11

첨부 4.

주미대사 발송 서한 국문 번역 내용 및 영문 서한

친애하는 "케리" 상원의원 귀하,

최근 귀하가 결의안에서 한국의 정치 발전에 관심을 표명하신 것에 대해 감사드립니다. 그런 점에서 본인은 다음과 같은 사실에 대하여 귀하의 주의를 환기시키고, 귀하와 우리 정부 및 본인이 관계되는 일들에 대해 좀 더 구체적으로 토론하고자 하는 본인의 솔직한 심정을 표하고자 합니다.

한국 정부는 한국내 정치 및 인권의 점진적 신장을 위해서 노력하고 있읍니다. 1980년 8월 제5공화국의 출범이후 한국은 정치적 민주화와 민족 화합에 있어서 눈부신 발전이 있었읍니다. 그러한 예로서 일부 정치인에 대한 정치활동 규제 조치가 해제되었고, 더우기 1985년 2월에 실시되었던 자유스럽고 공정한 선거는 그동안 이룩되었던 민주 발전과 동 민주 발전에 대한 한국 정부의 지속적인 공약을 극적으로 나타내 주는 것이었읍니다. 전두환 대통령 각하께서도 1988년도의 평화적 정권 이양을 약속하셨읍니다. 마지막으로 본인은 상황이 허락하는 경우 김대중의 법적 지위 제고를 포함한 민주화를 위한 추가 조치를 신중히 검토할 것임을 분명히 말씀드리고자 합니다. 결국 한국 정부와 국민이 열망하는 민주화와 화합의 추세는 점차 강화될 것입니다. 동시에 한국의 발전 속도는 1984년 미 국무성 인권보고서가 지적했듯이 우리의 지정학적 현실에 의해 영향을 받고 있읍니다. 호전적인 북한 공산주의자의 위협때문에 1948년 한국 정부 수립 이래 모든 한국 정부들은 국내의 안보 유지 문제에 최우선

0090

12

순위를 두어 왔읍니다. 이러한 위협은 실제적인 것임으로 한국의
우방들이 한국의 민주 발전 속도를 평가할때 이러한 요소를
충분히 고려하여 주실 것을 희망하는 바입니다.

본인은 이러한 문제와 한·미 우호 협력 증진을 위한 여타 문제에
관한 의견을 교환할 수 있도록 귀하와 직접 만날수 있게 되기를
희망합니다.

경 구

0001

13

Dear Senator Kerry,

I appreciate your interest in Korean political developments as expressed in the proposed concurrent resolution which you recently initiated. In that regard, I would like to draw your attention to the following facts and express my openness to our discussing in more detail the matters about which you, my government and I are concerned.

My government is committed to a course of progressive expansion of political and civil rights in Korea. Indeed, since the inauguartion of the fifth republic in August of 1980, Korea has made significant advances toward both political democratization and national reconciliation. Thus, for example, the ban on political activities which had previously been imposed on certain politicians has now been lifted.

Moreover, the free and fair elections which were held in February 1985 are a dramatic indication of the progress toward democratization which has already been made and of my government's continuing commitment to that process. President Chun himself remains committed to leaving office in 1988 and to a peaceful transfer of power at that time. Finally, I can assure you, as well, that my government will continue to give careful consideration to additional steps it might take to further this process, including possible review of Mr. Kim Dae Jung's status as circumstances permit. In sum, the trend toward further democratization and reconciliation, to which both the Korean government and the people are strongly committed, will continue to prevail.

At the same time, the pace of our progress is conditioned by our geo-political realities. As the U.S. State Department's 1984 human rights report noted.

Because of the threat from an aggressive communist regime in north Korea, all Korean governments since the Republic's founding in 1948 have felt it necessary to give top priority to maintaining external and internal security.

0092

14

This threat is very real, and we would hope that this factor would be fully taken into account by Korea's friends and allies when evaluating the pace of our progress towards democratization.

I would appreciate an opportunity to meet with you in person to exchange views on this matter and others relating to strengthening Korea-U.S. friendship and cooperation.

Sincerely,

Kyung-Won, Kim
Ambassador

0093

15

발 신 전 보

번 호 : WUS-0469   일 시 : 573/1930   전보종별 : _____

수 신 : 주   미   대사·송영사

발 신 : 장   관 (미북)

제 목 : Kerry 결의안

대 : USW-249, 480

연 : (1) WUS-192

　　(2) WUS-430

1. 대호 Kerry 결의안의 의회내 처리문제와 관련, 1.21 의회가 개회됨에 따라 동 결의안이 처리될 가능성에 대비해 최대한의 노력을 경주할 필요가 있다고 사료됨. 이와 관련, 귀관은 대호 귀하 명의 서신발송에 이어 현재 추진중인 Kerry ~~Kennedy~~ 등 공동발의 의원들과의 접촉 노력을 계속 ~~추진~~하기 바람.

2. 상기 주동의원들과의 접촉을 성공적으로 추진하기 위해서는 귀관에서 적절한 것으로 판단되는 방안을 적의 활용함과 동시에 가급적이면 아측 입장에 동조적인 의원들 (Fascell, Gilman, Solomon, Murkowski 의원등)에게 아측 입장 이해촉구와 아울러 이들을 통하여 주동의원들에 대한 설득을 시도하는 방안도 검토, 추진바람.

3. 귀관의 상기 활동 측면지원을 위하여 연호(2) 조찬회 참석 예정인 봉두완, 김현자 양의원이 방미기간중 관련 의원들을 접촉코자

양고제	86년 1월 31일	붕 미 과	기안자	과장	심의관	국장	세차관보	차관	장관
					추인		전결		

발신시간 :

외신과	접수자	과장

0094

하는 바, 아래 의원들 과의접촉을 주선 바람.

      o 상원 : Kerry, Pell, Eagleton 의원

      o 하원 : Fascell, Feighan, Dymally, Torricelli,

            Solarz 의원

4. 아울러 남미 순방후 2.25~3.10간 귀지 방문 예정인 리재형 국회의장도 방미 기획를 이용, 동 결의안 저지를 위한 적절한 활동 계획을 수립코자 하니 면담대상 인사등에 관한 귀견 보고바람. (방미일정은 별도 통보)

5. 공동 제안 의원 보좌관과의 접촉활동도 동 결의안 채택저지 저변을 확대하는 데 도움이 될 것으로 보이는 바, ~~대권 정무총산외~~ ~~의회담당 참사관외~~ 접촉 활동을 가일층 제고 바라며 동 접촉 시 동 결의안에 대한 향후 심의과정 및 전망과 결의안 관련 청문회 개최 가능 여부에 관해서도 탐문 보고 바람.

6. 한편, 국회측은 공동 제안 또는 외무위소속 의원들과 각별한 개인적 친분을 유지하고 있는 아국 경제계 인사들의 개인 서한발송을 계획하고 우선 하기 인사명의 서한 발송후 결과에 따라 확대 여부를 검토할 예정인 바, 동건 추진결과는 추후 통보 예정임.

      가. 삼성물산 박운서 부사장 : Torricelli 하원의원,

                            Murkowski 상원의원

      나. 동방생명 이동복 사장 : Solarz 하원의원

7. 대호로 요청한 아국 국회의원들의 개인 서신 발송 대상 의원명은 국회측 결정이 있는 대로 통보 예정임.

0095

8. 동 결의안 관련 보도문제는 관계부처에서 적절한 조치를 취하였음을 참고 바람. (차관)

예 고 : 86.12.31. 일반

0096

외 두 부   착신전듭

- 직접남께 안녹보고동(국회전담대)

번 호 : USW-0514   일 시 : 601312000   종 별 :

수 신 : 장 관 (미북)

발 신 : 주 미 대 사

제 목 : KERRY 결의안 대책

대: WUS-469

언: USW-5655(85.12.21.), 241, 480

표제 결의안 대책관련, 현황 및 당관의 향후 조치 계획을 아래 보고함.

1. 현황

가. 표제결의안은 하원의 경우 외무위 아태소위 및 인권소위에 등시 회부되었으며, 상원에서는 외교위로 송부되었음. 당관은 그간 의회측과 다각적으로 접촉, 등결의안 에 대한 심의 전망 및 향후 처리과정등을 탐문한바, 현재로서는 필리핀 사태등으로 인하여 등 결의안에 대한 관심이 상대적으로 높지않으며 2 월말경에나 검트가 시작될 것이라는 관측임.

나. 등 결의안 처리 관련, YATRON 인권 소위원장은 아국의 인권상황에 대해 비 교적 호의적 견해를 갖고 있으나 아태소위가 등 문제를 다루게될 경우 인권 소위르서 드 방관만 할수는 없다는 생각이므르 SOLARZ 소위원장의 음직임이 매우 중요한것 으르 판단되며, 상원에서는 예에 따라 LUGAR 외교위원장의 방침이 여타 의원들에 게 영향을 미치게될것으르 보임.

2. 향후 조치 계획

가. 표제 결의안 대책과 관련한 의회내 증점 접촉 대상은 아래와 같이 3 개 구룹으 르 구분될수 있을것인바, 이들에 대한 당관의 접촉 계획은 다음과 같음.

1) 공등제안 의원 및 진보계 등조가능 의원

본직은 1.16. 공등제안 의원 전운에 대하여 아측입장을 설명하는 서한 발송구 이들 과의 개별 면담을 추진증임. SIMON 상원의원은 이미 접촉한바 있고, PELL 상

미주국   차관실   1 차브   정훈국   청와대   안 기   0097

원의원 면담은 2.5. 르 결정되었으며   FEIGHAN 하원의원과드 내주중 접촉할수 있을것임. (2.5. 르 약속하였으나 등의원측 사정으르 연기) 본직은 등 면담을 통하여 이들의 아국 정세에 대한 이해를 제고하고 결의안 추진을 철회브록 요청할 예정이나 현 시점에서 설득 가능성은 의문시되며 다만 이들의 적극적 활등은 약화시킬수 있을것임.

2) 위원회 심의와관련한 핵심 의원

위원회 심의 과정에서의 결의안 저지를 위하여는 전항에서 언급한바 LUGAR 위원장 및 SOLARZ 소위원장에 대한 설득 활등이 가장 중요할것으르 판단됨.   SOLARZ 소위원장은 기 보그한바와 같이 결의안 내용조차 파악할 시간이 없는 상황이었는바, 앞으르 추이를 보아가며 계속 접촉할 예정임.   LUGAR 위원장은 2.4. 경 필리핀 선거 참관인단의 대프르 방비하는등 필리핀 문제르 경황이 없어 면담이 지연되고 있으며 등 선거후에나 면담이 가능할것으르 브임. 그러나 그간 등 위원장측과의 직접접촉 및 당관 콘설턴트를 통한 다각적 면담 주선과정에서 확인된 바와같이 지연 사유는 오르지 등 위원장의 바쁜일정 때문이므르 면담이 다스 지연되더타드 결의안 대책과 관련하여 시기적으르 문제는 없을것으르 판단하고 있음.

3) 친한의원 및 브수계 아국 입장 지지의원

결의안 대책과 관련한 측면 지원을 위하여 친한의원들을 등원하는 문제는 적절한 시기프착이 중요함. 현재로서는 대부분의 의원들이 등 결의안 제출 사실조차 므르고 있는바, 이러한 상황하에서는 접촉 효과가 의문시 되므르 당관으르서는 향후 결의안 처리등항을 주시하면서 필요하다고 판단되는 순간에 이들을 적의 등원, 활용할 계획임. 그러나 FASCELL 위원장과는 2.4. 본직 면담이 약속되어 있고, MURKOWSKI 소위원장드 2 월 휴회 직후 면담키르 원칙 합의 하였음.

나. 한편, 상기 의회 대책에 더하여 미행정부와 언론에 대한 대책드 병행되어야 할 것인바, SOLARZ 소위원장이 지적한대로 한국내 인권문제가 언론등에서 시끄럽게 되면 의회르서드 등 문제를 외면할수 없을 것이기 때문임. 이와관련, 특히 NYT, WP 등 유력지의 등경 독파원들 에의한 비판적 기사는 의회의 KERRY 결의안 처리에는 영향을 미칠 가능성이 큼. 또한 미행정부의 한득 인권 상황에 관한 대의회 브고

PAGE   2

0098

서가 금년에도 2 월 중순경 제출될 예정이며, 동 내용이 전년에 비하여 반드시 호의적이 아닐것이라는 관측이 있으므르 등사실드 결의안 대책에 불리하게 작용할 가능성이 큼. 이에 감하여 본직은 이미 국무성 BALL 차관브등과 이근제를 협의한바 있으며, 2.3. 에는 아국에 비판적 기사를 가끔 게재하고 있는 BALTIMORE SUN 지의 편집인들과 면담, 아국정세에 대한 이해를 제고시킬 예정임.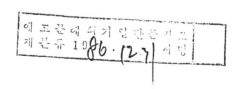

(대사김경원-차관)

예고 : 1986.12.31. 일반

면 담 요 록

1. 일   시 : 1986년 2 월 4 일(학 요일) 12:10시 ~ 13:00시

2. 장   소 : 장 원

3. 면 담 자 : 장선섭   미주국장

   　　　　　 이 양   북미과장

   　　　　　 이동복   삼성정밀사장

   　　　　　 박웅서   삼성물산 부사장

   　　　　　 (박인국 사무관 배석)

4. 내   용 :

미주국장 : (Kerry 결의안 관련 협조요청 내용 전달)

박 웅 서 : Torricelli 의원(민주、뉴저지)에 대해서는 영향력
　　　　　 행사가 가능하리라고 봄。 동 의원은 삼성과 계속 관계를
　　　　　 맺어오고 있기 때문에 어떤 형태로든지 입장 전달이
　　　　　 가능할 것으로 생각됨。 Murkowski   의원은 삼성
　　　　　 물산 사장께서 한번 만난데 불과하므로 개인편지를 보낼
　　　　　 형편이 아닌것 같음。

0100

이 동 복 : Solarz 하원의원과는 비교적 오랜 친분관계를 가져왔음.
그러나 대부분 직접 만나서 대화를 나누었지 편지를
보낸적은 없어서 동의원에게 갑자기 편지를 보냈을 경우
효과는 미지수라고 생각함. 과거의 경험으로 보아 대미
관계는 적극적인 action 보다는 차라리 가만 두어
두는 것이 효과적인 경우도 있었던것 같음.

미주국장 : 반드시 편지를 보내라는 것은 아님. 일부러 그럴필요는
없지만 직접 만날 기회가 있으면 더욱 좋을것임.
방법문제는 이사장에게 일임하겠음. 참고로 이번
결의안에 임하는 정부의 입장도 최대한 조용하게 처리
한다는 것임.

이 동 복 : 잘 알겠음. 여러가지 가능한 방법을 생각해 보겠음.
Solarz 의원이 제 5공화국 출범이후에는 두 차례
각하를 예방한 일도있고 그 때마다 매우 유익한 성과를
거둔것으로 알고 있음. 본인 생각으로는 황선필 청와대
대변인이 서신을 보내는것도 좋은 방법이 될것같음.
대변인의 편지는 바로 각하의 뜻을 직접 전한다는 것으로
받아들여지기 때문에 효과가 있을 것으로 생각됨.

Solarz 는 자신의 image make-up 을 위해
매우 영리하게 대처해 나가고 있음. 근 자에는 Nicaragua

- 2 -

0101

문제를 최대의 issue 로 하여 왔으나 조금 김이 빠진
감이들자 주관심을 비율빈 문제로 전환하였음. 비율빈
문제가 계속 hot issue 가 되는한 Solarz의원은
한국문제에 priority 를 두지 않을것이 분명함.

미주국장 : 비율빈 문제가 시끄러우면 한국에 대한 관심을 전환
시킬수 있어 유리한 점도 있으나 한국문제를 비율빈과
동일시 하려는 경향도 있기 때문에 염려됨.

이 동 복 : 물론임. 월남패망 이전에 미국의 여론은 한국을 월남과
동일하게 취급 하려 했던적이 있었음. 미국의 대한
여론을 순화시키기 위해서는 일반대중(grass-roots)
에 대한 문화적 접근이 매우 중요한 것임을 통감함.

미주국장 : 여러가지 도움 말씀에 감사함. 금번 서신발송과 관련,
필요 한일이 있으면 언제든지 연락 주시기 바람.

이 동 복 : 잘 알겠음. 곧 결과를 알려 드리겠음. 끝.

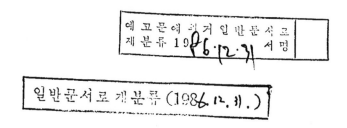

0102

Kerry 결의안 대책관련 주미대사관 향후 조치 계획
----

1. 현 황

   가. 결의안 회부

      ○ 하원 : 외무위 아태소위 및 인권소위에 동시 회부

      ○ 상원 : 외교위로 송부

   나. 심의 예상시기

      ○ 현재로서는 필리핀 사태등으로 인하여 동 결의안에 대한
        관심이 상대적으로 높지 않으며 2월말경에나 검토 개시예상

   다. 관련 소위원장 동정

      ○ 하원

         - Yatron 인권 소위원장은 아국의 인권상황에 대해
           비교적 호의적 견해를 갖고 있으나 아태소위가 동
           문제를 다루게될 경우 인권소위로서도 방관만 할수는
           없다는 생각이므로 Solarz 소위원장의 움직임이
           매우 중요한것으로 판단

      ○ 상원

         - Lugar 외교위원장의 방침이 여타 의원들에게 영향을
           미치게 될것으로 예상

2. 향후 조치계획

   : 의회내 중점 접촉 대상은 아래와같이 3개 구룹으로 구분
     접촉ㆍ계획 수립

0103

가. 공동제안 의원 및 진보계 동조가능 의원

　ㅇ주미대사는 1.16 대사명의 서한 발송후 이들과의 개별면담을
　　추진중
　　　- Simon 　상원의원 : 기접촉
　　　- Pell 　상원의원 : 2.5 면담결정
　　　- Feighan 　하원의원 : 내주중 접촉(2.3로 약속
　　　하였으나 동의원측 사정으로 연기)

　ㅇ 예상성과
　　　- 현 시점에서 결의안 철회 가능성은 의문시됨.
　　　따라서이들의 적극적 활동 약화가 목표

나. 위원회 심의와 관련한 핵심의원

　ㅇ 위원회 심의 과정에서의 결의안 저지를 위하여는 Lugar
　　위원장 및 Solarz 소위원장에 대한 섭득 활동이 가장
　　중요.

　-Solarz 소위원장
　　• 기 보고한 바와같이 결의안　내용조차 파악할 시간이
　　　없는 상황이었는 바, 앞으로 추이를 보아가며 계속
　　　접촉 예정

　- Lugar 　위원장
　　• 2.4경 필리핀 선거 참관인단의 대표로 방비하는등
　　　필리핀 문제로 경황이 없어 면담이 지연, 선거후에나
　　　면담이 가능할것 예상

0104

○ 면담이 다소 지연되더라도 위원장의 분주한 일정을
그려할때 시기적으로 문제는 없을 것으로 판단

다. 친한의원 및 보수계 아국입장 지지의원

○ 기본입장

- 결의안 대책과 관련한 측면지원을 위하여 친한의원
들을 동원하는 문제는 적절한 시기포착이 중요

- 현재로서는 대부분의 의원들이 동 결의안 제출 사실
조차 모르고 있는바, 이러한 상황하에서는 접촉효과가
의문시

- 향후 결의안 처리동향을 주시하면서 필요하다고 판단
되는 순간에 이들을 적의 동원, 활용할 계획

○ 면담 추진 현황

- Fascell 위원장 : 2.4 면담 약속

- Murkowski   동아.태 소위원장 : 2월 휴회(2.8-18)
직후 면담 원칙 합의

라. 대책건의

○ 상기 의회대책에 더하여 미행정부와 언론에 대한 대책도
병행되어야 할 것인바, Solarz 소위원장이 지적한대로
한국내 인권문제가 언론등에서 시끄럽게되면 의회로서도
동 문제를 외면할수 없을것이기 때문임.

- 특히 NYT 등 유력지의 동경 특파원들에 의한 비판적
기사는 의회의 Kerry 결의안 처리에 영향을 미칠

0105

가능성이 큼·

○ 아울러 미행정부의 한국 인권상황에 관한 대의회
  보고서가 금년에도 2월 중순경 제출될 예정이며,
  동 내용이 전년에 비하여 반드시 호의적이 아닐것
  이라는 관측이 있으므로 동 사실도 결의안 대책에
  불리하게 작용할 가능성이 큼·

0106

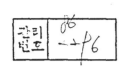

외 무 부 착 신 전 보

번 호 : USW-0548   일 시 : 602041038   종 별 :

수 신 : 장 관 (미북)

발 신 : 주 미 대사

제 목 : KERRY 결의안 대책

대: WUS-469

1. 대호 관련, 당관 장철규 서기관은 금 2.3 CRANSTON 상원의원(민주- CA) 의 대외관계 담당보좌관 L. KRUEGER 을 접촉한바 동인의 언급요지를 하기보고함.

가. KERRY 결의안관련, 최근 외교위 소속 의원들의 바쁜 일정으로 인하여 빠른 시일내 토의가 있을것으로는 보지않음 그러나 CRANSTON 의원은 한국의 인권 개선 문제에 깊은 관심이 있으므로 무역문제등 다른 사안으로 한국관계가 거론될 경우에도 인권문제와 88년 선거관계등을 언급할 가능성이 있음 동의원은 특히 김대중 복권가능성, 개헌문제를 위요한 여.야의 견해 차이, 문익환 목사의 구금 사실등에 관심을 갖고 있음

나. 동의원과 대사와의 면담 요청관련 동의원의 선거구활동 관계로 면담 주선이 지연되고 있음을 이해바람. 봉위원장의 당지 방문시는 동의원이 워싱턴에 없을예정이므로 면담이 불가능함.

2. 추후 대의회 접촉에 참고코자하니 문익환 목사관련 자료를 송부바람 ✓

(대사 김경원)

예고: 86.12.31일반

미주국   차관실   1 차브   청와대   안 기   정문국   0107

PAGE   1   86.02.05   09:49
                                                           외신 2과 통제관

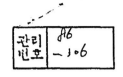
외 무 부

착신전보
지급

번 호 : USW-0579   입 시 : 602051605   종 별 : 지급

수 신 : 장관 (미북)

발 신 : 주 미 대사

제 목 : KERRY 결의안 대책

본직은 금 2.4. 표제결의안의 하원측 제안자인   FEIGHAN 의원을 면담한바 동내용을 아래 보고함. (장재룡참사관 수행)

1. 본직은 제5공화국하에서의 정치발전과 인권개선 상황을 소상히 설명하고, 88년의 평화적 정권 교체 실현을 위한 대통령각하의 확고한 결의를 재확인함. 본직은   정부의 이러한 민주발전 노력과 관련하여 외국의 공개적 압력이 있는듯한 인상   경우 오히려 부작용이 우려됨을 강조, FEIGHAN 의원이 표제결의안을 더 이상 추진하지 않을것을 강력히 권유함.

2. 동의원은 공개적이고 대립적인 자세가 한국의 인권개선에 도움이 되지않는다는 지적에 상당한 공감을 표시하면서도 1년전 바로 오늘 자신의 동행하에 이루어진 김대중 귀국시 공항 소요사태에서 나타난바와같이 아직도 문제점이 있음을 유의하지않을수 없다고말함. 이에 본직은 김의 귀국시 상황과 아국정부의 입장을 상세히 설명, 동사태가 보여주는바와같이 문제를 공개적으로 시끄럽게할 경우 부작용만 유발됨을 지적함. 본직은 미의회가 아국의 특수한 상황을 이해하고 그간의 착실한 민주화 성과등을 유의하여 좀더 인내심을 가져줄것과 공개적거론은 지양할것을 거듭 촉구함.

3. 이에대해 FEIGHAN 의원은 자신도 공개적 혼란을 야기할 생각은 없으므로 일단 본직의 요청을 존중하는 방향으로 재검토하겠으나, 동결의안에 포함된 내용이 한국민주화를 염원하는 다수 의원들의 뜻임을 한국측이 분명히 이해하여주기 바란다고 말함. 동의원은 이어 김대중 문제가 미국인들에게는 한국 민주화의 상징으로 생각되고 있음을 강조하면서, 다소 주제넘은 이야기이나 한국 정부가 김의 정치활동을 허용해줄수 있다면 한국민주화에 대한 시각 개선에 크게 도움이 될것으로 본다고 언급함.

∨ 미주국   차관십   1차보   정문국   청와대   안 기   0108

4.동의원은 상기 김대중 귀국과 관련한 공항사태를 언급하면서 동사태 직후의 김현
자의원 면담을 대우 유익하였던것으로 평가하고,김의원이 그후 요즈음도 한.미간 무
역관제등에 관하여 도움이 되는 많은 이야기를 해주고 있음을 고맙게 여기고 있다고
말함.
(대사 김경원)
예고:86.12.31.일반

0109

외 무 부 신 전 보

번 호 : USW-0586   일 시 : 602051852   종 별 : 지 급

수 신 : 장관 (미북)

발 신 : 주 미 대사

제 목 : KERRY 결의안 대책

1. 본직은 금 2.5. 표제 결의안의 공동 제안자인 PELL 상원의원을 면담한바 동
내용을 아래보고함. (장재룡 참사관 수행)

가. 본직은 KERRY 결의안 관련, 아국 인권문제에 대한 외국의 공개적 압력은 아
국정부의 입장을 난처하게 함으로써 민주화 노력에 오히려 역효과를 가져올것이 우려
됨을 지적하고, 그예로서 카터 행정부 당시 공개적 거론의 무익성을 환기시킴. 이에
대해 PELL 의원은 본직의 설명에도 일리는 있으나 한국의 인권문제에 대하여 미
의원들의 "강한 느낌" 을 토로할수 있는 기회가 있는것이 한국을 위하여 오히려 좋을
것으로 본다고 주장함.

나. 본직은 아국이 그간 이룩한 정치발전과 인권 개선 상황을 지적, 아국이 보다 개
방적이고 자유로운 사회를 이룩하기 위하여 노력중임을 누누이 설명한후 미의회가 이
러한 아국정부의 노력을 지지하고 성원하여야할것이며 KERRY 결의안과 같은 공개
적 압력으로 동 노력을 어렵게 만드는 일은 없어야 할것임을 강조. 동의원은 한국
의 민주발전이 보다빠른 속도로 진전된다면 KERRY 결의안과 같은 공개적 논의의
필요성이 없게될것이나 현재로서는 여사한 논의가 필요하다는 생각에 변함이 없다고
말함. 동의원은 KERRY 결의안이 한국의 인권문제와 관련한 보다 강경한 움직임의
가능성을 오히려 중화시킬수 있을것이므로 필요한 것으로 본다는 주장을 되풀이함.

2. 관측

가. 금일 면담을 통하여 나타난바, PELL 의원은 표제 결의안의 내용도 상세히
모르고 있었으며 김대중의 이름도 이억을 못하고 있었음.

나. 그러나 동의원은 시종일관하여 아국의 민주화 노력을 촉구하면서 동문제에 대한

미주국   차관실   1 차보   정문국   청와대   안 기   0110

PAGE 1   86.02.06 15:28
                                                      외신 2과 통제관

미 의원들의 "강한느낌" 만을 강조한바, 이는 동의원이 소위 진보적 사상의 대변인으로 자처코자하는 정략적 동기에서 비롯된것으로 보였음.

다. 상기와 같이 동의원의 아국 인권문제에 대한표면적 관심 (동의원은 아국의 민주화 노력과 현황에 대한 본직의 설명을 전혀 외면하고 일방적으로 자신의 종래 주장만을 되품이 말하였음. (이 자신의 정치노선 설정과 관련되어 있는 만큼 동의원의 생각과 활동 내용을 순화 시키는데 앞으로 상당한 시간이 필요할것으로 예상됨. 그러나 차기선거에서 민주당의 상원 지배시 동 의원이 외교위원장 서열 제 1 위임을 감안, 가능한 모든 방법으로 동의원에 대한 순화 활동을 시도하겠음.

(대사 김경원-차관)

예고 : 1986.12.31. 일반

예고문에 의거 일반문서로
재분류 1986.12.31 서명

PAGE 2

0211

외 무 부

착신전문
종 별 : 지급

번 호 : USW-0742   일 시 : 602131802

수 신 : 장 관 (미북)

발 신 : 주 미 대사

제 목 : 김대중 현황문의

연 : USW-579

1. EDWARD FEIGHAN 하원의원은 금 2.13. 김대중 가택연금설에 깊은 우려를 표명하고 김의권리와 자유가 즉시 회복되기를 희망하는 내용의 긴급 상용전문을 본직앞으로 타전하여 왔음.

2. 한편 KERRY 상원의원의 외교담당 보좌관 RICHARD MCCALL 은 금일 당관 장재룡 참사관에게 전화로 김의 가택연금 사실을 김씨측으로부터 연락받았다면서 여사한 심각한 사태는 계류중인 결의안의 중요성을 증명하는 것이라고 말함.

3. 본건은 KERRY 결의안 대책에도 영향이 있는것으로 보이는바, 본부지침 긴급 하시바람.

(대사 김경원)

예고 : 1986.12.31. 일반

예고문에 의거 일반문서로
재분류 1986.12.기 서명

0112

미주국 차관실 1차보 정문국 청와대 안기 보안사

PAGE 1   86.02.14 14:05
                          외신 2과 통제관

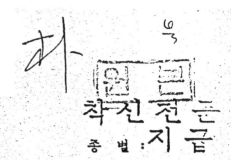

외　무　부

관리
번호 86
-38P

번　호 : USW-0760　　　　　일　시 : 602141624　　　종　별 : 지급

수　신 : 장　관 (미북)

발　신 : 주 미 대 사

제　목 : KERRY 결의안 대책

1. 당관 장재룡 참사관은 금 2.14. 하원 외무위 아태소위 공화당 전문위원　CINDY SP
RUNGER 와 면담, 최근의 국내사정과 아국정부의 민주화 조치등을 상세히 설명하고
FEIGHAN 결의안의 저지를 당부함.

이에대해 동 전문위원은 일응 이해를 표시하면서도 김대중 가택연금설을 지적, 평화
적방법에 의한 의사표시가 금지되는 상황 하에서는 한국내 민주발전문제에 관심을 갖
지않을수 없다고말 하고 여사한 사태가 지속되는한 미의회로서도 관심을 표명하지 않
을수 없음을 강조함.

2. 장참사관은 아국의 안보 현실, 개헌서명운동의 불법성, 김대중의 범법적 선동행위자
행과 이에 대한 예방조치등을 재차 설명한바, 동보좌관은 아측설명에 논리가 없는것은
아니나 문제는 미 국적 관념에서 이를 받아들이기 어렵다는데 있음을 지적. 이어 동
보좌관은 내주에 의회가 다시 열리면 현 한국정세발전에 대한 많은의원들의 우려표시
가 예상된다면서 그전에 상황이 개선되기만을 바란다고 말함.

동보좌관은 표제 결의안이 현재로서는 필리핀 사태때문에 부각되지않고 있으나 한국
정세가 계속 시끄럽게되면 필리핀사태가 일단락되는 대로 곧 동결의안에 대한 움직임
이 있을것으로 전망한다고 말함

(대사 김경원)

예고 : 86.12.31일반

대고문에 거일반관서료
재분류 19 86.12.31 서명

미주국　　차관실　　1 차보　　정문국　　청와대　　안 기　　　　　　0113

PAGE　1　　　　　　　　　　　　　　　　　　　　86.02.15　10:50
　　　　　　　　　　　　　　　　　　　　　　　　외신 2과　통제관

종별: 지급

번호: USW-0809   일시: 60218 1851

수신: 장관(미북)

발신: 주미대사

제목: 상원외교위 전문위원 접촉

대: WUS-728

1. 당관 한공사는 금 2.18(수) 상원 외교위 소속 TRIPPLETE (공화당) 및 RITCH(민주당)전문위원과 접촉 (장철균 서기관 배석), 동 위원들의 최근 국내정세에 관한 설명 요청에 대하여 정부의 민주화노력, 88년 평화적 정권교체, 헌법개정 서명운동의 헌정질서 위배, 김대중의 법적 지위, 야당 및 급진성향 학생의 가두시위의 목적등에 관해 대호 논지에 따라 상세히 설명하고 정부의 조치가 아국의 헌법질서유지를 위한 최소한의 조치였음을 강조함.

2. RITCH 위원은 평화적인 청원운동을 제재하는데 대하여 민주당 소속의원들이 부정적인 견해를 갖고있다고 언급하기에 평화적인 테두리를 벗어날 가능성이 있어 예방을 행하고 있다고 설명하였음.

TRIPPLETE 위원은 한국정세와 정부의 입장에 충분한 이해를 표시하고, 한국내 야당이 미 언론및 의회내 급진성향의 민주당 의원들과 연계되어 최근 한국내 정세를 미언론에 부각시킴으로써 상, 하의원들의 한국문제에 대한 관심을 고조시키는 징조가 보이고 있다고 언급함.

3. 동인은 KERRY 결의안 관련, 2.25(화)상원 외교위 BUSINESS MEETING 이 개최되는바, 동회의에서는 필리핀 선거 문제가 다루어질예정이나, 현 한국내 정세발전여하에 따라서는 민주당 의원에 의한 한국문제 거론가능성도 배제할수 없다고 말함.

1986. 2. 19

PAGE 1

0114

4. 향후 진전 사항에 관해 상호 긴밀히 협조키로함

(대사 김경원)

예고:86.12.31일반

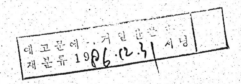

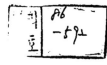

주 뉴 욕 총 영 사 관

주뉴욕(정) 700- 512   1986. 3. 3.

수신 : 장관 (사본 : 주미대사) 우편발송.
참조 : 미주국장
제목 : 김대중 복권 및 한국민주화 결의안

　　　1985.12.19. 미의회에 상정된 표제 결의안과 관련, 당관은 관내
주보소톤 J. Joseph Maloney 명예총영사로 하여금 동 결의안의 제안자중
1인인 Massachusetts주 출신 John F. Kerry 상원의원을 상대로
하여 김대중 문제와 아국내 정치상황에 관하여 올바른 인식을 하도록 하는
서한을 발송케 하였는 바, 동 서한 사본을 별첨 송부하오니 참고하시기
바랍니다.

　　　첨부 : 서한 사본.　　끝.

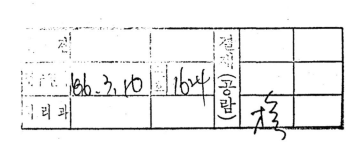

주　　　뉴　　　욕　　　총　　　영　　　사

0116

HONORARY CONSULATE-GENERAL OF THE REPUBLIC OF KOREA FOR BOSTON

J. JOSEPH MALONEY
HONORARY CONSUL-GENERAL

February 18, 1986

The Honorable Taezhee Kim
Consul General of the Republic of Korea
460 Park Avenue
New York, New York 10022

Dear Consul General Kim:

I am enclosing a copy of a letter which I have sent
today to Senator John F. Kerry of Massachusetts. I hope
it meets with your approval, and if I receive any response,
I will certainly keep you informed.

With warm regards,

Sincerely yours,

J. Joseph Maloney

JJM:ca
Enc.

0117

50 Congress Street, Suite 910, Boston, Massachusetts 02109   (617) 742-5550

J. JOSEPH MALONEY
HONORARY CONSUL-GENERAL

HONORARY CONSULATE-GENERAL
OF THE REPUBLIC OF KOREA
FOR BOSTON
February 18, 1986

Honorable John F. Kerry
Senate Office Building
Washington, D.C. 20510

Dear Senator Kerry:

We have never met, but I am taking the liberty of writing to you, presuming on my forty-seven years as a Boston lawyer. During all of those years I have been a working Democrat.

It has recently come to my attention that you have been one of the sponsors of a resolution in the Senate calling on the Republic of Korea to improve the climate for human life and civil liberties in Korea, and more particularly the rights of Kim Dae Jung. I would like to present a few thoughts for your consideration with respect to that resolution.

First, in the sixth paragraph of the preamble you cite the lack of due process and an independent and impartial judicial system in Korea. I am sure that you are aware that both of these concepts are products of western civilization, more particularly of the common law which we have inherited from England. Korea, like many Asian countries, has a very ancient culture and tradition - older than that of western Europe - to which these concepts are foreign. I think that the Korean people have done a remarkable job during the past thirty to forty years in adopting and adapting themselves to many of the concepts of democracy as we know it. I believe we should show them some patience in measuring their progress.

Second, we should not forget that Korea lives under the constant threat of an implacable enemy on its north. Less than forty miles from its capital city of Seoul there is an army of several hundred thousand men, well armed with modern weapons, whose leaders take every opportunity to proclaim loudly their intention to conquer the Republic of Korea by force of arms. They have demonstrated their hostile intent in many ways; for example, killing with an axe an American official who was performing a peaceful mission in the demilitarized zone, tunneling under the DMZ to gain access to the territory of South Korea, and sending innumerable parties by land and sea to infiltrate the south. The government of the Republic of Korea is very conscious of this threat and believes it is necessary to have a somewhat disciplined and authoritarian regime in the interests of the safety of its more than 10 million citizens who live in Seoul and other cities and towns in close proximity to the DMZ. It is easy for us to forget this situation since we live with no threat from invasion over either of our borders.

0118

Third, the Korean people are our friends. They have proven their friendship in a way that I am sure you understand. They sent a substantial body of fighting men- of division size, I believe,- to fight by the side of our soldiers and marines in Vietnam. They fought bravely and well and suffered substantial casualties. They did this not because they had any particular interest in the conflict in Vietnam but because we asked them to. We should not forget that they were there when we needed them or thought we did.

Fourth, I give you one final thought which to me is very revealing. We have recently had in our country two opposition leaders from Asian countries. Each of them lived for a period of time in our country and then returned to his homeland. I call to your attention the remarkably different greetings each received upon return to his homeland. I refer, of course, to Benigno Aquino who returned to the Phillipines and to Kim Dae Jung who returned to Korea.

I know that you have concerned yourself with the situation in the Phillipines; I hope that you will give equal time, attention and study to the situation in the Republic of Korea.

Sincerely yours,

J. Joseph Maloney
Honorary Consul-General
Republic of Korea

JJM:ca

0119

50 CONGRESS STREET, SUITE 910, BOSTON, MASSACHUSETTS 02109 (617) 742-5550

외 무 부

번 호 : USW-1139   일 시 : 603071638   종 별 :

수 신 : 장 관 (미북)

발 신 : 주 미 대사

제 목 : KERRY 결의안

연 : USW-5621

12.17 하원에 제출된 연호 결의안 (H.CPON.RES.261) 가담자는 그간 공동 제안자인 F EIGHAN 및 DIXON 의원에 머물러 있었으나, 2월 중순이후 동조 서명 의원이 다수 추가되었는바, 이들의 가담 일자 및 명단을 아래 보고함. (JEFFORDS 의원 이외 전원 민주당 소속임)

2.19: KOSTMAYER, FRAUNTROY, UDALL, MOAKLEY, MORRISON(CT), LOWRY(WA), TORRICELLI , SEIBERLING, MATSUI, HOWARD, BOXER, WALGREN, BEDELL, EDGAR, FRANK, BONIOR

- 2.20: FOGLIETTA, LEVINE(CA), JACOB, ROBINSON, GEJDENSON, BEILENSON, EDWARDS(C A), WOLPE, PEASE, ACKERMAN, EVANS(IL)

- 3.4: VENTO, RICHARDSON, RANGEL, HALL(OH), JEFFORDS, WEISS, BORSKI, GRAY(PA), KAPTUR, WILSON, GARCIA, OWENS, CROCKETT

(대사 김경원)

예 고 : 86.12.31. 일반

0120

미주국   차관실   1 차보   청와대   안 기

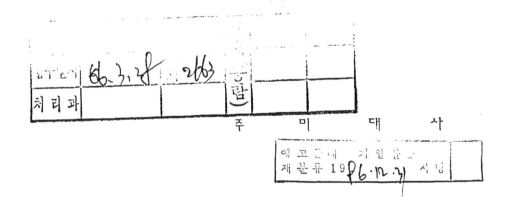

주 미 대 사 관

미국(정) 700-105   1986. 3. 25.

수신 : 장   관

참조 : 미주국장

제목 : Kerry   상원의원 결의안

         연 : USW-241 (86.1.16)

     Paul Simon   상원의원 (민주당, 일리노이주)은 연호

본직 서한에 대한 회신을 별첨과 같이 보내왔음을 보고합니다.

     첨부 :   Simon   의원 회신 사본 1 부. 끝.

     예고 :   86.12.31. 일반

PAUL SIMON
• ILLINOIS

COMMITTEES:
LABOR AND HUMAN RESOURCES
JUDICIARY
RULES AND ADMINISTRATION

United States Senate
WASHINGTON, DC 20510

February 13, 1986

The Honorable Kyung Won Kim
Ambassador
Embassy of the Republic of Korea
2370 Massachusetts Avenue N.W.
Washington, D.C 20008

Dear Mr. Ambassador:

Thank you for your letter regarding the concurrent resolution
that I sponsored calling for restoration of full civil and
political rights for Kim Dae Jung.

While I appreciate your points, recent reports that I have seen
from unbiased sources such as The New York Times indicate an
increase in repressive actions taken against political
dissidents in Korea.

In addition, Kim Dae Jung's status has not changed since the
introduction in Congress of the resolution. I think it would
be a wise and courageous action for your government to allow
Kim to participate fully in the political process. Political
dialogue and unfettered political participation by all the
elements of society is in the ultimate interest of the Korean
people, and it is likely to improve the overall climate of
Korean American relations. As I pointed out in the resolution,
America and Korea share many common bonds. We have an interest
in a stable, prosperous and democratic Korea. Restoring Kim
Dae Jung's civil rights would further that goal, and I can
assure you that it is an action that would be heartily
applauded by the Senate.

My best wishes.

Cordially,

Paul Simon
United States Senator

PS/ses

0122

230 S. DEARBORN
KLUCZYNSKI BLDG., 38TH FLOOR
CHICAGO, IL 60604

3 WEST OLD CÁPITOL PLAZA
SUITE 1
SPRINGFIELD, IL 62701

250 WEST CHERRY
ROOM 115-B
CARBONDALE, IL 62901

2. 자 료

0123

기 안 용 지

분류기호 문서번호	미북 700-99	(전화번호)	전결규정	조 항
				전결사항

처리기간		장 관			
시행일자	1986. 1. 13.				
보존연한					

보조기관	차 관	전결	제1차관보	협	
	국 장		심의관		
	과 장			조	
기안책임자	박인국	북 미 과			

경 유		발 신		통제	
수 신	주미대사				
참 조					

제 목   Kerry 결의안 관련 자료송부

연 : WUS-0079

Kerry 결의안에 대한 아측입장 자료작성과 관련,

국회측에서 작성한 연호 1항 자료를 별첨과 같이 송부합니다.

첨 부 : 상기자료 (제 1, 2, 3안) 각 1부.   끝.

예고 : 1986.12.31.일반.

예고문에 의기 일반문서로
재문규 1986.12.31 서명

0124

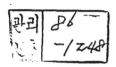

```
┌─────────────────────────────────────┐
│                                      │
│   Kerry 결의안 관련 조 찬획의 자료      │
│                                      │
└─────────────────────────────────────┘
```

1986. 1. 30.

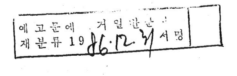

외   무   부

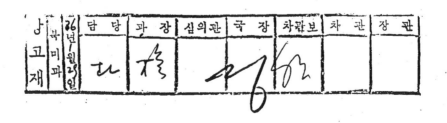

0125

1. 결의안제출 관련 주요일지

　가. 85.9.26.　　주미대사, 국무성 제보에 따라 9.27 Kerry
　　　　　　　　　의원이 결의안 발의 예정임을 보고

　나. 85.9.27.　　본부, 동 결의안 발의 철회 촉구 지시

　다. 85.9.28.　　주미대사대리, 의회담당 참사관의 Kerry
　　　　　　　　　의원 보좌관 면담결과 보고
　　　　　　　　　1) 아측입장 전달
　　　　　　　　　2) 결의안 구상 동기 문의
　　　　　　　　　　- 보좌관측, 선거구인 메사츄세츠주 내의
　　　　　　　　　　　인권문제에 대한 높은 관심 반영 설명

　라. 85.10.2.　　주미대사대리, Kerry 의원 면담신청에
　　　　　　　　　대한 회보 미접 보고

　마. 85.11.28.　주미대사, Kerry 및 Simon 상원의원이
　　　　　　　　　공동으로 김대중 복권 및 민주 발전을 희망하는
　　　　　　　　　내용의 결의안을 작성, 의원들의 동조를
　　　　　　　　　위해 회람중임을 보고

　바. 85.12.19.　Kerry 상원의원, 동 공동결의안 제출

　　o 공동제안의원 (8명)

　　　Edward Kennedy, Claiborne Pell,
　　　Allan Cranston, Christopher Dodd,
　　　Ernest Hollings, Paul Sarbanes,
　　　Donald Riegle, Tom Harkin

0126

사. 85.12.20. Feighan 및 Dixon 하원의원、하원측 결의안
제출

2. 대처경위

가. 85.12.24. 관계기관 대책회의(정무 제1수석 주재)

- 동 결의안을 계류 상태에서 천연시켜 99기획기
종료와 함께 사실상 폐기시키도록 노력

- 부처별 조치사항

• 의원성향별 그룹화 작업(외무부)

• 주동 배후세력 파악(안기부)

• 교포언론등 홍보문제(문공부)

• 반박논지 개발(최비서관)

• H.F.의 Plunk 연구원 활용(문공부)

• 아국 국회의원 활용방안 강구(최비서관)

- 1.10전후 제2차회의 개최

나. 85.12.24. 본부、주미대사관에 외무(고)위 소속의원의
예상 반응에 따른 성향별 그룹화 지시

- 핵심 주동의원

- 결의안 지지의원

- 단순 참여 또는 중립의원

- 아국입장 대변 가능의원

다. 85.12.27. 국회 대책회의

- 목표설정

0127

- 동 결의안이 의회심의 제단계에서(소위、
  외교위、본회의) 통과되지 않도록 전력

- 추진방향
  - 국회 주동하에 정부、민간간의 완벽한 협조
    체제 구축
  - 국회측에서는 동 결의안에 대한 반박자료
    작성후 각의원들에게 전달
  - 년초부터 의원들의 워싱톤 출장 적극 활용
  - Eagleton 등 관련의원 방한시 활용 검토

- 소위원회구성 : 현홍주의원
  - 실무지원 : 최창윤 비서관、도영심 전문
    위원、미주국장

- 부처별 지원사항
  - 결의안지지、동조에 대한 열성도 분류(외무부)
  - 김대중계 배후조종세력 파악 및 대책
    수립(안기부)
  - 반박자료 작성후 발송 대상、방법 및
    시기등 모색(외무부、주미대사관 의견 참조후)
  - 주동의원들의 대아국관계 파악、선거구
    내의 유력인사 동원 방법 강구(해협위)

0128

라. 85.12.27.   국회작성 반박자료 발송계획에 대한 주미
                대사관 의견 문의

마. 85.12.28.   주미대사, 상기 질문에 대한 의견회신
                - 극히 조용하면서도 효과적인 방법 추진이
                  바람직
                - 국회측 반박자료 별도 송부보다는 공동제안
                  의원들에 대한 대사의 면담추진과 함께
                  주미대사 명의 서한발송 건의

바. 85.12.31.   주미대사, 외무(고)위 소속의원의 예상 반응별
                분류 결과보고
                - 별첨참조

사. 86.1.4.   주미대사, William Ball.Ⅱ 국무성 의회
                담당 차관보 면담결과 보고
                - 면담경위
                  주미대사와 평소 친분이 두터운 슐츠 국무
                  장관 비서실장 Nicholas Platt 대사가
                  의회 문제에 경험이 많은 동 차관보와의
                  면담을 권장, 주선
                - Ball 차관보 언급사항
                  • 의회생리상 법적 구속력 없는 결의안
                    저지는 매우 어려운 실정

0129

- 서한 송부 자체가 해로울 것은 없으나 특별한
  기대는 하지 않는 것이 좋을 것임.
- 편지를 보내는 경우에도 그들의 주장을 정면으로
  공격하는 것은 오히려 역효과를 초래할 우려도
  있음.
- 서명을 한 의원들은 이미 Commit 를 한 것으로
  보아야 하므로 그들보다는 측면 지원인사, 예컨데
  영향력이 있는 위원장급 의원들과의 면담등
  접촉을 강화하는 것이 더욱 바람직함.

아. 36.1.8. 국회 (CSG) 정례 조찬회의
  - 개인적 친분을 바탕으로 극히 한정된 의원에
    대한 개별 서신 발송 필요

자. 86.1.13. 국회 작성 아측입장 자료 (제 1、2、3안)
    주미대사관 송부 및 발송시기와 대상에 대한
    의견 문의
  - 제 1、2안 : Kerry 상원의원등 핵심 추진
                 의원 대상
  - 제 3안 : 친분의원중 결의안과 유관한
             의원 대상

차. 86.1.17 주미대사 보고
  (1) 대사명의 서한발송 보고
  - 의회 개회시기 촉박으로 1.16 상기 국회자료

0130

참고후 발송 (서한내용 : 별첨 2)

- 대상의원
  - 원본 : 제안의원 12명
  - 사본 : 상·하원 외고 (무)위원장

(2) 별도 개인서한 송부에 대한 의견
  - 현 단계에서 아측이 과민한 반응을 보이는듯 한
    인상을 주지 않기 위해서 대상을 극히 제한하여
    각별한 친분관계에 있는 의원들에게만 발송
    - 서한내용은 제 3안보다 간결함이 효과적
    - 발송시기는 1월말 또는 2월초
    - 발송 대상의원 통보 요망

카· 86·1·17· 주미대사, 주미 특파원들을 통한 기사화 가능성에
            대비한 대책 강구 건의
  - 외무부, 문공부에 조치 요청

타· 86·1·17· 미주국장, Plunk 헤리티지 재단 정책분석관
            면담시 관련 견해 청취
  - 유사한 결의안이 매년 수 백개씩 나오고
    대부분은 Personal Statement에 그침
  - 주미대사관이 Kerry 결의안에 대해 공식
    적인 언급을 할 경우 여론의 관심을 끌게되어
    사태를 악화시킬 우려가 있으므로 이를
    피해야 할것임·

0131

3. 향후 대책

　가. 주미대사, William Ball 의회담당 차관보 및 Flunk
　　　의 의견과 같이 가능한한 조용히 동건을 처리토록 함.

　나. 최근 상원의 비율빈 결의안 통과 경우등을 비추어볼때,
　　　Ball 차관보의 관측처럼 결의안 통과를 기정사실로
　　　볼수도 있으나 미의회의 관행이 반드시 이와 일치하는
　　　것으로는 볼수없음. 따라서 정당하고 설득력있는 아측
　　　논리전개가 가능할 경우 적절한 설득활동을 병행할
　　　필요는 있는것으로 사료

　　　* 85.5 상원 본회의 비율빈 결의안 통과 결과
　　　　　- 찬성 89, 반대 8, 기권 3(심의 과정에서 반대발언
　　　　　　의원 전무)

　다. 주미대사 명의 서한에 대한 반응에 따라 향후 대응책 조정
　　　- 현재 상, 하원 외무(고)위는 비율빈 문제에 관심 집중

　라. 국회의장 및 외무위원장 방미시 미중진의원 및 관계의원
　　　접촉문제 검토
　　　- 국회의장 방미 :
　　　- 외무위원장 : 미의회 조찬기도회 참석(2.4-10)

0132

```
┌─────────────────────────────────────────┐
│                                          │
│  Kerry  결의안 제출 관련 참고 자료        │
│                                          │
└─────────────────────────────────────────┘
```

1986. 1.

외   무   부

0133

1. Kerry 결의안 제출관련 주요일지

가. 85.10.23 Kerry 및 Simon 상원의원, 김 대중
   복권 및 한국의 민주화를 촉구하는 공동결의안을 작성,
   동 제안 설명서를 상원내에 회람

나. 85.12.19 Kerry 상원의원 및 Simon 상원의원
   동 공동결의안 상원 제출
   ○ 공동제안 의원(8명)

   Edward Kennedy, Claiborne Pell,
   Allan Cranston, Christopher Dodd,
   Ernest Hollings, Paul Sarbanes,
   Donald Riegle, Tom Harkin

다. 85.12.20. Feighan 및 Dixon 하원의원,
   하원측 결의안 제출

라. 86.1.16 주 미 대사, 대사명의 아측 입장 설명 서한발송
   ○ 원본 : 상기 제안의원 12명
   ○ 사본 : 외교(무)위원장

0134

2. 향후 예상 심의과정

가. 일반적 처리절차

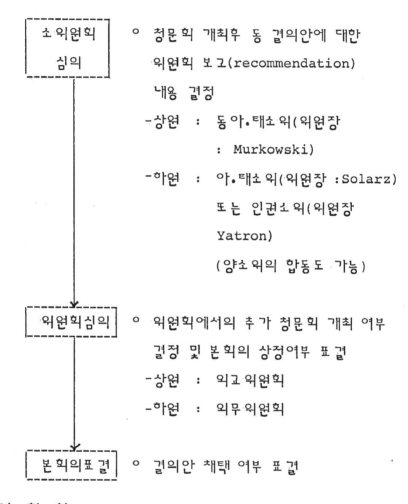

```
┌ ─ ─ ─ ─ ─ ┐
│ 소위원회  │    ° 청문회 개최후 동 결의안에 대한
│   심의    │        위원회 보고(recommendation)
└ ─ ─ ─ ─ ─ ┘        내용 결정
      │             -상원 : 동아·태소위(위원장
      │                       : Murkowski)
      │             -하원 : 아·태소위(위원장 :Solarz)
      │                     또는 인권소위(위원장
      │                     Yatron)
      │                     (양소위의 합동도 가능)
      ▼
┌ ─ ─ ─ ─ ─ ┐
│ 위원회심의 │    ° 위원회에서의 추가 청문회 개최 여부
└ ─ ─ ─ ─ ─ ┘        결정 및 본회의 상정여부 표결
      │             -상원 : 외교위원회
      │             -하원 : 외무위원회
      ▼
┌ ─ ─ ─ ─ ─ ┐
│ 본회의표결 │    ° 결의안 채택 여부 표결
└ ─ ─ ─ ─ ─ ┘
```

나. 현 황

상·하원 외교(무)위원회가 2.7 예정된 비율빈 총선
문제에 관심이 집중되어 있으므로 2월말부터 동결의안
문제가 거론될 것으로 전망

0135

Concurrent Resolution

Expressing the sense of the Congress that the
Republic of Korea should restore the civil and political rights of Kim Dae Jung and that true democracy should be instituted in the Republic of Korea

Whereas one of the primary purposes of the United
States Foreign Assistance Programs should be to
foster the growth of democratic institutions, the
holding of free, fair and honest elections, respect
for freedom of speech and freedom of the press and
the protection of individual civil rights and
liberties through the functioning of an independent
judiciary;

Whereas the people of the United States have
been more than generous in their commitment to the
security and economic well-being of the Republic
of Korea since its founding in 1948;

Whereas this commitment resulted in the loss
of the lives of 54,346 American servicemen and
103,248 Americans wounded during the Korean conflict
whereas the American people have contributed more
than $19 billion in economic and military assistance
to the Republic of Korea since 1948 and continue to
provide financial resources to support the presence
of 40,000 American servicemen on Korean soil;

Whereas recent developments, including the indictments of members of the national assembly and a

0136

resurgence in the use of torture against prominent
journalists and other democratic leaders, are cause
for grave concern over the commitment of the Government of the Republic of Korea to basic democratic
principles;

Whereas the right to due process for the people
of the Republic of Korea is virtually nonexistent,
and an independent and impartial judicial system, for
all itents and purposes, does not function, and

Whereas the prospects for any relaxation in
tensions between North and South in Korea is undermined
by political instability in the Republic of Korea;

Now, therefore
be it resolved by the House of Representatives(the
Senate concurring), that the Congress finds and
declares that the primary purposes of United States
assistance to the Republic of Korea shall be to
promote the return to true democracy in the Republic
of Korea. To that end, the Congress places the
highest priority on -

1) The replacement of the current climate of
   intimidation, abuses of basic human rights and
   civil liberties, and other antidemocratic actions,
   with an atmosphere of dialogue and trust between
   the Government of the Republic of Korea and the
   democratic opposition in that country

2) The full restoration of the political and individual
   rights of Kim Dae Jung and all others whose political
   rights are being restricted and

0137

3) The peaceful and fully democratic transfer of the
   presidency of the Republic of Korea in 1988
   through genuine popular elections open to all
   who are committed to the democratic process.

0138

대한민국이 김대중의 시민적, 정치적 권리를 회복시켜야하며

한국에서 진정한 민주주의가 이루어져야 한다는 미의회의 의사를

표명하는 공동 결의안

　　　　미국의 대외원조 계획의 주목적중 하나가 민주 제도의
신장, 자유롭고 공정하며 정직한 선거의 실시, 표현과 언론의
자유존중, 독립된 사법부의 기능을 통한 개인의 시민적 권리와
자유의 보호등을 촉진하는 것이어야 하며,

　　　　미국민은 1948년 대한민국 정부 수립 이래 대한민국의
안보와 경제적 번영에 대한 공약을 지키기 위해 매우 관대한
입장을 취해 왔으며,

　　　　이러한 공약으로 인해 한국동란시 54,346명의 미국 군인
들이 목숨을 잃고 103,248명의 미국인들이 부상을 당했고,
아울러 미국민들이 1948년이래 대한민국을 위해 190억불 이상의
경제 및 군사원조를 제공해 왔으며 한국 내의 40,000명의 미군
주둔을 지원하기 위해 재정적 지원을 계속해 왔음에 비추어,

　　　　또한 국회의원 기소, 유명 언론인 및 여타 민주 지도자
들에 대한 고문행위 재현등 최근 일련의 사태 발전이

0139

민주주의 　기본 원칙에 대한 대한민국 정부의 공약에 대해 심각한
우려를 야기시키고 있음에 비추어,

그리고 정당한 재판절차에 대한 권리는 대한민국 국민에게
사실상 존재하지 않으며, 독립적이며 공정한 사법부 역시 그 유의
기능을 상실하였으며,

남북한간 긴장완화에 대한 전망 역시 대한민국의 정치적
불안정으로 인하여 저해되고 있음에 비추어,

미의회가 미국의 대한민국에 대한 지원의 주된 　목적이
대한민국을 진정한 민주주의 국가로 복귀시키는 데 있다는 사실을
확인하고 이를 선언하도록 하원의 이름으로 (상원과 공동으로)
결의함. 　이를 위하여 미의회는 아래사항에 최대의 중점을 둠.

첫째, 위협, 기본적인권 및 시민적 자유의 침해,
그리고 기타 반민주적인 행위가 지배적인 현재의 분위기를 한국
정부와 민주적인 반대세력간의 대화와 신뢰의 분위기로 대체하는 것

둘째, 김대중과 기타 모든 미복권 정치인들이 정치적,
개인적 자유를 완전히 회복하는 것

0140

셋째, 민주적 절차에 승복하는 모든 인사들에게 개방된 진정한 직접선거를 통하여 1988년도에 대한민국 대통령직의 평화적이고도 완전한 민주적 이양이 이루어지는 것.

0141

4. 주 미 대사 명의 서한

Dear Senator Kerry:

I appreciate your interest in Korean
political developments as expressed in the
proposed concurrent resolution which you recently
initiated.   In that regard, I would like to
draw your attention to the following facts and
express my openness to our discussing in more
detail the matters about which you, my government
and I are concerned.

My government is committed to a course of
progressive expansion of political and civil
rights in Korea.   Indeed, since the inauguration
of the Fifth Republic in August of 1980, Korea
has made significant advances toward both political
democratization and national reconciliation.
Thus, for example, the ban on political activities
which had previously been imposed on certain
politicians has now be enlifted. Moreover, the
free and fair elections which were held in February,
1985 are a dramatic indication of the progress
toward democratization which has already been made

0142

and of my government's continuing commitment to
that process.   President Chun himself remains
committed to leaving office in 1988 and to a
peaceful transfer of power at that time.
Finally, I can assure you, as well, that my
government will continue to give careful consideration
to additional steps it might take to further this
process, including possible review of Mr. Kim Dae
Jung's status as circumstances permit.   In sum,
the trend toward further democratization and
reconciliation, to which both the Korean government
and the people are strongly committed, will
continue to prevail.

    At the same time, the pace of our progress
is conditioned by our geo-political realities.
As the U.S. State Department's 1984 human rights
report noted, because of the threat from an
aggressive communist regime in North Korea, all
Korean governments since the Republic's founding
in 1948 have felt it necessary to give top priority
to maintaining external and internal security.

0143

This threat is very real and we would hope that
this factor would be fully taken into account by
Korea's friends and allies when evaluating the
pace of our progress towards democratization.

I would appreciate an opportunity to meet
with you in person to exchange views on this matter
and others relating to strengthening Korea-U.S.
friendship and cooperation.

Sincerely,

Kyung-won Kim

Ambassador

0144

```
┌─────────────────────────┐
│                         │
│   참  고   자  료        │
│                         │
└─────────────────────────┘
```

1. 외교(무)위 소속의원 성향분석

2. 주미대사 명의 서한(영문)

3. Kerry 공동결의안(국·영문)

4. 한국 국내문제 관련 결의안 참고 사항

5. 국회 작성 아국입장 자료(I, Ⅱ, Ⅲ 안)

0145

(참고자료 1)

Kerry 공동결의안 관련기(당)위 소속의원 성향분석서

	상 원	하 원
핵심 추진 의원	KERRY, PELL, SARBANES, CRANSTON, DODD	FEIGHAN
결의안 지지가능 의원	BIDEN, EAGLETON, MATHIAS, PRESSLER	STUDDS, BARNES, CROCKETT, DYMALLY, TORRICELLI, WEISS, LEACH
수정 또는 중립입장 의원	BOSCHWITZ, TRIBLE, EVANS, ZORINSKY	SOLARZ, WOLPE, GEJDENSON, LANTOS, BERMAN, LEVINE, GARCIA
아직 입장 지지가능 의원	LUGAR, HELMS, KASSEBAUM, MURKOWSKI	BROOMFIELD, LAGOMARSINO, MICA, GILMAN, HYDE, SOLOMON, DORNAN

범 례

* ─────

Dear Senator Kerry:

I appreciate your interest in Korean
political developments as expressed in the
proposed concurrent resolution which you recently
initiated.   In that regard, I would like to
draw your attention to the following facts and
express my openness to our discussing in more
detail the matters about which you, my government
and I are concerned.

My government is committed to a course of
progressive expansion of political and civil
rights in Korea.   Indeed, since the inauguration
of the Fifth Republic in August of 1980, Korea
has made significant advances toward both political
democratization and national reconciliation.
Thus, for example, the ban on political activities
which had previously been imposed on certain
politicians has now be enlifted. Moreover, the
free and fair elections which were held in February,
1985 are a dramatic indication of the progress
toward democratization which has already been made

0147

and of my government's continuing commitment to
that process.   President Chun himself remains
committed to leaving office in 1988 and to a
peaceful transfer of power at that time.
Finally, I can assure you, as well, that my
government will continue to give careful consideration
to additional steps it might take to further this
process, including possible review of Mr. Kim Dae
Jung's status as circumstances permit.   In sum,
the trend toward further democratization and
reconciliation, to which both the Korean government
and the people are strongly committed, will
continue to prevail.

       At the same time, the pace of our progress
is conditioned by our geo-political realities.
As the U.S. State Department's 1984 human rights
report noted, because of the threat from an
aggressive communist regime in North Korea, all
Korean governments since the Republic's founding
in 1948 have felt it necessary to give top priority
to maintaining external and internal security.

0148

This threat is very real and we would hope that
this factor would be fully taken into account by
Korea's friends and allies when evaluating the
pace of our progress towards democratization.

I would appreciate an opportunity to meet
with you in person to exchange views on this matter
and others relating to strengthening Korea-U.S.
friendship and cooperation.

Sincerely,

Kyung-won Kim

Ambassador

0149

Concurrent Resolution

Expressing the sense of the Congress that the Republic of Korea should restore the civil and political rights of Kim Dae Jung and that true democracy should be instituted in the Republic of Korea

Whereas one of the primary purposes of the United States Foreign Assistance Programs should be to foster the growth of democratic institutions, the holding of free, fair and honest elections, respect for freedom of speech and freedom of the press and the protection of individual civil rights and liberties through the functioning of an independent judiciary;

Whereas the people of the United States have been more than generous in their commitment to the security and economic well-being of the Republic of Korea since its founding in 1948;

Whereas this commitment resulted in the loss of the lives of 54,346 American servicemen and 103,248 Americans wounded during the Korean conflict whereas the American people have contributed more than $19 billion in economic and military assistance to the Republic of Korea since 1948 and continue to provide financial resources to support the presence of 40,000 American servicemen on Korean soil;

Whereas recent developments, including the indictments of members of the national assembly and a

0150

resurgence in the use of torture against prominent
journalists and other democratic leaders, are cause
for grave concern over the commitment of the Government of the Republic of Korea to basic democratic
principles;

Whereas the right to due process for the people
of the Republic of Korea is virtually nonexistent,
and an independent and impartial judicial system, for
all itents and purposes, does not function, and

Whereas the prospects for any relaxation in
tensions between North and South in Korea is undermined
by political instability in the Republic of Korea;

Now, therefore
be it resolved by the House of Representatives (the
Senate concurring), that the Congress finds and
declares that the primary purposes of United States
assistance to the Republic of Korea shall be to
promote the return to true democracy in the Republic
of Korea.   To that end, the Congress places the
highest priority on -

1) The replacement of the current climate of
   intimidation, abuses of basic human rights and
   civil liberties, and other antidemocratic actions,
   with an atmosphere of dialogue and trust between
   the Government of the Republic of Korea and the
   democratic opposition in that country

2) The full restoration of the political and individual
   rights of Kim Dae Jung and all others whose political
   rights are being restricted and

0151

3) The peaceful and fully democratic transfer of the
   presidency of the Republic of Korea in 1988
   through genuine popular elections open to all
   who are committed to the democratic process.

0152

대한민국이 김대중의 시민적、정치적 권리를 회복시켜야하며

한국에서 진정한 민주주의가 이루어져야 한다는 미의회의 의사를

표명하는 공동 결의안

미국의 대외원조 계획의 주목적중 하나가 민주제도의
신장、자유롭고 공정하며 정직한 선거의 실시、표현과 언론의
자유존중、독립된 사법부의 기능을 통한 개인의 시민적 권리와
자유의 보호등을 촉진하는 것이어야 하며、

미국민은 1948년 대한민국 정부 수립 이래 대한민국의
안보와 경제적 번영에 대한 공약을 지키기 위해 매우 관대한
입장을 취해 왔으며、

이러한 공약으로 인해 한국동란시 54、346명의 미국 군인
들이 목숨을 잃고 103、248명의 미국인들이 부상을 당했고、
아울러 미국민들이 1948년이래 대한민국을 위해 190억불 이상의
경제 및 군사원조를 제공해 왔으며 한국 내의 40、000명의 미군
주둔을 지원하기 위해 재정적 지원을 계속해 왔음에 비추어、

또한 국회의원 기소、유명 언론인 및 여타 민주 지도자
들에 대한 고문행위 재현등 최근 일련의 사태 발전이

0153

민주주의 기본 원칙에 대한 대한민국 정부의 공약에 대해 심각한
우려를 야기시키고 있음에 비추어,

그리고 정당한 재판절차에 대한 권리는 대한민국 국민에게
사실상 존재하지 않으며, 독립적이며 공정한 사법부 역시 고유의
기능을 상실하였으며,

남북한간 긴장완화에 대한 전망 역시 대한민국의 정치적
불안정으로 인하여 저해되고 있음에 비추어,

미의회가 미국의 대한민국에 대한 지원의 주된 목적이
대한민국을 진정한 민주주의 국가로 복귀시키는 데 있다는 사실을
확인하고 이를 선언하도록 하원의 이름으로 (상원과 공동으로)
결의함. 이를 위하여 미의회는 아래사항에 최대의 중점을 둠.

첫째, 위협, 기본적인권 및 시민적 자유의 침해,
그리고 기타 반민주적인 행위가 지배적인 현재의 분위기를 한국
정부와 민주적인 반대세력간의 대화와 신뢰의 분위기로 대체하는 것

둘째, 김대중과 기타 모든 미복권 정치인들이 정치적,
개인적 자유를 완전히 회복하는 것

0154

셋째, 민주적 절차에 승복하는 모든 인사들에게 개방된 진정한 직접선거를 통하여 1988년도에 대한민국 대통령직의 평화적이고도 완전한 민주적 이양이 이루어지는 것.

0155

72년이후 한국 국내문제 관련 결의안 참고 사항

가. 76.9.   8.18 판문점 사건과 명동성당 사건에 관한 미하원
　　　　　　 국제관계위원회 결의안 채택
　　　　　　 ° 제안자 : Fraser   의원
　　　　　　 ° 결의안요지
　　　　　　　　 : 판문점 살해사건에 유감, 명동 사건 관련자에
　　　　　　　　　 대한 유죄선거에 유감, 동 철회 요청
　　　　　　 ° 결 과 : 본회의 상정 저지

나. 77.2.3. 하원 국제관계위원회, 국제기구소위(Fraser 소위)
　　　　　　 로하여금 한.미 관계의 비정상적인면을 전반적으로
　　　　　　 조사토록하는 결의안 채택
　　　　　　 ° 19:4로 통과

다. 77.2.9. 하원 본회의, 하원 윤리위원회로 하여금 미하원
　　　　　　 의원들의 한국정부 관련 불법비행(박동선 사건
　　　　　　 관계)을 조사토록 하는 결의안 (HR 252)   채택
　　　　　　 ° 박동선사건 조사 특별고문으로 Lacovara 임명
　　　　　　 ° 388:0으로 통과

라. 78.2.2. 미 하원 국제관계위, 박동선 사건 조사기간을
　　　　　　 78.10.31까지 2개월 연장하자는 Fraser
　　　　　　 소위원회의 지시 결의안 통과

0156

마. 80.11.20. Don Bonker 하원의원,김대중 구명과 한국의

　　　　민주화를 촉구하는 결의안을 외무위 국제기구

　　　　소위원회에 제출, 통과

　　　　(정족수 미달 상태에서 통과되었다하여 물의를

　　　　야기)

참 고 : 10.26 사태이후 미의회의 김대중 관련 동향

　　　o 상 원 : 서한발송 3회(4명)

　　　　　　　　　결의안제출 1회(5명)

　　　o 하 원 : 서한발송 2회(11명)

　　　　　　　　　결의안제출 2회(21명)

　　　* 결의안 채택 단 1건 : 하원 외무위 국제소위

0157

The Hon. John F. Kerry
The U.S. Senate
Washington, D.C.

Dear Sir:

The draft senate Resolution concerning the
Republic of Korea's political situation and Kim
Dae Jung only recently came to my attention.
As I was reading through it line by line, I was
rather astonished to note that the perception
of the draft resolution on Korean situation was
largely based on misinformation or a one-sided
point of view and that our official policy line,
which has not been held secret, was nowhere
acknowledged or appreciated.

Therefore, as one lawmaker to another,
please allow me to address you in this direct,
- maybe inadequate - manner in order not to
argue nor to protest, but only to round out
your information and provide you with our side
of the story. For this purpose, I feel the
following three questions should be answered.

- 1 -

0158

First, is any shift or change in our
government's initial committement to the
democratic principle occuring ?

Second, was Kim Dae Jung convicted on
trumpted up charges ?

Third, will the peaceful and democratic
transfer of the Presidency be realized in 1988 ?

First let me start by saying that I basically
agree with you that the Republic of Korea must
do its best to move toward democratization.
Indeed, this is the desire of every Korean citizen,
student, laborer, farmer, and yes, that of
government itself.

I cannot emphasize enough to you the changes
in the political atmosphere of the Republic of
Korea since that have taken place in 1980. It is
a phenomenon matched only by our economic progress
during the previous decade. The government of

- 2 -

President Chun has held its ultimate goal the
gradual, yet steady, democratization of Korea
through political development. We have
instituted concrete measures toward this goal
in both social and political spheres. These
measures are documented and their results are
visible for all to see. Allow me to enumerate
just a few of them for you.

In the social arena, much has been done to
"liberalize" the atmosphere of South Korea. For
the first time since the founding of the Republic
four decades ago, the midnight-to-four curfew was
lifted. More than ever in the history of our
country, Korean citizens are enjoying the privilege
to travel, study and work abroad at will, as
restrictions are gradually lifted. The rather
rigid looking school uniform worn for decades
by our young people and the strict hair code is
no longer required by law and has all but
disappeared.

- 3 -

0160

On a more political level, freedom of the
press, seriously restricted under the government
of the late President Park when all articles
critical to the government were taken out of
circulation and foreign journals were heavily
censored, has been freely circulated. Our
journalists no longer live in fear of persecution
as they d: in the 1970's.

    Also :any prisoners have been released
from priscr by amnesty measures and police were
removed from campuses in order to promote autonomy
among the Korean academic community.

    All these steps were nothing but the bold
initiative taken by   our government toward
democritization in order to accomodate growing
diversification and pluralization in Korean
society. The course is firmly set now and no
artificial force can reverse the trend of this
modernization and liberalization process.

Recent episode of indictment of several
lawmakers was nothing more than an ordinary
law enforcement action. No one is allowed to
incite violence by trying to rally students
who were staging a violent, unlawful demonstration. Especially for a person like National
Assembly member, our Confucian tradition calls
for a very high standard of ethics and respect
of laws. It should be also noted that the
proceeding against these legislators are
conducted in a very lawful manner with full
participation of defense counsels.

There have been some report on harsh treatment
against some journalists and other citizens. First
of all allegation presented by one side only should
be discounted and if there have been really such
irregularities, it must have happened as an isolated
case, and have nothing to do with the policy of
the government, which strongly denounces any form
of violence in conducting criminal investigation.

- 5 -

0162

Law enforcement effort by a responsible
government should not be construed as evil
scheme with political motive and isolated cases
of irregularities should not be treated as the
sign of shift in policy itself.

Secondly, it must be reminded that Kim Dae
Jung's political rights are restricted as a legal
consequence of his conviction. He was rightfully
found guilty of subversion by the Supreme Court
on January 20, 1981, as a result of his proved
direct responsibility for the student demonstration
of May 18, 1980, the demonstration which led to
the Kwangju incident. He was found to have
instigated the student unrest in the Kwangju area
by providing funds and by instructing those
students who led the demonstration.

It must be noted that when the supreme
Court which is composed of the most respected
civilian judges in Korea deliberated the Kim's
case, it made a very thorough and careful review
into the factual as well as legal aspects of the
conclusion that Kim is indeed guilty of instigating
the rebellion.

- 6 -

0163

Of course, Kim denied the charge after his
release. But it must also be pointed out that
a charge of subversion is indeed such a serious
one that admission of guilt cannot be easily
expected from the defendant.

Restrictions placed on Mr. Kim's political
rights (i.e. he cannot run for public office)
are the inevitable legal consequence of this
lawful conviction of subversion as is required
by our Criminal Code and the Code of Criminal
procedure, and they are not the result of any
arbitrary political decision.

He was released from confinement simply
out of humanitarian concern for his health and
was allowed to travel to the U.S.
His release means neither his innocence nor
his rehabilitation.

- 7 -

0164

In this connection, to the accusation made in the draft Resolution that the independent judiciary does not function in Korea, I would like to say that, on the contrary, our judiciary was always based on a solid tradition of political neutrality and any political affiliation has been considered toboo. Our courts have acted an their own in the past and they are continuing to do so today. For example, in 1984, Korean courts dismissed 8,092 warrants of arrest issued by the prosecution with complete impunity. Also, about 45% of bail applications were decided in the defendants favor. We have managed to produce an impressive judiciary system of which any nation would be proud of.

I would further like to take the example of Kim Dae Jung to point out to you just how far along our road to democracy our gradual, but steady, methods have taken us. Most observers in 1980, including one of the top officials under the Carter Administration, believed that Kim Dae Jung would be executed.

- 8 -

0165

Yet all have witnessed instead his release from
prison and travel to the U.S. and safe return to
Korea and to a relatively normal way of life.
Now Kim meets with the press, both foreign and
domestic, and appears regularly in public. I am
taking the liberty of enclosing some of the
articles where Kim is quoted in the Korean press.
These articles will show that, contrary to the
understanding of some of our friends in the U.S.,
Mr. Kim is now enjoying a normal life and is not
under   surveillance and harassment.

I do not preclude the possibility of restoration of rights for Mr. Kim in the future. As a
matter of fact, Korean government has hinted on
numerous occasions that an amnesty for Mr. Kim
can be favorably considered if he shows his
willingness to denounce his past tactic of
provoking mass uprising, like the one used in
1980, the chaotic period after President Park's
assassination.

- 9 -

0166

Finally, I would like to underline the fact
that the very measure your draft resolution promotes
as the next step toward the democratization of Korea,
i.e. free elections in 1988, is the stated intention
of this government. Indeed, President Chun Doo Hwan
has made it clear, that he has no intention of
acting as the President beyond his mandate which
ends in 1988. I firmly believe there will be a
peaceful change of presidential power as stipulated
in the constitution.

Though nothing out of the ordinary from the
Western perspective, the upcoming change of the
presidency will be a landmark in the 38-year
history of Korea's consitutional process.
Just remember that during this period there
took place eight constitutional changes with
an average life-span of four and half years.
Each time the primary purpose, was to prolong
the tenure of the Chief Executive. These have
of the Consitutional Revision
caused immense political turmoil and became
major obstacles to a stable and democratic form
of government. Given the long history of

- 10 -

0167

association between constitutional change and political retrogression, it is high time for us to think twice before seeking another revision to the existing constitution. The present constitution is firmly set on a course toward gradual democratization. It is not a perfect document, however, and in no way precludes constitutional revision. The critical concern is that a hasty revision out of partisan motives may not only chill the budding sign of democratization but might cause social and political instability.

Concluding this letter, I would like to assure you that we have never taken the support of the American people for granted and have always appreciated your support, written not so much in dollars but in the blood of your own people for the sake of ours. We are forever beholden to you and we recognize your concern for our continued development. We will continue to share your hope for us, and we will continue to move toward freedom for our people while holding the front line of Communism in Asia.

- 11 -

0168

We know that we cannot do so without your help
and your support. We only ask that you continue
to back us in every way, acknowledging our
progress and understanding our obstacles. The
Korean government is aware of the investment
made on our behalf by our American friends and
the free people of the world, and we are proud
to say that we are carrying out our obligation
and will not disappoint the aspirations of our
allies to hold us up as an example of
democratization in the developing world.

                    Very truly yours,

0169

Senator John F. Kerry
U.S. Senate
Washington, D.C.

Dear Senator Kerry:

The Senate Resolution concerning the Republic
of Korea and her political situation only recently
came to my attention. As I was reading through it
line by line, I was struck by the fact that our
country was under criticism by one of our closest
allies. I was further astonished to note that the
criticism was largely based on misinformation or a
one-sided point of view and that our real situation
was nowhere reflected.

Therefore, as one lawmaker to another, please
allow me to address you in this manner in order to
round out your information and provide you with our
side of the story. As I feel it is my duty to offer
you a different perspective I hope you will forgive

- 1 -

0170

my of such an inadequate medium as a letter to
communicate such an important point and will have
the patience to read this through with a open mind
to mutual understanding and dialogue.

I am in fundamental agreement with you that
the Republic of Korea must do its best to move
toward political development although the spirit
of ciriticism in your resolution leaves me quite
puzzled. Indeed, this is the desire of every
Korean citizen. However, your resolution reads
like a condemnation of the Korean government and
an intention to push us toward reform, without
taking into consideration our precarious situation
nor the progres already instituted from within
the government. I would like to take the opportunity
to point out these factors which were lacking in
your resolution.

The very fact that in the thirty eight years
since the foundation of the Republic of Korea we
have been through four vehement political changes,
none of which was peaceful, brings home the harsh
reality of Korean politics.

- 2 -

0171

We are faced with threats to our stability
and to our very lives that the American people,
with their 200 years of freedom and peace within
their borders, may find hard to understand. We
are living under the guns of communist North
Korea, under a shaky peace with a neighbor intent
on dominating and overthrowing us. The cruelty
and the taste for the international terrorism was
again proven when the North Korea carried out the
bloody Rangoon massacre. Any of your congressional
colleagues who visited the Demilitarized Zone will
share his astonishment to find the proximity of
the most heavily armed warfront with the bustling
10 million residents city of Seoul. The fact that
this artificial line of division is armed with
600,000 Korean soldiers along with 40,000 American
men one side and 800,000 North Korean soldiers the
other, is often underestimated by us. This is
where our misfortune and misery originates.

- 3 -

0172

If our Republic had not kept the vigilene
and if we had not put the question of survival
as our top priority, the economic growth through
which we were able to become the United States'
seventh largest trading partner leaving France
and Italy behind and fourth largest buyer of
U.S. agricultural products would not have been
possible.

Discussing the political development, I
feel it is appropriate to present you some
concrete facts about Mr. Kim Dae Jung whose
case is specifically mentioned in your resolution.
Contrary to what has been known about him there
is a truth, the truth that his various irresponsible
actions throughout his political career have
never been for the good of the Korean people.

For example, we are all familiar with the
Kwangju incident. A series of events led to that
tragedy, a nightmare in which Kim Dae Jung was
instrumental and which haunts us to this day.

- 4 -

0173

He must share the responsibility for the events
of early 1980, including the tragedy of Kwangju,
as it was he who took advantage of the already
confused masses to promote his own political
ambitions. He incited the violence in Kwangju
that bred more violence at a time when a true
political leader, concerned for the welfare of
the people, would have appealed to the peoples'
good sense. Recognizing this, the then U.S.
Ambassador to Korea, William Gleysteen, criticized
Kim's "lack of restraint" and his refusal to call
for moderation among dissident elements. Kim
persisted in choosing a course of extremism and
confrontation and should be held accountable for
the result. He was rightfuly found guilty of
subversion by the Supreme Court on January 20,
1981, as a result of his proved direct
responsibility for the student revolt demonstration
of May 18, 1980, the demonstration which led to
the Kwangju incident. He was found to have
instigated the student unrest in the Kwangju
area by providing funds and by instructing those
students who led the demonstration.

- 5 -

0174

In the humanitarian cause of his health,
and having obtained a statement of his repentance
and good intentions, he was allowed to seek
medical treatment in the United States on the
condition that he would cease all political
activities. He broke his promise, using the
foreign press and foreign influence to promote
disorder in this country and to promote his own
political goals. Having returned to this country
after two years in the States he has proven time
and again that he will continue to use the same
chaos-provoking mass-uprising methods to reach
his political goals that he used in 1980. This
is proof enough to us that his main concern is
to win the political game. Having seen his
performance to date, one has to wonder what
kind of a politician he would make.

- 6 -

0175

I would like to recall you how far the
treatment of Kim Dae Jung has been progressed
during the last five years. Most observers in
1980, including one of the top officials under
the Carter Administration, believed that Kim
Dae Jung would be executed. Yet all have
witnessed instead a gradual progression from
prison, two years' stay in the States, peaceful
return to Korea, and to normal way of life at
present. Kim meets with and is quoted in the
press, both foreign and domestic, and appears
in public. I am taking the liberty of enclosing
some of the articles where Kim is covered in the
Korean press.

I cannot emphasize enough to you the changes
in the political atmosphere of the Republic of
Korea since 1980. It is a phenomenon matched only
by our economic progress during the previous decade.
The current government has held its ultimate goal
the gradual, yet steady, political development.

- 7 -

0176

We have instituted concrete measures toward this
goal in both social and political spheres. These
measures are documented and their results are
visible for all to see. Allow me to enumerate
just a few of them for you.

Among other things, a set of liberalizing
reforms has been undertaken such as the lifting
of the midnight curfew for the first time since
the founding of the Republic 4 decades ago, the
easing of control on overseas travel, and the
increased autonomy given to the private sector
in economic activities including foreign trade.
Police ere removed from campuses in order to
promote campus autonomy, although this has
unfornately been abused by the activist sutents.
This trend toward liberalization will remain a
crucial feature of Korea's social-political
landscape throughout the 1980s. Korea is
firmly set on the course of liberalization
and opennes.

- 3 -

Freedom of the press, virtually unheard
of under the previous Adminstration when all
articles critical to the government were taken
out of circulation and foreign journals were
heavily censored, has been accepted in this
country for the first time ever. Our journalists
no longer live in fear of censorship or persecution
as they did until the end of the 1970s.

Despite some campus unrest, the current
administration has successfully maintained
socio-political stabillity during the last five
years. I would like to recall you that the
pervious administrations until the end of the
1970s have forged a semblance of stability,
usually using violence such as martial laws,
emergency decrees. In contrast, Korea after
1980 has never relied on such measures to
maintain the stability.

- 5 -

0178

To answer your charge that the judiciary
in Korea is less than satisfactory, I would
like to say that, on the contrary, our judiciary
has always been based on a solid tradition of
political neutrality and any political affiliation
has been considered taboo. The fact that not
one judge was ever the recipient of disciplinary
actions on the part of the government attests to
the guarantee of the status and independence of
the judiciary. In 1984, Korean courts dismissed
8,092 warrants of arrest issued by the Prosecution
with complete impunity. Also, about 45% of all
prisoners' bail applications were accepted.
We have managed to produce an impressive judiciary
system of which any government would be proud of.

Most importantly, I must emphasize the most
obvious, and the most hopeful, proof that Korea
is on the right road the political development.
The general election held under this current
government in February of 1985 produced a
healthy showing of 46% of the seat in the
National Assembly won by the Opposition Party.

- 10 -

Their strong showing warns those in power to
keep moving toward democracy, and it also
proves that these elections were conducted in
a free and open atmosphere. The fact that the
vociferous opposition, demonstrations and
criticism appear in print and are incresingly
discussed around the world attest to the
political development enjoyed by Koreans,
a healthy sign that democracy is being
achieved.

     Furthermore, I would like to underline the
fact that the very measure your resolution promotes
as the next step toward the democratization of
Korea, i.e. Free elections in 1988, is the
stated intention of this government. Indeed,
President Chun Doo Hwan has made it clear, that
he has no intention of acting as President beyond
his mandate which ends in 1988. Our goal is the
peaceful and orderly transfer of power according
to the laws of this country and the will of our
people.

- 11 -

0180

Finally, I would like to assure you that
we have never taken the support of the American
people for granted and have always appreciated
your support. We are forever beholden to you and
we recognize your concern for our continued
development. We will continue to share your
hope for us, and we will continue to move toward
freedom for our people while holding the front
line of Comunism in Asia. We know that we cannot
do so without your help and your support. We
only ask that you continue to back us in every
way, acknowledging our progress and understanding
our obstacles. The Korean government is aware
of the investment made on our behalf by our
American friends and the free people of the
world, and we are proud to say that we are
carrying out our obligation and will not
disappoint the aspirations of our allies
to hold us up as an example of democratization
in the developing world.

    With the best wishes, I remain,

                        Sincerely yours,

                    - 12 -

친분있는 의원중 결의안통과와 관련이 예상되는 의원 (Model Ⅲ)

Dear Congressman:

It is with great pleasure that I send new
year's greetings to you and express my sincere
feelings of admiration and appreciation for
the special attention you have paid for the
progress of our nation.

As you are well aware, for years Korea and
the US have put their efforts together for the
realization of peace in the world and freedom
for mankind in order to achieve a democratic
development. This was witnessed during the Korean
War when our friendly allies united their forces
to fight against the invasion of Communism.
Many US soldiers gave up their lives for freedom.
However, allow me to add that these deaths were
not in vain.

However, we find ourselves anxious because
the younger generations that haven't experienced
the war nor the vivid threats of Communism are
aggravating anti-American sentiments and views.

- 1 -

0182

Not only that, but we find ourselves unawarely
vigilant for the political powers that abuse
this situation.

Despite the turbulent situations and the
biggest threat to man's dignity--Communism,
the Korean people have guarded the security and
the gradual democratization of the nation for
a continuous 38 years.

Amid the apprehensive eyes of the world,
Korea has arrived to this point of democracy.
To reach this, the Korean government is guaranteeing
the absolute freedom for its citizens and the
rights of the people. The whole nation is now
participating in the process of a secure society
and the development of its people amid a trusting
atmosphere of harmony and dialogues.

1988 is two years away. It is a time in
the Korean history when the people's heartiest
desire and the government's determined will for
a peaceful change of political power will become

- 2 -

0183

a reality. It will be the first time when the
dream is no longer a dream but a realization.
This peaceful change of government to the essence
for the growth of the Korean people. In this
atmosphere of stability and trust, the 1988
election will take place freely and democratically.
This is the only truthful way believed by the
people and its government.

We find ourselves closer to this reality
as evidensed by the 1985 National Assembly
election where for the first time we have had a
fair and active election. The opposition party
obtained 102 seats of the Assembly, achieving 46%
of the legislators.

Mr. Kim Dae Jung, like all of us, is protected
by our laws, but like all of us, he must abide by
them. In the checks and balance system, where all
three of our government branches interact equally,
the judiciary branch is unique and independent.

- 3 -

0184

Mr. Kim, after a formal judiciary process, is presently on a suspension of imprisonment status. This is an internal matter that has been judicially processed and decided upon.

The resolution involving Mr. Kim is a distortion and exaggeration of the Korean political situation. This is not only a burden to the democratic progress of the Korean people but a hindrance. The prejudices and activities based upon these distortions and exaggerations will only invite chaos. The result of chaos, I would have to say is the most undemocratic and suppressice force on earth--Communism. Our people know that.

As someone representing the sentiment of the Korean people, I am confident that your knowledge and insight will lead you to make the wisest decision.

- 4 -

0185

It is our wish that with your understanding
of our difficult situation, you will help us
put our efforts together for a healthy democratic
development of our nation.

Wishing you health and prosperity, and a
successful year, I remain,

Sincerely,

p.s.   If you need any other information please
        do not hesitate to contact me.

0186

```
┌─────────────────────────────────────────────┐
╎                                               ╎
╎   Kerry  결의안 관련 국회대책회의 자료              ╎
╎                                               ╎
└─────────────────────────────────────────────┘
```

1986. 1.

앙 고 재	북 미 과	86년 1월 7일	담 당	과 장	심의관	국 장

미   주   국

0187

1. 결의안제출 관련 주요일지

  가. 85.9.26.   주미대사, 국무성 제보에 따라 9.27 Kerry
                의원이 결의안 발의 예정임을 보고

  나. 85.9.27.   본부, 동 결의안 발의 철회 촉구 지시

  다. 85.9.28.   주미대사대리, 의회담당 참사관의 Kerry
                의원 보좌관 면담결과 보고
                1) 아측입장 전달
                2) 결의안 구상 동기 문의
                   - 보좌관측, 선거구인 메사츄세츠주 내의
                     인권문제에 대한 높은 관심 반영 설명

  라. 85.10.2.   주미대사대리, Kerry 의원 면담신청에
                대한 획보 미접 보고

  마. 85.11.28.   주미대사, Kerry 및 Simon 상원의원이
                공동으로 김대중 복권 및 민주발전을 희망하는
                내용의 결의안을 작성, 의원들의 동조를
                위해 획람중임을 보고

  바. 85.12.19.   Kerry 상원의원, 동 공동결의안 제출

    ° 공동제안의원 (8명)

      Edward Kennedy, Claiborne Pell,
      Allan Cranston, Christopher Dodd,
      Ernest Hollings, Paul Sarbanes,
      Donald Riegle, Tom Harkin

0188

사. 85.12.20. Feighan 및 Dixon 하원의원, 하원측 결의안

제출

2. 대처경위

가. 85.12.24. 관계기관 대책회의(정무 제1수석 주재)

- 동 결의안을 계류상태에서 천연시켜 99기획기
종료와 함께 사실상 폐기시키도록 노력

- 부처별 조치사항

• 의원성향별 그룹화 작업(외무부)

• 주동 배후세력 파악(안기부)

• 고포언론등 홍보문제(문공부)

• 반박논지 개발(외비서관)

• H.F.의 Plunk 연구원 활용(문공부)

• 아국 국회의원 활용방안 강구(외비서관)

- 1.10전후 제2차회의 개최

나. 85.12.24. 본부, 주미대사관에 외무(고)위 소속의원의
예상 반응에 따른 성향별 그룹화 지시

- 핵심 주동의원

- 결의안 지지의원

- 단순 참여 또는 중립의원

- 아국입장 대변 가능의원

다. 85.12.27. 국회 대책회의

- 목표설정

0189

- 동 결의안이 의회심의 제단계에서(소위、
외고위、본회의) 통과되지 않도록 전력

- 추진방향
  - 국회 주동하에 정부、민간간의 완벽한 협조
    체제 구축
  - 국회측에서는 동 결의안에 대한 반박자료
    작성후 각의원들에게 전달
  - 년초부터 의원들의 워싱톤 출장 적극 활용
  - Eagleton 등 관련의원 방한시 활용 검토

- 소위원회구성 : 현흥주의원
  - 실무지원 : 최창윤 비서관、도영심 전문
    위원、미주국장

- 부처별 지원사항
  - 결의안지지、동조에 대한 열성도 분류(외무부)
  - 김대중계 배후조종 세력 파악 및 대책
    수립(안기부)
  - 반박자료 작성후 발송대상、방법 및
    시기등 모색(외무부、주미대사관 의견 참조후)
  - 주동의원들의 대아국관계 파악、선거구
    내의 유력인사 동원 방법 강구(해협위)

0190

라. 85.12.27.　　국회작성 반박자료 발송 계획에 대한 주미

　　　　　　　　　대사관 의견 문의

마. 85.12.28.　　주미대사, 상기 질문에 대한 의견회신

　　　　　　　　　- 국회 조용하면서도 효과적인 방법 추진이

　　　　　　　　　　바람직

　　　　　　　　　- 국회측 반박자료 별도 송부보 다는 공동제안

　　　　　　　　　　의원들에 대한 대사의 면담추진과 함께

　　　　　　　　　　주미대사 명의 서한발송 건의

바. 85.12.31.　　주미대사, 외무(고)위 소속의원의 예상 반응별

　　　　　　　　　분류 결과보고

　　　　　　　　　- 별첨참조

사. 86.1.4.　　　주미대사, William Ball.III 국무성 의회

　　　　　　　　　담당 차관보 면담결과 보고

　　　　　　　　　- 면담경위

　　　　　　　　　　주미대사와 평소 친분이 두터운 슐츠 국무

　　　　　　　　　　장관 비서실장　Nicholas Platt 대사가

　　　　　　　　　　의회 문제에 경험이 많은 등 차관보와의

　　　　　　　　　　면담을 권장, 주선

　　　　　　　　　- Ball 차관보 언급 사항

　　　　　　　　　· 의회생리상 법적 구속력 없는 결의안

　　　　　　　　　　저지는 매우 어려운 실정

0191

- 서한송부 자체가 해로울것은 없으나
  특별한 기대는 하지 않는것이 좋을것임.
- 편지를 보내는 경우에도 그들의 주장을
  정면으로 공격하는것은 오히려 역효과
  초래할(Counterproductive)우려도있음.
- 서명을 한 의원들은 이미 Commit 를
  한것으로 보아야 하므로 그들보다는 측면
  지원인사, 예컨데 영향력이 있는 위원장급
  의원들과의 면담등 접촉을 강화하는것이
  더욱 바람직함.

3. 향후 대책

가. 주미대사 및 William Ball의회담당 차관보의 의견에따라
   가능한한 조용히 동건을 처리토록함.

나. 최근 상원의 비율빈 결의안 통과 경우등을 비추어볼때,
   Ball 차관보의 관측처럼 결의안 통과를 기정사실로 볼수도
   있으나 미의회의 관행이 반드시 이와 일치하는 것으로는
   볼수없음. 따라서 정당하고 설득력있는 아측 논리 전개가
   가능할 경우 적절한 설득활동을 병행할 필요는 있는것으로
   사료됨.

   * 85.5 상원 본회의 비율빈 결의안 통과 결과
     - 찬성 89, 반대 8, 기권 3(심의 각정에서 반대발언
       의원 전무)

0192

다. 상기에 비추어 현재 국회측에서 작성하고 있는 반박
   자료를 예의 검토한후 이를 주미대사관에 송부하여
   현지에서 적의 활용토록 조치함.

라. 1.21 의회 개원후 상하원 관계(소)위원회 중 진의원에
   대해 주미대사가 적극 접촉토록하고 동 결과에 따라
   향후 대책을 재수립토록 함.

0193

Kerry 공동결의안 관련외교(무)위 소속의원 성향분석

	상 원	하 원
예상 추진 의원	KERRY, PELL, SARBANES, CRANSTON, DODD	FEIGHAN
결의안 지지가능 의원	BIDEN, EAGLETON, MATHIAS, PRESSLER	STUDDS, BARNES, CROCKETT, DYMALLY, TORRICELLI, WEISS, LEACH
소극적 동조 또는 중립의향 의원	BOSCHWITZ, TRIBLE, EVANS, ZORINSKY	SOLARZ, WOLPE, GEJDENSON, LANTOS, BERMAN, LEVINE, GARCIA
아직 입장 지지가능 의원	LUGAR, HELMS, KASSEBAUM, MURKOWSKI	BROOMFIELD, LAGOMARSINO, MICA, GILMAN, HYDE, SOLOMON, DORNAN

* _____ 는 공화당

Kerry 결의안 반박자료
----

1. 결의안 내용의 부당성 지적

   ○ 여당의 대화 기피 운운은 사실과 다름

   ○ 사법부 독립에 대한 전적인 부정은 한국 정부와 국민에
     대한 중대한 모독임.

2. 진행중인 남북 대화에 대한 악영향 초래 가능성 지적

   ○ '국내정치 불안이 남북 대화를 저해한다'는 결의안 표현은
     북한에게 남·북 대화 기피 구실을 줄 위험 내포.

3. 김대중 문제에 대한 정부입장 천명

   ○ 아국정부는 김대중이 정치활동을 하지 않겠다는 약속을
     파기하고 동인에 대한 형집행 정지 사유인 신병치료가
     종료되었음에도 불구하고, 관용을 베풀어 스스로 자숙할
     것을 기대하며 정치활동 이외의 행동에 자유를 부여하고
     있음.

   ○ 김대중의 복권여부는 동인의 반성과 법질서 존중등 향후
     동인의 행동 여하에 전적으로 달려있음.

   ○ 국회 및 학원문제등 현금의 아국 국내정세에 비추어
     여사한 결의안 상정은 관용과 화합을 위한 아국정부의
     노력과 김에 대한 관용조치를 오히려 어렵게 할
     가능성도 있음.

0195

4. 제 5공화국 출범이후 정부가 이룩한 민주화 업적에 대한
   평가 전무

   ○ 제 5공화국 정부는 출범후부터 학원자유화, 김대중、
     김영삼、 김종필을 포함한 정치활동 피규제자 전원해금、
     민주적인 2.12 총선등 파격적인 자유화 조치를 단행하여
     88년의 평화적 정권교체 달성을 위한 민주적 기반을
     성공적으로 조성하여 왔음.

   ○ 이러한 중요한 시기에 미의회에서의 여사한 결의안
     거론은 여·야간의 대립을 심화시켜 한국정치 발전 노력에
     저해요인이 됨으로써 결과적으로 한미 관계발전에 역행하게
     될것임.

5. 결   론

   ○ 한국은 '86 아시안게임과 '88 올림픽등 국제적인 행사
     개최와 함께 88년의 평화적 정권교체를 앞두고 그 어느때
     보다도 정치와 사회안정이 중요시되고 있음에 비추어
     우방국 의회에서의 여사한 결의안의 거론은 자제되어야
     할것임.

   ○ 김대중 추종세력의 준동에 의하여 발기된 편파적이고
     부당한 내용의 결의안을 미의회가 채택하지 않을것임을
     확신함.

0196

```
┌─────────────────────────────────────────────┐
│                                               │
│   Kerry    상원의원 결의안 관련 회의자료         │
│                                               │
└─────────────────────────────────────────────┘
```

1985· 12·

외   무   부

0197

목 차

0198

1. 결의안 제출 관련 주요일지

   85.9.26.   주미대사, 국무성 제보에 따라 9.27 Kerry
              의원이 결의안 발의 예정임을 보고.

   85.9.27.   본부, 동 결의안 발의 철회 촉구 지시

   85.9.28.   주미대사대리, 의회담당 참사관의 Kerry
              의원 보좌관 면담 결과 보고.
              1) 아측입장 전달
              2) 결의안 구상 동기 문의
                 - 보좌관측, 선거구인 메사츄세츠 주 내의
                   인권문제에 대한 높은 관심 반영 설명

   85.10.2   주미대사대리, Kerry   의원 면담 신청에 대한
              회보 미접 보고.

   85.11.28. 주미대사, Kerry및 Simon   상원의원이 공동으로
              김대중 복권 및 민주 발전을 희망하는 내용의 결의안을
              작성, 의원들의 동조를 위해 회람중임을 보고

   85.12.19.   Kerry 상원의원, 동 공동결의안 제출

   - 공동제안 의원 (8명)

   Edward Kennedy, Claiborne Pell,

   Allan Cranston, Christopher Dodd,

0199

Ernest Hollings, Paul Sarbanes,

Donald Riegle, Tom Harkin

85.12.20   Feighan및 Dixon   하원의원、하원측

결의안 제출

2. 향후 심의과정

가·일반적 처리 절차

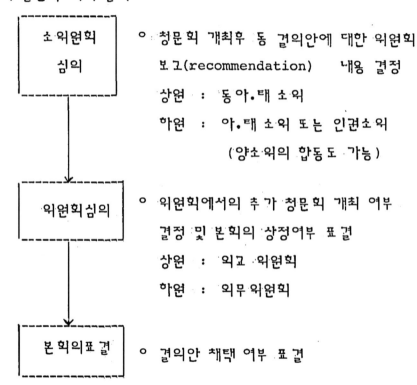

소위원회 심의
о 청문회 개최후 동 결의안에 대한 위원회
보고(recommendation)   내용 결정
상원 : 동아·태 소위
하원 : 아·태 소위 또는 인권소위
   (양소위의 합동도 가능)

위원회심의
о 위원회에서의 추가 청문회 개최 여부
결정 및 본회의 상정여부 표결
상원 : 외교 위원회
하원 : 외무위원회

본회의표결
о 결의안 채택 여부 표결

0200

나. 특기사항

  o 상하 양원이 동일한 내용의 결의안을 채택할 경우
    양원 협의회 심의는 불요

  o 소위원회와 위원회의 심의를 생략하고 바로 본회의에
    상정시키는 약식절차도 가능하나 이경우 다수당
    원내총무의 허락을 얻어야 하는 것이 관행임.

  o 본회의 표결에 많은 시간이 소요되는 것을 방지하기
    위하여 양정당이 기합의한 법안에 Non-Germane
    형태로 첨부시켜 통과시키려는 시도가 가능
    - 85.5 비율빈 결의안이 위원법안에 대한 수정안
      형태로 통과

3. 공동결의안 (Concurrent Resolution) 의 특징

  o 미의회(상하원)의 의사(Sense of Congress)를 표시하는
    것으로 합동결의안 (Joint Resolution) 과 달리 법적
    효력은 없음.

  o 결의안 (Resolution)과는 달리 상·하 양원의 통과가
    필요하나 대통령의 승인은 불요함.

0201

o Lugar 위원장은 외교위원장의 지위를 의식하여
  중립적인 입장을 취할 가능성도 있음.

o 민주당에서는 지금까지 아국 인권문제에 대해 매우
  비판적이었던 Cranston 의원이 중심이되어 금번
  결의안의 공동제안 의원인 Dodd 의원과 함께 동료
  의원 설득에 주력할 것으로 보임.

나. 외교위

1) 구 성(공화 9명、민주 8명、계 : 17명)

공 화 당 (8)	민 주 당 (7)
Richard Lugar	Claiborne Pell
Jesse Helms	Joseph Biden
Charles Mathias	Paul Sarbanes
Nancy Kassebaum	Edward Zorinsky
Rudy Boschwitz	Alan Cranston
Larry Pressler	Christopher Dodd
Frank Murkowski	Thomas Eagleton
Parul Trible	John Kerry
Daniel Evans	

2) 성향분석

o 민주당 소속의원 8명중 5명이 금번 결의안 공동 제안자
  이며、나머지 3의원중 Biden 의원은 84.2 김대중
  조기 귀국을 요청하는 레이건 대통령 앞 연서 서한에

0202

가담한바 있으며, Eagleton 의원의 진보적 성향을
감안할때 적어도 6-7명이상이 결의안을 지지할것으로
예상됨.

o 공화당의 경우 친한적 입장을 취해온 Lugar 위원장,
Helms, Murkowski, Evans   의원등이 정부 입장을
지지하는 것으로 예상되나 Lugar   의원은 위원장의
직위를 고려, 다소 중립적 입장을 취할수도 있음.

o 공화당의원 중에서 Pressler   의원이 80.12 김대중
구명을 요청하는 Tsongas   의원의 각하앞 서한에
연서한 사실이 있으며 Mathias   의원이 진보적
입장을 취해오고 있음을 고려할때 양의원이 금번
결의안에 동의할 가능성을 배제할수 없음.

o 여타 공화당 의원인 Kassebaum, Boschwitz, Trible
의원은 아국문제에 대해 비교적 무관심한 편으로
알려지고 있으나 Boschwitz 의원의 경우 지난 5월
채택된 비율빈 정부에 대한 상원 결의안을 제안
하였음을 고려할때 보다 적극적인 대처가 요망됨.

다. 결   론
상기에 비추어 볼때 동아·태 소위에서는 다소 유리한 입장이
라고 볼수 있으나 외교위에서는 결의안 채택 저지에 어려움이
예상됨. 아울러 동아·태 소위원장인 Murkowski   의원이
아국입장을 지지해 왔으나 동 의원이 지난 5월 비율빈

0203

결의안을 주도하였음을 고려할때 동아·태소위 심의시
의외의 입장을 취할 가능성도 있음·

```
┌─────────────┐
│  하     원  │
└─────────────┘
```

가·아·태소위

  1) 구   성(민주 6명、공화 4명、계 : 10명)

    민 주 당 (6)   **공 화 당 (4)**
    ----------------   ---------------

    Stephen Solarz   Jim Leach

    Mervyn Dymally   Toby Roth

    Robert Torricelli   Gerald Solomon

    Morris Udall   Doug Bereuter

    Michael Barnes

    Sam Gejdenson

  2) 성향분석

    ° 민주당 소속의원 6명 전원이 아국 인권문제에
      대해서는 비판적이며、특히 Barnes 의원은
      김대중 문제에 대한 의회의 여론을 주도해오고
      있음· 동의원중 Solarz 위원장과 Dymally
      의원은 인권문제를 제외한 여타문제에 대해서는
      비교적 친한적 입장을 취하고 있으나   자신들의
      image 를 고려、매우 신중한 반응을 보일
      것으로 예상됨·

0204

○ 공화당의원 4명중 친한의원은 Solomon 의원 1명
  이며, Roth 및 Bereuter 의원은 아국문제에
  비교적 무관심한 입장을 견지해 오고 있음.

○ 공화당의 Jim Leach 의원은 공화당내의 진보계
  중심인물로서 81.12 및 84.4 김대중의 안전귀국을
  촉구하는 각하앞 연서서한 작성을 주도한바 있으며,
  이번 결의안 심의시에도 적극적인 자세를 취할것으로
  예상됨.

나. 외무위

1) 구 성 (민주 25명, 공화 17명, 계 : 42명)

민 주 당 (25)

Fascell, Hamilton, Yatron, Solarz, Bonker

Studds, Mica, Barnes, Wolpe, Crockett,

Gejdenson, Dymally, Lantos, Kostmayer,

Torricelli, Smith Berman, Reid, Levine,

Feighan, Weiss, Ackerman, MacKay,Udall, Garcia

공 화 당 (17)

Broomfield, Gilman, Lagomarsino, Leach,

Roth, Snowe, Hyde, Solomon, Bereuter,

Siljander, Zschau, Dornan, Smith, Mack,

DeWine, Burton, McCain

0205

2) 성향분석

° 민주당 소속의원 25명중 13명이 80년이후 김대중문제
또는 기타 아국 인권문제에 대해 2회이상 비판적인
연서 서한에 가담한바 있으며 2명이 80년이후에는
침묵을 지키고 있으나 80년이전 2회이상 아국인권
문제에 비판적 입장을 취한바 있음. 또한Feighan
의원은 김대중 귀국시 동행인물로서 금번 하원
결의안의 제안자임.(무관심 또는 입장 미상의원 4명)

° 공화당의원 17명중 친한의원은 6명(Broomfield,
Gilman, Lagomarsino, Hyde, Solomon, Burton)
으로 결의안 통과를 적극 지지해 줄것으로 예상됨.

° 연이나 민주당과는 달리 3선이하 소장급 의원
대다수가 아국 문제에 무관심한 입장을 보여오고
있어(10명)Jim Leach 의원이 이들을 대상으로
중점적인 설득 활동을 전개할 것으로 예상됨.

다. 결 론

상기한 바와같이 하원의 경우는 민주당이 우위를 점하고
있는 객관적 정치상황외에도 공화당 소속의원들이 아국
문제에 비교적 무관심한 반면, 민주당 소속 의원들은 아국
인권문제에 대해 비판적인 입장을 견지해 왔음을 고려할때,
결의안 통과 저지에 보다 많은 어려움이 예상됨.

0206

5. 향후 전망

가. 전항에서 설명한 바와같이 상·하 양원외교(무)위원회에서
   금번 결의안이 통과될 가능성을 배제할수는 없는 상황이나
   동 결의안의 내용이 너무 강경하여 중립적 입장의 의원들을
   설득시키는 대 문제가 있을 것으로 보아 동 결의안 문안이
   그대로 통과 될 가능성은 적을 것으로 전망됨.

나. 따라서 동 결의안 주도의원측은 결의안 문구를 약화
   시킴으로써 중립적 입장을 취하고 있는 의원들의 지지를
   유도할 것으로 보임.   특히 동 유도 과정에서 주도
   의원측은 미의원들이 민감하게 반응할 고문 및 언론 자유
   문제를 부각시킬 것으로 예상됨.

다. 현재 의회 외무(교)위원회에서는 비율빈 정세등이 주요
   관심사로 되어있고 또 외무(교)위측이 동 결의안을 굳이
   서둘러 처리할 필요는 없는 것으로 보이므로 86년도 회기가
   시작되는 1.21 이후 즉각적인 조치 가능성은 많지 않은
   것으로 예상되며 오히려 동 결의안을 계류 상태에 두고
   아국 내 정치적 발전추세를 관망하는 전략을 취할 가능성도
   있음.

라. 동 결의안이 한·미 관계에 미치는 영향이나 남북 대화등에
   미칠 부정적 영향을 고려, 동 결의안이 위원회 심의 단계
   에서 저지되도록 최선을 다하여야 할것이나 상술한   의원
   성향으로 보아 이의 저지가 불가능할 경우 본회의에서는
   반드시 저지될수 있도록 보다 적극적인 대의회 활동을 전개
   하여야 할것임.

0207

6. 대   책

가. 동 결의안 내용에 대한 반박 또는 설득입장 정립

  ○ 결의안 내용의 부당성 지적

    - 여당의 대화 기피 운운은 사실과 다름

    - 제 5공화국 출범이후 정부가 이룩한 민주화
      업적에 대한 평가 전무

    - 사법부 독립에 대한 전적인 부정은 한국정부와
      국민에 대한 중대한 모독

  ○ 진행중인 남북 대화에 대한 악영향 초래 가능성 지적

    - '국내정치 불안이 남북대화를 저해한다'는 결의안
      표현은 북한에게 남·북 대화 기피 구실을 줄 위험
      내포

  ○ 김대중 문제에 대한 정부입장 천명

    - 최대의 관용 조치 기실시

나. 외무(고)위 소속 의원들에 대한 주미대사관 활동강화

  ○ 주미대사, 공사의 개별면담 강화 : 전의원 대상

  ○ 해당위원회 및 소위원회 전문위원과의 유기적 협조
    관계 강화

  ○ 소속의원들의 성향별 대책수립
    : 위원회간부, 친한의원, 비판적의원, 무관심 의원별

다. 양국 의회간 접촉강화

  ○ 국회의원 파견

0208

라. 로비스트 활용 강화

     ° 주미대사관 Consultant 활용극대화

       : Gray & Co., Baron & Canning

     ° 기타 아국관련 Lobbyist 회사 최대 활용

마. 국무성의 간접지원 유도

     ° 남·북 대화와 전반적 한·미 관계에 위해함을 의회측에
       설득토록 유도

     ° 한국의 상황이 비율빈과는 결코 비교될수 없음을
       강조토록 당부

바. 본회의 표결에 대비한 득표 전략 수립

     ° 아측입장 강력 옹호의원 사전물색

0209

(참고 자료 4)

미상원 비율빈 관련 결의안
----

1. 결의안 채택일 : 1985.5.15.

2. 채택형태 : FY   86 대외원조 수권법안 심의시 원조
   법안에 대한 수정안 형식으로 채택

3. 발의 및 공동제안 의원

   - 발 의 : Kerry 의원

   - 공동제안 : Murkowski, Dodd, Boschwitz   의원

4. 표결결과 : 찬성 89, 반대8, 기권 3

   - 반대의원 : Hecht, Heflin, Helms, Laxalt,
               McClure, Symms, Simpson, Wallop

   - 단, 심의과정에서 반대발언 의원은 전무

5. 주요 내용

   - 1986.87 선거의 자유, 공정선거 보장

   - 아키노 살해사건에 대한 완전 공정한 공개재판 보장

   - 언론 출판의 자유 보장

   - 구속적부 심사제 채택보장

   - 구속인사 석방

   - 필리핀군 또는 보안경찰에 의한 해외에서의 살해행위 중지

6. 결의안 채택이후 미의회의 대비율빈 정부 제재 조치

   - 미행정부의 대비율빈 군사원조액 1억불을 7천만불로 삭감,
     (대신 경제원조 9천 5백만불은 1억 1천만불로 증액)

0210

```
┌ ─ ─ ─ ─ ─ ─ ─ ─ ─ ─ ─ ─ ─ ─ ─ ─ ─ ┐
│                                     │
│  Kerry    상원의원 결의안 관련 회의자료  │
│                                     │
└ ─ ─ ─ ─ ─ ─ ─ ─ ─ ─ ─ ─ ─ ─ ─ ─ ─ ┘
```

1985. 12.

외   무   부

0211

목　　　　　차

(참고 자료)

0212

1. 결의안 제출 관련 주요일지

85.9.26. 주미대사, 국무성 제보에 따라 9.27 Kerry
의원이 결의안 발의 예정임을 보고

85.9.27. 본부, 동 결의안 발의 철회 촉구 지시

85.9.28. 주미대사대리, 의회담당 참사관의 Kerry
의원 보좌관 면담 결과 보고
1) 아측입장 전달
2) 결의안 구상 동기 문의
- 보좌관측, 선거구인 메사츄세츠 주 내의
인권문제에 대한 높은 관심 반영 설명

85.10.2 주미대사대리, Kerry 의원 면담 신청에 대한
회보 미접 보고

85.11.28. 주미대사, Kerry 및 Simon 상원의원이 공동으로
김대중 복권 및 민주 발전을 희망하는 내용의 결의안을
작성, 의원들의 동조를 위해 회람중임을 보고

85.12.19. Kerry 상원의원, 동 공동결의안 제출

- 공동제안 의원 (8명)

Edward Kennedy, Claiborne Pell,
Allan Cranston, Christopher Dodd,

0213

Ernest Hollings, Paul Sarbanes,

Donald Riegle, Tom Harkin

85.12.20   Feighan및 Dixon   하원의원、하원측

       결의안 제출

2. 향후 심의과정

가.일반적 처리 절차

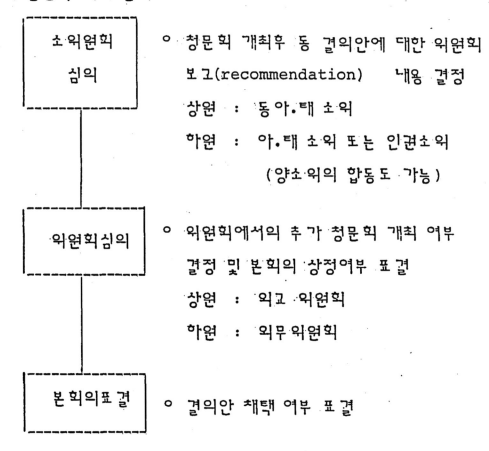

소위원회
심의

o 청문회 개최후 동 결의안에 대한 위원회
  보고(recommendation)   내용 결정
  상원 : 동아·태 소위
  하원 : 아·태 소위 또는 인권소위
        (양소위의 합동도 가능)

위원회심의

o 위원회에서의 추가 청문회 개최 여부
  결정 및 본회의 상정여부 표결
  상원 : 외교 위원회
  하원 : 외무위원회

본회의표결

o 결의안 채택 여부 표결

0214

나. 특기사항

　ㅇ 상하 양원이 동일한 내용의 결의안을 채택할 경우
　　양원 협의회 심의는 불요

　ㅇ 소위원회와 위원회의 심의를 생략하고 바로 본회의에
　　상정시키는 약식절차도 가능하나 이경우 다수당
　　원내총무의 허락을 얻어야 하는 것이 관행임.

　ㅇ 본회의 표결에 많은 시간이 소요되는것을 방지하기
　　위하여 양정당이 기합의한 법안에 Non-Germane
　　형태로 첨부시켜 통과시키려는 시도가 가능
　　　- 85.5 비율빈 결의안이 위원법안에 대한 수정안
　　　　형태로 통과

3. 공동결의안 (Concurrent Resolution) 의 특징

　ㅇ 미의회(상하원)의 의사(Sense of Congress)를 표시하는
　　것으로 합동결의안 (Joint Resolution) 과 달리 법적
　　효력은 없음.

　ㅇ 결의안 (Resolution)과는 달리 상·하 양원의 통과가
　　필요하나 대통령의 승인은 불요함.

0215

4. 의고(무)위 구성 및 성향분석

```
┌─────────┐
│ 상    원 │
└─────────┘
```

가. 동아·태소위

1) 구성(공화 4명, 민주 3명, 계 : 7명)

공 화 (4)	민 주 (3)
Frank Murkowski	Alan Cranston
Jesse Helms	Edward Zorinsky
Daniel Evans	Christopher Dodd
Richard Lugar	

2) 성향분석

° 공화당의원 4명 전원과 Cranston 의원을
  제외한 민주 당의원 전원이 지금 까지 김대중 문제나
  아국 인권문제에 대해 명시적인 비난을 표명한바
  없음.

° 특히 Helms 의원과 Evans 의원은 보수계
  중심의원들로서 아국입장을 지지할 것으로 예상됨.

° Murkowski 소위원장도 아국입장을 지지하여
  줄 것으로 생각되나, 자신의 관심사항인 한-알라스카
  어업 및 자원협력 문제에 대한 정부의 보 다 적극
  적인 협조를 요청할 것으로 사료됨.

0216

○ Lugar 위원장은 외교위원장의 지위를 의식하여
중립적인 입장을 취할 가능성도 있음.

○ 민주당에서는 지금까지 아국 인권문제에 대해 매우
비판적이었던 Cranston 의원이 중심이되어 금번
결의안의 공동제안 의원인 Dodd 의원과 함께 동료
의원 설득에 주력할 것으로 보임.

나. 외교위

1) 구 성 (공화 9명, 민주 8명, 계 : 17명)

공 화 당 (8)	민 주 당 (7)
Richard Lugar	Claiborne Pell
Jesse Helms	Joseph Biden
Charles Mathias	Paul Sarbanes
Nancy Kassebaum	Edward Zorinsky
Rudy Boschwitz	Alan Cranston
Larry Pressler	Christopher Dodd
Frank Murkowski	Thomas Eagleton
Parul Trible	John Kerry
Daniel Evans	

2) 성향분석

○ 민주당 소속의원 8명중 5명이 금번 결의안 공동제안자
이며, 나머지 3의원중 Biden 의원은 84.2 김대중
조기 귀국을 요청하는 레이건 대통령 앞 연서 서한에

0217

가담한바 있으며, Eagleton 의원의 진보적 성향을
감안할때 적어도 6-7명이상이 결의안을 지지할것으로
예상됨.

o 공화당의 경우 친한적 입장을 취해온 Lugar 위원장,
Helms, Murkowski, Evans 의원등이 정부 입장을
지지하는 것으로 예상되나 Lugar 의원은 위원장의
직위를 고려, 다소 중립적 입장을 취할수도 있음.

o 공화당의원 중에서 Pressler 의원이 80.12 김대중
구명을 요청하는 Tsongas 의원의 각하앞 서한에
연서한 사실이 있으며 Mathias 의원이 진보적
입장을 취해오고 있음을 고려할때 양의원이 금번
결의안에 동의할 가능성을 배제할수 없음.

o 여타 공화당 의원인 Kassebaum, Boschwitz, Trible
의원은 아국문제에 대해 비교적 무관심한 편으로
알려지고 있으나 Boschwitz 의원의 경우 지난 5월
채택된 비율빈 정부에 대한 상원 결의안을 제안
하였음을 고려할때 보다 적극적인 대처가 요망됨.

다. 결   론
상기에 비추어 볼때 동아·태 소위에서는 다소 유리한 입장이
라고 볼수 있으나 외교위에서는 결의안 채택 저지에 어려움이
예상됨. 아울러 동아·태 소위원장인 Murkowski 의원이
아국입장을 지지해 왔으나 동 의원이 지난 5월 비율빈

0218

결의안을 주도하였음을 고려할때 동아·태소위 심의시
외외의 입장을 취할 가능성도 있음.

```
┌─────────────┐
│  하    원    │
└─────────────┘
```

가. 아·태소위

1) 구 성(민주 6명, 공학 4명, 계 : 10명)

민 주 당 (6)	공 학 당 (4)
Stephen Solarz	Jim Leach
Mervyn Dymally	Toby Roth
Robert Torricelli	Gerald Solomon
Morris Udall	Doug Bereuter
Michael Barnes	
Sam Gejdenson	

2) 성향분석

   º 민주당 소속의원 6명 전원이 아국 인권문제에
     대해서는 비판적이며, 특히 Barnes 의원은
     김대중 문제에 대한 의회의 여론을 주도해오고
     있음. 동의원중 Solarz 위원장과 Dymally
     의원은 인권문제를 제외한 여타문제에 대해서는
     비교적 친한적 입장을 취하고 있으므로 자신들의
     image 를 고려, 매우 신중한 반응을 보일
     것으로 예상됨.

0219

o 공화당의원 4명중 친한의원은 Solomon 의원 1명
   이며, Roth 및 Bereuter 의원은 아국문제에
   비교적 무관심한 입장을 견지해 오고 있음.

o 공화당의 Jim Leach 의원은 공화당내의 진보계
   중심인물로서 81.12 및 84.4 김대중의 안전귀국을
   촉구하는 각하앞 연서서한 작성을 주도한바 있으며,
   이번 결의안 심의시에도 적극적인 자세를 취할것으로
   예상됨.

나. 외무위

1) 구 성 (민주 25명, 공화 17명, 계 : 42명)

   민 · 주 · 당 (25)

   Fascell, Hamilton, Yatron, Solarz, Bonker

   Studds, Mica, Barnes, Wolpe, Crockett,

   Gejdenson, Dymally, Lantos, Kostmayer,

   Torricelli, Smith Berman, Reid, Levine,

   Feighan, Weiss, Ackerman, MacKay,Udall, Garcia

   공 화 당 (17)

   Broomfield, Gilman, Lagomarsino, Leach,

   Roth, Snowe, Hyde, Solomon, Bereuter,

   Siljander, Zschau, Dornan, Smith, Mack,

   DeWine, Burton, McCain

0220

2) 성향분석

　　○ 민주당 소속의원 25명중 13명이 80년이후 김대중 문제
　　　　또는 기타 아국 인권문제에 대해 2회이상 비판적인
　　　　연서 서한에 가담한바 있으며 2명이 80년이후에는
　　　　침묵을 지키고 있으나 80년이전 2회이상 아국 인권
　　　　문제에 비판적 입장을 취한바 있음. 또한 Feighan
　　　　의원은 김대중 귀국시 동행인물로서 금번 하원
　　　　결의안의 제안자임.(무관심 또는 입장 미상의원 4명)

　　○ 공화당의원 17명중 친한의원은 6명(Broomfield,
　　　　Gilman, Lagomarsino, Hyde, Solomon, Burton)
　　　　으로 결의안 통과를 적극 지지해 줄것으로 예상됨.

　　○ 연이나 민주당과는 달리 3선이하 소장급 의원
　　　　대다수가 아국 문제에 무관심한 입장을 보여오고
　　　　있어(10명)Jim Leach 의원이 이들을 대상으로
　　　　중점적인 설득 활동을 전개할 것으로 예상됨.

다. 결　　론

　　상기한 바와같이 하원의 경우는 민주당이 우위를 점하고
　　있는 객관적 정치상황외에도 공화당 소속의원들이 아국
　　문제에 비교적 무관심한 반면, 민주당 소속 의원들은 아국
　　인권문제에 대해 비판적인 입장을 견지해 왔음을 고려할때,
　　결의안 통과 저지에 보다 많은 어려움이 예상됨.

0221

5. 향후 전망

가. 전항에서 설명한 바와같이 상·하 양원및고 (무)위원회에서
금번 결의안이 통과될 가능성을 배제할수는 없는 상황이나
동 결의안의 내용이 너무 강경하여 중립적 입장의 의원들을
설득 시키는데 문제가 있을것으로 보아 동 결의안 문안이
그대로 통과될 가능성은 적을 것으로 전망됨.

나. 따라서 동 결의안 주도의원측은 결의안 문구를 약화
시킴으로써 중립적 입장을 취하고 있는 의원들의 지지를
유도할 것으로 보임. 특히 동 유도 과정에서 주도
의원측은 미의원들이 민감하게 반응할 고문 및 언론 자유
문제를 부각시킬 것으로 예상됨.

다. 현재 의회 외무 (고)위원회에서는 비율빈 정세등이 주요
관심사로 되어있고 또 외무 (고)위측이 동 결의안을 굳이
서둘러 처리할 필요는 없는것으로 보이므로 86년도 회기가
시작되는 1·21 이후 즉각적인 조치 가능성은 많지 않은
것으로 예상되며 오히려 동 결의안을 계류 상태에 두고
아국내 정치적 발전추세를 관망하는 전략을 취할 가능성도
있음.

라. 동 결의안이 한·미 관계에 미치는 영향이나 남북 대화등에
미칠 부정적 영향을 고려, 동 결의안이 위원회 심의 단계
에서 저지되도록 최선을 다하여야 할것이나 상술한 의원
성향으로 보아 이의 저지가 불가능할 경우 본회의에서는
반드시 저지될수 있도록 보다 적극적인 대의회 활동을 전개
하여야 할것임.

0222

6. 대   책

가•동 결의안 내용에 대한 반박 또는 설득입장 정립

　　ㅇ 결의안 내용의 부당성 지적

　　　　- 여당의 대화기피 운운은 사실과 다름

　　　　- 제 5공화국 출범이후 정부가 이룩한 민주화 업적에 대한
　　　　　평가 전무

　　　　- 사법부 독립에 대한 전적인 부정은 한국정부와 국민에대한
　　　　　중대한 모독

　　ㅇ 진행중인 남북 대화에 대한 악영향 초래 가능성 지적

　　　　- '국내정치 불안이 남북대화를 저해한다'는 결의안 표현은
　　　　　북한에게 남•북 대화 기피 구실을 줄 위험 내포

　　ㅇ 김대중 문제에 대한 정부입장 천명

　　　　- 최대의 관용 조치 기실시

　　　　　• ~~비율빈의 아키노 살해와 파키스탄 Zia Ul Haq~~
　　　　　　~~대통령의 부토 처형과 비교~~

　　　　　• ~~복권문제는 국내 헌법문제로 미의회가 언급할 성질이~~
　　　　　~~아님.~~

나• 외무(교)위 소속의원들에 대한 주미대사관 활동 강화

　　ㅇ 주미대사, 공사의 개별면담 강화　 : 전의원 대상

　　ㅇ 해당위원회 및 소위원회 전문위원과의 유기적 협조 관계 강화

　　ㅇ 소속의원들의 성향별 대책수립

　　　　: 위원회간부, 친한의원, 비판적의원, 무관심의원별

0223

다. 양국 의회간 접촉 강화

　○ 국회의원 파견

라. 로비스트 활용 강화

　○ 주미대사관 Consultant 활용 극 대화

　　; Gray & Co., Baron & Canning

　○ 기타 아국관련 Lobbyist 회사 최대 활용

마. 국무성의 간접지원 유도

　○ 남·북 대화와 전반적 한·미 관계에 위해함을 의회측에
　　설득토록 유도

　○ 한국의 상황이 비율빈과는 결코 비교될수 없음을 강조토록 당부

바. 본회의 표결에 대비한 득표전략 수립

　○ 아측입장 강력 옹호의원 사전 물색

0224

대한민국이 김대중의 시민적, 정치적 권리를 회복 시켜야하며
한국에서 진정한 민주주의가 이루어져야 한다는 미의회의 의사를
표명하는 공동 결의안

미국의 대외원조 계획의 주목적중 하나가 민주 제도의
신장, 자유롭고 공정하며 정직한 선거의 실시, 표현과 언론의
자유존중, 독립된 사법부의 기능을 통한 개인의 시민적 권리와
자유의 보호 등을 촉진하는 것이어야 하며,

미국민은 1948년 대한민국 정부 수립 이래 대한민국의
안보와 경제적 번영에 대한 공약을 지키기 위해 매우 관대한
입장을 취해 왔으며,

이러한 공약으로 인해 한국동란시 54,346명의 미국 군인
들이 목숨을 잃고 103,248명의 미국인들이 부상을 당했고,
아울러 미국민들이 1948년이래 대한민국을 위해 190억불 이상의
경제 및 군사원조를 제공해 왔으며 한국 내의 40,000명의 미군
주둔을 지원하기 위해 재정적 지원을 계속해 왔음에 비추어,

또한 국회의원 기소, 유명 언론인 및 여타 민주 지도자
들에 대한 고문 행위 재현등 최근 일련의 사태 발전이

민주주의 기본 원칙에 대한 대한민국 정부의 공약에 대해 심각한 우려를 야기시키고 있음에 비추어,

그리고 정당한 재판절차에 대한 권리는 대한민국 국민에게 사실상 존재하지 않으며, 독립적이며 공정한 사법부 역시 고유의 기능을 상실하였으며,

남북한간 긴장완화에 대한 전망 역시 대한민국의 정치적 불안정으로 인하여 저해되고 있음에 비추어,

미의회가 미국의 대한민국에 대한 지원의 주된 목적이 대한민국을 진정한 민주주의 국가로 복귀시키는 데 있다는 사실을 확인하고 이를 선언하도록 하원의 이름으로 (상원과 공동으로) 결의함. 이를 위하여 미의회는 아래사항에 최대의 중점을 둠.

첫째, 위협, 기본적인권 및 시민적 자유의 침해, 그리고 기타 반민주적인 행위가 지배적인 현재의 분위기를 한국 정부와 민주적인 반대세력간의 대화와 신뢰의 분위기로 대체하는 것

둘째, 김대중과 기타 모든 미복권 정치인들이 정치적, 개인적 자유를 완전히 회복하는 것

셋째, 민주적 절차에 승복하는 모든 인사들에게 개방된 진정한 직접선거를 통하여 1988년도에 대한민국 대통령직의 평화적이고도 완전한 민주적 이양이 이루어지는 것.

0227

Concurrent Resolution

Expressing the sense of the Congress that the
Republic of Korea should restore the civil and political rights of Kim Dae Jung and that true democracy should be instituted in the Republic of Korea

Whereas one of the primary purposes of the United
States Foreign Assistance Programs should be to
foster the growth of democratic institutions, the
holding of free, fair and honest elections, respect
for freedom of speech and freedom of the press and
the protection of individual civil rights and
liberties through the functioning of an independent
judiciary;

Whereas the people of the United States have
been more than generous in their commitment to the
security and economic well-being of the Republic
of Korea since its founding in 1948;

Whereas this commitment resulted in the loss
of the lives of 54,346 American servicemen and
103,248 Americans wounded during the Korean conflict
whereas the American people have contributed more
than $19 billion in economic and military assistance
to the Republic of Korea since 1948 and continue to
provide financial resources to support the presence
of 40,000 American servicemen on Korean soil;

Whereas recent developments, including the indictments of members of the national assembly and a

0228

resurgence in the use of torture against prominent
journalists and other democratic leaders, are cause
for grave concern over the commitment of the Government of the Republic of Korea to basic democratic
principles;

Whereas the right to due process for the people
of the Republic of Korea is virtually nonexistent,
and an independent and impartial judicial system, for
all itents and purposes, does not function, and

Whereas the prospects for any relaxation in
tensions between North and South in Korea is undermined
by political instability in the Republic of Korea;

Now, therefore
be it resolved by the House of Representatives (the
Senate concurring), that the Congress finds and
declares that the primary purposes of United States
assistance to the Republic of Korea shall be to
promote the return to true democracy in the Republic
of Korea.   To that end, the Congress places the
highest priority on -

1) The replacement of the current climate of
   intimidation, abuses of basic human rights and
   civil liberties, and other antidemocratic actions,
   with an atmosphere of dialogue and trust between
   the Government of the Republic of Korea and the
   democratic opposition in that country

2) The full restoration of the political and individual
   rights of Kim Dae Jung and all others whose political
   rights are being restricted and

0229 ·

3) The peaceful and fully democratic transfer of the
   presidency of the Republic of Korea in 1988
   through genuine popular elections open to all
   who are committed to the democratic process.

0230

72년이후 한국 국내문제 관련 결의안 참고사항

가. 76.9. 8.18 판문점 사건과 명동성당 사건에 관한 미하원 국제관계위원회 결의안 채택

  ○ 제안자 : Fraser 의원

  ○ 결의안요지

    : 판문점 살해사건에 유감, 명동사건 관련자에 대한 유죄선거에 유감, 동 철회 요청

  ○ 결 과 : 본회의 상정 저지

나. 77.2.3. 하원 국제관계위원회, 국제기구소위(Fraser 소위) 로하여금 한·미관계의 비정상적인면을 전반적으로 조사토록하는 결의안 채택

  ○ 19:4로 통과

다. 77.2.9. 하원 본회의, 하원 윤리위원회로 하여금 미하원 의원들의 한국정부 관련 불법비행(박동선 사건 관계)을 조사토록 하는 결의안 (HR 252) 채택

  ○ 박동선사건 조사 특별고문으로 Lacovara 임명

  ○ 388:0으로 통과

라. 78.2.2. 미 하원 국제관계위, 박동선 사건 조사기간을 78.10.31까지 2개월 연장하자는 Fraser 소위원회의 지시 결의안 통과

0231

마. 80.11.20. Don Bonker 하원의원. 김대중 구명과 한국의

　　　　　민주화를 촉구하는 결의안을 외무위 국제기구

　　　　　소위원회에 제출、통과

　　　　　(정족수 미달 상태에서 통과되었다하여 물의를

　　　　　야기)

참　고 : 10.26 사태이후 미의회의 김대중 관련 동향

　　　　ㅇ 상　원 : 서한발송 3회(4명)

　　　　　　　　　　결의안제출 1회(5명)

　　　　ㅇ 하　원 : 서한발송 2회(11명)

　　　　　　　　　　결의안제출 2회(21명)

　　　　＊ 결의안 채택 단 1건 : 하원 외무위 국제소위

0232

김대중 관련 미상하의원 서한발송

서한발송 시기	서한발송자	내용	조치사항
81.12.11.	Jim Leach 등 하원의원 27명	o 김대중 및 관련자의 인권 특사 석방 지지	o 레이건 대통령 앞 연서 서한 (레이건)
84.2.28.	상원의원 28명	o 김대중 초기귀국 및 내방활동을 위한 정부의 영향력 행사 촉구	o
84.4.19.	하원의원 26명	o 인권 및 정치활동 규제법 폐지요구, 가계 등 인권 억압 및 민주안 시책에 맞는 조치안 활동 전개	o 주미대사 명의 외신방송 지시 촉신지역 충영사간에 연지 시책에 맞는 조치안 활동전개 지시
84.9.10.	케네디의원	o 김대중 귀국 시 신변안전보장 및 99명 비규 제재 해결 요망	o 주미대사 명의 외신방송 지시
84.10.16.	하원의원 64명	o 김대중의 안전귀국 및 정치활동 제재요구 3건 지원 접급 해결 요구	o 주미대사명의 서한발송 지시 (내용은 케네디 의원앞 서한 참조)
84.11.27.	케네디의원(주미 대사 앞 서한)	o 정치 탄압 복원의 부 단서 지지, 미국내 활동으로 기보 관 행사와이 80건무 선동 녹구 교 사노 사원무 군 실명	o 별도 외신발송 및 통보
85.2.1.	하원의원 34명	o 김대중 안전귀국 및 정치활동 재개 요망 요구	o 별도 외신 발송 대신 오찬, 면담 등 접의적 접촉 지시
85.1.28.	케네디의원등 상원의원 10명	o 김대중 정치귀국 및 정치활동 복귀 이용	o (청와대 지음)
85.5.31.	하원의원 31명	o 김대중 석방, 군문 및 인로 자유 회복, 수감자, 시착 강이완화 요구	o 주미대사 명의 외신발송 보류 (청와대는 무 사인장)

(참고자료 4)

미상원 비율빈 관련 결의안

1. 결의안 채택일 : 1985.5.15.

2. 채택형태 : FY 86 대외원조 수권법안 심의시 원조
    법안에 대한 수정안 형식으로 채택

3. 발의 및 공동제안 의원

    - 발 의 : Kerry 의원

    - 공동제안 : Murkowski, Dodd, Boschwitz 의원

4. 표결결과 : 찬성 89、반대8、기권 3

    - 반대의원 : Hecht, Heflin, Helms, Laxalt,
                McClure, Symms, Simpson, Wallop

    - 단、심의과정에서 반대발언 의원은 전무

5. 주요 내용

    - 1986.87 선거의 자유、공정선거 보장

    - 아키노 살해사건에 대한 완전 공정한 공개재판 보장

    - 언론출판의 자유보장

    - 구속적부 심사제 채택보장

    - 구속인사 석방

    - 필리핀군 또는 보안경찰에 의한 해외에서의 살해행위 중지

6. 결의안 채택이후 미의회의 대비율빈 정부제재 조치

    - 미행정부의 대비율빈 군사원조액 1억불을 7천만불로 삭감、
      (대신 경제원조 9천 5백만불은 1억 1천만불로 증액)

0234

Kerry 결의안 공동 제안의원 인적사항

0235

공　　　란

공 란

공 란

공   란

공 란

공 란

공　　　란

공   란

공 란

공   란

공   란

공 란

공 란

공   란

공　　　란

공　　　란

공 란

```
┌─────────────────────────────────────┐
│  관련위원회 소속 주요의원 인적사항   │
└─────────────────────────────────────┘
```

0253

공 란

공   란

공 란

공   란

공 란

공   란

공 란

공 란

공   란

공   란

공   란

공   란

공   란

공   란

공   란

공　　　란

공   란

공   란

공　　　　란

공   란

공　　　　란

공   란

공   란

공   란

공 란

공   란

공 란

공   란

공 란

공 란

공 란

공동 제안자 인적사항 및 아국에 대한 성향

가. 상원의원

성 명	연령	정당	출 신 구	방한사실	접 촉 인 물	대한태도	보 좌 관
John F. Kerry	42	민주	마사츄세츠				Dick McCall
Paul Simon	57	민주	일리노이	75.8.&11 정세파악	ㅇ 유일용 재미 교포(광주의거 기념사업 동지회 회장) ㅇ 김상현	ㅇ 안보지원 지지 ㅇ 국내문제 비판	Floyd Fithian
Edward Kennedy	53	민주	마사츄세츠		ㅇ 김정원 전뉴욕 교민회장 ㅇ 박정수 전국회 의원 ㅇ 최영희 전국회 의원 ㅇ 김대중 ㅇ 김상현		Andrea Young
Claiborne Pell	67	민주	로드 아일랜드		.	ㅇ 안보지원 지지	Joseph Lopes
Alan Cranston	71	민주	캘리포니아		ㅇ 신기수 경남 기업 사장 ㅇ 김창준 나성 한미정치협회 회장	ㅇ 안보지원 반대 ㅇ 국내문제 비판	Gerald Warburg
Christopher J. Dodd	41	민주	코네티컷			ㅇ 관심별무	Bob Dockery
Ernest Hollings	63	민주	사우스 캐롤라이나			ㅇ 관심별무	Ashley Thrift

0285

성 명	연령	정당	출신구	방한사실	접 촉 인 물	대한태도	보좌관
Paul Sarbanes	52	민주	메릴랜드			ㅇ 관심별무	Judith Davison
Donald Riegle Jr.	47	민주	미시간				Synthia Jurciukonis
Tom Harkin	46	민주	아이오와			ㅇ 안보지원 반대 ㅇ 국내문제 비판	Ed Long

나. 하원의원

성 명	연령	정당	출신구	방한사실	접 촉 인 물	대한태도	보좌관
Edward Feighan	38	민주	오하이오	85.2	*김대중귀국시 대동 반한		Kevin Sullivan
Julian Dixon	51	민주	캘리포니아				Gerwen Brown

0286

상원 외교위 소속위원, 보좌관 인적사항 및 아국에 대한 성향

성 명	연령	정당	출 신 구	방 한 사 실	접촉인물	대 한 태 도	보 좌 관
Lichard G. Lugar (위원장)	53	공화	인디아나			안보 지원 지지	Ann Sofios
Frank H. Murkowski (동 아.태 소위 위원장)	52	공화	암라스카	○ 82.1.14-18 농수산부 와 한. 암라스카 간 경협문제 협의 ○ 84.1.18-20 동자부 밋 농수산부 와 한. 암라스카간 경협문제 협의 ○ 84.4.17 친선 방문 ○ 84.12.6-11 한. 암라스카간 수산분야외 장기 협력문제 협외 ○ 85.4.8-11 암라스카 어업,임업 대표단 대동 방한, 대한 경협문제협의	○ 암라스카 산목제 구매 한국 6개 회사사장	○ 안보 지원 지지 ○ 경협문제 관심	Ron Murguluski

0287

성 명	연령	정당	출신구	방한사실	접촉인물	대한태도	보 좌 관
Rudy Boschwitz	55	공화	미네소타			관심별무	Tom Young
Thomas F. Eagleton	56	민주	미주리	○ 75.8.28-30 친선방문	○ 김용태 전외원 ○ 최영희 " ○ 김명회 "	○ 안보지원지지 ○ 국내문제비판	Jack Lewis
Daniel J. Evans	60	공화	워싱톤				Sam Spina
Jesse Helms	64	공화	노스 캐롤라이나			○ 안보지원지지 ○ 경제협력문제관심	Kathy Stoner
Nancy Landon Kassebaum	53	공화	켄사스			관심별무	Winslow Wheeler
Charles Mathias Jr.	63	공화	메릴렌드		○ 박동선 미롱 상사 대표	○ 안보지원지지	Steven Metalitz
Larry Pressler	43	공화	사우스 다코타			관심별무	Douglas L. Miller
Paul S. Trible Jr.	39	공화	버지니아				Andrew. Alford
Edward Zorinski	57	민주	네브라스카			관심별무	Grayson Fowler
John F. Kerry	42	민주	마사츄세츠				Dick McCall

0288

성 명	연령	정당	출 신 구	접 촉 인 물	대한 태도	보 좌 관
Clairbone Pell	67	민주	로드 아일랜드		○ 안보 지원 지지	Joseph Lopes
Alan Cranston	71	민주	캘리포니아	○ 신기수 경남 기업 사장 ○ 김창준 나성 한미정치협회 회장.	○ 안보 지원 반대 ○ 국내문제 비판	Gerald Warburg
Christopher J. Dodd	41	민주	코네티컷		○ 관심별무	Bob Dockery
Paul Sarbanes	52	민주	메릴랜드		○ 관심별무	Judith Davison
Joseph R. Biden, Jr.	43	민주	델라웨어		○ 관심별무	Mike Gelacak

0289

하원 외무위 소속의원, 보좌관 인적사항 및 아국에 대한 성향

성 명	년령	정당	출신구	방한사실	접 촉 인 물	대 한 태 도	보 좌 관
Dante B. Fascell (위원장)	68	민주	플로리다	74.4.15-17 한미 의원 간담회	김상현		Chales R. Oregon
Stephen J. Solaz (아.태 소위 위원장)	45	민주	뉴욕	°75.8.8-11 방한의원단 일원 °77.8.29-31 미일 정책 협의회 연석자료 수집 °80.7.12-14 평양방문에 앞선 자료 수집 °80.12.26- 27 아세아 정세파악차 °83.8.7-10 정세파악 (부산, 광주 시찰)	°차임석 전조선 호텔 사장 °노진관 전국회 의원 °김상협 전국무 총리 °김동길 교수 °임병규 재미 교포 변호사	°안보 지원 지지 °국내문제 비판 °남북대화 노력지지	Michael Lewan
Cus Yatron (인권 소위 위원장)	58	민주	펜실베니 아	75.8.8-11 정세 파악	김상현	°안보 지원 지지 °국내문제 비판	Joseph P. Gemmell

0290

성 명	년령	정당	출신구	방한사실	접촉인물	대한태도	보좌관
Samuel Cejdenson	37	민주	코네티컷		김대중	○ 국내문제 비판 ○ 아국 방산 물자 수출 억제주장	Maureen Gilman
Lee H. Hamilton	54	민주	인디아나	80.3.31-4.2 한반도정세 파악		○ 주한미군 축소주장 ○ 아국인권 실배비난	Casey Miller
Tom Lantos	57	민주	캘리포니아		김대중	○ 국내문제 비판	Robert King
Meldon E. Levine	42	민주	캘리포니아				Bill Anderson
Peter H. Kostmayer	39	민주	펜실바니아				F. H. BrewerⅢ
Michael D. Barnes	42	민주	메릴랜드			○ 국내문제 비판	Judith M. DeSarno
Howard L. Berman	44	민주	캘리포니아			○ 국내문제 비판	Tom Richle
Don Bonker	48	민주	워싱톤	80.3.31-4.2 한반도정세 파악	○ 김대중 ○ 김영삼 ○ 김종필	○ 안보지원 지지 ○ 야권인물 지지및 접촉	Mark Murray

0291

성 명	연령	정당	출신구	방한사실	접촉인물	대한태도	보좌관
George W. Crockett Jr.	76	민주	미시간		° 김대중	° 국내문제 비판	Joan T. Willough-by
Mervyn M. Dymally	59	민주	캘리포니아	81.8과 84.5 및 85.8 각각 방한	° 김상현 ° 이영 및 이상운 (마성고포) ° 김관석목사	° 안보지원 지지 ° 야권인물 지지 및 접촉	David Johnson
Robert Garcia	52	민주	뉴욕				Mildred Perez
Edward Feighan	38	민주	오하이오	85.2방한	° 김대중		Kelvin Sullivan
Buddy Mackay	52	민주	플로리다			° 관심별무	Greg Far-mer
Daniel A. Mica	41	민주	플로리다	° 83.4.1 친선 방한	° 강경식 전제무 장관	° 관심별무	Suzanne Stoll
Harry Reid	46	민주	네바다				Claude Zobell,Jr
Lawrence J. Smith	44	민주	플로리다			° 관심별무	Bernie Friedman
Gerry E. Studds	48	민주	마사츄세츠			° 대한안보 지원반대 ° 국내문제 비판	Steven Schavadron

0292

성 명	연령	정당	출 신 구	방한사실	접 촉 인 물	대 한 태 도	보 좌 관
Robert G. Torricelli	34	민주	뉴저지	85.6.29- 7.3 제2차 동북아 문제회의 참석차방한		○ 대한안보 지원지지 ○ 국내문제 비판	David Crane
Morris K. Udall	63	민주	아리조나	74.4.15-17 친선방한		○ 대한안보 지원반대	Bruce Wright
Ted Weiss	58	민주	뉴욕		김대중	○ 국내문제 비판	Patricia S. Fleming
Howard Wolpe	53	민주	미시간		김대중	○ 관심법무	Jeanne Baraka
Mark D. Siljander	34	공화	미시간			○ 관심법무	Robin Luketina
Christopher H. Smith	32	공화	뉴저지				Martin Dannen-felser
Olympia J. Snowe	38	공화	메인			○ 대한경제 협력관심	Kirk Walder
Gerald B.H. Solomon	55	공화	뉴욕	85.6.29-7.3 제2차 동북아 문제회의참석 차 방한		○ 대한안보 지원지지 ○ 국내문제 비판	Arthur A. Jutton

0293

성 명	연령	정당	출 신 구	방한사실	접촉인물	대 한 태 도	보 좌 관
Ed Zschau	45	민주	캘리포니아			○ 관심별무	Bill Pickens
Gary L. Ackerman	43	민주	뉴욕			○ 국내문제 비판	Leon Met
Robert J. Lagomarsino	59	공화	캘리포니아	80.3.31- 4.2 한국 정세자료 수집		○ 안보지원 지지	Chris Williams
Jim Leach	43	공화	아이오와		○ 김대중 ○ 김상현	○ 국내문제 비판	Doug Siglin
John McCain	49	공화	아리조나				John Timmons
Connie Mack Ⅲ	45	공화	플로리다				Mitch Bainwol
Joby Roth	47	공화	위스콘신			○ 관심별무	Jennifer White
Douglaok Bereuter	46	공화	네브라스카			○ 관심별무	Peter Schechter
William S. Broomfield	63	공화	미시간	○ 75.10.14 -17등 6회 친선방문 ○ 69.3.1-7 한반도 정세 파악		○ 안보지원 지지 ○ 국내문제 옹호	Kennon Nakamura

0294

성 명	년령	정당	출 신 구	방한사실	접촉인물	대한태도	보좌관
				º 74.4.15- 17 한미 의원간담회 참석			
Dan L. Burton	47	공화	인디아나	º 85.8.11 -15 친선 방문	º 쟈니윤 (라성거주 교포,연예인)		Saul Singer
Michael Dewine							Christopher Jones
Robert K. Dornan	52	공화	캘리포니아	º 86.1.10- 14 방북 추진취소 º 86.3월 방한예정		º 안보지원 지지	Jon Holstein
Benjamin A. Gilman	63	공화	뉴욕	º 75.8.8- 11 한반도 정세파악 º 79.1 친선 방문 º 85.6.30- 7.3 동북아 문제한.미 간담회 참석	º 문래준 전국회 의원 º 도영심 국회 외무 전무 위원	º 안보지원 지지 º 국내문제 비판	Linda Yassky
Henry J. Hyde	61	공화	일리노이	º 79.1.2-5 한국안보 정세시찰 및 주한 미군철수 문제협의		º 안보지원 지지	Michael Eaton

0295

미 외회의 김대중 복권 및 민주화 촉구 결의안 발의 관련대책

85. 12. 24

국 가 안 전 기 획 부

0296

1. 상황

    가. "존 케리" 상원의원(민주당, 마사추세츠주)은 12.19 "케네디" 상원의원
        (민주당, 마사츄세츠주), "패이건" 하원의원(민주당, 오하이오주)을
        포함한 상원의원 10명, 하원의원 2명등 12명의 진보파 의원을 공동
        제안자로 하여 "김대중등의 복권 및 민주화 촉구 결의안"을 상.하 양원
        외교 및 외무위원회에 발의

    나. 결의안 요지

        (1) 인권 및 시민 자유에 대한 침해와 여타의 비민주적 관행 분위기를
             한국 정부와 민주세력간 대화와 신뢰의 분위기로 전환 유도

        (2) 김대중을 비롯 정치적 권리가 제약받고 있는 모든 인사들에 대한
             정치적 개인적 권리 회복

        (3) 평화적이고 완전한 민주적 정권 이양을 위하여 1988년 한국
             대통령의 선거 절차의 민주화

2. 평가

    가. 금번 발의된 김대중 복권 및 한국 민주화 관련 결의안은 상.하 양원에서
        통과되더라도 의회의 견해표명으로 의사록에만 수록될뿐 미 행정부에는
        법적 구속력이 없음.

    나. 그러나 금번 결의안이 1980년 이후 5년만에 처음으로 제안된 미 의회의
        김대중 문제 및 한국 민주화 관련 결의안이며 최근 국내의 재야세력의
        동향과 관련, 다음과 같은 파급 효과가 예상됨.

        (1) 미 언론 및 반한 인권단체 등에서 한국의 인권 및 김대중 문제
             거론 계기 조성

0297

(2) 86년 미 중간선거와 관련, 민주당 진보파 의원을 중심으로 아국
    정치 발전 문제에 대한 거론이 미 조야에서 적극화될 가능성

(3) 국내 대정부 비판인물 활동 고무 및 관련 악성 유언비어 유포

    (가) 김대중은 자신이 미 민주당 인사들로 부터 전폭적인 지지를
        받고 있는양 과다 선전에 주력할 것으로 예상

        ○ 자파계 신한당 의원들을 통해 국회에서 자신의 사면
          복권문제 제론

        ○ 재야운동권 단체에 동 결의안 사실 전파 및 지지 성명
          발표 획책

        ○ 해외 불순고민을 활용한 국제 인권단체 지지 유도

        ○ 장외 개헌운동과 병행한 이른바 민주화 인권투쟁 가열화 기도

    (나) 김영삼은 김대중에 대한 미 민주당 인사들의 지지에 자극,
        김영삼 방미시 논의된 신한당-미 민주당간의 의원 교류 추진
        및 야권 개헌 서명운동 촉진 계기로 활용할 가능성이 있음.

3. 김대중 복권등 미 의회 결의안 발의 경위 및 예상 심의 절차 :

   가. 동 결의안은 그간 다수 의원의 호응을 얻지 못한 상태에서 여타 긴급한
       법안들의 심의로 인해 발의가 지연되어 왔으나, "케리" 의원은 동 결의안을
       금년도 회기 종료전에 일단 발의하여 86년도 회기 심의를 위한 근거를 마련하기
       위하여 휴회에 들어가기 하루 전에 이를 서둘러 제출한 것임.

   나. 동 결의안은 하기와 같이 상. 하원에 회부될 예정임. (재적의원 과반수 이상
       찬성이 통과)
       (1) 상원: 외교위 동아.태 소위 심의후 통과시 본 회의에 상정
       (2) 하원: 외무위 아.태 소위 및 인권소위에 동시 회부 심의후 통과시
                하원 본 회의에 상정

0298

다. 현지 비용빈 정세등 주요 관심사가 산적해 있으므로 미 외회가 동 겹외안을
서둘러 처리할 것으로는 간주되지 않으며, 오히려 동 겹외안을 게류 상태에
돈 채 아국내 정치 발전 추세를 관망하는 진슴을 취할 가능성이 있다는
견해도 있음.

라. 주미대사관 관계관이 상원 외교위 및 하원 외무위 전문 위원들과 접촉한
바에 의하면, 현재의 겹외안 문구가 너무 강경하여 관계 소위원회에서
현재 발의한 겹외안을 그대로 통과될 가능성이 적다는 것이 대체적 외견임.

마. 금번 겹외안 주도 외원들은 겹외안 문구를 약화시키는등 마협적 자세를
보여 다수 외원들의 지지를 유도할 가능성이 있음.

4. 대책

가. 기본 방침

(1) 정부, 여당 차원의 반박 분고력

(2) 제1단게로는 국내외 가용한 방법을 동원, 동 겹외안 통과를 최대한
지지하되, 겹외안이 통과되어 현지 언론에 보도되는 경우 아측의
반박 논리를 현지 언론에 게재

(3) 동 겹외안 국내 전파 최대 억제(미 의회에서 동 겹외안이 통과되더라도
국내에서는 보도관제)

(4) 동 겹외안 관련, 대정부 비판 인물들의 활동 첩저 견제

나. 세부 대책

(1) 국내분야

(가) 미 민주당 친분 국내 참여단체 및 인사의 국내정세 설명 서신 발송 유도

정치인	박동진, 김상구, 봉두완, 오세용, 현홍주 (이상 민정당), 유한업, 이태구 (이상 신한당), 박정수 (원외)
경제인	남덕우, 태완선, 김기환등

0299

(나) 재야권의 동 문제 부각 활용 기도 저지.

　　　° 김대중 에게 결의안 통과 악용 자제 경고

　　　° 김대중 사면 복권 문제 원내 계론 자제 유도

　　　° 심기섭, 이신범, 정동채등 재미 김대중 추종자 국내 연계 견제

　　　° 재야 운동권 단체 연계 결의안 부각 책동 차단

　　　° 관련 유인물 유언비어 유포등 단속

(다) 관련내용 보도 조정

　　　° 국내 언론 보도 관제

　　　° 필요시 재야의 사대주의적 책동 역홍보

(2) 국외분야

(가) 주미대사관의 미 의회 관계위원회 소속의원, 보좌관 섭독 활동 강화

　　　° 상원외교위 소속 의원 17명(공화10, 민주7)

　　　　－ 상원외교위 동아.태 소위의 공화당 친한 보수계 의원
　　　　　접촉: "머코스키"(소위원장), "헬롬즈", "루가"

　　　　－ 공화당 중도계 "예반스" 및 민주당 보수계 "조린스키"
　　　　　섭독 전개

　　　　　＋ 상원 동아.태 소위 의원 7명중 민주당 진보파는
　　　　　　"크랜스톤", "도드"등 "케리" 결의안 공동 제안
　　　　　　의원분임.

　　　° 하원 외무위 소속 의원 42명(공화17, 민주25)

　　　　－ 민주당 진보파 의원 및 동 의원들의 수석 전문위원급에
　　　　　대한 공사.참사관급 에서 집중 접촉 및 순화 노력 적극화

0300

(나) 유관 외원 교포 선거 구민을 활용한 영향력 행사(서신 및 전화).
　○ 각 지역 유력 교포단체
　○ 각 지역 교포 선거 구민
　○ 각 지역 친한 미국인.

(다) 미 각계 친한 인사들을 활용한 영향력 행사
　○ "알렌", "홀브루크", "디버", "머피"등 유관 전직 관리
　○ "록펠러", "벡텔"사등 유관 경제계 영향력 인사 및 회사
　○ 미 외회 전담 로비스트를 고용, 주미대사 지휘하에 활용
　　- 국익 관련법안 통과 및 저지를 위하여 외원 및 외회 전문위원을 접촉, 주미대사관 업무 보완
　　- 미 외회 전담 로비스트 선정은 청와대, 외무부, 안기부등 관계부처가 법도 추후 협의

(라) 관련 내용 보도 조정(결의안 통과후 언론 보도시)
　○ 교포 언론 보도 자제협조
　○ 주재국 언론에 대한 아국 입장 설명
　○ 주재국 언론에 아측의 반박 논리 전게

5. 미측 접촉시 아측의 대응 논리

　가. 김대중의 범죄 사실 및 사술적 정치 행각 설명

　나. 김대중 복권문제는 기본적으로 아국 국내법적 범위내에서의 문제인바,
　　미 외회등 외부 논란이 국내에 무영될 경우 아국 국내 정치발전을 저해하고
　　정부의 순리적 처리에 제동을 가하는 역효과를 초래함 파급영향을 야기

0301

다. 아국 정부는 현재 민주화를 위한 방향으로 정책을 추진중에 있으므로
   민주화 논의 자체를 막는 것은 아니며, 단, 민주화 추진 과정에서
   제반 사회 안정 저해 및 질서파괴, 폭력 수단을 동반하는 주장, 방법등
   민주주의 역행 행위는 규제

라. 정부의 민주화 일정 제환인 및 최초의 88 평화적 정권교체 노력의
   중요성 강조, 현 수준에서 실현 가능한 문제의 단계적 추진 필요성
   부각

첨부: 1. 결의안 내용
     2. 공동 제안자 인적사항 및 아국에 대한 성향
     3. 상원 외교위 소속 위원, 보좌관 인적사항 및 아국에 대한 성향
     4. 하원 외무위 소속 위원, 보좌관 인적사항 및 아국에 대한 성향. 끝.

0302

첨부 1.

결 의 안 내 용

1. 미 의회는 김대중의 복권과 대한민국에서의 진정한 민주주의 확립을 촉구함.

2. 미국의 대외 원조의 목적은 자유·공명선거의 실시, 언론·출판의 자유존중, 개인의 권리와 자유의 보존등을 통해 민주주의 제도의 성장을 강화하는 것임.

3. 미국은 1948. 한국정부 수립이래 한국의 안보와 경제적 번영을 위하여 다대한 기여를 해 왔으나, 국회의원에 대한 기소, 기자와 민주 인사들에 대한 고문재현 등을 비롯한 한국내의 최근 사태 발전은 민주주의의 기본 원리에 심각한 우려를 낳게 하고 있음.

4. 남북한간의 긴장완화 전망은 현재 한국의 정치적 불안으로 인하여 어둡게 되어지고 있는바, 미 상원은 하원과 함께 미국의 대한 원조가 한국의 진정한 민주주의 회복에 1차적 목적이 있으며, 동 목적 달성을 위해 다음 사항을 최우선으로 고려할 것을 결의함.

   가. 인권 및 시민 자유에 대한 침해와 여타의 비민주적 관행의 분위기를 한국 정부와 제야 민주세력간의 대화와 신뢰의 분위기로 전환시키도록 유도

   나. 김대중을 비롯한 정치적 권리가 제약받고 있는 모든 인사들에게 대한 정치적, 개인적 권리 회복

   다. 평화적이고 완전한 민주적 정권 이양을 위하여 1988년 한국 대통령 선거 절차의 민주화

0303

첨부 2.

공동 제안자 인적사항 및 아국에 대한 성향

가. 상원의원

성 명	연령	정당	출 신 구	방한사실	접 촉 인 물	대한태도	보 좌 관
John F. Kerry	42	민주	마사츄세츠				Dick McCall
Paul Simon	57	민주	일리노이	75.8.8-11 정세파악	○ 유일용 재미 교포 (광주의거 기념사업 동지회 회장) ○ 김상현	○ 안보지원 지지 ○ 국내문제 비판	Floyd Fithian
Edward Kennedy	53	민주	마사츄세츠		○ 김정원 전뉴욕 교민회장 ○ 박정수 전국회 의원 ○ 최영회 전국회 의원 ○ 김대중 ○ 김상현		Andrea Young
Claiborne Pell	67	민주	로드 아일랜드			○ 안보지원 지지	Joseph Lopes
Alan Cranston	71	민주	캘리포니아		○ 신기수 경남 기업 사장 ○ 김창준 나성 한미정치협회 회장	○ 안보지원 반대 ○ 국내문제 비판	Gerald Warburg
Christopher J. Dodd	41	민주	코네티컷			○ 관심범무	Bob Dockery
Ernest Hollings	63	민주	사우스 캐롤라이나			○ 관심범무	Ashley Thrift

0304

성 명	연령	정당	출신구	방한사실	접 촉 인 물	대한태도	보 좌 관
Paul Sarbanes	52	민주	메릴랜드			○ 관심별무	Judith Davison
Donald Riegle Jr.	47	민주	미시간				Synthia Jurciukonis
Tom Harkin	46	민주	아이오와			○ 안보지원 반대 ○ 국내문제 비판	Ed Long

나. 하원의원

성 명	연령	정당	출신구	방한사실	접 촉 인 물	대한태도	보 좌 관
Edward Feighan	38	민주	오하이오	85.2	*김대중귀국시 대동 방한		Kevin Sullivan
Julian Dixon	51	민주	캘리포니아				Gerwen Brown

0305

상원 외교위 소속위원, 보좌관 인적사항 및 이국에 대한 성향

성 명	연령	정당	출 신 구	방 한 사 실	접촉인물	대한태도	보 좌 관
Lichard G. Lugar (위원장)	53	공화	인디아나			안보 지원 지지	Ann Sofios
Frank H. Murkowski (동아.태소위 위원장)	52	공화	알라스카	○ 82.1.14-18 농수산부 와 한. 알라스카 간 경협문제 협의 ○ 84.1.18-20 동자부 및 농수산부 와 한. 알라스카간 경협문제 협의 ○ 84.4.17 친선 방문 ○ 84.12.6-11 한. 알라스카간 수산분야의 장기 협력문제 협의 ○ 85.4.8-11 알라스카 어업,임업 대표단 대동 방한, 대한 경협문제협의	○ 알라스카 산목재. 구매 한국6개 회사사장	○ 안보지원 지지 ○ 경협문제 관심	Ron Murguluski

0306

10

성 명	연령	정당	출 신 구	방 한 사 실	접 촉 인 물	대 한 태 도	보 좌 관
Rudy Boschwitz	55	공화	미네소타			관심별무	Tom Young
Thomas F. Eagleton	56	민주	미주리	ㅇ 75.8.28-30 친선 방문	ㅇ 김용태 전의원 ㅇ 최영희 " ㅇ 김명회 "	ㅇ 안보지원 지지 ㅇ 국내문제 비판	Jack Lewis
Daniel J. Evans	60	공화	워싱톤				Sam Spina
Jesse Helms	64	공화	노스 캐롤라이나			ㅇ 안보지원 지지 ㅇ 경제협력 문제관심	Kathy Stoner
Nancy Landon Kassebaum	53	공화	캔사스			관심별무	Winslow Wheeler
Charles Mathias Jr.	63	공화	메릴랜드		ㅇ 박동신 미륭 상사 대표	ㅇ 안보지원 지지	Steven Metalitz
Larry Pressler	43	공화	사우스 다코타			관심별무	Douglas L. Miller
Paul S. Trible Jr.	39	공화	버지니아				Andrew. Alford
Edward Zorinski	57	민주	네브라스카			관심별무	Grayson Fowler
John F. Kerry	42	민주	마사츄세츠			:	Dick McCall

0307

11

성 명	연령	정당	출 신 구	접 촉 인 물	대한태도	보 좌 관
Clairbone Pell	67	민주	로 드 아일랜드		○ 안보지원 지지	Joseph Lopes
Alan Cranston	71	민주	캘리포니아	○ 신기수 경남 기업사장 ○ 김창준 나성 한미정치협회 회장	○ 안보지원 반대 ○ 국내문제 비판	Gerald Warburg
Christopher J. Dodd	41	민주	코네티컷		○ 관심별무	Bob Dockery
Paul Sarbanes	52	민주	메릴랜드		○ 관심별무	Judith Davison
Joseph R. Biden, Jr.	43	민주	델라웨어		○ 관심별무	Mike Gelacak

0308

12

396 한국 인권문제 민주화 관련 기타 자료 1

첨부 4.

하원 외무위 소속위원, 보좌관 인적사항 및 아국에 대한 성향

성 명	년령	정당	출신구	방한사실	접촉 인물	대한 태도	보 좌 관
Dante B. Fascell (위원장)	68	민주	플로리다	74.4.15-17 한미 의원 간담회	김상현		Chales R. Oregon
Stephen J. Solaz (아.태 소위 위원장)	45	민주	뉴욕	○ 75.8.8-11 방한의원단 일원 ○ 77.8.29-31 미입 정책 협의회 언섬자료 수집 ○ 80.7.12-14 평양방문에 앞선 자료 수집 ○ 80.12.26-27 아세아 정세파악차 ○ 83.8.7-10 정세파악 (부산, 광주시찰)	○ 차임석 전조선 호텝 사장 ○ 노진환 전국회 의원 ○ 김상협 전국무 총리 ○ 김동길 교수 ○ 임병규 재미 교포 변호사	○ 안보 지원 지지 ○ 국내문제 비판 ○ 남북 대화 노력지지	Michael Lewan
Gus Yatron (인권 소위 위원장)	58	민주	펜실배니아	75.8.8-11 정세 파악	김상현	○ 안보 지원 지지 ○ 국내문제 비판	Joseph P. Gemmell

0309

13

성 명	년령	정당	출신구	방한사실	접 촉 인 물	대한태도	보 좌 관
Samuel Gejdenson	37	민주	코네티컷		김대중	○ 국내문제 비판 ○ 아국 방산 물자 수출 억제 주장	Maureen Gilman
Lee U. Hamilton	54	민주	인디아나	80.3.31-4.2 한반도 정세 파악		○ 주한미군 축소주장 ○ 아국인권 실태 비난	Casey Miller
Tom Lantos	57	민주	캘리포니아		김대중	○ 국내문제 비판	Robert King
Meldon E. Levine	42	민주	캘리포니아				Bill Anderson
Peter H. Kostmayer	39	민주	펜실바니아				F. H. Brewer III
Michael D. Barnes	42	민주	메릴랜드			○ 국내문제 비판	Judith M. DeSarno
Howard L. Berman	44	민주	캘리포니아			○ 국내문제 비판	Tom Richle
Don Bonker	48	민주	워싱톤	80.3.31-4.2 한반도 정세 파악	○ 김대중 ○ 김영삼 ○ 김종필	○ 안보지원 지지 ○ 야권인물 지지 및 접촉	Mark Murray

0310

14

성 명	연령	정당	출신구	방한사실	접촉인물	대한태도	보좌관
George W. Crockett Jr.	76	민주	미시간		○ 김대중	○ 국내문제 비판	Joan T. Willough-by
Mervyn M. Dymally	59	민주	캘리포니아	81.8과 84.5 및 85.8 각각 방한	○ 김상현 ○ 이영 및 이상운 (라성교포) ○ 김관석목사	○ 안보지원 지지 ○ 야권인물 지지 및 접촉	David Johnson
Robert Garcia	52	민주	뉴욕				Mildred Perez
Edward Feighan	38	민주	오하이오	85.2방한	○ 김대중		Kelvin Sullivan
Buddy Mackay	52	민주	플로리다			○ 관심범무	Greg Far-mer
Daniel A. Mica	41	민주	플로리다	○ 83.4.1 친선 방한	○ 강경식 전재무 장관	○ 관심범무	Suzanne Stoll
Harry Reid	46	민주	네바다				Claude Zobell,Jr
Lawrence J. Smith	44	민주	플로리다			○ 관심범무	Bernie Friedman
Gerry E. Studds	48	민주	마사츄세츠			○ 대한안보 지원반대 ○ 국내문제 비판	Steven Schavadro

0311

성 명	연령	정당	출신구	방한사심	접촉인물	대한태도	보좌관
Robert G. Torricelli	34	민주	뉴저지	85.6.29- 7.3 제2차. 동북아 문제회외 참석차방한		○ 대한안보 지원지지 ○ 국내문제 비판	David Crane
Morris K. Udall	63	민주	아리조나	74.4.15~17 친선방한		○ 대한안보 지원반대	Bruce Wright
Ted Weiss	58	민주	뉴욕		김대중	○ 국내문제 비판	Patricia S. Fleming
Howard Wolpe	53	민주	미시간		김대중	○ 관심범무	Jeanne Baraka
Mark D. Siljander	34	공화	미시간			○ 관심범무	Robin Luketina
Christopher H. Smith	32	공화	뉴저지				Martin Dannen- felser
Olympia J. Snowe	38	공화	메인			○ 대한경제 협력관심	Kirk Walder
Gerald B.H. Solomon	55	공화	뉴욕	85.6.29~7.3 제2차 동북아 문제회외참석 차 방한		○ 대한안보 지원지지 ○ 국내문제 비판	Arthur A. Jutton

U312

성 명	연령	정당	출 신 구	방한사실	접촉인물	대 한 태 도	보 좌 관
Ed Zschau	45	민주	캘리포니아			○ 관심별무	Bill Pickens
Gary L. Ackerman	43	민주	뉴욕			○ 국내문제 비판	Leon Met
Robert J. Lagomarsino	59	공화	캘리포니아	80.3.31- 4.2 한국 정세자료 수집		○ 안보지원 지지	Chris Williams
Jim Leach	43	공화	아이오와		○ 김대중 ○ 김상현	○ 국내문제 비판	Doug Siglin
John McCain	49	공화	아리조나				John Timmons
Connie Mack Ⅲ	45	공화	플로리다				Mitch Bainwol
Joby Roth	47	공화	위스콘신			○ 관심별무	Jennifer White
Douglaok Bereuter	46	공화	네브라스카			○ 관심별무	Peter Schechter
William S. Broomfield	63	공화	미시간	○ 75.10.14 -17등 6회 친선방문 ○ 69.3.1-7 한반도 정세 파악		○ 안보지원 지지 ○ 국내문제 옹호	Kennon Nakamura

0313

15

성 명	년령	정당	출 신 구	방한사실	접 촉 인 물	대한 태도	보 좌 관
				° 74.4.15-17 한미 의원간담회 참석			
Dan L. Burton	47	공화	인디아나	° 85.8.11 -15 친선 방문	° 쟈니윤 (라성거주 교포, 연예인)		Saul Singer
Michael Dewine							Christopher Jones
Robert K. Dornan	52	공화	캘리포니아	° 86.1.10- 14 방북 추진취소 ° 86.3월 방한예정		° 안보지원 지지	Jon Holstein
Benjamin A. Gilman	63	공화	뉴욕	° 75.8.8- 11 한반도 정세파악 ° 79.1 친선 방문 ° 85.6.30- 7.3 동북아 문제 한.미 간담회 참석	° 문래준 전국회 의원 ° 도영심 국회 외무전문 위원	° 안보지원 지지 ° 국내문제 비판	Linda Yassky
Henry J. Hyde	61	공화	일리노이	° 79.1.2-5 한국안보 정세시찰 및 주한 미군철수 문제협의		° 안보지원 지지	Michael Eaton

0314

18

정 리 보 존 문 서 목 록					

기록물종류	일반공문서철	등록번호	20733	등록일자	1995-05-29
분류번호	701	국가코드		보존기간	영구
명 칭	박종철 서울대생 고문치사 사건, 1987				
생 산 과	북미과	생산년도	1987~1987	담당그룹	북미국
내용목차	1. 기본문서 2. 언론보도 3. 국제사회반응				

0001

1. 기본문서

0002

관리 번호 81 -101

발 신 전 보

번 호 : WUS-0217   일 시 : 201171600   전보종별 : _____

수 신 : 주 미   대사 //총영사//

발 신 : 장   관   (미북)

제 목 : 박종철 관계

    1. 경찰조사중 사망한 박종철사건과 관련 검찰은 사인 규명을 위해 철저히 조사중이며 조사가 완료되는 대로 사실을 발표할 예정임.

    2. 상기 관련 귀관은 국무성과 접촉, 명확한 사인이 규명될때까지는 공개적인 논평을 삼가 하도록 촉구 바람.

    3. 아울러 금 1.17. 국내 석간은 1.16. 미국 무성이 "철저한 조사를 희망"한다는 논평을 하였다고 하는 바 동 내용 확인 보고 바람. (헉시 참조)

예고문에 의거 ___관 (1981___)
직위 ___ ___

(미주국장 장선섭)

검토필 (87.6.20.___

앙고재	87년 1월 17일 북미1과	기안자	과 장	국 장	차 관	장 관	발신시간 :
				추진	구두지시		외신과 접수자 과장

0003

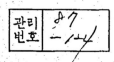

외 무 부   착신전문 지급

번 호 : USW-0246   일 시 : 701171906   종 별

수 신 : 장 관 (미북,해기)

발 신 : 주 미 대사

제 목 : 박종철 사건

대 : WUS-217

1. 김삼훈 참사관은 금 1.17(토) BLAKEMORE 한국과장을 접촉, 대호 박종철사건 관련 아국 검찰 당국에 의한 철저한 조사가 현재 진행중에 있는 만큼 조사결과가 밝혀질때까지 추가적인 공개논평을 삼가하여 줄것을 요청함.

2. 국무성은 작 1.16(금) 정오 브리핑시 동사건 관련 질의가 없어 논평하지 않았으나, 동일 오후늦게 동아태국 대변인실로 기자들의 개별질의가 있어 아래 PRESS GUIDANCE 에 의거 답변 하였다함.

Q : KOREAN PROSECUTORS ARE INVESTINGATING THE POSSIBLE TORTURE DEATH OF A STUDENT ACTIVITIST DURING POLICE QUESTIONING.

A : -- WE HAVE SEEN THE PRESS REPORTS OF THE PROSECUTORS' STATEMENT.

-- WE DEPLORE TORTURE AS A VIOLATION OF HUMAN RIGHTS.

-- WE NOTE THAT THE KOREAN AUTHORITIES HAVE ALREADY BEGUN AN INVESTIGATION. WE EXPECT IT TO BE THOROUGH AND THAT THEY WILL APPLY THE FULL FORCE OF THE LAW SHOULD ANY WRONGDOING BE UNCOVERED.

(대사 김경원-차관)

예 고 : 1987.12.31. 일반

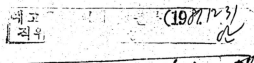

예고
직우   (1987.12.31)

검토필 (87 6 20 일

검토필 (1   X   일

미주국   차관실   1 차보   청와대   안 기   문공부

PAGE 1   87.01.18 10:45
                                                         외신 2과 통제관

                                                              0004

P/A─0084
NPO─0082

발 신 전 보

번 호: UHO─0084 일 시:_____   전보종별:

수 신: 주 수신처참조   대사·총영사 ↘   NPZ─0070
NSP─0071

발 신: 장   관 (정문)

재 목: 서울 대 박종철 사망 사건

1. 지난 1.14. 치안본부 에서 공안사건을 수사하는 과정에서 발생한 서울 대 박종철군 사망사건과 관련 치안본부 조사 결과를 아래와 같이 통보하니 필요시 주재국 정부·언론계 인사등 에게 적의 설명하고 특이사항 있을시 보고 바람.

— 아 — 래 —

가. 박종철 혐의사실

o 86.10.31. 서울 대 반혁명 책동 분쇄 및 제헌의회 소집을 위한 투쟁결의대회 시위 주도록

o 86.11.24. 용공 이적 단체로 규정된 서울 대 삼민투와 민민투의 배후 조직인 서울 대 민추위 사건 중요 수배자인 박종운을 1박 은닉하고 87.1.8. 도피자금을 제공하는등 수배자와 연계활동

나. 박종철 연행 경위

o 박종철이 서울 대 민민투 위원장 남택범 및 동 대 불순 지하조직 핵심책으로서 85년 미 문화원 농성사건, 경인지구 노학연계투쟁등 각종 반국가적 좌경용공 소요를 배후 조종해온 서울 대 민추위 사건 수배자 박종운 과 연계활동중이라는 정보를 입수하고

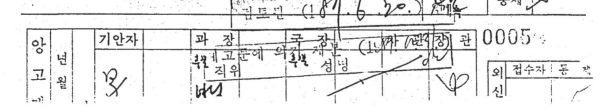

87.1.14. 하숙집 부근에서 잠복 근무하여 하숙집에서 동인을 임의 동행.

o 박 군은 대공 수사단 조사실에서 87.1.14.부터 조사관 경위 조한경, 입회 경사 강진규로 부터 상기 혐의 사실에 대하여 조사를 받음.

다. 박종철 사망 경위 조사

o 자체 특별 조사반 구성

   - 치안본부는 동 사건의 엄정한 사건 규명을 위해 치안본부 수사부장 이강년 경무관을 반장으로 조사요원 16명을 투입, 1.17-18. 양일간 박종철군의 수사를 담당했던 조한경, 강진규와 관련 민간인등 모두 16명을 철야신문하고 국립과학 수사 연구소의 부검 결과를 토대로 사망 경위를 집중 수사

   - 시체 부검은 1.15. 한양대 부속병원에서 국립과학 수사연구소가 동 병원 의사와 유가족 입회 아래 실시

o 사망 경위

   - 조사관 강진규가 서울대 민추위 사건 수배자 박종운의 소재를 알고 있음이 확실한 박종철로부터 사실을 알아내기위해 박종철의 두 팔을 뒤로 한후 다른 조사관 조한경이 머리를 강제로 욕조에 집어 넣었으나 계속 진술을 거부하자 다시 머리를 욕조 물에 집어 넣는 과정에서 급소인 목 부위가 욕조 턱에 잘못눌려 질식 사망 함

/계속

0006

ㅇ 시체 부검 결과

　－ 사망원인은 경부압박에 의한 질식사

　－ 복부 팽만은 조사관의 인공호흡과 초진 의사의 호흡주입기
　　사용으로 인해 공기가 위장에 들어가 생긴 일시적 현상

　－ 폐의 조직 검사 결과 수분 검출이 되지 않았으며, 폐 기공
　　현상은 과거 폐결핵 병력에 의한 폐손상 흔적

　－ 외촌 부위와 머리부위의 타박상은 연행 과정에서 저항으로
　　생긴 부상

　－ 상기 부검 내용은 군의 사망 원인과 직접 관계가 없는
　　것으로 판명

라. 경찰 조치

　ㅇ 조사 담당관 조한경 및 강진규는 특정범죄 가중 처벌법 위반 혐의로
　　구속 수사

　ㅇ 대공 수사 2단장 전석린 직위 해제

2. 김종호 내무부장관은 1·19·박종철 사망 사건과 관련 담화문을 통해 금번
　발생한 사고에 대해 국민에게 심심한 사과를 표했으며 강민창 치안본부장도
　경찰의 책임자로서 진심으로 유족과 국민앞에 사죄한다고 말했음을 참고로
　첨언함.　끝.

　　　　(정문국장 신두병)

수신처 : 화란, 덴마크, 스페인, 포르투갈　및 P.I. 수신공관

0007

內 務 部 長 官 談 話 文

1987. 1. 19.

국방 홍보실장
리랑
09:20 경
비서 건당
① 주비에서 배부한 것은 국어버려

0008

談 話 文

지난 14日 治安本部에서 公安事件을 搜査하는 過程에서 不幸한 事故가 일어난데 대하여 國民여러분 앞에 深甚한 謝過의 말씀을 드립니다.

또한 뜻하지 않게 숨진 故人에 대하여 깊은 哀悼의 뜻을 표하며 特히 不幸을 당한 遺族여러분께 깊은 謝罪와 아울러 慰勞의 말씀을 올립니다.

그동안 우리 警察은 國家安保와 社會秩序維持를 確固히 하며 自由民主主義 體制를 守護하고 國民의 生存權을 지키기 위하여 左傾容共不純勢力의 鬪爭에 不撤畫夜 全心全心을 傾注하여 왔읍니다만은.

이번에 뜻하지 않은 不幸한 事故로 因하여 國民여러분에게 많은 心慮를 끼치게 된 것을 眞心으로 謝過를 드립니다.

우리 12萬 警察은 이번의 不幸한 事故를 큰 敎訓으로 삼아 다시는 이러한 苟酷行爲가 再發되지 않도록 治安關係 職務遂行의 蓋底를 期해 갈것을 다짐하는 바 입니다.

이번 事件과 關聯하여 警察 스스로가 밝히는 것이 國民여러분에게 謝過드리는 길일뿐 아니라 警察의 名譽를 回復하는 것이라 생각하여 오늘 그 全貌를 밝혔으며 捜査擔任者도 關係法에 따라 處罰토록 했읍니다.

아무조록 國民여러분께서는 이와 같은 警察의 뼈를 깎는 反省과 反情을 깊이 혜아려 주시기를 懇曲히 바라오며.

또 한편으로는 容共左傾不純勢力의 拔本塞源과 對共捜査의 强化를 위하여 어려운 與件속에서 밤낮없이

0010

2

職務에 充實하고 있는 大多數 警察이 이런 不幸한

事故로 因하여 虛脫과 挫折에 빠지지 않도록

國民여러분께서 채찍과 아울러 激勵해 주시기를 付託

드리는 바 입니다.

0011

3

서울대생 박종철군 사망관련 치안본부 조사 발표문

1987. 1. 19.

0012

1. 개   요.

　　치안본부는 지난 1. 14 대공수사단에서 좌경용공 활동 혐의로
조사를 받고 있던 서울대생 박종철군의 사망과 관련하여 특별
조사반을 구성, 그동안 박군의 연행 수사 경위. 사망원인을
엄정하고 철저히 규명한 결과, 담당 수사관의 가혹 행위가
확인됨에 따라 당시 조사 수사관 경위 조한경. 경사 강진규를
특정 범죄 가중 처벌법(가혹 행위에 의한 치사) 위반혐의로 구속
하고 이에 대한 감독 책임을 물어 대공 수사 2단장을 직위 해제
조치 하였음.

2. 박종철의 수사 경위

　0. 박종철의 혐의 사실

　　． '86. 10. 31.

　　　서울대 아크로폴리스 광장에서 인문대 동원책으로 "반혁명
　　책동 분쇄 및 제헌의회 소집을 위한 투쟁결의 대회" 시위주도

　　． '86. 11. 24. 20:00 경

　　　용공이 적단체로 규정된 서울대 심민투와 민민투의 배후
　　조직인 서울대 민추위사건 중요 수배자인 박종운(서울대 사회
　　복지 4년)을 동인 하숙집에 1박 은닉시키고 '87. 1. 8 저녁
　　도피 자금을 제공 하는등 동 수배자와 연계 활동.

　＊． '85. 5. 24 사당동 가두 시위 가담으로 남부 지원에서 구류 5일
　　． '85. 6. 1 구로동 가두 시위 가담으로 위지원에서 구류 3일

　　　　　　　　　　　－ 1 －　　　　　0013

- '86. 4. 11 신당동 가두시위 주도로 '86.7.15 동부 지원에서 징역 10월에 집행유예 2년.

- '86. 9. 1 - 9. 21 간 (21일) 유기정학 등을 받음.

o. 박종철의 연행 경위

- 박종철이 서울대 민민투위원장 남택범(언어학과 4년)및 동대 불순 지하조직 핵심책으로서 '85년 이문학원 농성사건, 경인 지구 노학연계투쟁등 각종 반국가적 좌경용공 소요를 배후 조종해온 서울대 민추위사건 중요 수배자 동대 박종운(사회 복지 4년)등과 연계활동중 이라는 정보를 입수하고 '87.1.14. 06:00 부터 하숙집 부근에서 잠복 근무타가 08:10 경 하숙집 에서 동인을 임의 동행한 것임.

- 박군은 대공수사단 조사실에서 '87. 1. 4. 08:40 부터 조사 관 경위 조한경, 입회 경사 강진규로 부터 상기의 혐의 사실 에 대하여 조사를 받았음.

3. 박종철의 사망 경위 조사

o. 자체 특별 조사반 구성

- 치안본부는 동 사건의 엄정한 사건 규명을 위해 치안본부 수사 부장 이강년 경무관을 반장으로 조사요원 16명을 투입, 1. 17 - 1. 18일 양일동안 박종철군의 수사를 담당했던 경위 조한경, 경사 강진규와 관련 민간인등 모두 16명을 치안신문 하는 한편 국립과학 수사 연구소의 부검 결과를 토대로 박군의 사망 경위를 집중 수사 했음.

0014

- 2 -

• 사체 부검은 1. 15 서울 지검의 지휘를 받아 한양대 부속병원
  에서 국립과학 수사연구소가 동병원 의사와 유가족 입회 아래
  실시 하였음.

0. 사망 경위

    서울대 민추위사건 중요 수배자 박종운의 소재를 알고 있음이
  확실함에도 진술을 거부하고 있던 박종철로 부터 사실을 알아내
  기 위한 위협수단으로 조사관 경사 강진규가 박종철의 두팔을
  뒤로 잡고 조사관 경위 조한경은 머리를 강제로 한차례 욕조물
  에 잠시 집어 넣었다가 내놓았으나 계속 진술을 거부하면서
  완강히 반항하자 다시 머리를 욕조물에 밀어 넣는 과정에서
                              급소인 목부위가 욕조턱(높이 50센치、
너비 6센치)에   잘못눌려   질식 사망한 것임.

0. 사체 부검 결과

• 사망원인은 경부압박에 의한 질식사임.

• 복부 팽만은 조사관의 인공호흡과 초진 의사의 호흡주입기 사용
  으로 인해 증기가 외장에 들어가 생긴 일시적 현상임.

• 폐의 조직 검사 결과 수분 검출이 되지 않았으며、폐기공 현상
  은 과거 폐결핵 병력에 의한 폐손상 흔적임.

• 왼손 부위와 머리부위의 타박상은 연행 과정에서 저항으로 생긴
  부상임.

• 상기 부검내용은 박군의 사망 원인과 직접적 관계가 없는 것으로
  판명됨.

0015
- 3 -

4. 경찰 조치

o. 조사 담당관 경위 조한경, 경사 강진규 는

특정범죄 가중 처벌법 4조 2 - ② 위반 혐의로 구속 수사.

(가혹행위 치사 ... 무기 또는 3년 이상의 징역)

o. 대공수사 2단장 전석린 직위 해제

5. 사과 말씀

o. 이번의 뜻하지 않은 사건에 대하여 경찰의 책임자로서 진심으로 유족과 국민앞에 사죄를 드립니다.

o. 우라나라의 관계법률(특정범죄 가중 처벌법등)은 경찰이 사건 수사를 함에 있어 어떠한 경우에도 피의자에 대한 폭행은 물론 가혹행위를 용납할 수 없도록 규정하는 등 제도적 장치가 되어 있음에도 불구하고, 일부 수사관들의 지나친 직무 의욕으로 인해 이러한 불상사가 발생한 것은 매우 유감된 일로서 전경찰은 깊이 반성하고 있읍니다.

o. 우리 경찰은 이번 사건을 계기로 앞으로는 어떠한 경우에도 이러한 불상사가 재발되지 않도록   국민들의 생명 과 재산을 지키는 참된 봉사자로서의 책무를 다해 나갈것을 다짐 하는 바입니다.

o. 국민여러분께서는 이번과 같은 불상사를 엄히 꾸짖어 주심과 함께 이후 가혹행위가 철저히 근절된 가운데, 자유민주주의를 파괴하려는 극소수 좌경 용공분자를 완전히 척결할때까지 경찰의 주어진 책무를 성실히 수행할 수 있도록 계속 협조하여 주시기 바라는 바입니다.

- 4 -

0016

발 신 전 보

번 호: _WUS- 0239_ 일 시: _19 0119 1840_   전보종별: _____

수 신: 주   미   대사 ·/총영사/

발 신: 장   관 (미북)

제 목: 박종철 사망사건

연 : PIA-0004 , WUS-247

대 : USW-0246

1. 본부는 연호로 통보한 치안본부 수사결과및
내무부장관 담화문의 사본을 금 1·19(월) **발표**직전에
주한미대사관측에 통보한바 있음.

2. 금번사건과 관련, 귀관에서도 연호자료를 토대로
국무성측에 설명바람. 특히 정부의 강력한 인권보호 의지에도
불구하고 ~~일부조직의 법집행 과정애서~~ 가혹 행위가 ~~발생한데~~ 대한
~~막심한 유감의 뜻을 표명바람.~~ 아울러 금번사건의 철저한
사실조사및 관계자 인책조치 등으로 향후 유사사례의 재발
방지를 위해 정부가 최대한 노력하고 있음을 ~~설명하고~~
~~이~~에대한 미정부의 충분한 이해를 촉구하기 바람.

검토필 (1987.6 30.)

보존예고 의거 재분류 (19)
직위

(제1차관보 박수길)

앙 고 재	87 년 1 월 19 일	북미 과	기안자	과 장	심의관	국 장	차관보	차 관	장 관	발신시간:

0017

외 무 부 착 신 전 보

번 호 : USW-0258   일 시 : 8701201457   종 별 :

수 신 : 장 관(미북)

발 신 : 주 미 대사

제 목 : 박종철 사건

대 WUS-0239

1. 금 1.20(화) 당관 김삼훈 참사관이 DAVID BLAKEMORE 한국과장에게 대호 사건 조사결과 및 관계자 인책등 정부의 조치에 관해 설명 하였음.(1.19은 MARTIN LUTHER KING 추모 휴무 이었음)

2. 동 과장은 주한 미대사관에서도 보고 해온바 있다고 하면서, 금번 한국정부가 취한 조치는 매우 인상적(VERY IMPRESSIVE) 이었다고 말하고, 금일 국무성 정오 브리핑에서 이러한 평가가 반영될것 이라고 하였음.

(대사 김경원)

예고:87.12.31일반

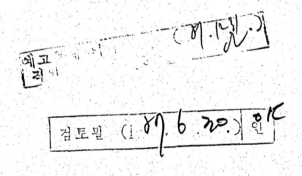

예고 적 니

검토필 (1 87.6.20. 기안

미주국 차관실 1 차보 청와대 안 기 정문국

PAGE 1   87.01.21 09:53
외신 2과 통제관

0018

관리 번호	87 -121

외 무 부 착신전문

번 호 : USW-0272   일 시 : 701201651   종 별 :

수 신 : 장 관(미북,해기)

발 신 : 주 미 대사

제 목 : 박종철 사건

대: WUS-0239

연: USW-0258

국무성 한국과는 금 1.20 박종철 사건 관련 아국정부의 조치등에 대해 아래 PRESS

GUIDANCE 를 준비 하였으나, 금일 정오 브리핑시 기자질의가 없어 사용 되지 않았다

함.

아 래

KOREA:STUDENT DEATH IN POLICE CUSTIDY

Q:DO YOU HAVE ANY COMMENT ON THE ROKG'S DISCLOSURE THAT A STUDENT DIED IN POLIC

E CUSTODY AFTER BEING TORTURED ?

A: WE HAVE SEEN PRESS REPORTS OF A STATEMENT BY PRESIDENT CHUN ON THIS MATTER.

WE WELCOME THE PRESIDENT'S EFFORTS TO ENSURE THAT SUCH A TRAGIC INCIDENTIS NEVE

R REPEATED.

AS WE SAID LAST WEEK,WE DEPLORE THE USE OF TORTURE.IN THIS CASE, THE KOREAN AUT

HORITIES HAVE SHOWN A COMMENDABLE DETERMINATION TO PURSUE AN INVESTIGATION AND

TO PUNISH THOSE RESPONSIBLE FOR THIS OUTRAGE TO THE FULL EXTENT OF THE LAW. PRES

IDENT CHUN HAS CLEARLY GIVEN HIS FIRM SUPPORT TO THIS EFFORT.

WE EXTEND OUR CONDOLENCES TO THE FAMILY OF THE VICTIM.

(대사 김경원)

예고:87.12.31일반

검토필 (87.6.30.

미주국   차관실   1차보   ... 문공부   정둥국

PAGE   1   87.01.21 09:29
                                                      외신 2과 통제관
                                              0019

분류기호 문서번호	장문 20501- 511	협 조 문 용 지 ( )	결 재	담당	과장	국장
시행일자	1987.1.30.					
수　신	수신처참조	발신 정보문화국장	(서명)			
제　목	박종철군 치사 사건					

1. 박종철군 치사사건과 관련, 또 위 고 박종철 국민추도회 준비
위원회는 2.7. 서울 명동 성당에서 박군 추도식 및 관련 행사를
계획하고 있읍니다.

2. 치안 당국은 상기 추도식등 관련 행사가 고 인의 명복을 비는
순수한 추념 행사가 아니라 현저히 사회적 불안과 공공의 안녕
질서를 해칠 불법 집회로서 만중봉기를 획책, 정권을 쟁취하려는
데 목적이 있다고 판단되어 민주적 헌정질서의 유지와 정국
혼란 예방을 위해 동 집회를 완전 차단 봉쇄 할 예정입니다.

3. 별첨 관련 자료를 참고로 하여 87.2.5. 하오에 귀국 관할
주한 외국 공관 대표를 동시에 초청하여 동 추도식의 불법
집회 성격과 당국의 동 집회 차단 봉쇄 조치의 불가피성을
설명하여 주시기 바라며, 동 설명 결과를 당국으로 회보하여
주시기 바랍니다.

0020

/계속

1505－8 일 (1) 190mm×268mm(인쇄용지 2 급 60g /㎡)

첨부 : 1. 2.7. 박종철 추도식에 따른 대책 1부.

    2. 야권 박종철 사건 확산기도 관련 대책 1부.   끝.

수신처 : 아주국장, 미주국장, 구주국장, 중동국장, 아프리카국장

情報文化局長

~~署名~~

2.7 朴鍾哲 追悼式에 따른 對策

0022

2.7 朴鍾哲 追悼式에 따른 對策

1 . 大會概要

○ 主 催 : 故 朴鍾哲君 國民追悼會 準備委員會

> 共同代表 : 桂勳悌 民統聯副議長 等 29 名
> 顧 問 : 金壽煥樞機卿 , 咸錫憲 , 洪南淳 ,
> 李敏雨 , 金大中 , 金泳三 等 8 名
> 準備委員 : 9,782 名

○ 行事內容

<서 울>

△ 2.7(土) 14:00 서울明洞聖堂 追悼會

(座席 1,500 名 , 立席 500 名 , 垈地 3,140 坪)

※ 收容能力 : 25,000 名

△ 參席豫想人員 : 10,000 ～ 30,000 名

△ 서울地域은 검은리본 , 흰喪章을 佩用하고
追悼會에 參席

<全 國>

△ 全國 新 · 舊敎 敎會 , 聖堂 및 寺刹에서 一齊히
5 分間 打鐘

△ 14:00 모든 車輛은 追悼警笛을 1 分間
울리면서 默念

※ 他市道의 追悼모임은 具體的으로 日程이
決定되지 않았으므로 確定되는대로 對策樹立
對處爲計임

1

0023

2 . 集會의 性格

○ 既히 政府에서 遺憾表示와 關係者引責 및
 關聯者拘束, 拷問根絶을 爲한 對策委構成
 等 一連의 諸般措置에도 不拘하고

○ 2.7 所謂「故 朴鍾哲君 國民追悼會 準備委員會」가
 主催하려는 서울 明洞聖堂에서의 朴君
 追悼式과 全國 教會・聖堂 및 寺刹에서
 一齊히 5分間 打鐘 및 모든 車輛의
 追悼警笛을 울리는 行爲 等은 純粹하게 故人의
 冥福을 빌고 追念하는 行事가 아니라

○ 民統聯, 民青聯, 民推協 等 問題團體와
 急進左傾學生, 拘束者家族, 問題宗教人,
 解職勤勞者 및 一部 野黨國會議員 等
 反政府勢力을 總網羅하여 顯著히 社會的
 不安과 公共의 安寧秩序를 害칠 不法集會
 로서

2

0024

○ 特히 首都 서울의 繁華街인 明洞한복판에서
追悼式을 憑藉하여 拷問事例 等을 誇張捏造
暴露 煽動하고

○ 이로 因하여 興奮한 群衆들로 하여금
暴力亂動事態를 惹起시켜 民衆蜂起를 劃策,
政權을 奪取하려는데 目的이 있다고 判斷
되므로

○ 民主的 憲政秩序의 維持및 社會不安을
加重시키는 政局混亂豫防과 國法秩序維持
次元에서 完全 遮斷封鎖해야 할것임

3

0025

3 . 主要　關聯動向

O 民推協 , 民統聯 , 宗教團體 等　在野圈은

急進左傾學生 , 問題宗敎人 , 解職勤勞者　및

野黨國會議員 等과　連繫하여

△ 人權鬪爭의　口實로　朴君事件을　對政府

鬪爭의　好材로　삼아　政治問題化시켜

△ 改憲　및　總選政局의　主導權掌握을　劃策

※ 朴君追慕와　關聯한　示威等　事例

(1.14 ～ 28 間)

徹夜籠城	糾彈示威	焚香所置	追悼式	追悼式副後策 示威	壁報揭示 플래카드	不穩油印物布 配	座談會 및 公聽會
8個團體 連 14 日 360餘名	30　回 4,810 餘名	73個所	20　回 7,700 餘名	5　回 4,000 餘名	69個所 150餘枚	94 個所 6,800 餘枚	2　回 200餘名

O 1.18　金壽煥樞機卿은　明洞聖堂　主日미사時

朴君을　爲한　祈禱會　開催

4

0026

○ 1.20 NCC 가 主體가 된 拷問 및 容共造作
沮止 共同對策委員會 (47個團體 連繫) 에서는
糾彈聲明을 내고

△ 1.20 ～ 26 까지 1週日間 朴君 追慕期間
으로 定하여 焚香所設置와 追慕禮拜

△ 朴君 追慕期間中 검은리본 佩用、

○ 1.24 桂勳悌 民統聯副議長 , 宋建鎬 民言協
議長 , 朴炯圭牧師 等이 朴君 國民追悼會
準備委員會를 構成 (各界人士 28名)

○ 1.26 基督教會舘 大講堂에서 「 故 朴君
國民追悼會 準備委員會 發足式 」劃策

(事前遮斷 瓦解)

○ 1.26 金大中 金泳三은 朴君 汎國民追悼會
開催對策을 協議하고

5

0027

△ 2.7 明洞聖堂 追悼會에 積極 協調
하기로 合意한 後에

△ 當局이 朴君 追悼式을 過剩沮止하면
豫測하지 못할 事態가 發生할것이다
고 言動

○ 1.27 民推協事務室에서 桂勳悌, 宋建鎬,
趙南基牧師, 金泳三, 金大中 等 20餘名이
「故 朴君 國民追悼會 準備委員會 發足式」을
갖고

△ 2.7 14:00 서울 明洞聖堂에서 追悼會를
갖기로 하는 한便

△ 拷問追放을 爲한 討論, 集會, 캠페인을
積極 展開하며

△ 拷問追放運動基金으로 1,000원씩 納付,
募金運動을 展開하기로 決定

6

0028

```
┌─ 送金處 ( 預金主  金祥根牧師 ) ─────────────┐
│                                                          │
│ 第 一 銀 行：125-10-058454   農    協：027-01-196541 │
│                                                          │
│ 서울信託銀行：14701-87000413  國民銀行： 008-010285-766 │
│                                                          │
│ 韓 一 銀 行：012-01-137678   朝興銀行：325-1-040851 │
│                                                          │
│ 商 業 銀 行：104-05-043030                           │
│                                                          │
└──────────────────────────────────────┘
```

○ 1.27   大韓辯協에서는   辯護士，宗教人，

  拷問被害者 및 拘束者家族 等 200 餘名

  參席裡에 拷問對策 公聽會를 갖고

  汎國民的次元에서 拷問追放運動을 第2建國

  運動으로 展開하기로 意見을 모음

○ 新民黨議員들은   1.26 ∼ 28 間 열린

  第132回 臨時國會에서 人權特委構成 및

  人權擁護 對政府建議案採擇 等이 與野

  異見으로 合意에 失敗된데 不滿

  1.27 24:00 ∼ 1.28 24:00 間 徹夜籠城

7

0029

4. 對策

基本方向

○ 源泉封鎖 概念下에   朴君 追悼式 瓦解

○ 行事前後 示威煽動等 不法行爲者
   强力 依法措置

○ 市民不便 最少化로 刺戟回避 (必要時
   最少限 交通統制)

全國對策

<情報對策>

○ 自制 및 警告的意味의 談話文 發表

─ 所謂 國民追悼會 準備委員會가 主催하는

   朴君 追悼行事의 性格 및 不法性集會임을

   알리고 對國民 協調要請 ─
                    (文公·法務·內務長官 共同)

8   0030

○ 政府次元의 對言論 醇化로 國民關心 轉換

○ 各級教會・聖堂 및 寺刹 教職者 等 積極醇化로
募金 및 追悼打鐘運動 瓦解

○ 各大學 指導教授로 하여금 問題學生
追悼會 參席沮止

○ 關係機關에서는 運輸業體와 事前協調로
追悼警笛行爲 遮斷

○ 拷問追放運動基金 募金 高次元的 工作 沮止

○ 情報活動強化로 不純策動 早期捕捉 瓦解

○ 大會關聯 不穩內容의 告知傳單・壁報・
플래카드 等 宣傳物 製作段階에서부터 團束
回收 및 押收

一 全國 印刷施設 事前點檢，印刷活動 封鎖

※ 集示法 第3條2項，廣告物 等 管理法 4條,
輕犯罪 處罰法   1條44號，道交法 63條

9

0031

○ 地域對策協議會 等 積極活用으로 追悼集會븜

全國擴散防止 및 集會瓦解

< 警 備 對 策 >

○ 全國警察 總動員體制 維持

△ 非常警戒實施로 總力對處

• 期 間 :87.2.6 09:00～2.8 09:00（ 3日間 ）

• 區 分 ┌ 甲號：서울·仁川·京畿

└ 乙號：餘他地域

△ 鎮壓部隊現況

區分 市道	計	機動隊	防巡隊	올림픽隊	戰警隊	署中隊
計	315	90	54	10	33	128
서 울	128	41	24	8	29	26
地 方	187	49	30	2	4	102

※ 軍配屬施設戰警 9個中隊 ┐
올림픽隊   8個中隊 ┘ 軍兵力으로 代替

10   0032

＜情 報 對 策＞

○　事前　明洞聖堂側에　場所不許　및　當日 一時

正門遮斷에　따른　協調要請

－ 政府次元에서　對處

○　大會當日　主導級人物 等　一時　自家保護措置

△　準備委員會　共同代表（29名）

△　顧問中　金大中・咸錫憲・洪南淳・金泳三

池學淳・尹犦熊（李敏雨總裁，金壽煥 樞機卿은

除外）

○　地方問題人物 等　集團上京　沮止

△　버스賃貸解約 等　遮斷

△　地方 核心的 問題人物　一時　自家遮斷

11

0033

○ 行事前日과 當日 서울市內一圓 檢問檢索
으로 示威用品 一齊收去

△ 大會場周邊 場所 및 旅舘

△ 各級 大學內

△ 其他 示威用品製作 및 保管容疑場所

※ 但, 敎會・聖堂 및 寺刹은 場內에 들어가지
않고 周邊에서 不審檢問强化로 事前發見 回收

<警 備 對 策>

○ 充分한 警察力으로 積極對處

總148個中隊 [서울旣存警察力 : 128個中隊
地方支援警察力 : 20個中隊

○ 明洞 行事場中心 群衆集結 拒否作戰 및
初場鎭壓

△ 有利한 地點에 3重先占配置 完全封鎖

△ 解散警告不應時 催淚彈發射 强制解散

12

0034

△ 國會議員 等 主要人物은 親切히 禮儀를

갖추어 101 作戰으로 歸家措置

○ 示威亂動 等 不法行爲時 初動鎭壓 强力解散

○ 情報 및 採證活動强化로 不法行爲主動者 嚴罰

○ 同時多發示威 및 偶發事態 對備徹底

△ 行事場·市街地·主要保護施設 同時對備

△ 主要脆弱個所에 機動打擊隊 運用

○ 協力鎭壓態勢 確立

△ 防犯員·巡視員 等 準警察力 最大動員
自體警備 强化

△ 消防車·韓電車·救急車·레카車 動員
前進配置

13

0035

5 . 關係部處　協調事項

○　外務部

　　△　外國公舘에　不法集會의　性格　等

　　　　事前說明

○　國防部

　　△　重要施設　軍配置　8個中隊　支援

　　△　올림픽施設　警備　9個中隊 → 軍兵力

　　　　으로　代替

○　文敎部

　　△　各大學　自體的으로　校內示威用品　收去

　　△　在京大學生　參席沮止策　講究

○　文公部

　　△　外信記者들에게　不法集會의　性格　等을

　　　　事前弘報

14

0036

△ 問題宗敎人 醇化 不參誘導

○ 民 正 黨

△ 黨代辯人 不法集會 非難聲明發表 等
　 事態進展에 따른 對應措置

15

0037

〈 別　　添 〉

「故 朴鍾哲君 國民追悼會 準備委員會」構成 名單

○　顧　　　問 (8 名)

金壽煥　池學淳　咸錫憲　尹攀熊　洪南淳　李敏雨

金大中　金泳三

○　共同代表 (29 名)

桂勳悌　金勝勳　申鉉奉　文正鉉　朴炯圭　白基琓

徐敬源　宋建鎬　李敦明　李小仙　李愚貞　李貞淑

趙南基　朴容吉　지 선　진 관　林基蘭　박영숙

李兌榮　高 銀　兪仁浩　明魯勤　張乙炳　高永根

金命潤　朴永祿　楊淳稙　崔炯佑　金鍾完

○　執行委員 (116 名)

金祥根　오인수　성유보　인재근　류동우　박병기

安承吉　黃明秀 등

○　準備委員

△　天主教　219 名　　　△　基督教　1,435 名

16

0038

△ 佛　教　173名　　　△ 民統聯　511名

△ 女性界　305名　　　△ 文　人　39名

△ 學　生1,332名　　　△ 拘束者家族615名

△ 政黨人2,665名

등　9,782名

0039

朴鍾哲事件　擴散企圖　關聯對策
（ 會議 資料 ）

1987 . 1 . 30.

ᄂ情報文化局長

黃揮曼

0040

目　　　　　次

0041

1. 槪　　況

○ 新韓黨과　民推協, 宗敎　및　在野　一部　問題圈에서는　朴鍾哲
　　事件을　契機로　2.7　「汎國民追悼大會」　等을　通해　國民的
　　關心을　誘導, 全國的인　糾彈雰圍氣　擴散을　企圖

○ 이는　旣存　搜査是非共同對策委(一名 : 共對委)가　主軸이
　　되어　새로　構成한　「朴鍾哲　國民追悼會　準備委」를　내세워
　　野圈을　網羅, 向後　改憲　및　總選政局에　至大한　惡影響을
　　미칠　것인　바　早期　鎭靜　對策　講究　必要

　　※ ╭共對委╮는　新韓黨·民推協　等　野圈에서　85.10
　　　金槿泰의　苛酷行爲　主張을　契機로　在野　結束을　위해
　　　組織한　汎野圈　團體임(組織現況　添附　#1　參照)

-1-

0042

2 . 關 聯 動 向

○ 1.24 朴燦鍾・金命潤 等이 記者會見 通해 金泳三・金大中・
      朴炯圭 等 28名을 發起人으로한 「故 朴鍾哲君 國民追悼會
      準備委員會」 發足을 公表(油印物 配布)

○ 1.26.16:00 基督教會舘 大講堂에서 「國民追悼會」發足式
      을 갖고자 企圖(沮止 霧散)

○ 1.27.10:10 民推協 事務室에서 金大中・金泳三・桂勳悌・
      宋建鎬 等 30餘名이 發足式을 兼해 內外信 記者會見
      갖고

      - 오는 2.7(土)을 朴鍾哲 國民追悼日로 定하고 同日
         14:00 明洞聖堂에서 國民追悼會를 開催할 것과

      - 國民追悼會 構成員(顧問:9名,共同代表:29名,
         執行委員:116名)과 準備委員 名單(1次 9,782名)
         및 8個項의 行動指針을 發表하는 한편

      - 一般 國民의 參加要領도 提示

-2-

＜準備委員 行動指針＞

　　o 各種 苛酷行爲事例 蒐集, 人權團體에 報告

　　o 搜査機關에 電話・書信 및 訪問 抗議

　　o 매스콤에 朴鍾哲事件 公正報道 促求

　　o 苛酷行爲 追放 爲한 討論・集會캠페인 展開

　　o 基金마련에 積極 同參 (1,000 원씩)

＜一般國民 參加要領＞

　　o 모든國民은 2. 7 14:00 追悼默念

　　o 검은色 또는 흰色 喪章 (리본) 佩用

　　o 自動車는 警笛을 울리고 모든教會・寺刹은 同時打鍾

　　※ 追悼會 構成員 및 準備委員名單 添附＃2, ＃3 參照

○ 한편 明洞聖堂에서는 1.26 18:00 金壽煥 樞機卿 執典으로

〃人權回復을 위한 미사〃를 開催 (1,800名 參席)

－ 金樞機卿은 講論을 通해 〃朴鍾哲의 死亡은 組織的인

殺人行爲〃라고 辛辣히 批判

－ 미사 終了後 흰祭禮服을 입은 神父 (100名)와 修女

(400名), 學生・信徒 等 1,000餘名은 1時間30分

동안 沈默示威로 抗議 表示 (各新聞 競爭的으로 報道)

－3－

0044

3 . 豫想展望과 問題點

　○　朴鍾哲 國民追悼會準備委 結成 等 〃共對委〃 活動을 實際
　　　背後에서 操縱하고 同調하는 人物은 金大中과 在野 追從
　　　勢力들인바

　　　※　李敏雨,金泳三側은 朴鍾哲 事件이 黨이미지 回復의 好機
　　　　　로 보고 對政府 對與黨 攻勢를 強化하고 있으나 基本的
　　　　　으로는 制度圈 안에서의 對與戰略을 摸索하고 있는만큼
　　　　　民衆革命으로 몰고 가려는 露骨的인 對國民 宣傳煽動
　　　　　行爲는 內心 不願하는 立場

　　　-　이는 朴鍾哲 事件이 非政治的 이슈로서 在野와 結束할
　　　　　수 있는 좋은 機會가 될 수 있다는 점에서

　　　-　차제에 過去의 苛酷行爲 是非事件을 모두 旣定事實化
　　　　　하여 對政府 不信을 擴散시키고

　　　-　窮極的으로는 改憲政局을 破局으로 몰고가는 한편 , 在野
　　　　　勢力과의 連帶活動을 通하여 支持 基盤을 擴充해
　　　　　나가려는 政治的 布石인 것으로 分析

-4-　　　　　　　　　　　　0045

○ 따라서 이들은

- 朴鍾哲 事件을 長期化하여 對政府 不信을 擴散시키는 한편,
  新學期 學園街에 불씨를 던져주고자

- 서울大會(2.7 明洞聖堂)를 마친後 各 市·道別로 追悼
  委員會를 結成, 地方大會를 開催함으로써 非暴力 市民抵抗
  運動으로 擴散시킬 計劃

- 特히 新學期 朴鍾哲 49齋(3.3)를 前後하여 大規模
  糾彈 群衆集會 等을 劃策할 可能性도 不無

- 또한 宗敎勢力의 呼應을 誘導하고자 大會場所를 聖堂·敎會
  로 擇하여 마치 宗敎全體의 支持를 받는 것으로 歪曲宣傳

※ 追悼大會를 2.7 明洞聖堂으로 定한 것도

- 이미 NCC側에서 2.8(日) 全國 傘下 敎會(現況 添附
  ♯4 參照)로 하여금 追慕禮拜를 갖도록 示達한 것과
  無關하지 않으며

- 場所 使用과 關聯 事前 諒解가 없었던 것으로 判斷(1.27
  金秉壽 明洞聖堂 主任神父를 接觸하였던바 場所 貸與 不許
  意思表明)

0046

-5-

4 . 基本 對處方案

① 1月末 (今週) 까지 全言論 擴大報道 止揚 및 쿨다운 誘導
(青瓦台 , 文公部 , 安企部)

○ 社說 , 論評 , 企劃報道 , 追跡 , 推理記事 等 一切 止揚

② 2月初에 局面 轉換 誘導 (青瓦台 , 文公部 , 安企部)

○ 國民 關心轉換 爲한 素材 開發
○ 金滿鐵 家族 脫出事件 等

③ 兩金 政治的 惡用事實 對國民 弘報 展開
(青瓦台 , 民正黨 , 外務部 , 文公部 , 安企部)

○ 國內 識者 , 輿論指導層
○ 特히 外國公舘 , 外信에 對應論理 開發 供給

④ 2.7 明洞聖堂 追悼大會 事前 對策講究
「 法務部 (檢察) , 內務部 (治安本部) , 文公部 , 安企部 」

○ 不法集會 事前 警告 醇化
○ 全面 遮斷 關聯 弘報論理 供給
○ 當日 治安 對策 講究 (自家遮斷 , 現場遮斷)

※ 現場 兵力 運用 計劃 樹立

-6-   0047

⑤ 來週初 全 市·道單位 地域對策協議會 開催
（ 內務部, 安企部, 警察 ）

　　○ 教會 不純集會 및 打鍾, 警笛
　　○ 學生 騷擾企圖 等 2.7 豫防對策 講究

⑥ 民心 刺戟要因 事前 發掘 早期 解消策 講究
（ 靑瓦台, 民正黨, 各 部處 ）

顧 問（9名）
李敏雨, 金泳三 金大中, 池學淳 洪南淳, 咸錫憲 金在俊, 尹㦲熊 文益煥

共 同 議 長 （14名）
崔炯佑, 楊淳稙, 朴永祿, 金命潤 白基琓, 金勝勳, 朴炯圭, 趙南基 宋建浩, 徐敬元, 李小仙, 李愚貞 李貞淑, 桂勳梯

會 員：260名

對 策 委 員 （241名）

- ○ 新韓黨（51名）：金東英, 金漢洙, 睦堯相, 朴燦鍾, 李宅敦 等
- ○ 民推協（50名）：金昌槿, 朴鍾泰, 尹奕杓, 金相賢, 金允植 等
- ○ 改新敎（33名）：金東完, 琴栄均, 高永根, 金祥根, 朴鍾基 等
- ○ 天主敎（24名）：金秉相, 文正鉉, 鄭鎬庚, 咸世雄, 黃相根 等
- ○ 仏 敎（10名）：境牛, 木牛, 碧牛, 玄基, 真寬 等
- ○ 在野圈（61名）：李敦明, 林采正, 郭泰栄, 李在五, 李昌馥 等
- ○ 拘束者家族（12名）：印在謹, 김영희, 崔貞順, 金春玉 等

所 在 地	非 常 設
沿 革	o 85.10.17 民靑聯 前議長 金槿泰 拷問 主張說 契機 民推協·民統聯 等 在野 10個團体 10人 実務小委 構成 o 85.11. 4 記者會見 通해 同機構 結成 發表

0049

 # 2　朴鍾哲　國民追悼會　準備委　構成員（ 154名 ）　名單

區　分	名　　　　　　　　　　單
顧　問 （ 9名 ）	金在俊 , 咸錫憲 , 尹攀熊 , 洪南淳 , 李敏雨 , 金壽煥 , 池學淳 , 金大中 , 金泳三
共同代表 （ 29名 ）	桂勳悌 , 金命潤 , 金勝勳 , 文正鉉 , 申鉉奉 , 朴永祿 , 朴炯圭 , 白基琓 , 서경원 , 宋建鎬 , 楊淳稙 , 李敦明 , 李小仙 , 李愚貞 , 이정숙 , 趙南基 , 崔炯佑 , 朴容吉 , 지 선 , 眞 寬 , 임기란 , 박영숙 , 李兌榮 , 高 銀 , 兪仁浩 , 明魯勤 , 張乙炳 , 金鍾完 , 高永根
執行委員 （ 116名 ）	金祥根 , 호인수 , 成裕普 , 黃明秀 , 柳濟然 , 印在謹 , 趙和順 , 류동우 , 정성헌 , 성 연 , 조병립 , 조준희 , 吳泰淳 , 安忠錫 , 朴炳基 , 朴昌信 , 鄭亨達 , 柳康夏 , 鄭鎬庚 , 安承吉 , 南才熙 , 金順浩 , 金煐式 , 吳忠一 , 崔聲默 , 姜信錫 , 李千洙 , 박영보 , 元亨洙 , 趙承赫 , 朴鍾基 , 高恒圭 , 印名鎭 , 朴德信 , 趙英來 , 이경석 , 柳淵昌 , 方鏞錫 , 李明俊 , 尹順汝 , 李吉載 , 김재규 , 이영진 , 윤기현 , 정상오 , 高光振 , 黃善鎭 , 奇 春 , 安永根 , 李至篇 , 金炳午 , 채영석 , 具玆鎬 , 元聖熙 , 崔鍾泰 , 朴龍來 , 김정웅 , 김지현 , 朴準喆 , 權亨澤 , 黃寅成 , 김영자 , 정광운 , 하연오 , 이명희 , 안순봉 , 김성순 , 정관수 , 최병욱 , 김상덕 , 정현찬 , 이정영 , 유병권 , 배용진 , 서정용 , 李總角 , 조경수 , 이태회 , 鄭明子 , 韓明姬 , 이영식 , 이형곤 , 정용식 , 김순희 , 김종성 , 許淑寧 , 이미경 , 윤영애 , 진 선 , 金希宣 , 손은하 , 木 愚 , 장 적 , 眞 常 , 해 조 , 황인민 , 김은숙 , 장병기 , 이 영 , 金炳傑 , 金圭東 , 李浩哲 , 千勝世 , 金正煥 , 蔡光錫 , 洪性宇 , 黃寅喆 , 고영구 , 姜信玉 , 金春玉 , 姜玉洙 , 李貞子 , 李信子 , 柳時春 , 김월금 , 이제학

0050

♯3

朴鍾哲 國民追悼會 準備委員(1 次名單 9,782名)

區 分	人 員	名　　　　　　單
政 治 人	2,665 名	李敏雨 , 金大中 , 金泳三　等
天 主 教	219 名	金勝勳 , 咸世雄　等　神父 , 修道士 , 修女
改 新 教	1,485 名	朴炯圭 , 趙南基 , 趙容述　等
佛 教	173 名	지 선 , 眞 觀 , 性 然　等
民 統 聯	511 名	姜希南 , 文益煥 , 桂勳悌　等
勞動貧民	579 名	方鏞錫 , 柳東佑 , 尹順汝　等
農 民	502 名	徐敬元 , 金英源 , 裵宗烈　等
女 性	305 名	李愚貞 , 朴英淑 , 李兌榮　等
法 曹 界	8 名	洪南淳 , 李敦明　等
學 界	4 名	兪仁浩 , 張乙炳 , 明魯勤 , 安炳茂　等
文 人	39 名	李浩哲 , 高 銀　等
靑 年	1,265 名	崔仁圭 , 朴準喆　等
學 生	1,382 名	이제학 , 조병립　等
拘束者家族	615 名	朴容吉 , 金春玉 , 李貞淑　等
市 民	32 名	박종찬　等

0051

4

全國 聖堂 및 教會現況

가. 天 主 敎

聖	堂	敎	職	者	
本 堂	公 所	神 父	修 士	修 女	計
659	1,701	1,057 (213)	261 (45)	3,472 (150)	4,790 (408)
	2,360個				

( )안은 外國人

나. 改 新 敎

區 分	敎 團	敎 會 數	敎 職 者	敎職者 構成比(%)
計	69	26,044	40,717	100
NCC 系	6	7,790	10,997	27.0
非NCC系	63	18,254	29,720	73.0

0052

비극적인 拷問事件
[再發防止노력 환영
美國務省 논평]

【워싱턴=金鎭文특파원】美
國務省은 20일 · 韓國경찰의
朴鍾哲군 拷問致死사건에관
해「우리는 이같은 비극적인
사건이 · 다시는 되풀이되지
않을것을」확고히 하되對한
국民의 … 의 노력을 환영
한다」고 말했다.

國務省은 또 「우리는 지
난秋에 韓국것처럼 … 의사
용을 규탄한다」고 말하면서
이의 경우… 責任있는자에대
한이의 … 엄격한 임자에대한 처벌
실시하기를 희망하는것과같대
하겠다」고, 嚴格한 罰의… 보
여줬다」고 말했다. 國務
부

성원 이 이 희생자의 「가족」에
게 위로의 뜻을 전했다.

朴鍾哲事件 관련 美国務省 論評

87.1.21

> 美國務省은 1.20 朴鍾哲事件 관련 我國政府의 措置를 歡迎하는 論評을 하였는 바, 要旨 아래 報告드립니다.

論評 要旨

o 美國은 今番과 같은 悲劇的 事件의 再發을 防止코자 하는 全斗煥 大統領의 確固한 努力을 歡迎함.

o 拷問은 慨歎할 일이나, 韓國 關係當局이 同 事件의 調査와 關聯者 處罰에 徹底를 기하려는 훌륭한 決意를 보여 주었음.

o 全斗煥 大統領은 이러한 關係當局의 努力을 明白하고도 確固하게 支持하였음.

o 犧牲者 家族에 弔意를 표함.

政務 1 (外交) 報告

0054

공 란

報 告 事 項

198 7. 1 . 31.

情報文化局　弘報文化課

題　目 : 박종철군 추도식

(要　約)

　소위 그 박종철군 국민추도회 준비위원회는 2.7. 서울 명동 성당에서의
박군 추도식 및 관련 행사를 계획중인 바, 동 추도식의 성격 및 동 추도식
에 대한 정부 대책에 관하여 아래와 같이 주한 주요 외국 공관에 브리핑을
실시 할 예정임을 보고합니다.

---

1. 일　시 : '87.2.5.(목) 하오

2. 장　소 : 해당지역 국장실

3. 브리핑 실시자 : 아주지역 : 아주국장

　　　　　　　　　미주지역 : 미주국 심의관 (미주국장 출장중)

　　　　　　　　　구주지역 : 아프리카국장 (구주국장 출장중)

4. 브리핑 대상 주요 공관명

　아주지역 (3개국) 일본, 호주 New zealand

　미주지역 (4개국) 미국, 카나다, 멕시코, 콜롬비아, ~~아르간아~~

　구주지역 (13개국) 영국, 불란서, 독일, 이태리, 벨지움, 그리스,

　　　　　　　　　　화란, 스페인, 덴마크, 오지리, 노르웨이, 핀란드,

　　　　　　　　　　스웨덴

5. 브리핑 내용 : 2.7. 박종철 추도식에 따른 대책(안) 내용

6. 기 타

　- 가능한 같은 시간에 각국 대사를 당부로 초치 설명 예정　　　　끝.

供覽	擔當	課長	局長	次官補	次官	長官
		Mg				

0056

공　　　　란

공   란

공   란

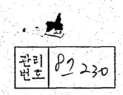

외 무 부

착신전문

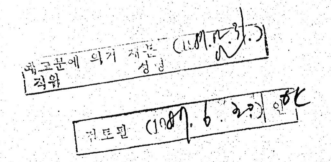

번 호 : USW-0459   일 시 : 702021639   종 별 : 긴급

수 신 : 장관(미북)

발 신 : 주미대사

제 목 : 인권차관보 면담

본직은 국무성의 긴급 요청으로 오는 2.4(수) 오전에 국무성 SHIFTER 인권담당

차관보와 최근 국내 인권상황관련 면담케 되어 있는바, 특별지시사항 있으면 회시바

람.

(대사 김경원-차관)

예고문: 1987.12.31. 일반

예고문에 의거 재분류 (1987.12.31.)

적 위   성 정

검토필 (1987. 6. 2)

미주국   1차보   청와대   안 기

87.02.03 10:06
외신 2과 통제관

0060

<table>
<tr><td>관리
번호</td><td>87
-231</td></tr>
</table>

발 신 전 보

번 호: WUS-0491 일 시: 20203 1830 전보종별: 지급

수 신: 주   미   대사·총영사

발 신: 장   관   (미북)

제 목: 인권차관보·면담

　　　　　　대 : USW - 0459

　　1. 대호·국무성 인권담당 차관보 면담시 명동 불법집회 (2.7)와 관련 별첨을 참고하여 아측 입장을 적절히 설명하기 바람.

　　2. 법무부장관은 2.5 (목) 담화문을 발표할 예정인 바 국민에 대한 사과와 가혹행위 근절을 위한 정부의 의지 및 명동 집회 관련 위법행위에 대한 엄중 대처 방침등이 포함 될 것임을 참고 바람.

　　　　　　　　　　　　(미주국장 대리 조기성)

첨 부 : 명동 불법집회 관련 설명자료

대표분에 의거 재분류 (19
해 위   예 고   성 명987· 12· 316 일반

검토필 (19   87 6 27 인

정보화과장

<table>
<tr><td rowspan="3">양
고
재</td><td>87
년
월
일</td><td>북
미
과</td><td>기안자</td><td>과 장</td><td></td><td>국 장</td><td>1차관보</td><td>차 관</td><td>장 관</td><td colspan="3">발신시간 :</td></tr>
<tr><td></td><td></td><td rowspan="2">조</td><td rowspan="2"></td><td></td><td rowspan="2"></td><td></td><td></td><td rowspan="2"></td><td rowspan="2">외
신
과</td><td>접수자</td><td>과 장</td></tr>
<tr><td></td><td></td><td></td><td></td><td></td><td></td><td></td></tr>
</table>

0061

명동 불법집회 관련 설명자료

o 정부는 박종철 사건 관련 대통령 각하의 유감표시와 내무장관, 치안
  본부장등 관계자 인책 및 관련자 구속은 물론 고문근절을 위한 대책위
  구성등 실질적 개선책 마련을 위해 제반 조치를 취하고 있음.
  - 대통령각하의 인권보호 특별기구 설치 검토지시 (1.21)
  - 민정당 인권기구 설치 (2.2)
  - 경찰 쇄신책 수립발표 (2.3)
  - 정부 인권기구의 기능 및 구성원칙 발표 (2.4)

o 2.7 예정된 소위 "고 박군 국민추도회"는 민통련, 민추협등
  반정부 단체와 급진좌경 학생, 구속자 가족, 문제 종교인, 해직
  근로자 및 일부 야당 국회의원등 반정부 세력이 모두 가담한 집회
  로서 단순히 고인의 명복을 비는 추도집회가 아니라 정치적 목적을
  가진 불법 옥외 집회로서 금번사건을 자신들의 정권야욕 달성을 위한
  기회로 활용, 대규모 군중집회를 통해 민심을 자극, 국민을 반정부
  적으로 몰아 궁극적으로 폭력에 의한 민중봉기로 연결시키려 하고
  있음.

o 금번 명동 집회는 민추협등 상습적인 반정부 활동 주동 재야 문제권이
  종교세력의 호응을 유도하고 종교계 전체의 지지를 받는 것으로 왜곡
  선전하기 위해 천주교측과 사전 협의없이 일방적으로 명동성당을 집회
  장소로 선정하였음.

0062

○ 준비위원 22,064명과 10만명 이상의 대규모 군중 동원 계획(명동 성당
   최대 수용 인원 2,200명), 모든 국민들에게 검은색 리본 및 흰색 상장
   폐용, 자동차 경적, 교회, 사찰의 타종등을 권유하는 점에서 순수
   추도회라기 보다는 정치목적의 대규모 군중집회로서 극도의 사회적
   불안을 야기할 우려가 명백하여 그 불법성이 명약관화 함.
   더욱이 집회 전후의 가두시위로 5.3. 인천 소요사태등에서 나타난
   화염병 부척, 공공기물 파괴, 건물 점거 방화, 인명 피해등 폭력
   난동사태로 발전될 가능성이 농후함.

○ 정부는 순수한 종교집회 및 추도회 성격의 집회는 계속 허용해 왔고
   앞으로도 허용할 것이나, 금번 집회처럼 민중선동과 사회불안을 야기
   하려는 종교행사를 위장한 불순 정치집회는 북괴와 대치하고 있는
   안보상의 특수한 여건과 국민의 생명과 재산 및 순수한 종고활동을
   보호한다는 예방적 차원에서 법에 의해 엄정히 다스려 져야 할 것임.

○ 정부, 여당은 민주적 헌정질서의 유지를 통해 88년 평화적 정부 이양을
   달성하고 나아가 올림픽의 성공적 개최를 이룩하는데 최선을 다하고
   있는 바 이를 위해서는 무엇보다 정치적, 사회적 안정이 중요한 것임.

○ 따라서 정부는 동 집회가 당국의 허가를 받지 않은 욱의 집회이며
   "현저히 사회적 불안을 야기시킬 우려가 있는 집회 이므로"집 시 법 "
   제 3조 1항등 관련 법규에 의거 동 집회를 강력 저지할 예정임.

0063

長官님報告事項

1987. 2. 3.

美洲局 北美課

題 目 : 명동 불법집회 관련 조치결과 보고

概 要

04 1330

o 북미과장은 금 2.3(화) 오전, Dunlop 주한미 정무참사관에게 명동 불법집회
관련 아측입장을 설명하고 Talking Point 수교
(동내용을 2.3 오후 Miller 1등서기관에게도 구두로 설명)

o 주미대사와 미국무성 인권차관보와의 면담시 (2.4 예정) 명동집회의 불법적
성격 및 정부의 입장을 설명토록 2.3 상세 지침 하달

駐韓美大使舘 反應

o 아측의 사전 설명에 감사하며 어떤 경우에도 폭력사태가 발생하지 않기를
희망

0064

박종철사건

면 담 요 록

1. 면담일시 : 1987. 2. 3. 12:30-14:00

2. 면담장소 : 라칸티나 (오찬)

3. 면 담 자 : 아 측 : 북미과장

　　　　　　　　　　　박인국 북미과 사무관

　　　　　　　미 측 : 피어스 1등서기관

　　　　　　　　　　　밀러 1등서기관

4. 면담내용 :

　(비자 관계)

아 측 : ○ 지난번에도 언급한 바 있는데 최근 미국대사관 비자
　　　　　신청과 관련된 민원이 급증하고 있음. 상용비자도
　　　　　보통 비자신청후 2주간이 걸린다고 하며 거부되는
　　　　　경우도 많다고 함. 또한 비자신청서를 접수시키기
　　　　　위하여 대사관 밖의 인도에 까지 길게 줄을서서
　　　　　기다리는 것을 보았음.

　　　　○ 영사과는 컴퓨터 고장이라고 하면서 국무성에 지원을
　　　　　요청했으나 우선순위가 낮아 아직 충분한 지원을 받지
　　　　　못하고 있다 함.

(명동 추도 집회)

아 측 :　ㅇ 금일 던롭 참사관에게도 Talking point 를 전달하고
　　　　　설명한 바와 같이 정부로서는 법질서 유지가 최대의
　　　　　중요 과제임.

　　　　ㅇ 평화적 실내 집회까지 막을려는 것은 아니나 재야 및
　　　　　야당이 계획하는 집회는 그런것이 아님.　　2만여명
　　　　　이상을 좁은 명동에 운집 시키려는 정치적 목적이
　　　　　있는 바 이는 십중팔구 인천사태와 비슷한 소요가
　　　　　예상되기 때문에 부득이 저지하려는 것임.

　　　　ㅇ 서울에서 인천소요와 같은 무질서와 방화가 발생한다면
　　　　　여야 모두 불행한 사태가 불가피하게 전개 될 것임.
　　　　　국가가 존재해야만 정치가 있는것이지 국가없는 정치도
　　　　　인권도 있을수 없음.　　　우리는 아직 월남을 잘
　　　　　기억함.

　　　　ㅇ 많은 미국인은 한국의 실정을 잘모르고 무조건 인권
　　　　　또는 민주화 운운하고 있으며 북한을 동구의 어느 한
　　　　　공산권과 비슷하게 생각하고 있는 것같음.

미 측 :　한국정부 여당의 입장과 고충을 잘 이해하고 있음.
　　　　88년 평화적 정부이양 보다 중요한 것은 없음.

0066

면 담 요 록

면담일시 : 1987.2.3(화) 11:00-11:30

장   소 : 북미과

면 담 자 : 아측 : 유명환 북미과장

김원수 북미과 사무관

미측 : Thomas Dunlop 주한미 정무참사관

Dennis Droney 주한미 3등서기관

면담내용 :

 북한의 대화관련 제의

Dunlop : 램버슨 공사가 박수길 차관보에게도 설명한 바 있지만,
워싱턴은 최근의 북한 제의를 의미있다고 (significant)
보고 있음을 다시한번 이야기해 두고자 함. 물론 한국의
입장은 설명들어 잘 알고 있으나 국무성의 지시가 있기
때문에 전달하는 바임.

 슐츠장관 방한

(일정주선)

Dunlop : ○ 슐츠장관 방한 관련 다음과 같이 일정 주선을 희망함.

3.6(금) 10:00 서울공항 (K-16) 도착

(상해발 특별기편)

10:45 의무장관 희담

11:30 청와대 예방

0067

o 슐츠장관의 여행에는 통상 30-40명의 대규모 기자단이
수행하는 바, 상기 기자회견은 특히 한국 기자들에게
슐츠장관과 만날 기회를 주기 위한 것임.

(통역배석 문제)

Dunlop : o 슐츠 장관은 외국여행시 반드시 통역을 모든 회담에
배석시키고 있음.

o 외무장관 회담시에는 필요없을 것으로 생각하나,
청와대 예방 및 오찬시에는 통역의 배석이 필요할
것인 바, 협조를 부탁함.
- 물론 배석하더라도 작년과 마찬가지로 실제
통역은 하지 않고, 슐츠장관 옆에서 슐츠장관만을
도와주게 될 것임.

북미과장 : 관계부서와 협의후 결과를 알려 주겠음.

③ 명동 불법 집회(2.7) 관련

북미과장 : o 정부는 박종철 사건 관련 유감표시와 관계자 인책
및 관련자 구속은 물론 고문근절을 위한 대책위
구성등 실질적 개선책 마련을 위해 제반 조치를
취하고 있음.

0068

o 2.7 예정된 소위 "고 박군 국민추도회"는 민통련,
   민추협등 문제 반정부 단체와 급진좌경 학생,
   구속자 가족, 문제 종교인, 해직근로자 및 일부
   야당 국회의원등 반정부 세력이 모두 가담한 집회
   로서 단순히 고인의 명복을 비는 추도집회가 아니라
   정치적 목적을 가진 불법 옥의 집회임.

o 국민의 생명과 재산을 보호하고 법질서 유지의
   책임을 지고 있는 정부 입장에서 볼때 동 집회는
   86.5.3 인천 소요사태와 유사한 성격으로 현저히
   사회적 불안과 공공의 안녕질서를 해칠 우려가
   있다고 판단되고 있음.   특히 집회장소인 명동성당은
   수용인원이 2,000명에 불과하고 서울수도의 번화가인
   명등에 위치하고 있기 때문에 다수의 군중이 운집할
   경우 모든 교통이 마비되고 불순세력이 건물점거,
   방화등 폭력난동사태를 야기시키기 쉬운 장소임.

o 정부.여당은 민주적 헌정질서의 유지를 통해 88년
   평화적 정부 이양을 달성하고 나아가 올림픽의
   성공적 개최를 이룩하는데 최선을 다하고 있는 바
   이를 위해서는 무엇보다 정치적, 사회적 안정이
   중요한 것임.

- 5 -

0069

ㅇ 따라서 정부는 법 질서의 차원에서 동 집회가 당국의
　허가를 받지 않은 옥외집회인 점등을 감안 "집시법"
　3조 1항등 관련법규에 의거 동 집회를 강력 저지할
　방침임.

Dunlop : 귀측의 사전 설명에 감사하며 어떤 경우에도 폭력사태가
　발생하지 않기를 희망함.　　　　　끝.

예고 : 1987.12.31. 일반.

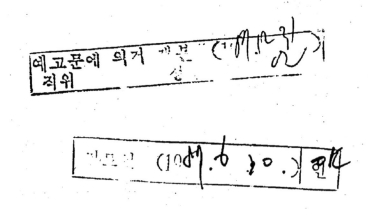

외 무 부   착신전보

번 호 : USW-0488   일 시 : 70203 1646   종 별 : 지급

수 신 : 장 관(미북,해기)

발 신 : 주 미 대사

제 목 : 명동 불법집회 관련 국무성 논평

국무성 한국과는 금 2.3(화) 명동 불법집회와 관련 아래와같이 PRESS GUIDANCE 를
준비하였으나 금일정오 브리핑시는 기자질의가 없어 사용되지않았다함.
그러나 금일 오후 동아태국으로 동건 관련 기자들의 논평요구가 있어 동 GUIDANCE
에 따라 알려주었다함.

아 래

질의 : DO YOU HAVE ANY COMMENTS ON THE KOREAN GOVERNMENT'S DECLARING THE OPPOSIT
ION RALLY FOR FEB,7 ILLEGAL ?

답변 : WE HAVE SEEN PRESS REPORTS OF A STATEMENT BY CHUNGHO YONG, THE NEW MINIST
ER OF INTERIOR ON THIS. WE CONSIDER IT THE DUTY OF A GOVERNMENT TO PROTECT NOT O
NLY THE SECURITY OF ITS CITIZENS,BUT ALSO THEIR RIGHTS TO PEACEABLE ASSEMBLY.

(대사 김경원)

미주국   차관실   1 차보   문공부   정문국   청와대   안 기

PAGE 1   87.02.04 07:47
                                                 외신 1과 통제관

                                             0071

長 官 님 報 告 事 項 不報告

1987. 2. 6.

美洲局　北美課

題 目 ： 명동 불법집회관련 조치결과 보고

| 概　要 |

o　북미과장은 87.2.5(목) 16:00 Sheppy 주한카나다 참사관을 면담,
　　박종철 추도회와 관련한 정부입장을 설명

| 駐韓 카나다 大使館 反應 |

o　성당내 추도회는 허용하는 점에서 작년 11월 신민당 서울 집회에
　　비해 금번 한국정부의 조치가 더 유연한 것으로 평가

o　박군의 가족이 불교신자로 불교식 추도회가 거행되었음에도 주최측이
　　천주교식 추도회를 계획하고 있는 점을 지적한 아측의 설명에 공감

o　카나다 시민 반응이 더욱 관심 돌때

0072

면 담 요 록
----

1. 일   시 :   1987. 2. 5. 16:00 - 16:30

2. 장   소 :   외무부 북미과

3. 면 담 자 :   아   측 : 유명환 북미과장

                           조백상 북미과 사무관

                카나다측 : Sheppy   주한 카나다 대사관 참사관

                           Gwozdeeky 주한 카나다 대사관 3등 서기관

4. 면담내용 :

    (명동집회 관련 정부입장 설명)

    북미과장 : ○   2.7로 예정된 박종철 추도회는 민통련, 민추협등

                   40여개의 불법단체 및 신민당등 반정부 세력이

                   모두 가담한 집회로서 단순히 고인의 명복을 비는

                   추도 집회가 아니라 반정부 과격단체에 의해

                   고무되어 추진되는 불법 옥외 집회임.

               ○   정부는 박종철 유가족, 종교인 및 신도등에

                   대해서는 명동성당 <s>수용인원(2,000 명) 범위 내에서</s>

                   성당내의 추도회는 허용할 방침이나, 문제는 준비

                   위원만 20,000 여명 인데다 주최측이 10만명 이상의

                   대중 동원계획을 세워놓고 있는데 서울 수도의

박종철 서울대생 고문치사 사건, 1987 **475**

번화가인 명동에서 다수군중이 운집할 경우 고통
마비 및 불순세력에 의한 건물점거, 방화등 5.3
인천사태와 유사한 폭력사태가 발생할 가능성이
매우 크다는 점임.
이러한 점을 감안, 정부는 금번 옥외 집회를 허용
하지 않을 방침임.

o 또한 박종철군의 가족은 불교도로서 불교식으로
이미 추도회가 거행된 바 있으나 주최측은 천주교를
움직여 명동성당에서 대규모 추도회를 계획하고
있는 점도 그들의 저의가 순수한 것이 아니란 것을
입증함.

Sheppy   : o 정부의 방침을 주최측에 통보하였는지 또한 그들이
참사관   이를 수락했는지 ?

북미과장   : o 통보 하였으나 그들이 이를 수락하지 않았음.

Sheppy   : o 경찰측과 주최측의 충돌이 예상되는데 쇼핑을
참사관   위한 외국인의 명동출입이 안전한지 또한 내
                   외신 기자의 추도회 취재는 가능한지 ?

북미과장   : o 순수한 쇼핑이나 취재 자체는 허용될 것으로 보나
                   소요가 발생할 경우 이들이 안전에 문제가 있을
                   가능성도 있어 우려됨.

0074

Sheppy
참사관
: o 지난해 11.29의 신민당 서울집회에 비해 성당내
추도회 자체는 허용하는 점에서 금번 한국정부의
조치가 더 유연한 (flexible)것으로 평가 됨.

o 박종철군의 가족이 불교신자로 이미 불교식으로
추도회가 거행 되었는데 천주교식 추도회를 주최
측이 계획하고 있는 점은 납득키 어려운 점이
있음.

o 카나다 시민의 안전에 관심을 가지고 있는 우리
로서는 외무부의 사전 설명에 감사를 표함.

0075

報　告　事　項

.　. 198 7 . 2 . 5 .

美洲局

題　　目 :　Zambrano 주한 콜롬비아 대사 면담

---(要　約)---

　조기성 미주국 심의관이 87.2.5(목) Zambrano 　주한
콜롬비아 대사를 면담(10:00-10:30), 박종철 추도 미사와 관련한
정부입장을 설명하였는 바, 동인의 반응을 아래와 같이 보고
드립니다.

1. Zambrano 　대사는 재야세력이 야당과 합세해서 추진예정인
   박종철 추도미사가 정치사회 불안요인이 되고 소요 사태로 발전할
   가능성이 있으므로, 한국정부의 우려와 대응조치는 이해한다고 말함.

2. 추도미사와 관련, 주한 미주 및 구주 외교단들은 대부분 카톨릭
   국가이므로 종교적 추도미사는 허용되어야 한다고 생각하고 있음.
   동 정부입장을 주한 로마교황 사절을 통해 외교단의 여론을 순화함이
   필요하다고 생각되어 suggest 함.

供覽	擔當	課長	審議官	局長	次官補	次官	長官

0076

報　告　事　項

198 7. 2. 5.

美洲局

題　　目 : Galan 주한 멕시코 대사 면담

(要 約)

조기성 미주국 심의관이 87.2.5(목) Galan 주한
멕시코 대사를 면담 (10:30-11:00)、박종철 추도 미사와 관련한
정부입장을 설명하였는 바、동인의 반응을 아래와 같이 보고드립니다.

---

1. 박종철의 추도미사는 <u>종교적으로는 허용되어야 한다고 언급함</u>.
   멕시코는 과거 카톨릭이 국교였으나、종교계의 정치 개입을
   막기위해 정치와 종교를 분리했다함.

2. 한국의 경우、<u>종교계와 야당이 박종철 미사를 정치적으로 이용하려고
   한다면、이를 저지하려는 한국정부의 입장은 정당하다고 생각함</u>.

3. 동 대사는 2.7. 명동성당 미사와 관련、참석자와 경찰간에 충돌이
   야기되지 않을지 우려를 표함.

供覽	擔 當	課 長	審議官	局 長	次官補	次 官	長 官

0077

외 무 부

착 신 전 보

번 호 : USW-0573   일 시 : 702061717   종 별

수 신 : 장관(미북)

발 신 : 주 미 대사

제 목 : 아마코스트 차관 면담

1.본직은 금 2.6.당지 방문중인 봉두완 국회 외무위원 장과함께 ARMACOST 국무성 정부차관을 면담한바, 동 차관은 명동성당 추도 집회 계획에 대한 정부의 입장을 문의함.

이에대해 본직은 대학생 사망사건과 관련하여 대통령각하께서 내무장관 해임조치, 유감표시,경찰책임자 처벌,향후 인권보호를 위한 제도적 장치등 즉각적이고도 명백한 시정조치를 취하였음에도 불구하고 재야세력이 추도식을 빙자하여 민중선동을 획책하는것은 순수한 의미에서 고인에 대한 추도 또는 인권보호에 대한 관심에서 나온 것이 아니라 동 사망사건을 악용하여 정치적,사회적 혼란을 조성하려는 저의로 밖에 볼수 없다고 설명하고 따라서 당국으로서는 이를 방치할수 없는 상황임을 강조함.

2.특히 본직은 금번 사건과 관련하여 공식 야당 지도층보다도 김대중,김 영삼등 재야세력이 더욱 과격한 태도로 나오고 있음을 볼때 이는 그간 수세에 몰려있던 반정부세력이 대학생 사망사건을 계기로 자신들의 입장을 공세화하여 봄에 예상되는 학생소요사태 까지 몰고가려는 책략임에 틀림없음을 지적 함.

본직은 이러한 상황하에서 정부가 명일의 군중데모 계획을 방치한다면 이는 무책임한 태도로밖에 볼수 없음을 강조함.

3.상기 본직의 설명에 대해 ARMACOST 차관은 이해를 표시하면서 대학생사망 사건 직후 한국 정부가 매우 적절한 조치를 취한 것으로 생각한다고 말함.

동 차관은 한국정부가 명일의 군중데모 계획을 기본적으로 봉쇄할수 밖에 없다는 본직의 설명에 이견을 제시하지 않았으나 명일의 추도식이 큰 문제없이 조용히 끝나기를 기대한다는 태도를 보임 (대사 김경원)

예고 : 87.12.31 일반   검토필 (1)87. 6 30.) 필

미주국   차관실   1차보   정문국   청와대   총리실   안 기

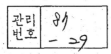

외 무 부

원 본

작전전문

번 호 : USW-0571   일 시 : 702061703   종 별 :

수 신 : 장관(미북)

발 신 : 주미대사

제 목 : 인권차관보 면담

대: WUS-0471

연: USW-459

1. 본직은 연호 국무성의 요청으로 금 2.6(금) 15:00 RICHARD SCHIFTER 인권차관

보와 면담하였음.

2. 먼저 SCHIFTER 차관보는 최근 고문 사건과 관련 아국정부의 조치 및 미국정

부의 입장에 대해 아래와같이 언급하였음.

가. 금번 사건에 대한 한국정부의 신속한 시정조치는 매우 고무적이었으며 이번일을

계기로 경찰의 수사방법등이 새로운 방향으로 발전될수 있기를 희망함.

나. 미국은 한국이 보다 발전된 국가로 성장하는가운데 최상의 한.미관계를 유지할수

있기를 희망하고 있는바 금번사건으로 한국이 국제적 손실을 가져온면도 없지않다는

점을 안타갑게 생각하고 있음.

다. 미국은 여사한 사건의 재발방지를 위한 한국 최고위층의 의지가 잘 실천될수 있

기를 희망하고있으며, 국무성측은 어떤형태로든 도움이 될수 있는 방안을 검토해 왔는

바, 하나의 방안으로 한.미 경찰당국간의 수사훈련을 위한 교류를 생각해 보았음.

3. 동 차관보는 동 경찰수사 교육 제의가 어디까지나 한국측의 의향을 물어보는데

그치는 비공식적인 제의라고 전제하면서 아래와같이 부연 설명하였음.

가. 과거 미국경찰도 현재 한국경찰이 가지고있는 수사방법상의 문제점을 가지고 있

었으며 지금도 완전히 해결된것은 아님.

나. 한국경찰간부가 단기간이나마 미국을 방문, 경찰제도 및 수사방법등을 수습 시찰

할경우 한국의 수사 방법개선에 도움이 될수도 있을것으로 봄.

- - - - - - - - - - - - - - - - - - - -

미주국   차관실   1 차보   정문국   청와대   총리실   안 기

PAGE 1

87.02.07 09:53
외신 2과 통제관

0079

박종철 서울대생 고문치사 사건, 1987 **481**

다. 한·미간에는 군사분야등 많은 분야에서 훈련교류가 있었음에 비추어 경찰훈련 교류를 가지는것이 이상하 지않을것이며, 실현된경우 이는 대외 공개되지않는 방법으로 이루어질수 있음.

라. 한국측에서 관심이 있을경우 국무성은 한국경찰 당국과 FBI 및 다른 국내 경찰당국과의 협조를 주선할 용의가 있음.

4. 이에대해 본직은 대호와같이 여사한 사건 재발방지를 위한 대통령각하의 확고한 의지 천명과 구체적이고 단호한 조치에 대해 설명하고, 경찰훈련 교류문제에 대해서는 본직의 일시귀국시 본국당국과 협의한후 알려주겠다고 하였음.

(대사 김경원).

예고: 88.12.31일반

外交擔當
金斗圭 秘書官

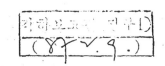

┌─ 韓·美兩国 警察当局間 交流 ─┐
└─ 國務省 人權擔當次官補 提議 ─┘

1987. 2. 9

┌──────────────────────────────────────┐
│ 美國務省 人權次官補는 2.6 駐美大使에게 朴鍾哲事件과 관련한 │
│ 我國 政府의 신속한 措置를 歡迎하면서 韓·美 兩國 警察當局間의 │
│ 交流를 提議하였는 바, 要旨 아래 報告드립니다. │
└──────────────────────────────────────┘

人權次官補 言及要旨

o 朴鍾哲事件에 대한 韓國政府의 신속한 措置는 매우 고무적
  이었으며 이를 契機로 警察의 搜査方法이 새로운 方向으로
  發展되기를 希望

o 再發防止를 위한 韓國 最高位層의 意志가 잘 實踐되기를 希望

o 美國務省은 韓國側의 努力에 도움이 될수 있는 方案을 檢討해
  왔는바, 하나의 方案으로서 "兩國 警察當局間 搜査訓練을
  위한 交流"를 생각해 보았음.

  - 韓國 警察幹部가 美國의 警察制度 및 搜査方法등을 訓練,
    視察할 境遇 搜査方法 改善에 도움이 될수 있을것임.

  - 韓·美間에는 過去 軍事등 여러분야에서 交流가 있었음에
    비추어, 警察分野 交流를 갖는 것이 이상한 일은
    아니며 實現 경우 非公開로 할수 있을 것임.

  - 韓國側이 關心 있을 경우 國務省은 美國關係當局의 協調를
    주선할 용의가 있음.

措置事項

o 駐美大使 歸國時 關係機關間 協議 豫定

┌─────────────────┐
│ 政務 1 (外交) 報告 │
└─────────────────┘
0081

外 務 部

번 호 : USW-0596   일 시 : 70209 1537   종 별 : 지급

수 신 : 장 관 (미북,해신) 사본: 김경원대사

발 신 : 주 미 대사대리

제 목 : 박종철군 추도집회-국무성 정오 브리핑

금 2.9(월) 국무성 정오브리핑시 박종철군 추도집회관련 논평요구가 있었는바, REDMAN 대변인은 아래와같이 답변함.

    아 래

Q: DO YOU HAVE ANYTHING ON THE RIOTS AND THE ARRESTS IN SEOUL AND OTHER SOUTH KOREAN CITIES OVER THE WEEKEND?

MR. REDMAN: NO, I DON'T.

(공사 한탁채)

미주국   차관실   1 차보   문공부   청와대   안 기   대 사

PAGE 1   87.02.10 09:39
                                           외신 1과 통제관

0082

人權問題와 우리의 覺悟

海外公報舘

〈 人權問題에 대한 敎訓的 契機 〉

　　우리의 경찰이 국민의 生命과 財産, 나아가 自由와 人權을 앞장서 보장하는 民主警察의 使命을 다하기 위해 지속적인 노력을 기울여 오던 터에 최근 左傾容共 嫌疑事件 수사와 관련하여 뜻밖의 사건이 일어난 것은 매우 유감스럽고 가슴아픈 일이었다.

　　서울대 朴鍾哲군 사건발생 닷새만인 1.19, 捜査 全貌를 발표하는 자리에서 강민창 前 치안본부장은 "경찰이 事件捜査를 할때는 어떠한 경우에도 피의자에 대한 폭행은 물론 苛酷行爲를 할 수 없도록 규정하고 있음에도 불구하고, 일부 수사관들의 지나친 職務意慾으로 인해 이러한 불상사가 발생한 것은 매우 유감된 일로서 全 警察은 깊이 반성하고 있다"라고 밝혔으며,

　　金宗鎬 前 내무부장관도 "公安事件을 수사하는 과정에서 불행한 사고가 일어난데 대해 국민 여러분 앞에 심심한 사과를 드리며 故人에 대하여 깊은 애도의 뜻을 표하고 불행을 당한 遺族 여러분께 깊은 謝罪와 아울러 慰勞의 말씀을 드린다"고 밝혔으며, 1.26 개회한 제132회 臨時國會 본회의와 소관상임위에서도 신임 鄭호용 내무장관과 李영창 치안본부장이 누누이 깊은 사과의 의사를 밝혔으며, 苛酷行爲 根絶을 위해 모든 努力을 경주할 것을 굳게 約束한 바 있다.

　　더구나 이 불의의 사건을 두고 國政의 最高責任者가 국민앞에 유감의 뜻을 표명하고 즉각 사건관계자에 대한 責任을 물은 것은 이번 사건과 관련하여 정부가 국민에 대해 취할 수 있는 最大의 謝過表示를 한 것으로 보아야 할 것이다.

-1-

0084

이처럼 이번 사건이 주는 충격과 상처는 너무나 큰 것이었다.
그러나 한편으로 이번 사건은 人權保護問題와 搜査公權力의 運用問題에 대한 새로운 반성과 앞으로 우리가 지향해 나아갈 방향을 제시해 주었다는 데서 비온뒤 땅이 더욱 굳게 다져지듯이 커다란 교훈적 계기가 될 수 있을 것이다.

〈 正直한 政府, 責任지는 政府 〉

이번 사건에 대한 各 政黨 및 一般輿論을 종합해 본다면

   1) 신속·철저한 眞相調査와 관련자의 엄중 문책
   2) 치안책임자 및 관계장관에 대한 정치·도의적 문책
   3) 정부당국의 對國民 謝過
   4) 인권보호를 위한 制度的 裝置 마련

등으로 집약되었다.

이번 사건에 대해 경찰 당국은 국민에게 사과와 더불어 그 경위를 신속·소상하게 발표하면서 關係搜査官 2명을 拘束하고, 그 次上級責任者 2명은 解任, 直上級者 2명을 懲戒하는 등 자신의 살을 도려내는 아픔을 스스로 감수하였다.

사건 발생후 경찰이 이처럼 빨리 또 이처럼 솔직하게 事件全貌를 밝히고 자기 과오를 시인한 것은 전례없는 일이었다. 또한 사건을 이첩받은 검찰은 警察의 未盡한 搜査部門을 엄정하게 조사하여, 警察側 發表의 相異部分을 있는 그대로 밝히고 관련수사관 2명을 구속기소하였다.

따라서 이번 발표를 바라보는 内外의 視角도 사건 자체의 심각성보다 事件收拾을 위한 努力에 더욱 더 초점이 모아지기도 했다.

-2-

더구나 사건경위의 早期發表에 이어 사건의 최종책임자라 할 수 있는 内務部長官과 治安本部長을 즉각 문책 해임하는 등 이번 사건에 임하는 政府의 意志가 얼마나 단호하며 反省의 態度가 얼마나 심각한 것인지를 확실하게 드러내 주었다.

　　이는 바로 〈正直한 政府〉〈責任지는 政府〉의 면모를 여실히 보여주었으며, 대통령의 統治理念과 民主發展意志를 실천적으로 구현한 자세라 할수 있다.

　　또한 이와 같은 정부의 조치가 일시적인 것에 그치지 않고, 장기적이고 종합적인 차원에서 人權保護對策을 수립하기 위하여 全大統領은 "국민의 人權을 보호하기 위한 特別機構"를 政府內에 상설할 것을 검토하도록 지시하였다.

　　아울러 민정당의 盧泰愚 代表委員도 1.22 年頭記者會見을 통해 朴鍾哲군 사건에 대해 심심한 유감의 뜻을 표시한 뒤 "捜査上의 苛酷行爲가 재발하는 것을 制度的으로 막기 위해 최선을 다하겠으며, 우리 黨이 국회에 제출한 改憲案에는 人權伸張에 관한 부분이 포함되어 있고 필요하다면 이 부분을 더욱 보완해 나가겠다"고 말하고, 野黨側도 人權伸張에 대한 좋은 방안이 있으면 國會 改憲特委에 제출해줄 것을 촉구했다.

　　이처럼 정부는 이번 사건의 刑事的·法的책임은 물론, 道義的·政治的 책임 등 모든 책임을 통감하고 앞으로의 改善方案 講究에 최선을 다하고 있다.

-3-

0086

이제 앞으로 구성될 〈人權保護特別機構〉는 사회 각계각층의 지도급인사가 참여하여 국민의 기본적 권리를 보호하고 선진민주를 지향하는 制度的 裝置로 그 기능을 다해 나갈 것이다.

이처럼 조속한 시일내에 野黨의 요구를 포함한 각계의 여론을 허심탄회하게 수렴한 것은 바로 正義社會의 具現을 제시한 第5共和國 國政指標를 행동으로 실천한 조치였으며, 그늘진 구석없이 완전한 정부를 이양하겠다는 全大統領의 솔직담백한 意志에 따른 것임은 두말할 나위가 없다.

〈 國家公權力은 尊重되어야 〉

피의자에 대한 調査·取調·審問 등은 범죄와 관련된 사실을 밝히기 위한 法節次 遂行에 반드시 필요한 과정이다. 또 관계법률의 테두리내에서 모든 可用한 方法으로 범죄의 진상을 밝히는 것은 警察의 任務이기도 하다.

이 경우, 본능적으로 자기를 보호하려는 被疑者와 公益을 보호하려는 수사관은 사실상 對立關係에 있는 것이 수사과정의 속성이라 하지 않을 수 없다.

특히 對共관계나 思想관계 피의자의 경우는 자기의 思想을 확신하고 자신의 범죄적 행위에 대한 倫理的 正當性을 신봉하는 경향이 강하기 때문에 공권력이 공익보호를 위해 필요로 하는 事實과 眞相의 糾明이 매우 어려운 것이 사실이다.

이러한 사실은 바로 公權力 執行의 限界와 애로이기도 하다. 외국의 경우 역시 이러한 사실은 마찬가지이다.

-4-

0087

그러나 분명한 것은 國家의 公權力이 국가안보 및 국민의 生命과 權利와 財産을 보호하는 마지막 보루이므로 반드시 존중되고 확립되어야 한다는 사실이다. 이것이 어떤 일부요인때문에 그 기반이 크게 동요될 경우 社會不安 狀況을 제어할 수가 없으며, 나아가 國家安保上 커다란 危機가 초래될 수 밖에 없다는 점을 결코 간과해서는 안된다.

더우기 우리나라는 南北의 分斷과 對峙라는 특수상황에 처해있는 만큼 그 어느나라보다도 公權力이 제대로 발휘될 수 있는 與件確立이 긴요한 것이다.

그러므로 國家公權力은 부당하게 남용되어서도 안되지만 그 누구에게 침해되어서도 안될 것이다. 그래서 정부 안에는 이에 대한 〈制度的 裝置〉가 마련되어 있을 뿐 아니라 國會와 言論이 주요한 監視者 역할을 하고 있다.

이를 위해 捜査要員의 자질향상과 捜査體系의 科學化와 高度化가 전제되어야 함은 두말할 필요조차 없다.

〈 捜査要員 士氣昂揚도 時急 〉

일선 수사요원들은 대부분 어려운 捜査與件과 薄俸에도 불구하고 오직 使命意識으로 고된 업무를 수행하고 있다. 특히 對共擔當 수사관들은 北傀工作員들의 테러 등 언제 어느때 닥칠지도 모를 신변의 위험을 무릅쓰고 불철주야 헌신 봉사하고 있다.

과거 對間諜作戰 수행중에 희생된 사람, 強·窃盗者를 검거하려다 목숨을 잃은 사람, 심지어는 暴力示威를 막다가 숨진사람 등 그 사례는 일일이 열거할 수 조차 없다.

-5-

이들도 엄연한 대한민국의 국민이자 시민이요 善良한 人間들이며, 오로지 國家와 國民을 위해 일하다가 희생된 사람들임을 잊어서는 안될 것이다. 즉,˙罪는 미워해도 사람은 미워하지 말라는 옛말은 이 시접에서 새로이 되새겨 볼만 하다.

이번에 뜻하지 않은 불상사를 가져왔던 對共關係 搜査官들 가운데는 오랫동안 이 분야에만 종사해온 베테랑이 있었는가 하면, 정년퇴직을 얼마 안남긴 無事故의 모범요원도 있었으며, 남의 뺨 한대 때릴줄 몰랐던 연약한 心性의 요원도 있었다.

또 이번 사건과 관련된 어떤 警察幹部는 "내 인생도 망쳤지만 무엇보다 國家에 누를 끼쳤다는 것이 견딜 수 없다"면서 "차라리 나를 총살시켜달라"고 몸부림을 치기도 했다. 이번 사건을 지켜본 다른 많은 對共搜査要員들은 국민의 지탄 앞에 謝罪하는 마음을 감추지 못하면서 "이제 앞으로 어떻게 빨갱이를 잡아들일 것인가"라고 한숨을 내쉬기도 했다.

그러나 대학가의 左傾意識 범람과 北傀의 對南心理戰 공세강화로 인해 우리 사회의 理念 葛藤은 점차 격심해지는 추세로서 대공수사요원들의 士氣昂揚이 무엇보다도 시급한게 우리의 현실이다.

< **政治的 惡用은 破局 自招** >

정부 당국이 輿論의 흐름을 좇아 가능한 모든 조치를 취했거나 확실한 改善努力을 보이고 있음에도 불구하고 일부 정치세력들은 이 사건을 政權鬪爭의 방편으로 이용하기 위해 政治問題化하여 그들에게 불리하게 전개되던 政局 局面을 뒤엎으려 획책하고 있다.

0089

또 野圈은 이번 사건을 계기로 집요하게 體制是非論을 벌여 궁극적으로 그들의 執權野慾을 채우기 위해 與論을 誤導하기 위한 불법적 책동을 기도하고 있다.

이와 관련하여 최근 사회일각의 朴군 추모행사에 편승하여 이를 대중봉기의 절호의 기회로 악용하려는 일부 정치세력의 企圖는 철저하게 경계되지 않으면 안될 것이다. 어떠한 종교적행사도 순수한 차원의 추모행사로 국한되어져야 할 것이며, 비합법적 정치투쟁의 場으로 이용되어서는 안된다.

특히 兩金 등 일부 정치세력이 진정한 인권신장을 위한 합법적 투쟁에 관심을 가지기보다는, 煽動과 暴力을 통한 극도의 불안고조의 소재로 이를 악용함으로써, 정치파국을 초래하여 궁극적으로 정권탈취의 야욕을 탐하려하는 것은, 국민생활 전체의 희생 위에 소수 특정 정치인만이 정치적 전리품을 독식하겠다는 이기적이고 독선적인 발상이 아닐 수 없다.

野圈이 이번 사건의 성격을 오판하여 이를 政略的으로 이용할 경우, 또다시 社會不安이 조성되고, 나아가 국민에게 크나큰 고통을 안겨주게 될 것이며, 이 사건과 관련한 不法的 煽動集會를 잇달아 열고 악의적인 유언비어를 유포하게 되면 자연 學生·在野를 더욱 자극, 결국은 과거의 예와 같은 위험한 騷擾事態를 초래할 것이 너무나 분명하다.

友邦 美國의 論評은 우리 정부의 신속·솔직한 사건발표와 후속조치에 대해 肯定的 反應을 보내왔으며, 日本 등의 外國 言論들도 이 사건에 대한 비판보다 이로 인한 우리 사회의 騷擾事態 내지 불안조장을 더 우려하고 있는 실정이다.

-7-

0090

騷擾事態가 발생되면 당장 국민의 생업을 파괴함은 물론 우리 경제에도 큰 악영향을 미쳐 安定과 發展을 해치게 될 것이다. 금년도 우리 경제는 선거철에 따른 물가오름세심리, 石油價 仰騰조짐, 선진국의 개방요구 및 保護貿易主義 강화로 인해 상당한 어려움에 부딪치게 될 것으로 전망된다.

만일 다시 物價上昇率이 80년초와 같이 30~40%로 치솟게 되면, 국민 대다수인 俸給生活者는 생활의 안정을 잃고 엄청난 곤란을 당하게 될 것은 자명한 일이다.

따라서 野圈의 사회불안 조장은 결과적으로 全體 國民을 拷問하는 격이 된다고 하겠다. 이는 어떤 일이 있어도 安定만은 유지되기를 갈망하고 있는 대다수 국민의 염원과 소망을 무참히 짓밟는 처사라 하지 않을 수 없다.

또한 이 사건의 政略的 利用과 사회혼란 획책은 차츰 소멸되어가고 있는 左傾·容共勢力들이 다시 발호하는 기회를 제공해 주는 셈이 될 것이다. 비록 뜻하지 않은 불상사가 있었다고해도 이를 이유로 우리의 自由民主主義 體制를 顚覆하려는 좌경·용공세력의 부추김에 편승하는 행위는 결국 누구를 利롭게 할 것인지 깊이 생각해야만 한다.

모든 국민들은 이처럼 明若觀火한 事態惡化를 사전에 직시, 스스로 경계하고 인내하는 슬기를 발휘해야 할 것이다.

〈 지금은 民主發展에 더 盡力해야 할 때 〉

지금 우리 앞에는 合意改憲 및 單任制 實現과 평화적 정부이양, 지속적인 경제발전, 그리고 '88 서울올림픽의 성공적 개최 등 民族史의 進運을 가름할 국가적 과제가 산적해 있다. 특히 합의 개헌으로부터 平和的 政府移讓으로까지 이어지는 민주정치의 발전은 가장 긴요한 과제이자 오랜 국민적 염원이다.

이러한 큰 과제들을 앞에 놓고 지나간 아픈 상처를 계속해서 헤집고, 시종일관 과열된 시비논쟁에만 집착한다는 것은 國論分裂을 惹起하고, 民主政治 發展까지 저해할 우려가 있다.
오히려 이러한 진통과 시련은 民主道程을 더욱 크게 열어갈 수 있는 轉禍爲福의 계기로 삼아져야 할 것이다.

이제 우리는 이번 사건을 계기로 우리의 人權問題를 더욱 개선하려는 國民的 覺悟를 다지고 우리 앞에 놓여있는 國家大事를 수행하는데 全國民的 力量을 投入하는 슬기로운 자세를 보여야 한다.

아울러 국민 모두는 냉철한 理性을 바탕으로 조속히 상처를 치유하면서 우리가 직면한 左傾容共勢力의 위험성을 망각하지 말고 그에 대해 능동적으로 대처하는 한편, 민주정치의 발전과정을 순리적으로 풀어나가야 하겠다.

이렇게 된다면 산적한 國家的 課題가 성공적으로 완수된 가운데 先進圈으로 進入하게됨은 물론 국민생활도 더욱 안정되고 윤택해질 것이다.

-9-

0092

The Human Rights Issue in Korea

and

Our Determination to Resolve It

KOREAN OVERSEAS INFORMATION SERVICE

An Object Lesson

It is most unfortunate and regrettable that,
during the course of a recent police investigation
into suspected pro-Communist activities, a student
died from police brutality. This shocking development
occurred even though the police have been making
steadfast efforts to faithfully perform their duties
as a democratic law-enforcement organization to
safeguard the lives, property, freedom and rights of
citizens.

On January 19, the police made public the result
of their investigation into the tragic death of Pak
Chong-ch'ŏl, a student of Seoul National University,
which occurred five days earlier. In making the
announcement, Kang Min-ch'ang, then director of the
National Police, said, "The laws and regulations
strictly prohibit police officers from resorting to
any act of cruelty, including beating, in investigating
suspects. It is truly regrettable that this tragedy
occurred owing to the excessive zeal of some police
officers to accomplish their assignments. The entire
police are deeply reflecting upon this."

Kim Chong-hoh, then minister of home affairs,
said, "I profoundly repent before the public for this
unfortunate development which occurred in the course
of investigation into breaches of public security.
I also express my heartfelt repentance and condolence
to the bereaved family." At the 132nd extraordinary
session of the National Assembly which was convened

-11-

0004

on January 16 and at the meetings of the standing
Assembly committees, the newly appointed home minister,
Chong Ho-yong, and the newly-named director of the
National Police, Lee Young-chang, both repeatedly
expressed their regrets over the affair as well as
their firm pledges to stamp out police brutality.

Furthermore, President Chun Doo Hwan also publicly
expressed regret over the tragedy and swiftly effected
personnel changes to put the political and ethical
blame where it is due. The government has thus offered
its utmost repentance to the nation.

The death of Pak was a great shock and has caused
severe distress. On the other hand, this affair has
made the nation reflect deeply on the human rights
issue and the proper exercise of law-enforcement
authority and has also pointed up the right direction
to be followed in the future. It thus serves as a
great object lesson. It is imperative to ensure that
"the ground will be firmer after a rain," as an old
saying goes.

Honest and Responsible Government

In a capsule, the political parties and the general
public made several demands regarding the affair.

-- Swift and thorough investigation of the affair
and stern action against those responsible for it;

-- The placing of the political and ethical blame
on the chief of the National Police and the government
minister in charge of public security;

-- Expressions of governmental repentance to the
public; and

-- The establishment of an institutional device
for the more effective protection of human rights.

In connection with the affair, the police expressed
their regrets to the public and expeditiously announced
the result of an investigation. They arrested the two
police investigators implicated in the affair, took
disciplinary action against two immediate supervisors
and dismissed two ranking police officers higher up
in the police chain of command.

There have been few precedents in which the police
so quickly and frankly admitted their errors and
published the full picture of such an affair. The
prosecutors office, to which the case was referred,
also thoroughly investigated and published its
results, including discrepancies with the earlier
police announcement. The prosecutors have indicted
the two police investigators and put them under
physical detention. Accordingly, domestic and international attention has been focused more on the official
remedial actions than on the tragedy itself.

The resoluteness of the government in dealing
with the affair and the seriousness of its reflection
upon it have been clearly demonstrated by the speedy

-13-

0096

announcement about the tragedy and the prompt dismissal
of the home minister and the national police chief.
This is in line with the Fifth Republic's pursuit
of an honest and responsible government. This also
illustrates the unflagging determination of President
Chun to promote democratic development, as well as his
ideals of national administration. In order to ensure
that the renewed concern about human rights will not
be a short-lived one, President Chun has instructed
the Cabinet to develop plans to establish a permanent
government commission to more effectively protect
the rights of citizens by charting and enforcing a
comprehensive long-term human rights policy.

On January 22, the chairman of the ruling
Democratic Justice Party, Roh Tae-woo, expressed deep
regret over the death of Pak at a press conference.
He said, "The Democratic Justice Party will do its
best to create institutional devices to prevent the
recurrence of police brutality. Our proposed bill
for amending the Constitution, which has been submitted
to the National Assembly, contains provisions designed
to promote human rights. We are prepared to alter
the provisions, if deemed necessary, to reinforce
their effectiveness." Roh then invited the opposition
parties to refer their own good ideas for promoting
human rights, if they have any, to the ad hoc
National Assembly committee on constitutional reform.

Both the administration and the ruling party are
thus working hard to improve the human rights situation
with an acute sense of legal, ethical and political
responsibility. The planned human rights commission,

0097

expected to be participated in by prominent citizens
from all walks of life, will serve as a major
institutional device to protect and promote the
rights of citizens and to foster the development of
a mature democracy.

The swift acceptance of the views and demands of
various segments of society, including the political
opposition, symbolizes the resolve to translate the
goal of a just society into reality, which is one
of the priority tasks of the Fifth Republic. Needless
to say, this also reflects the unflagging determination
of President Chun to hand over a spotlessly clean
government.

Law Enforcement Vital

The investigation, examination and interrogation
of suspects is an indispensable legal procedure to
determine the facts in a criminal case. It is the
responsibility of the police to employ all methods
permitted by law to ferret out criminals. In such
a process, it is inevitable that an adversary
relationship should develop between the suspect, who
instinctly tries to defend himself, and the criminal
investigator, who must protect the public interest.
Especially in cases involving those suspected of
committing Communism-related or ideologically motivated
crimes, it is often quite difficult to determine the

-15-

0098

truth because such suspects tend to have deep faith
in their ideologies and believe in the ethical
justifiability of their criminal acts. This often
poses limitations and obstacles to the exercise of
law-enforcement authority. The situation is virtually
the same in foreign countries.

It is obvious that the law-enforcement authority
must be respected and supported, because it is vital
to safeguarding public security and protecting the
lives, rights and property of citizens. If the law-
enforcement authority is weakened for any reason,
there would be social unrest, threatening national
security. Especially in the case of Korea, which is
faced with such peculiar circumstances as territorial
division and confrontation, effective exercise of the
law-enforcement authority is even more crucial than
in most other countries.

Although the law-enforcement authority of the
state must not be abused, it also should not be
undermined. This is why an institutional device to
ensure its correct exercise is built into the government.
Furthermore, the National Assembly and the press also
serve as major watchdogs. It is also essential that
the professional competence of criminal investigators
be improved and the police capabilities for scientific
investigation be further upgraded and systematized.

0099

Police Morale Must Be Boosted

The great majority of criminal investigators are
faithfully carrying out their demanding duties with
a keen sense of mission, in spite of difficult
circumstances and inadequate remuneration. In
particular, anti-Communist investigators must work
around the clock in the face of the constant threat
of terrorist attacks by North Korean undercover
agents and other ceaseless threats to their personal
safety. As is widely known, numerous police officers
have been killed, wounded or injured in the course
of counter-infiltration operations, in trying to
arrest robbers and burglars, and in dealing with
violent demonstrations. It must never be forgotten
that the majority of police officers are good and
honest citizens of the Republic who dedicate themselves
to preserving public security at the risk of their lives.

The corps of anti-Communism investigators--two
of whom were implicated in the recent tragedy--
includes many veteran police officers who have spent
many years exclusively in this line of activity. There
are model officers who are about to reach the mandatory
retirement age after having served long investigative
careers without blemish.

A certain ranking police officer who was supervising
anti-Communism investigations, exclaimed, "My career
has been ruined. But what pains me even more is the
disgrace this has brought to the state. I'd rather
be shot dead by a firing squad." Upon hearing the

-17-

0100

news of the incident, other anti-Communism investigators
also felt deep regret. At the same time, they sighed,
"How can we continue to ferret out Commies in the
future?" In view of the rise of leftist radicalism
on the campuses and also of the intensification of
North Korea's psychological warfare against the South,
boosting the morale of the anti-Communist investigators
is a very urgent task in dealing with social unrest
caused by ideological strife.

Politicizing the Affair Dangerous

With due respect for public opinion, the government
has already taken all possible remedial steps and is
taking effective measures to prevent its recurrence.
And yet, some politicians are attempting to make a
political issue out of the incident so that they can
turn around the political situation which has been
unfavorable to them and thus further their struggle
to grab power. In addition, the opposition camp is
trying to use the affair to fan controversy over the
justifiability of the current political system. The
ultimate purpose of their illegal activities is to
mislead public opinion to fulfill their political
ambitions.

In this connection, thoroughgoing caution must be
exercised against some political groups which are
scheming to take advantage of memorial services for

-18-

0101

Pak Chong-ch'ol to incite popular uprisings. All such
religious services should be purely commemorative
events and should not be abused as occasions to wage
illegal political strife.

In particular, some political forces, including
the two Kims--Kim Young-sam and Kim Dae-jung--are not
so much interested in lawful efforts to promote human
rights as in abusing the Pak affair to further their
scheme to foment unrest through demagoguery and
violence. They are thus intent on creating a political
catastrophe with the ultimate aim of attaining their
ambition to grab power. This handful of politicians
are so egoistic and self-righteous as to seek to
monopolize political booty at the sacrifice of the
general public.

If the opposition camp misjudges the nature of
the Pak affair and attempts to use it to advance its
partisan interests, social unrest would be triggered
once again, inflicting great hardship upon the public.
If illegal and demagogic rallies are held in connection
with the affair and disseminate malicious and groundless
rumors, students and dissidents would be naturally
agitated. It is obvious that such agitation would
lead to grave disturbances, as was often the case in
the past.

The press in the United States, which is a friend
of Korea, has taken an affirmative attitude toward the
government's expeditious and frank announcements on
the Pak affair and the remedial actions it has taken.
The press in Japan and other countries have also

expressed concern about possible disturbances and
unrest in Korea stemming from the incident, rather
than voicing criticisms.

If disturbances should occur, this would not only
immediately disrupt and inconvenience the people but
would also undermine the growth and stability of the
nation's economy. Even without such disturbances,
the Korean economy is expected to face considerable
difficulties this year on account of rising oil prices,
increasing foreign pressures on Korea to open its
markets more widely, mounting protectionism in the
developed nations, and the general tendency among
the Korean public to assume that inflation will be
rekindled by general elections anticipated to be held
within this year. Should the annual rate of inflation
bounce back to the 30-40 percent level that prevailed
in the early 1980s, most Korean families, especially
wage and salary earners, would be hard hit.

Should social unrest be caused by opposition
agitation, this would be torture for the entire public.
It would callously disregard the fervent wish of the
majority of the people to see stability maintained by
all means. Furthermore, if social confusion is
created by attempts to abuse the Pak affair in quest
of narrow partisan gains, the pro-Communist leftist
forces, which have been gradually going out of existence,
would be afforded an opportunity to recover their
strength and go on the rampage again. Even though
the Pak affair was a shocking tragedy, the potential
consequences of using the incident to embolden pro-
Communists and leftists intent on toppling the

-20-

0103

Republic's liberal democratic system must never be
underestimated. The public, therefore, must act with
wisdom, caution and self-restraint in view of the
potential consequences.

Time for Greater Democratic Development

     Korea now has at hand a string of crucial national
tasks that will determine the Republic's fortunes--
constitutional reform by consensus, a peaceful change
of government following the conclusion of President
Chun's seven-year term of office, and the staging of
the 1988 Olympics. In particular, a host of important
legislative and administrative steps will be required
to implement the process of democratic development
ranging from constitutional revision to a peaceful
transfer of power, a long-cherished goal of the Korean
people.

     To keep rubbing salt into the wound--and to remain
engrossed in overheated controversy over this issue--
would only divide the nation and impede democratic
development. Instead, the nation must turn the
tragic death of Pak and the trials it has occasioned
into an opportunity to spur the progress toward mature
democracy. Learning a lesson from the tragedy, the
nation should renew its determination to vigorously
protect and advance human rights, while focusing all
its wisdom and energies on accomplishing the major
national tasks at hand.

-21-

0104

All Korean citizens are called upon to coolheadedly
exercise reason with a view to healing the wounds
resulting from the affair as soon as possible, to
keep a watchful eye on and actively counter the
menace of the pro-Communist left, and to cooperate
actively in promoting democratic development in a
peaceful and reasonable fashion. In that way, the
Republic should be able to successfully carry out
its many urgent tasks, thereby advancing into the
ranks of the developed countries. With this, the
Korean people should come to enjoy a more affluent
and more secure life.

-22-

0105

人權問題를 政治問題의 媒介로 惡用

- 〈3.3 不法示威 策動〉관련 分析 解說資料 -

1 9 8 7 . 2 .

不法策動의 底意分析

o 박종철군의 4.9재판 빙자, 국민감정을 자극 선동함으로써, 현정부에 대한 반감을 유발하는 동시에 야권이 의도하는 바대로 대건국면의 현정국을 악화시키려는 정치적 책략의 일환임.

o 야권은 겉으로는 "평화행진"운운하나 일반 다중이 집결하면 무질서하게 마련인 군중심리를 선동하여 폭력적인 반정부 가두시위와 집단당중사태를 유발하려 하고 있음.

o 야권은 이번 불법시위의 감행시점을 대학가 개학, 신민당 지구당 개편대회, 제5공화국 출범 6주년, 슐츠 국무장관 방한 등의 계기에 맞춤으로써 정치권의 불순세력을 모조리 끌어들여 이들을 자기들의 지원세력으로 삼아 반정부 내지 반체제투쟁을 강화하는데 정치적으로 악용하고 있음.

o 특히 제5공화국 출범 6주년에 즈음한 이번 불법시위 계기로 현정부의 정통성을 훼손시키는 한편, 이들 발판으로 봄철의 학원시위 및 노동계의 상습적인 "춘투"를 부추기고 년중 내내 사회혼란 분위기를 점증 고조시킴으로써, 비합법적 방법으로 정권을 타도하거나 폭력혁명으로 체재를 전복하기 위한 결정적 시기를 포착하려 하고 있음.

o 야권은 이 불법시위를 강행함으로써, 최근 침체되어있는 학원 및 재야운동권의 사기를 끌어올리는 한편, 당국의 좌경척결의지를 약화시키고 공권력의 권위를 실추시키려고 획책하고 있음.

o 외세의존의 사대반상적인 "인권" 명분을 내세워 야권에 대한 미국 조야의 두둔 내지 지원을 얻어내는 한편, 현정부에 대한 미국의 지지철회를 은밀 책동함으로써, 대여우위 확보와 민심이반을 기도하고 있음.

-1-

0107

o 대여 강경자세의 고수를 통해 양김의 입장을 강화하고 당내의 온건타협론을 억제함으로써, 내분으로 4분5열 되고있는 야당의 흐트러진 전열을 재정비하고 자신들의 당권장악 계기로 삼고자 하는 저의임.

3.3 示威策動의 不法 不當性

< 社會不安 誘發시킨 不法示威가 分明 >

o 동 시위관련 책동은 현행법 규정에 의하여 그 불법·부당성이 명백히 입증됨.

- <집회 및 시위에 관한 법률> 제3조에서는 "현저히 사회적 불안을 야기시킬 우려가 있는 시위의 주최 또는 참가"를 금지하고 있으며, "집시법" 제2조는 이러한 시위가 "다수인이 공동목적을 가지고 도로 기타 옥외장소를 진행하거나 위력 또는 기세를 보여 불특정 다수인의 의견에 영향을 주거나 제압을 가하는 행위"라고 규정하고 있음.

- 형법 제144조는 "단체 또는 다중의 위력을 보이거나 위험한 물건(예: 화염병, 보도블럭)을 휴대하여 경찰관 등의 공무집행을 방해"한 경우 <특수공무집행방해죄>를 적용, 엄벌에 처하도록 하고 있음.

- 또한 <폭력행위 등 처벌에 관한 법률위반> 제2조에서도 "2인 이상이 다른 사람을 폭행·상해하거나 재물을 손괴"한 경우, 의법조치토록 규정하고 있음.

-2-

0108

o 현재 야권은 "평화적 도보행진이므로 불법시위가 아니다"라고 강변하고 있으나,

- 장소가 협소한 파고다공원에 엄청난 규모의 군중 동원
- 서울 도심의 주요 간선도로를 일시에 점거
- 화염병·흉기소지 등에 대하여 사전대응 곤란
- 학원가 등 과격용공세력의 데거 시위시 종래와 같이 저지 불 가능한 사태 우려
- 불법시위로 인한 도심지 마비, 생업지장, 국민불안감 조성 등 각종 부작용 초래

동을 감안해 볼때 동 시위의 불법성과 위험성은 명백하다 할 것임.

< 人權은 暴力鬪爭의 美化名分 될수 없어 >

o 인권이란 사람이 "압박과 공포", "빈곤", "차별과 박해"로 부터 해방되어 떳떳하게 인간으로서 살아 갈 수 있는 최저한의 권리란 뜻하며, 자유민주주의 국가에서 인권문제는 제도상 기본 적으로 보장되어 있으며, 이의 개선을 지속적으로 추구하는 것 은 민주사회의 본질임.

o 인권문제는 날로 제기되는 새로운 문제점에 부응하여 법적·제도 적·경제적 문제 및 국민의식수준 등과 관련지어 개선방법을 점 진적으로 연구 검토하고 실천해 나가야할 성질의 것임.

o 따라서 인권문제를 편협하게 정치적 측면에서만 보고 정치적 공 정의 제물과 정치적 쟁점으로 삼아 국력을 소모하는 시비를 부 지하 세월로 따지고 있을 성질이 아니며, 보다 본원적이며 보다 사회발전 주도적인 측면에서 파악해야 하는 것임.

-3-

'0109

o 또한 인권문제를 혁명적 방법으로 일시에 해결하기 위해 폭력투쟁의 목표로 삼는 것은 결국 폭력과정에서 인권을 毁손하는 반인권의 이율배반성을 자초하게 될 것임.

o 우리나라와 같은 특수상황 아래서 인권문제를 내세워 불안과 혼란을 자초하는 반정부·반체제투쟁을 벌이는 것은 사회혼란과 국기문만을 야기시킬 뿐 본질적인 인권문제 개선에는 아무런 도움이 되지 못함.

< 印□은 □☐만 생기면 城外□☐ >

o 박종철군 사건에 대해 정부는 즉각 국민에게 솔직히 사과하고 ✓ 관계자들을 엄중 문책했으며, 나아가 총리 직속의 인권독위 가동 등으로 인권보호를 위한 제도적 개선방안 마련에 전력을 다하고 있음.

  - 그러나 야권은 국민의 인권향상에 대한 관심보다 이를 일방적인 대여정치공세의 호재로만 여기고, 정권타도를 위한 장외투쟁에 악의적으로 이용하고 있음.

  - 개헌정국으로 요약되는 작금의 정치상황에서 야권이 개헌문제는 제쳐놓고, 또 국회의 인권독위 구성도 외면한 채, 아스팔트 위의 정치투쟁에만 일관하는 것은 인권은 외면하고 대권에만 연연하는 소인배들임을 반증하고 있음.

o 특히 현재 야권이 인권문제를 순전히 정략적, 당리당략적으로 악용하는 것은 교활한 정치술책의 일환이며, 진정한 인권의 개선을 바라는 국민염원에 등을 돌리는 파렴치한 작태임.

-4-

0110

< 49齋의 政治的 濫用은 故人을 모멸하는 行爲 >

o 불교의식인 49재는 고인의 집안식구 및 아주 가까운 친구만이
   모여 조용하고 엄숙하게 의식을 갖는 것이 판례임.

   - 그럼에도 야권이 이를 빙자하여 대대적인 군중동원과 소란스
     러운 불법 가두시위를 획책하고 있는 것은, 고인추모에는 전
     혀 뜻이 없음을 반증하고 있음.

   - 야권이 준비하고 있는 49재 추모용 수만개의 고무풍선과 태
     극기가 과연 종교추모행사에 걸맞는 것인지, 시민을 자극하는
     도보시위나 선동구호가 박군의 죽음을 마음으로부터 애도하는
     진정한 의사표시인지 묻고 싶음.

o 야권은 이미 박군사건을 여러차례 정략적으로 악용, 서울과 지
   방에서 폭력시위를 자행해왔고 국회기능을 마비시켰으며, 이번에
   또다시 49재를 빙자하여 폭력시위와 불법집회를 획책하는 것은
   박군의 추도보다는 이번 사건을 무한정 확대하여 현정부·현체제
   의 전복을 기도하는 정치책략을 내비치고 있음.

o 이와 같은 야권의 저의는 고인의 죽음을 타고앉아 폭력소요와
   민중봉기를 유발함으로써 사회혼란의 가중과 국법질서의 교란을
   초래하여 정권을 타도하겠다는 어처구니 없는 것임.

< 野圈은 政治投爭의 細略政署에만 執着 >

o 야권이 이처럼 인권문제를 정략적으로 이용하고 있는 것은, 어
   떤 명분이나 방법으로든 국민 속에 대정부 적대감을 고취, 확산
   시켜 보겠다는 일념으로 좌충우돌의 혁명적 위기상황을 조성하려
   는 것임.

-5-

0111

- 이에 따라 야권은 현 정부를 조산(粗散)으로 규정함과 아울러 현정 권을 타도하지 않고서는 인권문제가 영원히 해결되지 못할 것 이라는 식으로 국민을 현혹하고 있음.

o 야권이 이와 같이 인권보호냐 정권타도냐 하는 반선적 흑백논리 에만 집착해 있는한 야권내에서 어떤 건설적인 인권개선 대안이 마련될 가능성은 전혀 희박한 뿐만 아니라 여·야간 정상적인 대 화정치도 무망함.

o 실제로 이번 3.3 불법시위 책동을 앞두고 종전과 같이 야권은 시위의 위장전술로 "용공조작" "민주인사 단압" 등 북괴주장과 유사한 왜곡·날조된 흑색선동구호와 주장을 합부로 표방하고 있 으나, 이는 최근 "친북괴 반미 공산혁명 음모사건" 수사발표에 서도 명백히 입증된 바와 같이 "월북모의" "병사혁명운동조" 등 반국가적 범죄가 횡행하고 있는 엄연한 현실을 전적으로 외 면한 것이며, 정권쟁취를 위해서는 민주의 적과도 어깨동무를 할 수 있다는 무분별하고 무책임한 작태를 계속하고 있는 심정 임.

o 야권의 "3.3 불법시위" 획책은 단순한 수모행사나 다발적인 불법시위가 아닌 정권담취와 체제전복의 음모를 이면에 숨기고 있음.

- 야권은 이 불법시위 책동을 통해 봅천 이후의 갖가지 가두시 위와 폭력난동, 또는 반정부활동을 접화시킴과 아울러 그들의 투쟁전열을 정비 강화하여 음해안에 결정적 시기를 조성하여 기필코 현정권을 타도하는 것을 목표로 삼고 있음.

-6-

< 野圈은 "3.3不法示威에 어린이·老弱者까지 動員 >

○ 이에 따라 현재 야권은 이 행사에 대규모 군중을 조직적으로 동원함은 물론, 국민의 반정부 적대감정을 의도적으로 유발시키고자 평화적 시위를 위장한 유언비어와 간교한 폭력시위 유도술책을 은밀리에 강구·준비하고 있음.

  - 야당 및 참여단체에 부녀자·어린이·노약자까지 동원하도록 독려하여 경찰의 제지시 신체허약자 폭행·인권탄압·무차별 진압 운운의 허위사실 조작과 날조·모략 선동기도
  - 3월3일 전국 사찰에서 동시에 타종토록 강요
  - 신민당은 반정부 구호를 부착시킨 수천개의 풍선을 준비
  - 신민당은 서울·경기지역 지구당에 각각 200명 이상을 동원하여, 일시에 파고다공원으로 행진할 것을 지시
  - 서울대·고대·연대 등에서는 야권의 불법시위와 함께 좌경용공 세력의 "연합투쟁"을 획책
  - 민민투·자민투 등 급진좌경 학생들은 3월3일 명동·종로2,3가 등 시내 6개지역에서 폭력시위를 동시다발 감행 기도

○ 이밖에도 야권은 3월6일 미국 슐츠 국무장관의 방한일을 기해 장충체육관, 남산 야외음악당, 서울운동장, 한강 고수부지 등 4개장소에서 동시 개최, 또는 이중 1개소를 채택하여 외세의존의 사대망상적인 소위 "고문 등 인권탄압규탄 범국민대회" 개최를 책동하고 있음.

○ 이러한 간악한 불법시위책동은 신민당과 재야세력을 배후에서 조종하고 있는 김대중·김영삼씨가 앞장서 지휘하고 부추기고 있어 양김씨의 불순한 저의가 분명하게 드러나고 있음.

-7-

0113

< 전대 平和的 示威도 끝날 수 없어 >

o 야권은 매번 그들의 불법집회 및 시위때마다 걸핏하면 "평화적
  집회" "질서있는 시위" 운운하지만, 지금까지의 실례가 입증하듯
  이 이번 "3.3 불법시위" 또한 평화적으로 끝날 가능성은 전혀
  없음.

  - 지난 해 신민당 개헌현판식 및 5.3 인천소요사태, 11.29
    신민당서울대회, 또 최근 "2.7 명동불법집회"가 과연 그들
    의 말대로 평화적이고 질서정연하게 끝났었는지 한번 확인할
    필요가 있음.

  - 당시 경찰의 확고한 예방조치가 없었다면, 차량과 상점 등에
    방화하고 공공기관을 파괴했던 난동소요사태가 이번에 또다시
    재현될 것은 불문가지의 사실임.

o 지난 2월 25일 저녁 김대중씨는 외신기자들과 만난 자리에서
  이번 행사에 "민민투 소속 학생들이 500명 정도 참여하여 폭
  력시위를 벌일 것"이라고 밝히고 자신은 이들의 폭력시위와 불
  법행동은 용재할 수 없다면서 스스로 3.3 불법시위의 폭력과
  불법을 자인하고 있음.

  - 김대중씨가 재야 및 운동권학생들과 밀접한 관계를 맺고 있다
    는 것은 세상이 다 아는 사실인데, 폭력획책 학생들을 용재
    한 수 없다는 것은 스스로 이 행사의 폭력난동화를 방조 내
    지 조장하고 있음을 분명히 드러낸 것임.

-8-

0114

- 통제 불가능한 과격운동학생들이 폭력소요를 **입으로** 무대를 상습적으로 마련해주는 것은 이들의 폭력소요와 **난동사태를** 방조 내지 지원하는 행위와 다름없으며, 나아가서는 **과격학생** 들의 친북괴적 폭력소요를 정치적 목적에 이용하려는 저의를 지닌 것으로 밖에 볼수 없음·

< 社會秩序과 民生保護 위해 公權力 動員 不可避 >

o 현재 야권은 개헌과 관련한 여·야 협상을 거부하고, **국회까지도** 외면하면서 오로지 장외투쟁에만 전념하고 있음·

- 박종천군 49재 때 "평화행진" 운운하는 것도 양김씨의 압력 에 굴복하여 또 다시 거리로 나서기 위한 명분 **찾기에** 불과 한 것임·

o 아무리 야권이 평화적 도보시위라고 강변하고 있으나, **상식적으** 로 판단할때 다중이 운집하면 군중심리에 따라 순시에 **치안질서** 문란과 인명피해가 유발될 가능성이 없지 않으며, **더우기** 과격 세력 내지 불순세력의 무차별 폭력과 모략선동의 **난무에 따라** 단순한 불법집단 난동사태로 번진될 가능성이 농후함·

- 견국 이번 시위는 그 동안의 야권과 과격학생 **및 재야의** 상 습적 극단투쟁 책동으로 미루어 보아 이를 방치할 **경우** 그야 말로 폭력과 파괴의 대행진이 될 수밖에 없을 것임·

o 따라서 정부는 사회질서 유지와 국민생활 보호를 위해 **공권력으** 로 이러한 불순책동을 사전에 예방·봉쇄하는 조치를 **취하지** 않 을 수 없음·

-9-

0115

o 단, 가족·친지애 의한 순수한 박군의 추모모임은 이제까지 허용
  되어 온대로 앞으로도 얼마든지 가질 수 있고 또 보호될 것임.

< 野黨의 反省을 促求하는 國民輿論 >

o 일반국민은 야권의 정치적 책략을 직시하여 이에 악용 당하는
  일이 없도록 해야할 것임.

  - 특히 야권이 이번 기회에 다소 소원됐던 학원의 운동권 학생
    과 재야 및 노동계와의 연합전선 형성은 피해 사회혼란과 안
    정파괴를 기도하고 있음을 깊이 인식해야 할 것임.

o 야권이 진정한 정책정당이라면 단순한 정치적 책략에만 매달리지
  말고, 국회에서 진지한 연구와 토론을 통해 국민여망에 부응하
  는 그야말로 "政策의 政治"를 보여주는 본분을 다해야 할 것임.

  - 이 경우 여권도 허심탄회하게 야권의 대안을 받아들여 함께
    협의하는 자세가 필요한 것임. (끝)

-10-

0116

明洞 不法集会(2.7)관련 説明資料

1 9 8 7 . 2

政 務 1

(弘報)

1. 2.7 명동집회는 왜 불법인가

일부 정치인과 불순재야단체 및 좌경운동권이 강행하려 하는
소위 "박종철군 국민추도회"라는 명목의 2.7집회는

현저히 사회적 불안을 야기시킬 우려가 있는 집회(집시법
제3조 1항)로서 법률상 금지대상 집회일뿐 아니라

위반하는 경우, 처벌대상(집시법 제14조 1항)으로서
이를 불법집회로 보는 근거는 다음과 같음.

〈 불순세력의 불법집회 주동 〉

과거부터 불법집회와 폭력시위를 상습적으로 일삼아온 민통련과
산하가맹기구 등 불순재야단체의 주요간부들과 좌경운동권세력들이
추도행사를 빙자하여 또다시 정치선동 목적의 불법집회 개최를
주도하고 있음.

〈 도심지를 집회장소로 선정 〉

명동은 상시 인파가 운집하고 상점·회사등이 즐비한 수도경제권의
요충지이자 도심의 최번화가로서 소요발생시 경제생활과 시민생활의
불편을 초래하고 치안질서를 파괴할 우려가 심대한 지역임.

〈 다중집회로 치안질서 파괴 〉

소위 "국민추도회"의 준비위원회 고문8명. 공동대표29명.
집행위원 116명 등 준비위원 9,782명으로 예상참가인원이
1만여명에 육박할 것임. 특히 이들은 대부분 성향이 극한적일
뿐만 아니라 상습적인 과격시위의 전력을 지니고 있어 이번
불법집회의 심각성이 가중되고 있는 것임.

-1-

0118

그밖에 주최측인 재야단체가 학원가·주택가 등지에 참가를 선동
하는 다량의 불온유인물을 살포하고 있어 문제학생·근로자·기타
불순분자들까지 모여들고, 현장주변의 상주인원까지 혼입되는
경우, 약 2만명이 운집할 가능성이 있음.

명동성당 최대수용인원이 2,000명인 점을 감안할 때,
본 집회는 당초부터 불법 옥외집회로 계획되고 있는 것이
분명함.

〈 예상 불순동향 〉

주최측에서 당일 하오 2시 모든 자동차는 경적을 울리고,
모든 교회·성당·사찰은 동시 타종토록 하며, 검은색 리본
또는 흰색 상장을 달고 추도묵념토록 유도하는 등 순수종교
행사와는 거리가 먼 대규모 불법 정치집회의 선동적 분위기
조성을 기도하고 있음.

명동불법집회는 5.3인천소요사태 등에서 목격한 바와 같이
이를 방치할 경우, 구호 및 노래제창, 플래카드와 유인물
살포, 집회 전후의 가두시위 감행 등의 몇단계 과정을 거쳐
화염병 투척, 공공기물 파괴, 건물접거 방화, 인명피해 등
으로 번지는 폭력난동사태가 예상됨.

따라서 순수한 종교행사가 아닌 정치목적의 대규모 군중집회의
저의가 분명하고, 현저한 사회적 불안을 야기시킬 우려가
어느 때보다도 농후하므로 그 불법성이 명백한 것임.
(집시법 3조 1항)

-2-

0119

< 정부의 불법집회 저지방침 >

여러가지 정황과 사실에 비추어 볼때 이번 집회는 종교행사장
에서 소위 추도행사를 빙자하여 현저한 사회불안을 야기시킴으로써
특정의 정치목적을 달성하기 위한 불법불순집회라 아니할 수
없음.

정부는 순수한 종교집회 및 추도회 성격의 집회는 계속 허용해
왔고, 앞으로도 허용할 것이나 이번의 경우처럼 종교행사를
위장한 불법정치집회는 계속 불허할 것임.

주최측이 살포하고 있는 소위 "민통련"등의 집회참가 선동 불온
유인물을 보더라도 국민 선동과 사회혼란을 야기. 폭력으로
정부를 전복하려는 저의가 명백한 이번 불법집회는 국민의 생명과
재산을 보호하는 차원에서 절대로 허용될 수 없음.
(경찰관 직무집행법 제6조)

따라서 이와 같은 범법행위를 자행하려 하는 경우에는 법에
따라 이를 예방·단속할 것이며, (경찰관 직무집행법 제5조)
위반행위가 있을 경우에는 관계법에 따라 엄중 처벌할 것임.

2. 야권은 불법집회로 무엇을 노리고 있나

< 고문문제를 투쟁잇슈로 삼아 정치적 악용 >

양김과 불순재야단체 및 좌경운동권 등 장외의 야권세력은
2.7로 예정된 소위 "박종철군 추모범국민대회"를 계기로
고문과 인권문제 등에 관한 사실을 날조하여 폭로하는 한편,
신민당과 인권단체에 계속 압력을 가해 대정부 공격을 가열
시키려 하고 있음.

-3-

0120

즉, 박군사건에 대한 국민의 감정과 관심을 고문문제에 집중시켜, 이를 정부·여당을 공격하려는 주무기로 삼음으로써, 불법·불순한 방법으로 정국의 파탄국면을 유도하여 결국 체제를 전복하겠다는 저의를 드러내고 있음.

< 혼란조성의 장외투쟁에만 혈안 >

이에 따라 신민당은 당분간 원내활동, 대여협상, 여·야대화나 통상적인 정당활동보다는 장외투쟁에 당력을 집중시켜나갈 것임.

이민우 신민총재가 1.30 "이재형 국회의장이 귀국하는 2월 하순, 임시국회를 열어 인권특위구성과 국정전반을 다루자"고 했으나, 이는 1월 임시국회에서 인권특위구성을 외면함으로써 받은 비난여론을 만회하려는 명분상의 요구일 뿐 실제로는 전혀 관심의 대상이 되지 못하고 있음.

또, 국회가 열린다고 해도 장외투쟁을 계속하면서 국회를 장외투쟁을 더욱 가열시키는 무대로 만들려는 것임.

야권의 장내외투쟁이 병행되면 정국불안은 가중되고, 치안질서를 파괴하는 불법시위와 극렬소요가 연발하게되면 사회혼란이 극도에 달하리라는 것은 불문가지임.

< 재야에 예속된 신민당 >

고문·인권문제에 대한 시비의 확산은 지금까지 인권문제의 개선과 보 .나보다는 체제전복의 정치투쟁에 목적을 두고 행동해온 재야단체·반체제인사들의 불순책동의 반경을 크게 넓혀주게 됨 으로써 제도권 야당이 이들의 압력에 굴복하는 위험한 결과를 초래하여 모든 문제가 불순재야의 주도하에 끌려갈 것으로 보임.

-4-

0121

이에 따라 신민당은 현실정치에서의 제1야당이라는 위치를
지키지 못하고, 좌경용공세력이 잠복해 있는 불순재야단체에
예속되는 과정을 더욱 촉진하게 될것임.

이같은 신민당의 재야예속은 의회민주주의의 파괴와 폭력에 의한
정치투쟁이 가속화되는 위기현상으로 비화될 우려마저 없지 않음.
사태의 심각함은 장외의 김대중·김영삼씨가 이들 불순재야세력의
편을 들고, 물심양면으로 비호하는데 있음.

< 두김씨의 당 주도권과 영향력 확대 >

김대중씨는 북괴의 "통일전선"과 같은 성격의 범야권기구를 발족
시켜 신민당을 그 기구의 일원으로 참여시키려고 오래전부터
획책해 왔음. 이번 고문·인권문제가 중요 정치·사회적 이슈로
등장함에 따라 그는 정권탈취의 최대의 기회를 포착했다고 스스로
생각하고 있으며, 실제 신민당을 재야에 예속화시키는 작업에
박차를 가해 나갈 움직임을 보이고 있음.

김영삼씨도 김대중씨의 재야포섭작업에 뒤지는 것에 초조하여
경쟁적으로 신민당의 장외투쟁을 부채질 할 것이 분명함.
이같은 강경일변도의 투쟁노선은 이른바 "이민우구상"으로 한때
당내에서 고개를 들었던 합의개헌 지지세력의 대여협상파,
정풍파나 중도계의 설 자리를 더욱 좁게 만들것이고, 이총재
등도 당분간 합의개헌에 대한 성취노력을 감추고 강경의 대세에
따를 것으로 보임.

두김씨는 당내 의원들의 최대관심이 개헌과 선거에 쏠려있는
사실을 잘 알고 있으며, 이 두가지 관심사가 현실문제로 등장될
경우, 온건세력의 발언권이 강화되어 강경세력이 열세로 밀릴
우려가 있기때문에 인권·고문문제를 장기간 끌묘감으로써, 신민당을
자신들의 정권탈취 기도에 한껏 악용할 속셈임.

-5-

< 명동집회는 "봄의 위기" 부채질 >

이같이 제도권 정당보다는 장외의 불순제야세력에 추파를 던지고
있는 두김씨는 인권문제와 관련한 장외투쟁을 봄까지 이끌어서
오는 3~4월 대학의 개학과 더불어 대대적인 학원 안팎의
소요와 연결하여 사회안정과 경제질서까지 교란시키겠다는 책략을
세우고 있음.

이에 따라 오는 봄을 결정적인 국면전환의 계기로 만들어 국가
사회의 안정은 아랑곳하지 않고, 자신들이 기도하는 정권타도를
이룩하거나, 사태악화의 주도권을 잡겠다는 계산임.

< 사실상 개헌의 포기이며, 정치의 포기 >

두김씨의 투쟁강화노선이 신민당을 지배하고 있어 당내에서는
개헌의 "改"자도 꺼내기 어려운 실정에 있으며, 더우기
개헌을 위한 여·야대회를 제의했다가는 당장 "사꾸라"로 몰릴
처지임.

또한 두김씨는 민추협의 한 회의에서 앞으로 개헌의 "改"자도
꺼내지 말고, "고문"과 "인권"투쟁만 하라고 지령했다고
전해지고 있음. 이는 사실상 개헌의 포기이며 정치의 포기라
할 수 있음.

두김씨는 현재 "이민우구상"에 동조했거나, 이를 성원한 것
으로 알려진 소위 "반발세력"에 대해 협박 또는 회유책을
폄으로써 강경세력 일변도로 신민당을 이끌어 나갈 구상을
펴고 있음.

-6-

0123

3. 고문시비의 확산은 더 큰 것을 잃는다.

〈 강경 장외투쟁의 결과는 파국 뿐이다 〉

정당이 본래의 사명인 국민을 위한 정치를 포기하고 거리의 소요투사로 나서 "힘"을 사용한다면 정부의 대응 또한 질서 유지를 위해 "힘"의 사용이 불가피할 것이므로 결국 힘과 힘의 대결은 정치부재와 사회불안을 야기할 것이며, 끝내는 희생과 파국을 재촉하는 결과를 초래할지도 모름.

〈 불순재야의 주도는 폭력과 파괴만 낳는다 〉

일부 불순재야단체는 국법질서를 전면 부정하고 현체제를 파괴·전복시키는데 주목적이 있고, 야당은 국법질서와 체제긍정의 테두리 내에서 현실을 비판·개선하며, 대안을 제시하는 것으로 역할분담을 하고 있음.

그런데 현실에 대해 하등의 책임을 지려하지 않고, 책임을 질수도 없는 무분별한 재야가 야당을 압도해 재야의 임의대로 정국까지 좌지우지 하게 된다면 야당도 재야와 함께 폭력과 불법에 의한 체제파괴에 나서는 결과가 될 수밖에 없음.

이는 국민이 야당에 걸고 있는 일말의 기대마저 배신하는 것으로써, 폭력과 파괴에 따른 모든 책임을 양김씨와 야당이 져야 할것임.

〈 인권문제는 거리의 외침만으로 해결 안된다 〉

인권문제는 정치문제화하여 여·야가 공방만 한다고 해서 금방 해결될 성질의 것이 아님.

-7-

0124

따라서 정치인을 포함한 각계인사가 참여하는 인권기구 등에서
차분하고 실질적으로 접근해야 개선책이나 해결방안이 나올 수
있을 것임.

그런데도 굳이 이를 정치문제화하려는 것은 박군의 죽음을
악용해 자신의 정치목적을 달성하려는 비열한 권모술수라는
비난을 면키 어려움.

인권문제는 감성적인 대처 보다는 이성적인 접근이 있어야
구체적이고 현실적인 해결방안이 나올 수 있지, 거리의 외침과
소요와 폭력만으로 해결될 수 없는 일인데도 이번 대회를 강행
하려는 그 저의를 의심치 않을 수 없음.

〈 혼란의 토양위에 인권의 나무는 자라지 않는다 〉

국법질서가 파괴되어 사회가 혼란해지고 국가안보가 위태로워진
상황에서는 인권의 보호나 신장이 이루어지지 못하며, 오히려
그러한 상황에서는 대다수 국민의 인권이 침해될 뿐이라는
사실은 동서고금의 진실임.

따라서 정부는 전체 국민의 인권을 보호하고 신장하기 위해
박군사건을 악용하여 법질서를 파괴하고 자유민주체제를 동요
시키는 어떠한 소요행위 내지 소요유발행위도 용납하지 않을
것임.

-8-

0125

< 인권문제의 궁극적인 해결주체는 정부·여당이다 >

박군사건을 계기로 정부·여당은 대통령의

- 인권보호 특별기구 설치검토지시(1.21)에 이어
- 민정당 인권기구 설치(2.2)
- 경찰쇄신책 수립 발표(2.3)
- 정부 인권기구의 기능 및 구성원칙 발표(2.4) 등

신속한 일련의 조치들로 실질적인 개선책을 마련하고 있음.

그러나 이것과 비교할 때 야당이 정치문제화하고 있는 것은
큰 차이가 있음. 야당이 이 문제를 이용하여 정치공세를
위한 구태의연한 공세만을 펴고 있는 것은 문제해결이나 인권
문제 개선에 전혀 도움을 주지 못하는 공허한 투쟁에 지나지
않음.

따라서 인권문제의 해결주체는 궁극적으로 정부·여당이지 결코
아무런 대안과 권한을 갖지 못하고 있는 야당이 아님.

< 좌경세력은 "살판 났다"고 날뛰고 있다 >

그동안 안정을 희구하는 대다수 국민들로부터 외면당해 위축되어
숨어있던 좌경용공세력은 박군사건을 계기로 국민선동으로 민중
봉기의 호기를 맞은 것으로 "살판 났다"며 날뛰고 있음.

박군사건을 악용하여 군중집회 등 소요행위가 있게 되면 그것은
결과적으로 좌경용공세력의 활동영역을 확대해 주는 잘못을
범하게 될 것임.

-9-

0126

< 개헌문제 외면은 본말전도이다 >

지금 우리 정치의 가장 중요한 과제는 개헌문제이며, 이것은
헌정 40년의 정치 악순환을 청산하는 역사의 명제이고,
온 국민의 한결같은 여망이기도 함.

인권문제도 민주발전의 일면인 것은 사실이지만, 그것이
전반적인 민주발전의 근간인 개헌을 촉진하는 계기가 돼야하지,
어떤 이유로도 개헌을 방해하거나 무시하는 결과가 초래되어서는
안될 것임.

< 야당은 좀더 솔직해야 한다 >

야당의원들의 겉과 속이 다른 야누스와 같은 성격이 요즘
더욱 두드러지고 있음. 속마음은 하루빨리 개헌이 성사되기를
바라고, 그에 따라 온 신경이 다음 선거의 공천과 당선에
집중돼 있는게 현 실정임.

그런데도 두 김씨의 눈치, 불순제야나 운동권 학생들의 비난이
두려워 개헌하자는 소리나 선거소리 조차 꺼내놓지 못하고
있는 형편임.

이는 야당의 불행에 그치지 않고, 현실 정치의 불행임.
신민당은 하루빨리 현실정치에 참여하고 있는 자신의 위치와
역할을 되찾아 정상적인 수권정당의 면모를 갖춰야 할 것임.

-10-

0127

< 누구를 위한 불안조성인가 >

국가 현실을 외면한 불순재야세력 및 두김씨의 인권문제 시비 확산과 장외투쟁 강화는 결과적으로 개헌을 포기하고, 정치를 외면한채 오로지 정권쟁취 투쟁만으로 승부를 결하려는 무모한 파국자초 행위가 아닐 수 없음.

이에 따라 우리의 정치·사회가 불안해지고 경제가 위축되고 안보가 위태로워지면 결국 국가가 위기에 처할 수밖에 없음.

따라서 이러한 예측할 수 없는 우리사회의 불안과 위기는 인권 문제 해결에 아무런 도움이 되지 못할 뿐 아니라, 개헌이나 평화적 정부이양에도 방해가 될 것은 뻔한 일임.

누구를 위한 불안조성인가. 우리 모두가 현실을 똑바로 보고, 이성과 냉정을 되찾아야 할 때임.

-11-

0128

주 미 대 사 관

미국(정)700-51   1987. 2. 10.

수신 : 장관(사본: 김경원 주미대사)

참조 : 미주국장

제목 : 하원의원 서한

    연 : USW-606 (87.2.9.)

    박병적이기(~~~~)
    Edward F. Feighan 하원의원(민주-오하이오)등의 George P.
Shultz 국무장관앞 연서서한을 별첨 보고합니다.

첨부 : 상기서한 사본 1부. 끝.

예고 : 87.12.31. 일반

                    주 미 대 사 대

1223 LONGWORTH BUILDING
WASHINGTON, DC 20515
202-225-5731

2951 FEDERAL OFFICE BUILDING
1240 EAST NINTH STREET
CLEVELAND, OH 44199
216-522-4382

Congress of the United States
House of Representatives
Washington, DC 20515

February 6, 1987

The Honorable George P. Shultz
Secretary of State
U. S. Department of State
2201 C Street, N.W.
Washington, D.C. 20520

Dear Mr. Secretary,

We write to express our concern about increasing repression in the Republic of Korea.

The recent murder of a student named Park Jong Thol during interrogation by police in South Korea was the tragic -- if inevitable -- consequence of widespread abuse, torture, and beatings of political suspects by the police. While the Chun government has acted promptly to charge the police with the murder and has dismissed several top officials, the appointment of Chung Ho Yong -- the former commander of the South Korean Special Forces which carried out the coup bringing Chun Doo Hwan to power and later conducted the massacre of hundreds of civilians at Kwangju in 1980 -- does not inspire confidence that the Korean Government is taking a new and positive approach on human rights matters. Moreover, Korean church sources have reported six previous deaths allegedly due from police beatings since 1985 which have not been prosecuted.

The torture and abuse of political detainees; the sentencing and imprisonment of thousands of Koreans, including journalists, students, clergy, and human rights monitors for the nonviolent expression of their political views; restrictions on political activity, press, and assembly; and police attacks on demonstrators characterize the rule of General Chun Doo Hwan. Such practices violate the basic human rights of the Korean people, contribute to instability and political upheaval within Korea, and erode Korea's standing in the community of nations.

Many Koreans associate our own government with Chun's repression because of public expressions of support for his rule and U.S. reluctance to condemn publicly restrictions on democratic participation and gross violations of human rights. We respectfully urge you to seek opportunities to convey U.S. concern to the Chun government about South Korea's deteriorating

0130

The Hon. George P. Shultz
Secretary of State
U. S. Department of State
February 6, 1987
Page two

human rights situation. We respectfully request that President
Chun be encouraged to investigate all deaths in detention or
allegations of police brutality and to take strong action against
those responsible, as well as to release all persons jailed for
the nonviolent expression of their political views.

                    Sincerely,

0131

발 신 전 보   3

번 호 :＿＿＿＿＿   일 시 : 445-746＿＿＿＿＿   전보종별 :＿＿＿＿＿

수 신 : 주 L. A.   대사·총영사 (내무 주 재관) 사본: 주미대사

발 신 : 장   관   치안본부장

제 목 : 수사 전문학 과정 조사 계획

　　당부는 아래 기준에 따른 수사전문학 과정에 고급수사관의 파견 수학으로
수사의 과학학를 기하고저 하니 다음과 같은 사실을 지급 조사 보고하기 바람.
동 수사전문학과정 (Criminalistics Course) 은 채증으로부터 기소에 이르는
모든 수사절차를 집중적으로 교육하는 과정이라야 됨을 참고하시기 바람.

　　1. FBI 에 설치되어 있는 수사 전문학 과정

　　　FBI 학교에 설치되어 있는 수사과정중 국립학교 (National Academy)
보다 장기간이며 전문 수사요원을 양성하는 과정이 있는지 여부와 교육기간,
참가자격자(어느 계급), 고 과목의 편성, 필요한 비용과 기타 유학 희망자 파견에
관한 기타 참고사항

　　2. 주경찰 (State Police) 과 시경찰 (City Police)의 경찰학교에
설치되어 있는 수사전문학 장기과정의 설치운영 여부와 제 1항과 같은 제사항

　　3. 일반대학에 수사전문학과정(Criminalistics)이 설치운영되는
대학과 1항과 같은 제사항. 동건은 Criminal Justice 가 아닌 순수한 수사
전문요원 과정이어 중요하니 참고하기 일반문서로 재분류 (1981. 2. 23.)

(예고: 독후일반)

보안
통제

양 고	87 년 2 월 23 일	치 안 본 부	기안자	계장	과 장	부 장	국 장	차 관	장 관	0132
										외 신	접수자	통 제

미국 관계 주요활동 (박종철)

Michael E. LOWRY (하원, 민주, WA-07)
  1987. 2.11 : 박종철 사건관련, 한국정부에 대한 영향력 행사를 요청하는 하원의원 36명의
       : 슐츠 국무장관 앞 연서서한 가담

Nicholas MAVROULES (하원, 민주, MA-06)
  1987. 2.11 : 박종철 사건관련, 한국정부에 대한 영향력 행사를 요청하는 하원의원 36명의
       : 슐츠 국무장관 앞 연서서한 가담

Howard WOLPE (하원, 민주, MI-03)
  1987. 2.11 : 박종철 사건관련, 한국정부에 대한 영향력 행사를 요청하는 하원의원 36명의
       : 슐츠 국무장관 앞 연서서한 가담

Thomas M. FOGLIETTA(하원, 민주, PA-01)
  1987. 2.11 : 박종철 사건관련, 한국정부에 대한 영향력 행사를 요청하는 하원의원 36명의
       : 슐츠 국무장관 앞 연서서한 가담

Barney FRANK (하원, 민주, MA-04)
  1987. 2.11 : 박종철 사건관련, 한국정부에 대한 영향력 행사를 요청하는 하원의원 36명의
       : 슐츠 국무장관 앞 연서서한 가담

Tom LANTOS (하원, 민주, CA-11)
  1987. 2.11 : 박종철 사건관련, 한국정부에 대한 영향력 행사를 요청하는 하원의원 36명의
       : 슐츠 국무장관 앞 연서서한 가담

Gary L. ACKERMAN (하원, 민주, NY-07)
  1987. 2.11 : 박종철 사건관련, 한국정부에 대한 영향력 행사를 요청하는 하원의원 36명의
       : 슐츠 국무장관 앞 연서서한 가담

Herbert H. BATEMAN (하원, 공화, VA-01)
  1987. 2.11 : 박종철 사건관련, 한국정부에 대한 영향력 행사를 요청하는 하원의원 36명의
       : 슐츠 국무장관 앞 연서서한 가담

Jim BATES(하원, 민주, CA-44)
  1987. 2.11 : 박종철 사건관련, 한국정부에 대한 영향력 행사를 요청하는 하원의원 36명의
       : 슐츠 국무장관 앞 연서서한 가담

Barbara BOXER(하원, 민주, CA-06)
  1987. 2.11 : 박종철 사건관련, 한국정부에 대한 영향력 행사를 요청하는 하원의원 36명의
       : 슐츠 국무장관 앞 연서서한 가담

Edward F. FEIGHAN(하원, 민주, OH-19)
  1987. 2.11 : 박종철 사건관련, 한국정부에 대한 영향력 행사를 요청하는 하원의원 36명의
       : 슐츠 국무장관 앞 연서서한 주도

Marcy KAPTUR (하원, 민주, OH-09)
  1987. 2.11 : 박종철 사건관련, 한국정부에 대한 영향력 행사를 요청하는 하원의원 36명의
       : 슐츠 국무장관 앞 연서서한 가담

0133

Mel LEVINE (하원, 민주, CA-27)
    1987. 2.11 : 박종철 사건관련, 한국정부에 대한 영향력 행사를 요청하는 하원의원 36명의
              : 슐츠 국무장관 앞 연서서한 가담

Buddy MACKAY (하원, 민주, FL-06)
    1987. 2.11 : 박종철 사건관련, 한국정부에 대한 영향력 행사를 요청하는 하원의원 36명의
              : 슐츠 국무장관 앞 연서서한 가담

Matthew G. MARTINEZ(하원, 민주, CA-30)
    1987. 2.11 : 박종철 사건관련, 한국정부에 대한 영향력 행사를 요청하는 하원의원 36명의
              : 슐츠 국무장관 앞 연서서한 가담

Robert J. MRAZEK (하원, 민주, NY-03)
    1987. 2.11 : 박종철 사건관련, 한국정부에 대한 영향력 행사를 요청하는 하원의원 36명의
              : 슐츠 국무장관 앞 연서서한 가담

Robert G. TORRICELLI (하원, 민주, NJ-09)
    1987. 2.11 : 박종철 사건관련, 한국정부에 대한 영향력 행사를 요청하는 하원의원 36명의
              : 슐츠 국무장관 앞 연서서한 가담

Edolphus TOWNS (하원, 민주, NY-11)
    1987. 2.11 : 박종철 사건관련, 한국정부에 대한 영향력 행사를 요청하는 하원의원 36명의
              : 슐츠 국무장관 앞 연서서한 가담

Chester G. ATKINS(하원, 민주, MA-05)
    1987. 2.11 : 박종철 사건관련, 한국정부에 대한 영향력 행사를 요청하는 하원의원 36명의
              : 슐츠 국무장관 앞 연서서한 가담

Albert G. BUSTAMANTE (하원, 민주, TX-23)
    1987. 2.11 : 박종철 사건관련, 한국정부에 대한 영향력 행사를 요청하는 하원의원 36명의
              : 슐츠 국무장관 앞 연서서한 가담

Tommy ROBINSON (하원, 민주, AR-02)
    1987. 2.11 : 박종철 사건관련, 한국정부에 대한 영향력 행사를 요청하는 하원의원 36명의
              : 슐츠 국무장관 앞 연서서한 가담

Mike ESPY(하원, 민주, MS-02)
    1987. 2.11 : 박종철 사건관련, 한국정부에 대한 영향력 행사를 요청하는 하원의원 36명의
              : 슐츠 국무장관 앞 연서서한 가담

0134

아국 관계 주요활동 (박종철)

Morris K. UDALL(하원, 민주, AZ-02)
    1987. 2.11 : 박종철 사건관련, 한국정부에 대한 영향력 행사를 요청하는 하원의원 36명의
               : 슐츠 국무장관 앞 연서서한 가담

Don EDWARDS(하원, 민주, CA-10)
    1987. 2.11 : 박종철 사건관련, 한국정부에 대한 영향력 행사를 요청하는 하원의원 36명의
               : 슐츠 국무장관 앞 연서서한 가담

John CONYERS, Jr.(하원, 민주, MI-01)
    1987. 2.11 : 박종철 사건관련, 한국정부에 대한 영향력 행사를 요청하는 하원의원 36명의
               : 슐츠 국무장관 앞 연서서한 가담

Ronald V. DELLUMS(하원, 민주, CA-08)
    1987. 2.11 : 박종철 사건관련, 한국정부에 대한 영향력 행사를 요청하는 하원의원 36명의
               : 슐츠 국무장관 앞 연서서한 가담

Gerry E. STUDDS(하원, 민주, MA-10)
    1987. 2.11 : 박종철 사건관련, 한국정부에 대한 영향력 행사를 요청하는 하원의원 36명의
               : 슐츠 국무장관 앞 연서서한 가담

Stephen L. NEAL(하원, 민주, NC-05)
    1987. 2.11 : 박종철 사건관련, 한국정부에 대한 영향력 행사를 요청하는 하원의원 36명의
               : 슐츠 국무장관 앞 연서서한 가담

James L. OBERSTAR(하원, 민주, MN-08)
    1987. 2.11 : 박종철 사건관련, 한국정부에 대한 영향력 행사를 요청하는 하원의원 36명의
               : 슐츠 국무장관 앞 연서서한 가담

James H. SCHEUER (하원, 민주, NY-08)
    1987. 2.11 : 박종철 사건관련, 한국정부에 대한 영향력 행사를 요청하는 하원의원 36명의
               : 슐츠 국무장관 앞 연서서한 가담

Anthony C. BEILENSON (하원, 민주, CA-23)
    1987. 2.11 : 박종철 사건관련, 한국정부에 대한 영향력 행사를 요청하는 하원의원 36명의
               : 슐츠 국무장관 앞 연서서한 가담

Peter H. KOSTMAYER (하원, 민주, PA-08)
    1987. 2.11 : 박종철 사건관련, 한국정부에 대한 영향력 행사를 요청하는 하원의원 36명의
               : 슐츠 국무장관 앞 연서서한 가담

Vic FAZIO(하원, 민주, CA-04)
    1987. 2.11 : 박종철 사건관련, 한국정부에 대한 영향력 행사를 요청하는 하원의원 36명의
               : 슐츠 국무장관 앞 연서서한 가담

Tony P. HALL (하원, 민주, OH-03)
    1987. 2.11 : 박종철 사건관련, 한국정부에 대한 영향력 행사를 요청하는 하원의원 36명의
               : 슐츠 국무장관 앞 연서서한 가담

0135

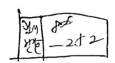

통 화 요 록

1. 일   시 : 1987.2.24(화) 15:00-15:30
2. 송 화 자 : 외무부 북미과장
3. 수 화 자 : 치안본부 외사 1과장
4. 통화내용 :

수사전문화 과정 조사

북미과장 : 치안본부장의 LA 내무 주재관에 대한 수사전문화 과정
        파악 지시와 관련, 주미대사는 한.미 경찰 훈련 교류
        문제와 관련한 조치인지 문의해 왔는 바, 치안본부의
        입장을 알려주기 바람.

외사과장 : 치안본부장의 LA 내무 주재관에 대한 자료 조사 지시는
        주미대사의 건의를 긍정적으로 검토하라는 내무부
        장관의 지시에 따른 것임.
        금번 미측의 제의는 종전 일반 정규과정 연수와는 달리
        처음있는 수사전문 연수이므로 과정선택, T/O, 예산등에
        대한 실무적 검토가 우선되어야 하므로 우선 비공식으로
        내무주재관을 통해 자료를 수집하기로 한 것임.

0136

미국무성에 대해서는 우리의 의도를 통보하고 수사전문화

과정에 대한 자료 조사를 요청하되, 연수실시 여부는

아직 확정적으로 방침이 결정된 것이 아닌것을 설명하여

주시기 바람.

북미과장 : 상기 내용을 주미대사관에 통보하겠음.   끝.

예 고 : 1987.12.31 일반.

검토필 (1.87. 6. 3 이후 ~

일반문서로 재분류 (1987.3.1

0137

외 무 부 착 신 전 문

번 호 : USW-0839   일 시 : 702231807   종 별 :

수 신 : 장관(미북)

발 신 : 주미대사

제 목 : 수사전문화 과정조사

대 : WUS-796

연 : USW-571

1. 대호 아국 수사관의 미국파견 수학에 관한 치안본부장의   LA   내무주재관에 대
한 지시가 연호 본직과 국무성   SCHIFTER   인권차관보의 면담시 동 차관보가 제의
한 한.미간 경찰훈련 교류문제와 관련이 있는지 지급 회시바람.

2. 상기 지시가 국무성 인권차관보의 제의와 관련이 있을경우, 미측제의에 대해 본
직이 일단   SHCIFTER   차관보에게 아측 입장을 전달한후 공식경로를 통해 사전 참
고사항을 파악하는 것이 좋을것으로 생각되어 건의함.

(대사 김경원-차관)

예고문: 1987.12.31. 일반

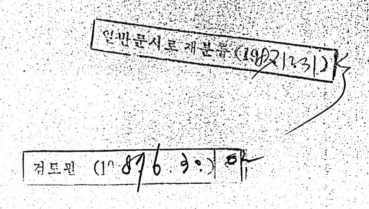

일반문서로 재분류(1987.12.31.)

검토필 (1987.6.30.)

분류번호	보존기간

발 신 전 보

번 호 : WUS-0864 일 시 : 702271030 전보종별 : 지급

수 신 : 주   미   대사 · /총영사/

발 신 : 장   관 (미북)

제 목 : 수사 전문화 과정 조사

　　　　연 : WUS-796

　　　　대 : USW-0839, 0571

　　1. 대호, 치안본부장의 L.A 내무주재관에 대한 자료 조사 지시는 귀관 건의를 긍정적으로 검토하라는 내무부장관의 지시에 따른 것이라 함.

　　2. 금번 미측 제의는 종전 일반 정규과정 연수와는 달리 처음 있는 수사전문 연수이므로 실무적 검토 (과정선택、 T/O、 예산등)가 우선 되어야 함으로 아직 연수계획을 확정한 것은 아니라고 함.

　　3. 따라서 내무부는 공식 경로를 거치지 않고 우선 내무주재관을 통해 자료를 수집하기로 한것이라고 함. 상기를 감안 미국무성측 에는 아측의 의도를 통보하고 연호사항에 대한 자료를 요청하되 연수실시 여부는 아직 확정된 방침이 결정된 것이 아님을 설명하기 바람.

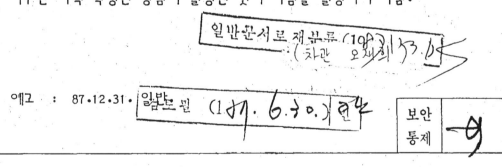

예고 : 87·12·31· 일반 (187. 6.30.)연후

보안 통제	영

앙고재	년월일	봉미과	기안자 3	과 장	국 장	1차관보	차 관	장 관 2·26 장관보고필	0139	외신과	접수자	통 제

외 무 부 착 신 전 보

번 호 : USW-0979   일 시 : 703021853   종 별 원 본

수 신 : 장관(미북,김경원대사)

발 신 : 주미대사대리

제 목 : 수사전문화

대: WUS-864

연: USW-571

1.대호 금 3.2(월) 당관 송민순 서기관이 국무성 인권국 THOMAS MURPHY 아태담
당관에게,연호 경찰 수사교육에 관한 SCHIFTER 차관보의 비공식 제의를 아측이
긍정적으로 검토하고 있음을 통보하고 연수관련 사항에 대해 문의하였음.

2. 이에 대해 동 담당관은 지난 2.6 자 제의가 어디까지나 국무성 내부에서 비공식
적으로 검토중이라고 하므로 국무성측도 FBI 등 관계기관과 보다 구체적인 협의
를 가진후 연수 참고 사항을 알려주겠다고 하였음.

(공사 한탁채)

예고:87.12.31일반

검토필 (1987. 6. 1여 훈)

일반문서로 재분류 (1992.1.23.)

- -

미주국 대사 안기 내무부

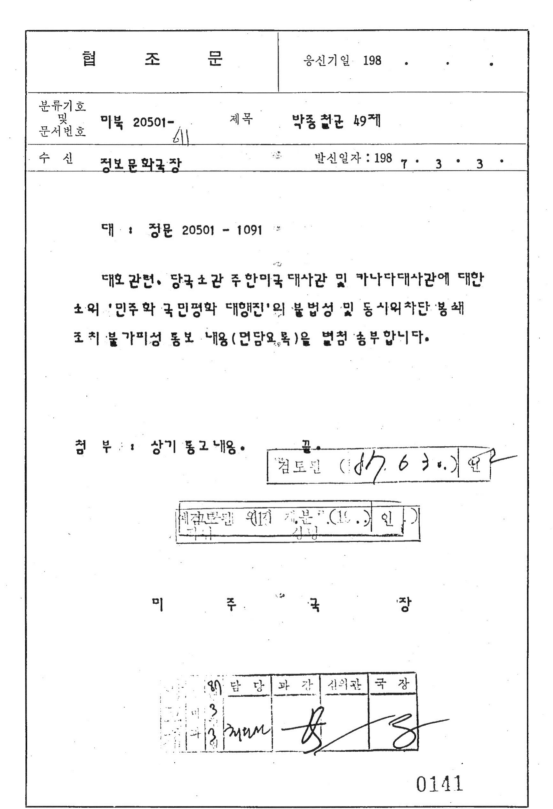

협 조 문	응신기일 198 . . .

분류기호 및 문서번호	미북 20501- 611	제목	박종철군 49제

수 신	정보문화국장	발신일자 : 198 7 . 3 . 3 .

대 : 정문 20501 - 1091

대호 관련, 당국소관 주한미국 대사관 및 카나다대사관에 대한
소위 '민주학 국민평학 대행진'의 불법성 및 동시위차단 봉쇄
조치 불가피성 통보 내용(면담요록)을 별첨 송부합니다.

첨 부 : 상기 통고 내용. 끝.

검토필 (87. 6. 30.) 완

재검토필 완료 처분 (19. .) 인

미 주 국 장

87 미 3 3	담당 계계계	과장 	심의관 	국장

0141

1205—8A
1981. 12. 1 승인

190mm×268mm (인쇄용지(2급)60g/㎡)
가 40—41 1985. 9. 5

면 담 내 용

---

1. 면담일시 : 87.3.3(화) 09:30-10:15
2. 면담장소 : 미주국장실
3. 면 담 자 : 장선섭 미주국장

   유명환 북미과장

   Dunlop 주한미국대사관 참사관

   (배석 : 최원선 사무관)

4. 면담내용 :

(3.3. 민주 대행진)

국 장 : o 불순 재야단체와 좌경용공 세력 및 일부 정치인들이
         박종철군 추도를 빙자해 금일 소위 '고문추방 민주화
         국민대행진 '을 준비하고 있음.

        o 우리 정부는 순수히 종교적 차원에서 추모를 위한
           행사등은 최대한 허용 보호할 방침이지만 이를
           빙자한 일부의 정치적 책략 실현을 위한 대규모
           집회등 사회불만을 의도적으로 야기시키려는 불법
           집회는 강력 저지할 방침임.

Dunlop : o 귀국정부의 입장을 잘 알고 있음.

        o 미대사관으로서도 금번 3.3. 집회는 참어하는
           사람들의 숫자도 적을 것으로 보고 있으며 단지
           도심교통 혼란정도가 있을 것으로 예상함.

0142

면 담 요 록

1. 면담일시 : 1987.3.3(화) 10:30-11:00

2. 면담장소 : 북미과

3. 면 담 자 : Mark Gwozdecky 3등서기관 [주한 카나다 대사관]

   최원선 사무관

4. 면담내용 :

최사무관 : ㅇ 금일 일부 불손 재야단체와 좌경용공세력 및 일부
         정치인들이 소위 '고문추방 민주화 국민 대행진'을
         서울, 부산, 대구, 광주등 주요 도시에서 동시에
         개최하려 하고 있음.

       ㅇ 금번 집회는 불순 재야단체 급진좌경학생 및 일부
         반체제적인 인사들이 박종철군의 추모를 빙자하여
         체제전복을 위한 정치적 책략실현을 위해 사회
         불안을 의도적으로 야기하려는 불법 집회임.

       ㅇ 따라서 정부는 법질서의 차원에서 국민의 생명과
         재산을 보호하고 치안질서 확립을 위해 동 집회를
         강력 저지할 방침임.

       ㅇ 또한 우리정부는 박종철 추모등 순수한 종고행사는
         최대한 허용하고 보호할 방침임.

Gwozdecky : ㅇ 귀국 정부입장을 잘 알겠음.   끝.

공 람	북 미 과	보낸신 3인	담 당	과 장	심의관	국 장	차관보	차 관	장 관
			최원선						

0143

3.3. 소위 '민주 대행진' 관련 설명자료

o 정부는 박종철 사건과 관련, 그간 정부의 유감표시와 관계자 인책
(내무장관, 치안본부장, 대공 수사단장) 및 관련자 (관련형사 2명)
구속은 물론, 고문 근절을 위해 2.12 총리실 직속인 인권보호 특별
위원회를 신설하는등 제반 노력을 다해왔음.

o 그럼에도 불구하고 불순 재야단체와 좌경용공세력 및 일부 정치인들은
박종철군의 추도를 빙자해서 2.7 명동 불법집회 강행을 시도한데
이어 이번 3.3에도 박종철의 49일제를 기화로 소위 '고문추방 민주화
국민 대행진'을 서울, 부산, 대구, 광주등 전국 주요도시에서 동시에
개최하려고 시도하고 있음.

o 정부여당은 민주적 헌정질서 유지를 통해 88년 2월의 평화적 정부
이양을 달성하고 나아가 올림픽의 성공적 개최를 이룩하는데 최선을
다하고 있는 바, 이를 위해서는 무엇보다도 정치적, 사회적, 안정이
중요한 것임.

o 금번 집회는 지난 2.7 명동집회와 마찬가지로 불순재야단체 급진좌경
학생 및 일부 반체제적인 인사들이 박종철군의 추모를 빙자하여 정권
타도와 체제전복을 위한 그들의 정치적 책략 실현을 위해 사회불안을
의도적으로 야기하려는 불법 집회임.

0144

o 국가를 보위하고 국민의 생명과 재산을 보호하며 치안 질서 확립의
   최종적 책임을 가진 정부는 불법가두시위를 통해 수도 서울의 기능
   마비를 초해할지도 모를 금번 집회를 허용할 수 없음.

o 따라서 정부는 법질서의 차원에서 동 집회가 당국의 허가를 받지 않은
   불법 옥외집회인 점을 감안, 집회 및 시위에 관한 법률 3조 1항에 의거
   동 집회를 강력 저지할 방침임.

o 그러나 박종철 추모 49제등 순수한 종교행사 및 합법적 정치집회나
   건전한 학생 및 노동운동은 민주발전 및 국민 기본권 차원에서 최대한
   허용하고 보호할 방침임.

0145

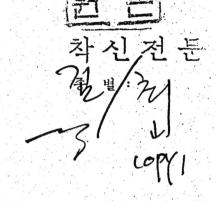

외 무 부

착 신 전 보

번 호 : USW-1008   일 시 : 703031853

수 신 : 장관(미북,김경원주미대사)

발 신 : 주미대사대리

제 목 : 박종철 49 제

표제관련, 국무성 한국과는 금일 정오 브리핑용으로 아래와 같은 PRESS GUIDENCE
를 작성하였으나, 사용치 않았다함.

Q: WHAT DO WE KNOW ABOUT THE DEMONSTRATIONS IN KOREA AND THE GOVERNMENT'S RESPO
NSE ? WHAT COMMENT DO WE HAVE ON WHAT IS GOING ON, ESPECIALLY IN VIEW OF THE SEC
RETARY'S UPCOMING VISIT ?

A: OPPOSITION GROUPS PLANNED A   GRAND PEACE MARCH NATIONWIDE IN MEMORY OF TORT
URE VICTIM PAK CHONG-CHOL. MEMORIAL SERVICESWERE SLATED FOR TODAY BECAUSE THE 49
TH DAY AFTER DEATH IS OF SPECIAL SIGNIFICANCE IN BUDDHIST FUNERARY RITES.
WE UNDERSTAND THAT POLICE LARGELY BLOCKED THIS PROTEST AS THEY HAVE OTHER RECEN
T DEMONSTRATIONS.

LET ME RE-EMPHASIZE THAT WE CONSIDER IT THE DUTY OF A GOVERNMENT TO PROTECT NOT
ONLY THE SECURITY OF ITS CITIZENS BUT ALSO THEIR RIGHT TO PEACEABLE ASSEMBLY.

(공사 한탁채-국장)

예고문: 1987.12.31.일반

예고문에 의거 재분류 (1987.12.31)
직위   성명

미주국   차관실   1 차보   정문국   청와대   총리실   안 기   대 사

외 무 부

번 호 : USW-1025　　　　　일 시 : 70304 1749　　　종 별 : 지급
수 신 : 장 관 (미북,해신,김경원주미대사)
발 신 : 주 미 대사대리
제 목 : 박종철군 49재-국무성 논평

국무성은 금 3.4(수) 박종철군 49재 관련 기자질의에 대해 동사태가 슐츠 국무장관
의 방한에 영향을 미치지는 않을것이라고 작일 보도지침에 따라 아래와같이 답변함.

-아 래-

Q: CONCERNING THE SITUATION IN KOREA. IS THERE SOME CONCERN NOW, WITH RENEWED DE
MONSTRATIONS, ANTI-GOVERNMENT DEMONSTRATIONS, ESPECIALLY WITH THE SECRETARY OF S
TATE GOING THERE ON FRIDAY ?

MS.OAKLEY: I DON'T THINK THERE HAS BEEN ANY SPECIFIC CONCERN ABOUT ANY POSSIBILI
TY OF CHANGING THE SECRETARY'S PLANS. IT'S OBVIOUS THAT OPPOSITION GROUPS HAVE PL
ANNED A GRAND PEACE MARCH, NATIONWIDE, IN MEMORY OF TORTURE VICTIM PAK CHUNG CHU
L(?) THE MEMORIAL SERVICES WERE SLATED FOR MARCH 3, BECAUSE THE 49TH DAY AFTER DEA
TH IS OF SPECIAL SIGNIFICANCE IN BUDDHIST FUNERARY RITES.

WE UNDERSTAND THE POLICE LARGELY BLOCKED THIS PROTEST, AS THEY HAVE OTHER RECEN
T DEMONSTRATIONS. LET ME REEMPHASIZE THAT WE CONSIDER IT THE DUTY OF A GOVERNMEN
T TO PROTECT NOT ONLY THE SECURITY OF ITS CITIZENS, BUT ALSO THEIR RIGHT TO PEACE
ABLE ASSEMBLY.

(공사 한탁채)

미주국　차관실　1차보　문공부　정문국　대 사　청와대　안기

PAGE 1

87.03.05 09:56
외신 1과 통제관

0147

발 신 전 보

번 호: WUS-1810   일 시: 0429/9 ⊙   전보종별: _____

수 신: 주 미   대사 ·총영사/

발 신: 장   관 (마북)

제 목: 수사전문화

    대 : USW - 0979

    대호, 표제관련 진전사항 파악보고 바람.

(미주국장   장선섭)

    예 고 : 87. 12. 31. 일반.

앙 고 재	87 년 8 월 21 일	주 미 과	기안자	과 장	국 장 전결	차 관	장 관

발신시간 :

외 신 과	접수자	과 장

0148

<table>
<tr><td>관리
번호</td><td>87
-/01P</td></tr>
</table>

발 신 전 보

번 호: WUS-2071　일 시: 70/13 1130　　전보종별: _____

수 신: 주　미　　　　대사·高領사11

발 신: 장　　　　관　　　　(미북)

제 목: 수사전문화

　　　　　대 : USW - 2350

　　　　　연 : WUS - 1810

1. 대호, 문공차관의 5.5 Schifter 인권 차관보 면담시 동
차관보는 경찰관 훈련계획을 아측에 상기시킨 바 있음.

2. 상기관련, 미측의 자료협조준비등 진전사항이 있는지 파악
보고 바람.

3. 동건에 관해 내무부에서 계속 문의가 있음을 첨언함.

　　　　　　　　　　　　　　　(미주국장　장선섭)

일반문서로 재분류 (1987.12.5.)

예 고 : 87.12.31. 일반.

검토필 (19)87. 6. 30까지

<table>
<tr><td rowspan="2">앙
고
재</td><td>7
년
5
월
12
일</td><td>미
주
과</td><td>기안자</td><td>과 장</td><td>심의관</td><td>국 장</td><td></td><td>차 관</td><td>장 관</td></tr>
<tr><td></td><td></td><td>2</td><td></td><td></td><td>전결</td><td></td><td></td><td></td></tr>
</table>

발신시간 :

<table>
<tr><td rowspan="2">외
신
과</td><td>접수자</td><td>과 장</td></tr>
<tr><td></td><td></td></tr>
</table>

0149

외 무 부

착 신 전 문

번 호 : USW-2570   일 시 : 705191752   종 별 :

수 신 : 장 관 (미북)

발 신 : 주 미 대 사

제 목 : 수사 전문화

대 : WUS-2071,796

연 : USW- 979,571

1. 대호에 관해 그간 국무성 인권국과 접촉, 훈련 참고사항 및 자료를 요청해오고
있으나 금 5.19 인권과 MURPHY 과장대리는 미측 사정을 다음과같이 알려왔음.

가. 아측의 경찰 수사 교육 (CRIMINALISTICS) 관심표명을 받고 국무성은 미국내 관
련 기관에의 위탁교육 가능 방안을 검토하였으나, SCHIFTER 차관보가 고려한 형식
의 외국경찰 미국내 교육관련한 예산 및 법적 제약 요소로 아직 적절하다고 판단되는
교육과정을 찾지못하고 있음.

나. 현재로서는 미국내 경찰 훈련에 관한 일반적인 자료만을 제공해줄수 있는 입장
임.

다. SCHIFTER 인권차관보는 아측에 대해 비공식적이나마 연호와 같은 목적의 훈
련주선 용의를 표명한바 있으나 상기와같은 예산 및 법적 제약 요소를 감안 다른 방
안을 생각중에 있음.

2. 상기 훈련에 관한 일반적 자료를 차파편 송부함.

(대사 김경원)

예 고 : 87.12.31. 일반

일반문서로 재분류 (1987.12.31)

검토필 (1981.6.30)

미주국   차관실   1 차보   청와대   안 기

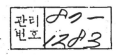

외 무 부

관리
번호 87-
1283

번 호 : USW-2666   일 시 :-705221547   종 별 : 지급

수 신 : 장관(미북,정홍)

발 신 : 주 미 대사

제 목 : 박종철 사건

대 : AM-0111

1. 대호 박종철 사건 관련, 국무성 인권과는 조사진행등에 대해 계속 관심을 표시해
온바 있으므로, 금 5.22. 당관 송서기관은   THOMAS MURPHY   부과장에게 대호 연루
자 3명 추가 구속과 조사 진행계획등 정부발표 요지를 설명하였음.

2. 이에 대해 동 부과장은 5.6자 하원 아태소위 청문회(USW-2258   참조)에게도 제
기된바와 같이 이문제에 관해 의회는 물론 인권단체등 여러곳으로 부터 국무성에 문
의해 오고 있음을 지적하면서 동 사건처리 경과는 인권문제 개선을 위한 한국정부
의지의 하나의 척도가 될수 있을것으로 보인다고 하고, 이러한 면에서 금번 한국정부
가 조사를 철지히 진행시키겠다는 의사를 밝힌것을 바람직하게 생각한다는 반응을 보
였음.

(대사 김경원)

예 고 문 예고 : 87. 12. 31까지 로
재 분류 1급 일반문서화 서명

검 토 필 (1987. 6. 30.)

미주국   차관실   1 차보   2 차보   정문국   청와대   총리실   안 기

외 무 부

번 호 : USW-2681   일 시 : 70522 1753   종 별 :

수 신 : 장 관 (미북,정홍,해신)

발 신 : 주 미 대사

제 목 : 국무성 논평-(박종철 사건)

대 : AM-111

연 : USW-266

국무성 동아태국은 금 5.22(금) 대호 박종철 사건 관련 언론의 논평요구 (전화 질문)
가 있어 아래와 같이 답변 F하였다함

Q: DO YOU HAVE ANY COMMENT ON THE ARREST OF THREE MORE POLICE OFFICERS IN THE P
ARK CHONG CHUL CASE AND ACCUSATIONS THAT THERE WAS A KOREAN GOVERNMENT COVER-UP
IN THE INITIAL INVESTIGATION ?

A: AS WE HAVE SAID MANY TIMES, THE U.S. ABHOR TORTURE. IT IS THE RESPONSIBILITY
OF THE GOV'T TO INVESTIGATE VIGOVOUSLY, APPREHEND AND PUNISH PERPETRATORS OF SUC
H ATS. THE ARREST OF MORE OFFICERS BELIEVED RESPONSIBLE IS A STEP IN THE RIGHT D
IRECTION.

NEVERTHELESS, THE LATEST REVELATIONS UNDERSCORE THE NEED FOR GREATER ATTENTION T
O HUMAN RIGHTS ABUSES IN KOREA. WE CALL UPON THE KOREAN GOV'T TO PROTECT HUMAN R
IGHTS AND PREVENT TORTURE

(대사 김경원)

미주국   1 차보.   정문국   문공부   청와대   안 기

PAGE 1

32

관리	81
번호	260

외 무 부 착신전문

긴급

번 호 : USW-2732   일 시 : 705261754   종 별 : 긴급

수 신 : 장관(미북,정홍,해기)

발 신 : 주 미 대사

제 목 : 청와대 대변인 발표(박군사건)

대: AM-0112,0113

1. 대호 청와대 대변인 발표관련, 금 5.26(화) 오전 당관 정태익 참사관이 국무성 JACK GOSNELL 한국과장대리와 접촉, 정부의 인권개선을 위한 각별한 관심과 진상 규명을 위한 계속적 노력을 강조하면서 인권개선을 위해 정부가 취하고 있는 제반조 치에 대해 설명하였음.

2. 이에대애 동 과장대리는 아국정부가 동 사건의 진상을 밝히기 위해 만호한 조치 를 취하고 있는것은 국내외로 부터 긍정적 반응을 받는데 도움이 될것으로 본다고하 면서 아국 개각에 대해 금일 정오 브리핑시 논평요구가 있을 것으로 예상되나, 국무 성은 이에대한 논평을 하지 않을 것이라고 말하였음.

3. 한편 금일 정오브리핑시 아국 개각에 관해 질문이 있었는바, REDMAN 국무성대 변인은 논평할것이 없다고 답변하였음.

질의응답 내용은 다음과 같음.

Q: CHUCK, DO YOU HAVE ANY COMMENT OR THOUGHTS ON THE CABINET RESHUFFLE IN SEOUL ?

MR. REDMAN: NO

(대사 김경원)

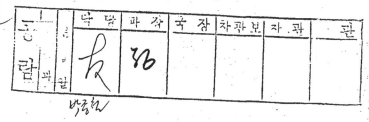

동		담당	과장	국장	차관보	차관	관
람							

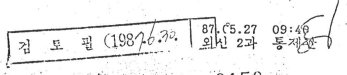

미주국   차관실   1 차보   2 차보   정문국   청와대   안 기   문공부

PAGE 1   87. 05.27 09:40

검 토 필 (1987.6.30.   외신 2과 통제관

0153

박종철 서울대생 고문치사 사건, 1987 **555**

2. 언론보도

0154

외 무 부 착 신 전 보

번 호 : CGW-0069   일 시 : 701201600   종 별 :

수 신 : 장 관 (정문)
발 신 : 주 시카고 총영사
제 목 : 아국관계기사

1.19.자 시카고 트리뷴지는 8면 WORLD REPORT 란에. 2SEOUL COPS CHARGED IN STUDENTS
DEATH 제하, 1.20.자 CHICAGOSUN TIMES 는 25면 2단 기사로 SOUTH KOREA POLICE ADMI
T TORTURE IN DEATH 제하에 각각 서울대 박종철의 경찰 수사중 사망사실을 보도함.
(총영사 이승곤-국장)

정문국   차관실   1차보   청와대   안 기   미주국

0155

변 호 : USW(F)- 49

수 신 : 장관 (미북, 정문, 해산)

제 목 : 소요대학생 구금중 사망

01610

발 신 : 주미대사

/매

The Washington Times

PAGE 6A / FRIDAY, JANUARY 16, 1987

Korean student dies in custody

SEOUL, South Korea — A university student detained for anti-government activities died while being questioned by police, the Joongang Ilbo reported yesterday. The newspaper said police reported the student, Park Jong-chol, 21, died of "shock" Wednesday. The paper said state prosecutors were investigating whether his death was caused by torture. Human rights campaigners have accused police of torturing dissidents to make them falsely confess to pro-communist activities, punishable by death in South Korea. The government denies the charge.

0156

전 보 : USW(F)- 60

수 신 : 장관 (미북.정문.해신)   발신 : 주 미 대사

제 목 : 박종철 사망사건   1 매

The Washington Times | .MONDAY, JANUARY 19, 1987 / PAGE 6A

Prosecutor suspects police torture

SEOUL, South Korea — A student who died after being questioned by police apparently underwent water torture, a senior prosecutor was quoted yesterday. Park Jong-chul, 21, a linguistics student at Seoul National University, was pronounced dead at a city hospital Wednesday.

Yesterday's Chosun Ilbo newspaper quoted Seoul district Chief Prosecutor Chung Ku-yong as saying Mr. Park is believed to have died after "brutal acts of police officers, apparently involving torture with water." The Korea Times quoted Oh In-sang, the first doctor called in to examine the student, as saying "breathing had almost stopped upon my arrival at the police interrogation room. The abdominal area of his body was swollen. It was filled with water." It quoted another prosecutor as saying a preliminary examination showed bruises on the body and a blood clot in the lung. Mr. Chung was quoted as saying final autopsy results would be available soon, possibly in a couple of days.

번 호 : USW(F)- 64   이자1500.
수 신 : 장 관 (미북정문,혁신,내무부)   발 신 : 주 미 대 사
제 목 : 박 종 철 사망 사건   4매

The Washington Post   TUESDAY, JANUARY 20, 1987 **A15**

Opposition in Seoul Urges Torture Inquiry

Resignations Sought in Student's Suffocation

By John Burgess
Washington Post Foreign Service

TOKYO, Jan. 19—South Korea's main opposition party today demanded a special National Assembly investigation and the resignation of senior officials following the disclosure that police tortured and killed a student during interrogation.

The opposition also pressed for a statement from President Chun Doo Hwan. "President Chun must personally apologize to the people for this," Kim Young Sam, one of the New Korea Democratic Party's unofficial leaders, said in an interview.

The party's call followed a formal admission today by South Korea's national police chief that a 21-year-old university student died of suffocation last week after his head was forced into water in a bathtub during a police interrogation.

National police chief Kang Min Chang said two officers had been arrested and charged in connection with the death, which he called "very regrettable" and a violation of a ban on using violence against prisoners.

The opposition has frequently alleged that the South Korean police use torture against persons arrested on politically related charges. In all but a small number of cases, the government has labeled the charges false.

According to an official account, the student, Park Chong Chul, was arrested at about 8 a.m. Jan. 14, taken to a central Seoul police facility and questioned about alleged antigovernment activities.

Interrogators pushed his head into the water-filled bathtub twice, Kang said. The second time, his neck was pressed against the top of the tub and he suffocated. He died at about 11:20 a.m. the same day.

Two interrogators, Lt. Cho Han Kyung, 42, and Sgt. Kang Chin Kyu, 30, were arrested and charged under a South Korean law involving special crimes, officials said. A police superintendent, Chun Suk Rin, was relieved of his duties in connection with the incident.

Park was a junior majoring in linguistics at Seoul National University, South Korea's most prestigious learning center. According to a Seoul newspaper, he had twice been arrested in connection with antigovernment demonstrations and had been sentenced to 10 months in jail. He had not served the sentence, however, because it was suspended for two months.

After his death became known last week, police said he died of "shock." With rumors circulating widely, they formed a special committee to investigate the incident and today Kang acknowledged in a press conference that he had been tortured.

Kim Young Sam said the opposition party had called for convening a special session of the National Assembly to discuss the case and forming an assembly committee with broad investigative powers. He said the police chief and home affairs minister should take responsibility and resign.

The opposition has frequently called unsuccessfully for the resignation of members of Chun's cabinet.

Last summer, the party led a campaign against the government's alleged use of sexual torture against female prisoners. These protests, which the government attempted to ban by force, focused on a 22-year-old female labor organizer who said a policeman had forcibly committed a variety of sexual acts against her during a night-time questioning session in a police station.

Prosecutors, however, said that an investigation found that the officer had made her take off her jacket, used abusive language and struck her lightly on the breasts and that this did not constitute sexual abuse. The policeman was dismissed but not prosecuted.

Over the years, dissident groups have made detailed allegations of torture of prisoners.

Amnesty International, the London-based human rights organization, said in a recent report that it knows of many credible reports of torture in South Korea but only two cases of officials being prosecuted for it.

0158

The New York Times

TUESDAY, JANUARY 20, 1987   A11

Seoul Admits Dissident Died of Police Brutality

SEOUL, South Korea, Jan. 19 (AP) — The national police director said today that police brutality caused the death of a dissident student last week, and he announced the arrest of two officers and apologized.

The official, Kang Min Chang, said at a news conference that the student "suffocated to death" Wednesday when his throat was pressed against the edge of a bathtub as the two officers stuck his head into the water in an effort to extract statements.

Mr. Kang said the student, Park Jong Chul, 21 years old, who had been accused of anti-Government activities, had refused to talk during the questioning at a special police investigation center in Seoul.

The two officers, Lieut. Cho Han Kyong, 38 years old, and Sgt. Kang Chin Kyoo, 33, have been charged with homicide through brutal acts, Mr. Kang said. He said Col. Chun Suk Rin, who is in charge of Counter-Communism Investigation Group No. 2, had been relieved of his post for failure to supervise his subordinates.

Mr. Kang said that as the official in charge of the police, he "sincerely offers my apology to the family of the student and the entire people for the incident."

It was the first time in years that the police had acknowledged such treatment of a political detainee, although dissidents have said the police have used torture against them.

The Washington Times

TUESDAY, JANUARY 20, 1987 / PAGE 5D

S. Korea apologizes for death of student

SEOUL, South Korea (Agence France-Presse) — Home Minister Kim Jong-ho apologized to Koreans yesterday after the chief of the National Police admitted at a news conference that a dissident student died last week while being tortured by police.

The political opposition and dissidents immediately seized on Park Chong-chul's death to attack President Chun Doo Hwan's government and demand greater democracy in the country.

Leaders of Mr. Chun's ruling Democratic Justice Party (DJP) said the 21-year-old student's death came at an inopportune moment because a general election was expected to be held this year after the constitution is amended.

But they said the government acted swiftly to reveal the truth and allay public distrust of the National Police.

The home minister, who oversees the police, expressed "profound" apologies after National Police chief Kang Min-chang announced that the Seoul National University student was suffocated last Wednesday as two interrogators struggled to submerge his head in a tub of water at the Police Counter-Communism Bureau here.

Mr. Kim said Lt Cho Han-kyong and Sgt. Kang Jin-kyu have been arrested on homicide charges and face three years to life in prison if convicted. Their superior, Col. Chun Suk-lin of the Police Counter-Communism Bureau, has been relieved of his post, the minister added.

The minister urged citizens to support the great majority of police officers who "are faithfully performing their duties around-the-clock under difficult conditions to ferret out pro-communist radicals."

Opposition politician Kim Young-Sam said the bureau was a "vicious place to torture conscientious citizens to maintain the dictatorial regime."

The opposition New Korea Democratic Party said in a written statement after a meeting of party leaders that Mr. Park's death was only one of the "brutal acts" committed by police with the "tacit permission" of the government.

It demanded the dismissal of the home minister and the police chief and the immediate convening of Parliament to look into Mr. Park's death

Sources said the ruling DJP was considering convening the parliamentary Home Affairs Committee instead.

DJP Chairman Roh Tae-Woo canceled a press conference scheduled for today to announce plans for greater democracy in South Korea, his spokesman said.

0159

6 11-2

박종철 서울대생 고문치사 사건, 1987   **561**

Chicago Tribune Tuesday, January 20, 1987 4 Section 1

Two South Korean police charged in protester's death

SEOUL—The national police director said Monday a dissident student's death last week was due to police brutality. Kang Min Chang announced the arrest of two officers and apologized. He said the student "suffocated to death" last Wednesday when his throat was pressed against the edge of a bathtub as the two officers stuck his head into the water trying to extract statements from him. Kang said the student, Park Jong Chul, allegedly accused of antigovernment activities, had refused to talk during the questioning at a special police investigation center in Seoul. The two officers, Lt. Cho Han Kyong, 38, and Sgt. Kang Chin Kyoo, 33, have been charged with homicide through brutal acts, Kang said.

THE SUN TUESDAY, JANUARY 20, 1987 2A

Seoul admits student died of torture

2 policemen held; superior dismissed

Deutsche Presse-Agentur

SEOUL, South Korea — South Korea's police headquarters officially admitted yesterday that the death of 21-year-old Seoul student Wednesday was caused by police torture and said two police officers were detained in connection with the affair.

Park Chong-Chol collapsed Wednesday during police questioning and later died. Police said two members of a special anti-communist squad who were suspected of having been responsible for his death were detained and their superior was dismissed.

An investigation found that Mr. Park suffocated to death when his head was pushed under water several times to compel him to give information about the whereabouts of a student leader wanted by police, a police statement said.

The statement said swelling of the student's abdomen, diagnosed by a doctor who examined him at the police station, was caused by "efforts to revive" him.

Mr. Park was questioned on suspicion of pro-communist activities.

64-3

0100

562 한국 인권문제 민주화 관련 기타 자료 1

Los Angeles Times 12 Part I/Monday, January 19, 1987

Torture by Police Suspected in Death of South Korean Student

SEOUL, South Korea (AP)—A 21-year-old student who died after being questioned by police about purported anti-government activities apparently had undergone water torture, a senior prosecutor was quoted as saying Sunday.

Park Jong Chul, a linguistics student at Seoul National University, was pronounced dead at a city hospital Wednesday. The initial police report said that he fainted and went into shock after questioning began. Police denied torturing Park.

The opposition New Korea Democratic Party accused police of torturing the student and said the incident was "only the tip of an iceberg."

The newspaper Chosun Ilbo on Sunday quoted Seoul district chief prosecutor Chung Ku Yong as saying Park is believed to have died after "brutal acts of police officers, apparently involving torture with water." He did not say how water was used.

Chung was quoted as saying the preliminary findings were based on statements from a doctor who was called in to examine Park and from other doctors who subsequently performed the autopsy.

The Korea Times quoted the first doctor, Oh In Sang, as saying that "breathing had almost stopped upon my arrival at the police interrogation room. The abdominal area of his body was swollen. It was filled with water."

Bruises Found

Another press report quoted the doctor as saying he tried to resuscitate the student and that the floor of the room was wet with water.

An investigative team said that when a police investigator tried to resuscitate Park, the student's upper body was unclothed and the pants Park was wearing were not his own and were stained with feces.

The Korea Herald quoted another prosecutor as saying the autopsy showed bruises on the body and a blood clot in the lung.

64-4

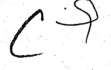

The Washington Post

A18 WEDNESDAY, JANUARY 21, 1987

South Korean President Fires Interior Minister, Police Chief

SEOUL—President Chun Doo Hwan, acting to defuse a political crisis, yesterday fired his interior minister and national police chief after the government's admission that police had tortured a student.

Chun had earlier made an unprecedented public apology for last week's "shocking incident" in which Park Chung Chul, 21, died of suffocation during interrogation by two officers of the country's special anticommunist police squad.

Interior Minister Kim Chong Hoh and National Police Chief Kang Min Chang formally resigned, accepting political and moral responsibility for Park's death.

Chun named a new interior minister, close associate Chung Ho Yong, a former general who as commander of the South Korean Special Forces helped stage the 1979 coup that brought Chun to power.

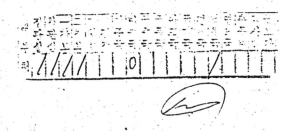

THE NEW YORK TIMES, WEDNESDAY, JANUARY 21, 1987   A8

2 Top South Korean Officials Dismissed in Student's Death

SEOUL, South Korea, Jan. 20 (Reuters) — President Chun Doo Hwan, acting to defuse a political crisis, dismissed his interior minister and his National Police Chief today after the Government's admission that the police had tortured a student to death.

Mr. Chun had earlier made a public apology for what he called the "shocking incident" last week in which the student, Park Chong Chol, 21 years old, died of suffocation during interrogation by two officers of the country's special anti-Communist police squad.

The Interior Minister, Kim Chong Hoh, and the National Police Chief, Kang Min Chang, formally resigned today, accepting responsibility for Mr. Park's death.

President Chun quickly named a new Interior Minister, Chung Ho Yong, a former general who, as commander of the South Korean Special Forces, helped stage the 1979 coup. He named the Seoul police commander, Lee Yong Chang, to replace Mr. Kang.

Head Plunged Into Water

The moves today came after an outburst of public anger over the death of Mr. Park, a linguistics student at Seoul National University who was picked up last Wednesday, accused of anti-Government agitation.

Police Chief Kang told reporters on Monday that Mr. Park was suspected of having sheltered a fugitive leftist radical. Mr. Kang said the two officers twice plunged Mr. Park's head into a bath filled with water in an attempt to make him reveal the fugitive's whereabouts. On the second occasion, he said, they crushed his throat against the bath rim, suffocating him. The two officers were said to have been arrested.

News of the death stirred public outrage, with opposition leaders and dissidents claiming it was just "the tip of the iceberg" of widespread, institutionalized torture of political offenders.

Officials of the opposition New Korea Democratic Party said the death illustrated common police practices, in trying to make Government critics admit to pro-Communist sympathies.

Killing Called Isolated Case

The Seoul Government, which has been trying to forge a better image in advance of the 1988 Summer Olympic Games to be held in Seoul, has called the Park incident an isolated case. It has also denied consistently that the country holds political prisoners.

0162

The New York Times

A relative of a student detainee swinging her handbag at a riot-police officer who was trying to arrest protesters at a memorial rally in Seoul yesterday. The rally was for a student who died after being tortured by police.

The Washington Times WEDNESDAY, JANUARY 21, 1987 / PAGE 7A

Seoul National University students march in protest after a memorial service for torture victim. Park Chong-choi.

69-2

0163

Two fired in South Korea over death of a dissident

Seoul

President Chun Doo Hwan fired his home minister and the head of the National Police yesterday as a result of the death of a student activist while in police custody, Mr. Chun's office announced.

The announcement said Kim Chong Hoh was replaced as home minister by Chung Ho Yong, a former Army chief of staff, and Kang Min Chang was replaced as director general of National Police by the Seoul metropolitan police director, Lee Yong Chang.

Two police investigators have been arrested on charges of torturing the student to death.

Protester at a Seoul university carries photo of a fellow student who died during police interrogation.   ASSOCIATED PRESS

SOUTH KOREA
2 high officials fired in youth's torture death

President Chun Doo Hwan, acting to defuse a political crisis, fired his interior minister and national police chief yesterday after the government's admission that police had tortured a student to death.

Mr. Chun had earlier made an unprecedented public apology for last week's "shocking incident" in which Park Chong Chol, 21, died of suffocation during interrogation by two officers of the country's special anti-communist police squad.

The Seoul government, which has been trying to forge itself a better image in advance of the 1988 Seoul Summer Olympics, calls the incident an isolated case.

Opposition politicians and students staged a number of anti-government protests yesterday in connection with the killing. Top dissident Kim Young Sam and a group of supporters were blocked by police when they attempted to give a news conference.

69-3

0164

The Washington Times

Chun fires two aides in student's death

SEOUL, South Korea (Reuters) — President Chun Doo Hwan, acting to defuse a political crisis, fired his interior minister and national police chief yesterday following the government's admission that police tortured a student to death.

Mr. Chun earlier made an unprecedented public apology for the "shocking incident" in which Park Chong-chol, 21, died of suffocation last week during interrogation by two officers of the country's anti-communist police squad.

Interior Minister Kim Chong-hoh and National Police Chief Kang Min-chang formally resigned, accepting moral responsibility for the student's death. They had made public apologies on Monday.

Mr. Chun quickly named a new interior minister, close associate Chung Ho-yong, a former general who as commander of the South Korean Special Forces helped stage the 1979 coup which brought him to power.

He also promoted Seoul Police Commander Lee Yong-chang to replace Mr. Kang.

Opposition politicians and students staged a number of anti-government protests yesterday in connection with the student's death.

Dissident Kim Young-sam and a group of supporters were blocked by police when they attempted to enter a Christian human rights center to give a press conference.

Later Mr. Kim, one of the New Korea Democratic Party leaders, joined a 36-hour sit-in by dissidents in a city center office demanding an end to police brutality.

Another prominent critic of the government, former presidential candidate Kim Dae-jung, stayed with protesters throughout the night Monday.

More than 1,000 students took part in memorial demonstrations at three Seoul campuses for the student, whose body was cremated Friday.

An outburst of public anger followed the death of Mr. Park, a linguistics student at Seoul National University who was picked up last Wednesday for alleged anti-government agitation.

Police chief Kang told reporters that Mr. Park was suspected of having sheltered a fugitive leftist radical.

Mr. Kang said the two officers twice plunged Mr. Park's head into a bath filled with water in an attempt to make him reveal the fugitive's whereabouts. On the second occasion they crushed his throat against the bath rim, suffocating him.

The NKDP said it illustrated police practice in trying to make government critics admit to pro-communist sympathies.

The Seoul government, which has been trying to forge itself a better image in advance of the 1988 Seoul Summer Olympics, called the death an isolated case. It constantly denies the country has any political prisoners.

4A • WEDNESDAY, JANUARY 21, 1987 • USA TODAY

South Korean President Chun Doo Hwan replaced his home affairs minister and national police chief in connection with the torture-death of a student.

69-4

0165

주 라 성 총 영 사 관

주 라 성 (정) 840- ㄱㄱㄱ   1987. 2. 3.

수신 : 장관
참조 : 영사교민국장, <u>미주국장</u>, 정보문화국장
제목 : 기사 송부

　　　연 : WLA - 0126

　　　연호, 박종철군 사망 추도 대회 관련 L.A.TIMES 지 기사를
별첨과 같이 송부합니다.

첨부 : 상기 기사 1부.

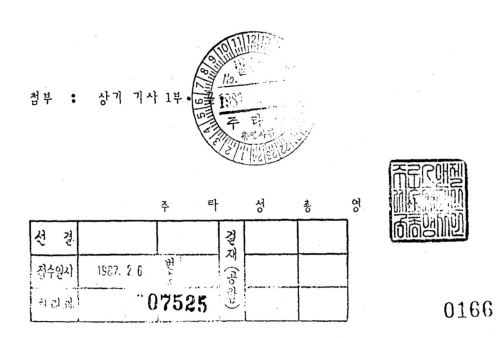

Los Angeles Times (87 2. 1)

Koreans Protest Death of Student

Olympic Blvd. Marchers Say Police in Seoul Killed Him

By TRACEY KAPLAN, *Times Staff Writer*

Carrying signs reading "Torture and murder must stop in South Korea" and "Death to killer Chun," about 100 demonstrators marched along Olympic Boulevard in Koreatown on Saturday to protest the recent death of a South Korean student who died while being interrogated by police.

The protesters carried a mock coffin and wore white to symbolize their sorrow and anger at the Jan. 14 death of Park Jong Chul, 21, a linguistics student at Seoul National University. Park suffocated when two policemen repeatedly shoved his head into a tub of water, crushing his throat in the process.

"Park's death is a manifestation of systematic oppression by President Chun Doo Hwan's government," said Lee Sang-yon, 26, a member of Young Koreans United of Los Angeles. "There have been many such tortures."

South Korean authorities initially reported that Park had died of shock but later acknowledged that he had been tortured to uncover the whereabouts of a campus radical leader. President Chun ordered the arrest of the two policemen on charges of homicide and fired his home minister and national police chief.

The incident has had a profound impact on Korean politics. About 80 opposition members of the South Korean Parliament staged a sit-in Wednesday to protest the government's refusal to allow a special committee to investigate police and prosecution departments.

Spokesmen for the Korean Institute for Human Rights, an umbrella organization that represents 18 groups in Southern California, said the dismissals and arrests were not sufficient. Leaders played a tape recording of Park's mother crying over the loss of her son during an emotional memorial ceremony in Ardmore Park before the demonstration.

"Concern is growing among Korean residents here," said Myong Jae Hwi, a member of the Southern California Congress for Restoration of Democracy in Korea, one of the 18 groups represented by the institute. "We vow to make the most of this incident to show that South Koreans are one of the most suppressed, unfortunate people in the world."

Shin Hyung Kim, spokeswoman for the Korea Task Force of Southern California, said fear kept more people from showing up to protest.

"The Korean dictator has the means to suppress and torture anyone, even in America, who speaks out," Kim said. "But we know the people's heart is with us."

Officials from the South Korean Consulate in Los Angeles declined to comment on the Saturday protest.

0167

연 오 : USW(F)- 82　1.25 1100 :

수 신 : 장 관 (미북, 정문)　　　발신 : 주미대사

제 목 : 박 준 철 사건

The New York Times SUNDAY, JANUARY 25, 1987 　 10

2 Policemen in South Korea Are Indicted in Torture Case

SEOUL, South Korea, Jan. 24 (Reuters) — Two South Korean policemen were formally charged today with torturing a student to death.

The indictment against Lieut. Cho Han Gyong, 38 years old, and Sgt. Kang Jin Gyu, 30, accused them of plunging the head of Park Chong Chol into a bathtub full of water to make him confess to anti-Government activities.

The 21-year-old student suffocated when his throat was crushed against the bathtub rim, it said.

The two officers face a maximum penalty of life imprisonment if found guilty, prosecutors said.

Aides of a leading dissident, Kim Dae Jung, said he was placed under house arrest again today to stop him from attending a meeting with other dissidents and human rights campaigners to discuss holding nation-wide rallies in memory of Mr. Park.

0168

韓国関係主要外信

1987.1.27(火) 07:20

(第 1 便)

外 信 名	内　　　　　容	페이지
Reuter,AP (마드리드發)	[盧信永]國務總理, 스페인 訪問	1
AFP (서울發) AP (東京發)	北韓 亡命人 事件 關聯 動向 - 필리핀으로 向發 가능성 대두 - [최광수]外務部長官, 駐韓 日大使에 自由意思 확인위한 亡命者와의 面談 許容 要求 - 北韓, 亡命者 北送 要求	3
外信綜合 (서울發)	[박종철]君 拷問致死事件 關聯 動向 - 臨時國會 召集 - [정호영]內務部長官, 拷問根絶 노력 다짐 - 警察, 拷問抗議 集會 强制 解散	7

0169

NNNN

¤ YK0946

261200 :AM-KOREA (EXPECT PIX)
SEOUL DISSIDENTS CLASH WITH RIOT POLICE OVER TORTURE CASE
SEOUL, JAN 26, REUTER - RIOT POLICE FIRING TEAR GAS TODAY
BARRED ABOUT 300 DISSIDENTS AND HUMAN-RIGHTS WORKERS FROM
ATTENDING A MEMORIAL SERVICE FOR A STUDENT WHO DIED UNDER
POLICE QUESTIONING, WITNESSES SAID.
ABOUT 150 PEOPLE ENTERED A CHURCH TO ATTEND THE SERVICE
BEFORE POLICE SEALED OFF SURROUNDING STREETS, OPENING FIRE
WITH TEAR GAS. SEVERAL PROTESTERS WERE DETAINED BUT THERE WERE
NO INJURIES, WITNESSES SAID.
LEADING DISSIDENT KIM YOUNG-SAM WAS AMONG THOSE TURNED
BACK BY POLICE AND HIS FELLOW DISSIDENT, KIM DAE-JUNG, AND
SEVERAL OTHER OPPOSITION POLITICIANS WERE PUT UNDER HOUSE
ARREST AND PREVENTED FROM ATTENDING, AIDES TO THE KIMS SAID.
TWO POLICE OFFICERS HAVE BEEN FORMALLY CHARGED WITH
TORTURING TO DEATH PARK CHONG-CHOL, A 21-YEAR-OLD LINGUISTICS
STUDENT. THEY ARE ACCUSED OF PLUNGING HIS HEAD INTO A BATH OF
WATER TO MAKE HIM CONFESS TO ANTI-GOVERNMENT ACTIVITIES.
THOUSANDS OF STUDENTS, WORKERS AND WOMENS' RIGHTS
CAMPAIGNERS HAVE DEMONSTRATED TO PROTEST OVER HIS DEATH AND
INTERIOR MINISTER KIM CHONG-HOH AND NATIONAL POLICE DIRECTOR
KANG MIN-CHANG HAVE BEEN DISMISSED OVER THE AFFAIR.
PRESIDENT CHUN DOO HWAN HAS MADE AN UNPRECEDENTED PUBLIC
APOLOGY FOR THE INCIDENT AND ORDERED THE GOVERNMENT TO SET UP
A SPECIAL BODY TO HELP END PHYSICAL ABUSE OF CRIMINAL
SUSPECTS.
MORE

NNNN

¤ YK0947

261203 :AM-KOREA =1.1
GOVERNMENT OFFICIALS TOLD PARLIAMENT THEY WOULD DO THEIR
BEST TO IMPROVE SOUTH KOREA'S HUMAN-RIGHTS RECORD, QUESTIONED
BECAUSE OF FREQUENT ALLEGATIONS OF TORTURE AGAINST POLITICAL
DETAINEES.
REUTER

7

0170

NNNN
ø YK0061

261529 :AM-KOREA 1STLD (EXPECT PIX)
SOUTH KOREAN CHRISTIANS DEMONSTRATE AGAINST TORTURE
SEOUL, JAN 26, REUTER - MORE THAN 2,000 CHRISTIANS ANGERED
BY THE DEATH OF A STUDENT IN POLICE CUSTODY DEMONSTRATED IN
SEOUL TODAY FOR A WORLD FREE OF TORTURE, WITNESSES SAID.
LED BY ABOUT 200 BANNER-WAVING PRIESTS, THE ROMAN CATHOLIC
DEMONSTRATORS MARCHED FOR AN HOUR OUTSIDE MYONGDONG CATHEDRAL
TO PROTEST AGAINST THE DEATH OF STUDENT ACTIVIST PARK
CHONG-CHOL, 21, UNDER POLICE INTERROGATION EARLIER THIS MONTH.
THE PLACARDS READ +DRIVE OUT MILITARY DICTATORSHIP+ AND
+WE WANT TO LIVE IN THE WORLD FREE OF TORTURE+.
ABOUT 1,000 POLICEMEN SURROUNDED THE CHURCH AND STOPPED
HUNDREDS OF YOUNG PROTESTERS, MARCHING IN THE CATHEDRAL
GROUNDS, FROM TAKING TO THE STEETS, THE WITNESSES SAID.
TWO POLICE OFFICERS HAVE BEEN FORMALLY CHARGED WITH
TORTURING PARK TO DEATH. THEY ARE ACCUSED OF PLUNGING THE
LINGUISTICS STUDENT'S HEAD INTO A BATH OF WATER TO MAKE HIM
CONFESS TO ANTI-GOVERNMENT ACTIVITIES.
EARLIER RIOT POLICE FIRED TEAR GAS TO PREVENT ABOUT 300
DISSIDENTS AND HUMAN RIGHTS CAMPAIGNERS FROM ENTERING A
CHRISTIAN HUMAN RIGHTS CENTRE WHERE THEY PLANNED TO DISCUSS
ORGANISING A MASS PROTEST RALLY AGAINST TORTURE.
HORE

0171

¤ YK0062

261531 :AM-KOREA 1STLD =1.1
    POLICE SEALED OFF STREETS LEADING TO THE CENTRE AND
DETAINED SEVERAL PEOPLE DEFYING ORDERS TO DISPERSE BUT THERE
WERE NO INJURIES, WITNESSES SAID. ABOUT 150 PEOPLE WHO ENTERED
THE BUILDING EARLIER HELD A MEMORIAL SERVICE FOR PARK.
    LEADING DISSIDENT KIM YOUNG-SAM WAS AMONG THOSE TURNED
BACK FROM THE CENTRE BY POLICE AND HIS FELLOW DISSIDENT, KIM
DAE-JUNG, AND SEVERAL OTHER OPPOSITION POLITICIANS WERE PUT
UNDER HOUSE ARREST AND PREVENTED FROM ATTENDING, AIDES TO THE
KIMS SAID.
    PRESIDENT CHUN DOO HWAN HAS MADE AN UNPRECEDENTED PUBLIC
APOLOGY FOR PARK'S DEATH AND ORDERED THE GOVERNMENT TO SET UP
A SPECIAL BODY TO HELP END PHYSICAL ABUSE OF CRIMINAL
SUSPECTS.
    GOVERNMENT OFFICIALS TOLD ... (PICK UP 7TH PARA AM-KOREA)
REUTER
                                    9

R I
    KOREA-1STLD-PICKUP4THGRAF 1-26
    (MORE PROTESTS)
    SEOUL, JAN.26 (UPI) -- POLICE MONDAY FIRED TEAR GAS PROFUSELY TO
BREAK UP TWO VIOLENT ANTI-GOVERNMENT DEMONSTRATIONS PROTESTING THE
RECENT TORTURE DEATH OF A COLLEGE STUDENT DURING AN INVESTIGATION,
WITNESSES SAID.
    THERE WERE NO IMMEDIATE REPORTS OF ARRESTS OR INJURIES IN THE
TWO VIOLENT CLASHES REPORTED IN DOWNTOWN SEOUL DURING THE DAY, THE
WITNESSES SAID.
    IN ONE CLASH, POLICE, FIRING TEAR GAS, BATTLED FOR MORE THAN ONE
HOUR SOME 700 ROCK-THROWING STUDENTS WHO WERE TRYING TO MARCH OFF
THEIR SCHOOL, SUNGKYUNKWAN UNIVERSITY, THE WITNESSES SAID.
    SHOUTING, +POLICE, MURDERER,+ THE STUDENTS HURLED ROCKS AT RIOT
POLICE WHO RETALIATED WITH TEAR GAS, THE WITNESSS SAID. THE STUDENTS
ENDED THE PROTEST ABOUT ONE HOUR LATER.
    ABOUT 1,500 METERS AWAY, SOME 500 PEOPLE CLASHED WITH RIOT POLICE
WHO BLOCKED OFF THE KOREA NATIONAL COUNCIL OF CHURCHES (KNCC) WHERE
28 PROMINENT RELIGIOUS, CIVIC AND DISSIDENT LEADERS WERE TO
INAUGURATE A MEMORIAL COMMITTEE FOR THE DEAD STUDENT, THE WITNESSES
SAID.
    DELETE 3RDGRAF AND PICKUP 4THGRAF BGNG:THE PROTESTS MONDAY ETC.
    (UPI) PS
CCCCQQE ZCZ
=01261118   16   0172
NNNN

GLGL

EXR0123 3 /AFP-AE62

SKOREA-TEARGAS

POLICE USE TEARGAS TO DISPERSE SEOUL GATHERING

SEOUL, JAN 26 (AFP) - RIOT POLICE USED TEARGAS TO DISPERSE SEVERAL HUNDRED PEOPLE WHO HAD GATHERED FOR A MEETING HERE MONDAY TO DISCUSS A PLANNED MEMORIAL SERVICE FOR A STUDENT WHO DIED UNDER POLICE TORTURE, EYEWITNESSES SAID.

HUNDREDS OF PLAINCLOTHES POLICE AND RIOT POLICE FORMED A TIGHT CORDON OUTSIDE THE NATIONAL COUNCIL FOR CHURCHES (NCC) BUILDING IN SEOUL, WHERE THE MEETING WAS TO BE HELD, WITNESSES SAID.

WHEN SEVERAL HUNDRED PEOPLE TRIED TO PUSH THEIR WAY INTO THE BUILDING, POLICE FIRED A BARRAGE OF TEAR GAS BOMBS TO CHASE THEM AWAY, AS SOME DISSIDENTS ALREADY INSIDE THE BUILDING POURED BUCKETS OF COLD WATER ONTO THE POLICE OUT OF THE WINDOWS IN RETALIATION.

OPPOSITION AND DISSIDENT LEADERS HAD ANNOUNCED THAT THEY WOULD MEET AT THE NCC BUILDING MONDAY TO STUDY PLANS FOR A NATIONAL MEMORIAL SERVICE FOR SEOUL UNIVERSITY STUDENT PARK CHONG-CHUL WHO DIED UNDER POLICE TORTURE 12 DAYS AGO.

PKW/SJK

AFP 260922 GMT JAN 87

0173

AP-NY-01-26-87 0939GMT

BB
W201
    R
    LEAD SOUTH KOREA-KIM INSERT
    RA
    SEOUL - LEAD SOUTH KOREA-KIM, TO COVER DEVELOPMENTS, INSERT
AFTER 6TH GRAF: PARTICIPANTS.
    LATER, POLICE FIRED ABOUT 30 TEAR GAS SHELLS TO DISPERSE PEOPLE,
NUMBERING ABOUT 800 AT ONE TIME, WHO GATHERED OUTSIDE THE BUILDING,
DISSIDENT SOURCES SAID. THEY SAID SOME OF THE PEOPLE ATTEMPTED TO
ENTER THE BUILDING.
    AN ESTIMATED 300 PEOPLE IN THE CROWD CLASHED WITH POLICE WHILE
PROTESTING THE POLICE BLOCKADE, AND ONE FEMALE STUDENT WAS INJURED
AND TAKEN TO A HOSPITAL, THEY ADDED. THERE WERE NO IMMEDIATE
REPORTS OF ARRESTS.
    THE SOURCES, WHO INSISTED ON ANONYMITY, SAID THE MEETING PLANNED
INSIDE THE BUILDING COULD NOT BE HELD, BUT THAT ABOUT 100
DISSIDENTS WHO HAD SNEAKED INTO THE BUILDING HELD A BRIEF MEMORIAL
SERVICE FOR THE STUDENT WHO WAS TORTURED TO DEATH.
    TWO POLICE, 7TH GRAF SEOUL - LEAD SOUTH KOREA-KIM
AP-NY-01-26-87 0943GMT   18

                                                        0174

GLGL
EXR0144 3 /AFP-RF03
SKOREA 1
   S. KOREAN POLICE TEAR GAS CROWD HEADED FOR MEETING ON TORTURED
STUDENT

   SEOUL, JAN 26 (AFP) - RIOT POLICE USED TEAR GAS TO DISPERSE
SEVERAL HUNDRED PEOPLE TRYING TO ATTEND A MEETING HERE MONDAY TO
DISCUSS A MEMORIAL SERVICE FOR A DISSIDENT STUDENT WHO DIED UNDER
POLICE TORTURE, WITNESSES SAID.
   DISSIDENT LEADERS, INCLUDING KIM DAE-JUNG, WERE PLACED UNDER
HOUSE ARREST TO PREVENT THEM ATTENDING, DISSIDENT SOURCES SAID.
   WITNESSES SAID A TIGHT CORDON OF HUNDREDS OF PLAINCLOTHES
POLICEMEN AND RIOT POLICE HAD BEEN DEPLOYED OUTSIDE THE NATIONAL
COUNCIL FOR CHURCHES BUILDING TO FOIL THE GATHERING OF OPPOSITION
AND DISSIDENT LEADERS.
   WHEN A CROWD OF SEVERAL HUNDRED TRIED TO PUSH THEIR WAY INTO
THE BUILDING, POLICE FIRED A BARRAGE OF TEAR GAS BOMBS TO CHASE
THEM AWAY.
   IN RETALIATION SOME DISSIDENTS ALREADY INSIDE THE BUILDING
POURED BUCKETS OF COLD WATER ONTO POLICE OUTSIDE, WITNESSES SAID.
   SOME 28 OPPOSITION AND DISSIDENT LEADERS HAD ANNOUNCED THEY
WOULD MEET THERE TO STUDY PLANS FOR A NATIONAL MEMORIAL SERVICE FOR
THE SEOUL UNIVERSITY STUDENT PARK CHONG-CHUL, WHO DIED WHILE BEING
TORTURED BY POLICE 12 DAYS AGO.
   MEANWHILE, 1,500 RIOT POLICE WERE DEPLOYED AROUND SEOUL'S
MYUNG-DONG ROMAN CATHOLIC CATHEDRAL WHERE A MASS FOR PARK WAS DUE
TO BE HELD, WITNESSES SAID.
   ONE OF MR. KIM'S AIDES SAID A POLICE CONTINGENT HAD BEEN POSTED
OUTSIDE THE 61-YEAR-OLD OPPOSITION LEADER'S HOME TO PREVENT HIM
ATTENDING MONDAY'S MEETING.
   MORE PKM/JM
AFP   261005 GMT JAN 87   13

                                    -   0175

GLGL
EXR0145 3 /AFP-AF04
SKOREA 2-LAST
(SEOUL)

IT WAS THE 43RD TIME MR. KIM HAD BEEN PLACED UNDER HOUSE ARREST
SINCE HE RETURNED HOME IN FEBRUARY 1985, AFTER TWO YEARS OF
SELF-IMPOSED EXILE IN THE UNITED STATES, TO LEAD A CAMPAIGN FOR
GREATER DEMOCRACY IN SOUTH KOREA.

DISSIDENT SOURCES SAID AT LEAST FIVE OTHER DISSIDENT LEADERS
HAD ALSO BEEN PUT UNDER HOUSE ARREST.

MEANWHILE, PARLIAMENT CONVENED A THREE-DAY EXTRAORDINARY
SESSION DEMANDED BY THE OPPOSITION TO LOOK INTO MR. PARK'S DEATH.

HOME MINISTER CHUNG HO-YONG ASSURED PARLIAMENT THAT EVERY
EFFORT WOULD BE EXERTED TO ELIMINATE TORTURE BY POLICE.

PARLIAMENT IS SET TO CREATE A SPECIAL PARLIAMENTARY BODY TO
ENSURE THE PROTECTION OF HUMAN RIGHTS.

BUT SOME OPPOSITION MEMBERS SAID THE CREATION OF SUCH A BODY
WOULD BE MEANINGLESS IF IT WERE NOT GIVEN INVESTIGATIVE POWERS.

OPPOSITION NEW KOREA DEMOCRATIC PARTY MEMBERS ALSO SAID THE
GOVERNMENT SHOULD THOROUGHLY INVESTIGATE THE RECENT DEATHS OF TWO
UNIVERSITY STUDENTS AND AN ANTI-GOVERNMENT DEMONSTRATOR IF IT WAS
REALLY DETERMINED TO ERADICATE TORTURE.

THEY ALSO DEMANDED THAT THE GOVERNMENT FULLY EXPLAIN HOW A
TOTAL OF 238 PEOPLE WHO THEY BELIEVED HAD BEEN TORTURED DURING
INTERROGATION HAD BEEN DETAINED WITHOUT ARREST WARRANTS IN THE LAST
THREE MONTHS.

PKM/JM
AFP 261009 GMT JAN 87

14

0176

```
ØQ
W149
   R
   LEAD SOUTH KOREA-KIM
   RA
   NO PICKUP
   EDS: UPDATES WITH ASSEMBLY OPENING, OTHER DEVELOPMENTS
   SEOUL, SOUTH KOREA (AP) - THE NATIONAL ASSEMBLY OPENED A SPECIAL
THREE-DAY SESSION MONDAY TO TAKE UP THE TORTURE DEATH OF A SOUTH
KOREAN UNIVERSITY STUDENT AT THE HANDS OF POLICE.
   QUESTIONING OF GOVERNMENT OFFICIALS BY OPPOSITION LAWMAKERS
BEGAN QUICKLY AFTER THE ASSEMBLY WAS CONVENED IN THE EARLY
AFTERNOON.
   THE MAJOR OPPOSITION NEW KOREA DEMOCRATIC PARTY, JOINED BY THE
MINOR KOREA NATIONAL PARTY, HAD DEMANDED THE HOLDING OF THE SPECIAL
SESSION. THE RULING DEMOCRATIC JUSTICE PARTY AT FIRST WAS
RELUCTANT, BUT OVER THE WEEKEND AGREED TO THE OPPOSITION DEMANDS.
   DESPITE THE AGREEMENT, THE FUROR CONTINUED IN OTHER AREAS OVER
THE DEATH OF 21-YEAR-OLD PARK JONG-CHUL, A SEOUL NATIONAL
UNIVERSITY STUDENT WHO DIED JAN. 14 WHILE BEING INTERROGATED BY
POLICE IN CONNECTION WITH ANTI-GOVERNMENT ACTIVITIES.
   FOR THE SECOND TIME IN THREE DAYS, DISSIDENT LEADER KIM DAE-JUNG
WAS PUT UNDER HOUSE ARREST TO KEEP HIM FROM ATTENDING A MEETING
AIMED AT MAKING PLANS FOR A PROTEST RALLY.
   DISSIDENT SOURCES SAID THREE OTHER LEADERS IN THE MOVEMENT ALSO
WERE PLACED UNDER HOUSE ARREST, AND THAT ''HUNDREDS'' OF POLICE HAD
BEEN DEPLOYED OUTSIDE THE NATIONAL COUNCIL OF CHURCHES OFFICE
BUILDING, WHERE THE MEETING WAS TO HAVE BEEN HELD, TO PREVENT
ENTRANCE BY OTHER PARTICIPANTS.
   TWO POLICE OFFICERS HAVE BEEN ARRESTED AND CHARGED WITH CAUSING
THE STUDENT'S DEATH BY BRUTAL ACTS. THE HOME MINISTER AND THE
DIRECTOR OF NATIONAL POLICE WERE FIRED, WHILE A POLICE
SUPERINTENDENT WAS REMOVED FROM HIS POST IN STEPS TO FIX
RESPONSIBILITY.
   MORE
AP-NY-01-26-87 0708GMT                    15
```

BB
W150
    R
SEOUL - LEAD SOUTH KOREA-KIM 2
    RA
    IT WAS ANNOUNCED ON MONDAY THAT TWO MORE POLICEMEN HAD BEEN
RELIEVED OF THEIR DUTIES, BUT DETAILS WERE NOT IMMEDIATELY
AVAILABLE.
    SHORTLY BEFORE THE SPECIAL ASSEMBLY SESSION OPENED, LEE MIN-WOO,
PRESIDENT OF THE MAJOR OPPOSITION PARTY, CALLED FOR THE LAUNCHING
OF A NATIONWIDE CAMPAIGN TO PREVENT POLICE FROM TAKING PEOPLE INTO
CUSTODY OR MAKING SEARCHES OF PROPERTY WITHOUT OBTAINING WARRANTS
THROUGH LEGAL PROCEDURES.
    ''A SPECIAL ANTI-TORTURE COMMITTEE, WHICH THE RULING AND
OPPOSITION PARTIES HAVE AGREED TO SET UP IN THE NATIONAL ASSEMBLY,
SHOULD BE EMPOWERED TO THOROUGHLY INVESTIGATE ALL CASES OF
TORTURE,'' LEE SAID.
    HE SPOKE AT A NEW YEAR NEWS CONFERENCE, WHERE HE ALSO URGED THE
GRANTING OF AMNESTY AND RESTORATION OF CIVIL RIGHTS TO POLITICAL
DETAINEES, THE POLITICAL NEUTRALITY OF PUBLIC SERVANTS AND A
GUARANTEE OF FREE POLITICAL PARTY ACTIVITIES.
    LEE ALSO TOLD REPORTERS THE NATIONAL ASSEMBLY SHOULD REVISE THE
ELECTION LAW AS SOON AS POSSIBLE BECAUSE THE GOVERNMENT OF
PRESIDENT CHUN DOO-HWAN AND HIS RULING POLITICAL PARTY HAVE SAID
THEY FAVOR THE HOLDING OF A GENERAL ELECTION THIS YEAR.
    THE TWO POLITICAL SIDES ARE DEEPLY DIVIDED OVER APPROACHES TO
CHANGES IN THE CONSTITUTION. AFTER STANDING STRONG AGAINST ANY
REVISIONS, THE RULING AUTHORITIES NOW ADVOCATE A PARLIAMENTARY TYPE
OF GOVERNMENT WITH A STRONG PRIME MINISTER AND A LARGELY FIGUREHEAD
PRESIDENT.
    MORE
AP-NY-01-26-87 0710GMT   16

                                                    0178

W151

R

SEOUL - LEAD SOUTH KOREA-KIM 3

RA

THE OPPOSITION IS SEEKING A SYSTEM PROVIDING FOR THE DIRECT,
POPULAR ELECTION OF THE PRESIDENT. IT MAINTAINS THAT A
PARLIAMENTARY SETUP AND THE PRESENT ELECTORAL COLLEGE SELECTION OF
THE PRESIDENT BOTH WOULD FAVOR THOSE IN POWER AND SERVE TO KEEP
THEM THERE.

CHUN'S SEVEN-YEAR TERM ENDS IN FEBRUARY 1988, AND HE HAS SAID HE
WILL STEP DOWN AT THAT TIME TO GIVE SOUTH KOREA ITS FIRST PEACEFUL
TRANSFER OF POWER. WHILE A BITTER POLITICAL STRUGGLE HAS GONE ON
FOR MONTHS, GOVERNMENT FORCES APPEARED TO BE ON THE OFFENSIVE UNTIL
THE TORTURE DEATH OF THE UNIVERSITY STUDENT INJECTED AN EMOTIONAL
NEW ISSUE AND BROUGHT FRESH, UNIFIED ACTION BY THE OPPOSITION.

END

AP-NY-01-26-87 0712GMT

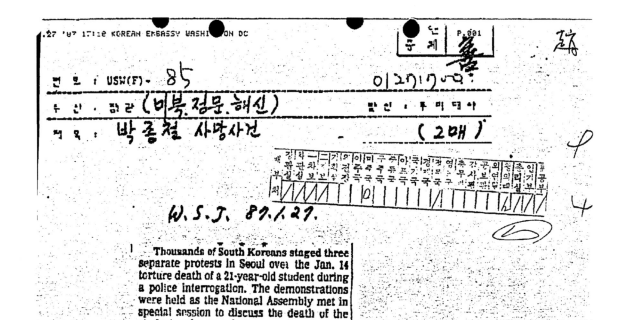

W.S.J. 87.1.27.

Thousands of South Koreans staged three separate protests in Seoul over the Jan. 14 torture death of a 21-year-old student during a police interrogation. The demonstrations were held as the National Assembly met in special session to discuss the death of the student, who was being questioned about anti-government activities.

W.T. 87.1.27.

Asia

Torture-death protests dispersed

SEOUL, South Korea — Police dispersed thousands of demonstrators at three separate protests yesterday as the National Assembly met in special session to discuss the Jan. 14 death of student activist Park Chong-chol, 21. The government has admitted Mr. Park was a victim of police torture but argued that it was "an unfortunate and isolated case." Its critics, however, say the case is "only a tip of the iceberg" of South Korea's human rights violations.

The most violent clash of the day was reported at Sungkyunkwan University in a central residential area, where 1,000 riot policemen battled 700 rock-throwing students shouting "Police murderers" for more than an hour, witnesses said. Almost simultaneously, hundreds of people were dispersed outside the National Council of Churches building downtown, where 28 prominent religious, civic and dissident leaders were to inaugurate a memorial committee for the dead student. At least five civic and opposition leaders, including Kim Dae-jung, were confined to their homes by police to prevent them from attending the meeting.

After a one-hour evening Mass at Myongdong Catholic Cathedral in central Seoul, thousands of people led by white-robed priests and nuns carrying banners reading "Drive out military dictatorship," and "We want to live in a world free of torture," stood in silent protest for 90 minutes as 1,500 riot police formed human barriers, blocking off the entrance to the cathedral. After most of the priests and nuns withdrew, about 600 youths scuffled with police, witnesses said.

0180

□ Chicago Tribune, Tuesday, January 27, 1987   Section 1   5

S. Korean protesters, cops clash

SEOUL [AP]—Hundreds of dissidents clashed with police Monday as the National Assembly met in special session to discuss the torture death of a 21-year-old university student under police interrogation.

Police fired about 30 tear-gas shells to disperse protesters, who numbered about 800 at one point, outside the National Council of Churches office building, dissident sources said.

A meeting had been called inside the building to plan a protest rally over the student's death, said the sources, who spoke on condition of anonymity.

They said about 300 people in the crowd tangled with police and a female student was hurt and taken to a hospital.

In the National Assembly, opposition lawmakers immediately questioned government officials about the Jan. 14 death of Park Jong Chul of Seoul National University, who died while being questioned by police about antigovernment activities.

The major opposition New Korea Democratic Party, joined by the smaller Korea National Party, had demanded the special three-day session that opened Monday. President Chun Doo Hwan's governing Democratic Justice Party balked at first, but agreed to it over the weekend.

For the second time in three days, dissident leader Kim Dae Jung was put under house arrest to keep him from attending the protest planning meeting. Dissident sources said three other leaders in the movement also were placed under house arrest.

Two police officers have been arrested on charges of causing Park's death by brutal acts. The home minister and national police director were fired, and a police superintendent was removed from his post.

It was announced Monday that two more policemen were relieved of duty, but details were not available.

Before the special session began, Lee Min Woo, president of the New Korea Democratic Party, called for a national campaign to prevent police from taking people into custody or searching property without warrants.

He said the party in power has agreed that a special committee be set up in the assembly with power to investigate all cases of torture.

0181

外務部 情報1課

韓国関係主要外信

1987. 1. 28(水) 07:30

(第 1 便)

外 信 名	内　　　　容	페이지
AFP (東京發)	集團 脫出 北韓住民 11名, 亡命 希望地 관련 異見	1
AP, AFP, Reuter (서울發)	[박종철]君 拷問 致死 事件 - 野黨 및 反政府團體. 2.7 全國的인 　추도식 거행 예정 - 서울市内 大學生 500名, 연세大學에서 　拷問 反對 示威	3
AP (서울發)	政局動向 - [盧泰愚]民正黨 代表委員, 民正黨 　主催 세미나에서 内閣責任制는 1人 　長期執權 防止에 寄與 言及 - 國家保安法 違反嫌疑 言論人 3名 起訴	11
UPI (앵커리지發)	美 地方法院, 美 漁業 監督人 暴行嫌疑 韓國人船長 公判위한 陪審員 選出	15
UPI (LA發)	휴즈社 헬機 北韓 密輸出 관련 美國人 2名, 無罪 主張	16

0182

GLGL

EXR0093 3 /AFP-AJ47

SKOREA-TORTURE 1

SOUTH KOREAN OPPOSITION TO HOLD MEMORIAL SERVICE ON FEBRUARY 7

SEOUL, JAN 27 (AFP) - SOUTH KOREAN OPPOSITION AND DISSIDENT GROUPS JOINTLY ANNOUNCED TUESDAY NATIONWIDE MEMORIAL SERVICES TO BE HELD ON FEBRUARY 7 FOR A DISSIDENT STUDENT WHO DIED UNDER POLICE TORTURE TWO WEEKS AGO.

SOME 20 OPPOSITION AND DISSIDENT LEADERS INCLUDING KIM DAE-JUNG AND KIM YOUNG-SAM MANAGED TO GATHER AT THE HEADQUARTERS OF THE DISSIDENT COUNCIL FOR PROMOTION OF DEMOCRACY IN SEOUL TO ANNOUNCE THE PLANNED SERVICE.

WITNESSES SAID POLICE WERE UNAWARE OF THE MEETING.

ON MONDAY, SEVERAL HUNDRED THOUSAND RIOT POLICE BLOCKED THE CHRISTIAN COUNCIL BUILDING IN SEOUL, PREVENTING A SIMILAR MEETING FROM BEING HELD.

PARK CHONG-CHUL WAS A 21-YEAR-OLD SEOUL NATIONAL UNIVERSITY STUDENT.

A TOTAL OF 9,782 PEOPLE HAVE SIGNED UP THROUGHOUT THE COUNTRY TO BECOME MEMBERS OF THE PREPARATORY COMMITTEE FOR PARK'S NATIONAL MEMORIAL SERVICE, A STATMENT ISSUED AFTER THE TUESDAY MEETING SAID.

THE COMMITTEE COMPRISES REPRESENTATIVES OF OPPOSITION POLITICAL PARTIES, DISSIDENT ORGANIZATIONS, ALL RELIGIOUS CIRCLES AND UNIVERSITY STUDENTS.

THE PREPARATORY COMMITTEE SAID THAT SEOUL'S MYONGDONG ROMAN CATHOLIC CHURCH WILL HOLD A MASS ON FEBRUARY 7 AT 2 P.M. WITH SIMULTANEOUS MASSES OR PRAYER MEETINGS AT ALL CHURCHES AND BUDDHIST TEMPLES THROUGHOUT THE COUNTRY.

MORE/PKM/PS   3

AFP   270545 GMT JAN 87

0183

GLGL
EXR0094 3 /AFP-AJ48
SKOREA-TORTURE 2-LAST
    (SEOUL)

    BELLS WOULD BE RUNG SIMULTANEOUSLY THROUGHOUT THE COUNTRY AT
WHICH TIME THE ENTIRE NATION WOULD OFFER ONE MINUTE OF SILENT
PRAYERS FOR THE REPOSE OF MR. PARK'S SOUL, THE COMMITTEE SAID.
    EVERYONE WILL BE ENCOURAGED TO WEAR BLACK RIBBONS ON THE DAY.
    THE COMMITTEE SAID THAT IT WILL CONTINUE TO CALL FOR FOR THE
ERADICATION OF TORTURE AND OTHER VIOLATIONS OF HUMAN RIGHTS IN
SOUTH KOREA, THE PRESENT GOVERNMENT HAVING PERPETRATED ''NUMEROUS''
HUMAN RIGHTS VIOLATIONS, ILLEGAL DETENTIONS AND TORTURES.
    PARK'S DEATH SERVED AS ''AN OCCASION TO AWAKEN ALL THE PEOPLE
FROM A LONG SUBMISSION AND RESIGNATION''.
    LATE MONDAY, SOME 2,000 PEOPLE STAGED A SILENT DEMONSTRATION
FOR MORE THAN AN HOUR IN FRONT OF A 1,500-MAN RIOT POLICE FORCE
DEPLOYED AT THE ENTRANCE TO THE MYONGDONG CATHEDRAL, AFTER
ATTENDING A MASS BY CARDINAL STEPHAN KIM.
    CATHOLIC PRIESTS AND NUNS HELD BANNERS DEMANDING THE OUSTER OF
THE ''MILITARY DICTATORSHIP''.
    CARDINAL KIM SAID AT THE MASS THAT PARK'S TORTURE AND DEATH WAS
NOT SOMETHING WHICH OCCURRED ''ACCIDENTALLY'' AND DEMANDED THAT
''ALL PRISONERS OF CONSCIENCE'' BE FREED FROM PRISON.
    PKM/PS
AFP 270548 GMT JAN 87

GLGL
EXR0117 3 /AFP-AJ83
SKOREA-TORTURE CORRECTION
    ≈≈≈CORRECTING EXR 093 EX-SEOUL

    ATTN. EDS, IN SKOREA-TORTURE,1 FOURTH PARA PLS READ X X X
SEVERAL HUNDRED RIOT POLICE X X X (STED SEVERAL HUNDRED THOUSAND
AS SENT).

                                        4
AFP 270654 GMT JAN 87

0184

R
.LEAD SOUTH KOREA-TORTURE
RA
EDS: UPDATES WITH DISSIDENTS SCHEDULING MEMORIAL SERVICES
SEOUL, SOUTH KOREA (AP) - A GROUP OF DISSIDENTS LED BY KIM DAE-JUNG AND KIM YOUNG-SAM DECIDED TUESDAY TO HOLD MEMORIAL SERVICES IN SEOUL AND PROVINCIAL CITIES ON FEB. 7 TO MOURN THE TORTURE DEATH OF AN ACTIVIST STUDENT, THE COUNCIL FOR THE PROMOTION OF DEMOCRACY ANNOUNCED.

THE DECISION CAME IN A MEETING AT THE DISSIDENT COUNCIL, CO-CHAIRED BY THE TWO KIMS. THE GROUP FORMED A COMMITTEE TO ORGANIZE THE MEMORIAL SERVICES.

THE COMMITTEE ALSO DECIDED TO HAVE CHRISTIAN CHURCHES AND BUDDHIST TEMPLES ACROSS THE COUNTRY RING BELLS AND MOTORISTS BLOW HORNS AT 2 P.M. FEB. 7, THE SCHEDULED TIME OF THE MEMORIAL RITES.

THE DISSIDENTS ORIGINALLY PLANNED TO FORM THE COMMITTEE MONDAY IN A MEETING AT THE DOWNTOWN NATIONAL COUNCIL OF CHURCHES OFFICES BUT THEY COULD NOT MEET BECAUSE OF POLICE INTERVENTION. KIM DAE-JUNG AND SEVERAL OTHER KEY DISSIDENTS WERE PLACED UNDER HOUSE ARREST TO KEEP THEM FROM TAKING PART IN MONDAY'S GATHERING AND POLICE SEALED OFF THE MEETING SITE.

MEANWHILE, PUBLISHED REPORTS SAID TUESDAY THAT TWO POLICEMEN ACCUSED OF THE STUDENT'S TORTURE DEATH LIKELY WOULD BE PUT ON TRIAL IN LATE MARCH OR EARLY APRIL AFTER PUBLIC FUROR HAS SUBSIDED.

QUOTING UNIDENTIFIED OFFICIALS AT THE SEOUL DISTRICT CRIMINAL COURT, THE YONHAP NEWS AGENCY SAID THE TRIAL WILL BE OPEN TO THE PUBLIC. UNDER PERTINENT LAWS AND REGULATIONS, CLOSED TRIALS CAN BE HELD HERE IN WHAT ARE TERMED ''SERIOUS MATTERS,'' INCLUDED CASES INVOLVING NATIONAL SECURITY.

MORE
5
AP-NY-01-27-87 0729GMT

0185

00

W198

R

SEOUL - LEAD SOUTH KOREA-TORTURE 2

RA

PARK CHONG-CHUL, A 21-YEAR-OLD SEOUL NATIONAL UNIVERSITY
STUDENT, DIED JAN. 14 WHILE UNDERGOING POLICE INTERROGATION IN
CONNECTION WITH ANTI-GOVERNMENT ACTIVITIES. OFFICIAL ANNOUNCEMENTS
HAVE SAID HE SUFFOCATED WHEN HIS THROAT WAS FORCED AGAINST THE RIM
OF A BATHTUB WHILE HIS HEAD WAS PUSHED UNDER WATER.

THE TWO POLICE OFFICERS, LT. CHO HAN-KYUNG AND SGT. KANG
JIN-KYU, WERE ARRESTED AND HAVE BEEN INDICTED ON CHARGES OF CAUSING
HIS DEATH ''BY BRUTAL ACTS.'' IF CONVICTED, THEY COULD FACE UP TO
LIFE TERMS IN PRISON.

IN ADDITION TO THE ARRESTS OF THE TWO POLICEMEN ALLEGEDLY
INVOLVED DIRECTLY, A POLICE SUPERINTENDENT WAS REMOVED FROM HIS
POST AND THE HOME MINISTER AND DIRECTOR OF NATIONAL POLICE WERE
REPLACED.

DESPITE THESE ACTIONS ON THE PART OF GOVERNMENT AUTHORITIES,
PUBLIC OUTCRY OVER THE CASE CONTINUED, RANGING FROM DENUNCIATIONS
AND CALLS FOR REFORM AND DEMOCRATIZATION BY THE POLITICAL
OPPOSITION AND DISSIDENT ELEMENTS TO RALLIES, PROTESTS AND
DEMONSTRATIONS.

ON MONDAY NIGHT, ABOUT 3,000 PEOPLE WERE REPORTED TO HAVE HELD A
''SILENT'' SERVICE MARKING THE STUDENT'S DEATH DURING A PRAYER
MEETING AT MYONGDONG CATHEDRAL, THIS COUNTRY'S MAIN ROMAN CATHOLIC
CENTER, IN THE HEART OF THE CAPITAL.

SOURCES SAID, 3RD GRAF SEOUL - SOUTH KOREA-TORTURE 2
AP-NY-01-27-87 0731GMT

6

00

0186

270728 :PM-KOREA (PIX SE001)
THOUSANDS TO SPEARHEAD NATIONWIDE PROTEST AGAINST TORTURE
    SEOUL, JAN 27, REUTER - NEARLY 10,000 SOUTH KOREANS WILL
LEAD A NATIONWIDE PROTEST AGAINST TORTURE NEXT WEEK TO MOURN
THE DEATH OF A STUDENT IN POLICE CUSTODY, DISSIDENTS KIM
DAE-JUNG AND KIM YOUNG-SAM SAID TODAY.
    CHURCH BELLS WILL TOLL, CAR HORNS WILL BLARE, FLAGS WILL
BE HOISTED AT HALF MAST AND PEDESTRIANS WILL BE URGED TO PRAY
IN THE STREETS DURING THE PROTEST ON FEBRUARY 7, THE TWO
DISSIDENTS TOLD A NEWS CONFERENCE.
    THEY SAID ALMOST 10,000 PEOPLE, INCLUDING SOME 1,800 ROMAN
CATHOLIC, PROTESTANT AND BUDDHIST CLERGYMEN, HAD AGREED TO
ORGANISE THE PROTEST TO DEMAND AN IMMEDIATE END TO TORTURE IN
SOUTH KOREA.
    A MEMORIAL SERVICE WILL ALSO BE HELD ON THE DAY AT SEOUL'S
LARGEST CHURCH, MYONGDONG CATHEDRAL, FOR PARK CHONG-CHOL, 21,
WHO DIED WHILE BEING QUESTIONED BY POLICE ABOUT
ANTI-GOVERNMENT ACTIVITIES.
    TWO POLICEMEN FACE TRIAL ON CHARGES OF TORTURING PARK TO
DEATH EARLIER THIS MONTH. THEY HAVE ADMITTED PLUNGING THE
LINGUIST STUDENT'S HEAD IN A TUB OF WATER DURING QUESTIONING.
    LAST NIGHT MORE THAN 2,000 ANGRY CHRISTIANS, LED BY 200
PLACARD-CARRYING PRIESTS, DEMONSTRATED AT MYONGDONG CATHEDRAL
IN PROTEST AT PARK'S DEATH. THE PLACARDS READ +DRIVE OUT
MILITARY DICTATORSHIP+ AND +WE WANT TO LIVE IN THE WORLD FREE
OF TORTURE.+
    MORE   7

0187

NNNN

ม YK0472

270730 :PM-KOREA =1.1

HOURS BEFORE THE DEMONSTRATION BY THE ROMAN CATHOLICS, KIM
YOUNG-SAM WAS AMONG 300 DISSIDENTS AND HUMAN RIGHTS
CAMPAIGNERS WHO CONFRONTED TEAR GAS-FIRING RIOT POLICE OUTSIDE
A CHRISTIAN HUMAN RIGHTS CENTRE.

KIM DAE-JUNG AND SEVERAL OTHER DISSIDENTS WERE YESTERDAY
PLACED UNDER HOUSE ARREST TO STOP THEM GOING TO THE CENTRE,
WHERE THE 300 WERE DUE TO DISCUSS ORGANISING NEXT WEEK'S
RALLY.

SPEAKING AT A SPECIAL PARLIAMENTARY SESSION CALLED TO
DISCUSS ALLEGATIONS OF WIDESPREAD TORTURE OF DISSIDENTS,
INTERIOR MINISTER CHUNG HO-YONG SAID THERE WOULD NEVER BE
FURTHER CASES OF TORTURE OR HUMAN RIGHTS ABUSES BY POLICE.

CHUNG WAS APPOINTED AFTER PRESIDENT CHUN DOO HWAN FIRED
HIS PREDECESSOR THIS MONTH TO DEFUSE NATIONAL OUTRAGE OVER
PARK'S DEATH.

REUTER

8

0188

270832 :PM-KOREA =2 SEOUL (REOPENS)
    ABOUT 500 STUDENTS CHANTING +DOWN WITH DICTATORSHIP+ AND
+GO AWAY MURDERER REGIME+ CLASHED WITH RIOT POLICE AT SEOUL'S
PRESBYTERIAN YONSEI UNIVERSITY TODAY, EYEWITNESSES SAID.
    THEY SAID AT LEAST TWO STUDENT LEADERS WERE DETAINED BY
POLICE.
    THE PROTESTERS GATHERED AT THE CAMPUS TO MOURN THE DEATH
OF PARK ALTHOUGH THEY WERE ON A WINTER VACATION. THEY HURLED
STONES AND PETROL BOMBS AT RIOT POLICE WHO RETALIATED WITH
TEAR GAS SHELLS.
    HUNDREDS OF POLICEMEN ENTERED THE CAMPUS TO BREAK UP THE
PROTEST AFTER THE STUDENTS TRIED TO MARCH ON TO THE STREET
WITH THEIR ARMS LINKED.
    THE STUDENTS PLEDGED THAT THEY WOULD ACTIVELY TAKE PART IN
NEXT WEEK'S PROTEST RALLIES.
                                              9
    REUTER

0189

2ND LEAD SOUTH KOREA-TORTURE

RA

EDS: UPDATES WITH STUDENT-POLICE CLASH

SEOUL, SOUTH KOREA (AP) - STUDENTS AND POLICE CLASHED BRIEFLY AT YONSEI UNIVERSITY TUESDAY FOLLOWING A MEMORIAL SERVICE AND RALLY FOR A STUDENT WHO DIED WHILE UNDERGOING POLICE INTERROGATION.

SOURCES SAID ABOUT 500 STUDENTS FROM SEVERAL UNIVERSITIES IN SEOUL GATHERED ON THE YONSEI CAMPUS AND THEN MARCHED OUT THE MAIN GATES AND CONFRONTED ABOUT 1,000 RIOT POLICE. THE STUDENTS WERE REPORTED TO HAVE SHOUTED SLOGANS DENOUNCING THE TORTURE DEATH AND TO HAVE HURLED ROCKS.

THE SOURCES, WHO INSISTED ON ANONYMITY, SAID POLICE MOVED ON TO THE CAMPUS AND FIRED ABOUT 15 TEAR GAS ROUNDS TO DISPERSE THE DEMONSTRATORS. ONE WOMAN STUDENT WAS SEEN BEING TAKEN AWAY BY POLICE, BUT NO INJURIES WERE REPORTED.

SLOGANS SHOUTED BY PROTESTORS WERE SAID TO HAVE INCLUDED ''DOWN WITH THE VIOLENT REGIME INDULGING IN MURDEROUS TORTURE. ... CLARIFY THE TRUTH OF THE INCIDENT. ... DISBAND THE DEFENSE SECURITY COMMAND AND THE AGENCY FOR NATIONAL SECURITY PLANNING, THE HOTBEDS OF ILLEGAL INVESTIGATION. ...''

MEANWHILE, A GROUP OF DISSIDENTS LED BY KIM DAE-JUNG AND KIM YOUNG-SAM DECIDED TO HOLD MEMORIAL SERVICES IN SEOUL AND PROVINCIAL CITIES ON FEB. 7 TO MOURN THE TORTURE DEATH OF THE STUDENT, THE COUNCIL FOR THE PROMOTION OF DEMOCRACY ANNOUNCED.

THE DECISION, 2ND GRAF SEOUL - LEAD SOUTH KOREA-TORTURE

AP-NY-01-27-87 0855GMT

10

0190

韓国關係主要外信

1987.1.28(水) 16:00
(第 2 便)

外 信 名	内 容	페이지
AFP, Reuter (서울發)	[박종철] 拷問事件 - 新民黨 議員, 人權特委 構成 關聯, 無期限 籠城 突入	1
AP (워싱톤發)	美 國防省,韓國에 6,500萬弗의 美製 航空機 部品 供給 合意	5
AP (서울發)	政府, 美國産 담배販売所를 1,000個所로 늘리기로 決定	7
AP (서울發)	KAL, 向後 5年間 20億弗 相當 新型 제트機 導入 發表	8
Reuter (서울發)	韓國 株式市場,外國人의 直接投資 期待로 好況	9

0191

GLGL

EXR0087 3 /AFP-A002

SKOREA-TORTURE 1

<u>SOUTH KOREAN OPPOSITION MP'S LAUNCH INDEFINITE SIT-IN</u>

SEOUL, JAN 28 (AFP) - <u>OPPOSITION MP'S BEGAN AN INDEFINITE</u>
<u>SIT-IN IN PARLIAMENT HERE WEDNESDAY TO PRESS THEIR DEMAND THAT A</u>
<u>PROPOSED COMMITTEE ON HUMAN RIGHTS BE EMPOWERED WITH BROAD</u>
<u>INSPECTION RIGHTS INTO NATIONAL AFFAIRS, OPPOSITION LEGISLATORS</u>
<u>SAID.</u>

<u>THE SIT-IN BY DEPUTIES OF THE NEW KOREA DEMOCRATIC PARTY (NKDP)</u>
<u>BEGAN EARLY WEDNESDAY AFTER THE MAJOR OPPOSITION PARTY AND THE</u>
<u>RULING DEMOCRATIC JUSTICE PARTY (DJP) FAILED TO NARROW THEIR</u>
<u>DIFFERENCES OVER FORMATION OF THE PROPOSED PARLIAMENTARY COMMITTEE</u>
<u>TO INVESTIGATE INFRINGEMENT OF HUMAN RIGHTS.</u>

THE OPPOSITION AND RULING PARTIES AGREED TO SET UP THE
COMMITTEE AFTER PRESIDENT CHUN DOO-HWAN'S GOVERNMENT CAME IN FOR
WIDESPREAD CRITICISM OVER THE DEATH OF A DISSIDENT STUDENT DURING
POLICE TORTURE TWO WEEKS AGO.

WITH THE SIT-IN STRIKE UNDER WAY, THE CURRENT THREE-DAY SPECIAL
SESSION OF THE NATIONAL ASSEMBLY, CONVENED TO LOOK INTO THE TORTURE
CASE, WAS EXPECTED TO END WEDNESDAY WITHOUT HOLDING THE MAIN
SESSION DURING WHICH THE COMMITTEE WAS TO HAVE BEEN SET UP,
PARLIAMENTARY SOURCES SAID.

<u>THE DJP OBJECTED TO THE OPPOSITION DEMAND THAT THE COMMITTEE BE</u>
<u>CONVENED WITH A QUORUM OF ONE-THIRD OF COMMITTEE MEMBERS AND HAVE</u>
<u>TWO SUB-COMMITTEES -- ONE TO INVESTIGATE THE TORTURE DEATH OF</u>
<u>UNIVERSITY STUDENT PARK CHONG-CHUL AND THE SECOND TO DEAL WITH</u>
<u>OTHER ALLEGATIONS OF HUMAN RIGHTS VIOLATIONS.</u>

MORE/CKP/KH

AFP 280402 GMT JAN 87   1

0192

GLGL
EXR0088 3 /AFP-A003
SKOREA-TORTURE 2-LAST
    (SEOUL)

    THE RULING PARTY SAID THE OPPOSITION HAD BROKEN A PREVIOUS
AGREEMENT THAT DETAILED GUIDELINES FOR THE OPERATION OF THE
COMMITTEE WOULD BE DISCUSSED AFTER THE COMMITTEE WAS SET UP.
    MEANWHILE, HOME MINISTER CHUNG HO-YONG TOLD PARLIAMENT LATE
TUESDAY THAT HE WOULD ORDER INVESTIGATION TO BE CONTINUED INTO THE
OPPOSITION'S ALLEGATION THAT ELECTRICITY WAS USED TO TORTURE THE
21-YEAR-OLD SEOUL NATIONAL UNIVERSITY STUDENT.
    HE ALSO SAID POLICE WOULD REOPEN INVESTIGATION INTO WHAT THE
OPPOSITION DESCRIBED AS TWO OTHER UNIVERSITY STUDENTS' MYSTERIOUS
DEATHS -- IN OCTOBER 1985 AND JUNE 1986 -- AND THE CASE OF A LABOR
ACTIVIST WHO WAS REPORTEDLY TAKEN AWAY BY POLICE LAST YEAR AND
LATER FOUND DEAD.
    MR. CHUNG WAS REPLYING TO THE OPPOSITION'S DEMAND THAT POLICE
MAKE PUBLIC THE RESULTS OF AN AUTOPSY AND PICTURES OF MR. PARK'S
BODY.
    THE OPPOSITION HAS CHARGED THAT POLICE HURRIEDLY CREMATED MR.
PARK'S BODY IN A BID TO DESTROY EVIDENCE OF TORTURE.
    CKP/KH
AFP 280405 GMT JAN 87

0193

280451 :PM-KOREA (EXPECT PIX)

SOUTH KOREAN OPPOSITION M.P.S STAGE PROTEST IN PARLIAMENT

SEOUL, JAN 28, REUTER - ABOUT 80 OPPOSITION MEMBERS OF PARLIAMENT STAGED A SIT-IN AT SOUTH KOREA'S NATIONAL ASSEMBLY TODAY TO PROTEST AT WHAT THEY ALLEGED WAS A GOVERNMENT ATTEMPT TO COVER UP TORTURE OF POLITICAL OFFENDERS, AN OPPOSITION SPOKESMAN SAID.

DURING THE NIGHT THE M.P.S, FROM THE NEW KOREA DEMOCRATIC PARTY (NKDP), PULLED OUT OF A SPECIAL ASSEMBLY SESSION CALLED TO DEBATE THE DEATH OF A STUDENT IN POLICE CUSTODY AND OCCUPIED A ROOM NEAR THE CHAMBER, DEMANDING THAT PARLIAMENT BE EMPOWERED TO INVESTIGATE THE ACTIVITIES OF GOVERNMENT AGENCIES.

THE RULING DEMOCRATIC JUSTICE PARTY (DJP) HAS AGREED TO FORM A SPECIAL PARLIAMENTARY COMMITTEE TO LOOK INTO ALLEGATIONS OF HUMAN RIGHTS ABUSES BUT HAS REFUSED TO ACCEPT THAT IT COULD PROBE POLICE AND PROSECUTION DEPARTMENTS.

THE DJP ACKNOWLEDGES A NEED TO CREATE SAFEGUARDS AGAINST FUTURE POLICE HUMAN RIGHTS ABUSES BUT CALLS THE OPPOSITION'S PROPOSAL UNCONSTITUTIONAL.

KIM HYON-KYU, THE NKDP'S PARLIAMENTARY LEADER, TOLD REPORTERS HIS PARTY LAUNCHED TODAY'S PROTEST BECAUSE THEY SUSPECTED THE DJP SOUGHT TO FORM A +COMMITTEE IN NAME ONLY, WITHOUT SUBSTANCE+.

MOST OF THE PROTESTING M.P.S HAVE PLEDGED TO TAKE PART NEXT WEEK IN A PLANNED NATIONWIDE DAY OF PROTEST AGAINST TORTURE TO MOURN THE DEATH OF PARK CHONG-CHOL, 21, WHILE UNDER POLICE INTERROGATION.

MORE   ЗЗ

0194

NNNN
ø YK0033

280454 :PM-KOREA =1.1
    DISSIDENT LEADERS KIM DAE-JUNG AND KIM YOUNG-SAM SAID
YESTERDAY THE ORGANISERS OF THE PROTEST DAY WOULD INCLUDE
LAWYERS, PROFESSORS AND POLITICIANS AS WELL AS ROMAN CATHOLIC,
PROTESTANT AND BUDDHIST CLERGY.
    DISSIDENTS ACCUSE POLICE OF USING TORTURE TO MAKE CRITICS
FALSELY CONFESS TO BEING PRO-COMMUNIST. THE GOVERNMENT DENIES
THIS BUT HAS ADMITTED POLICE TORTURED PARK TO DEATH WHILE
QUESTIONING HIM ON THE WHEREABOUTS OF A WANTED RADICAL.
    PRO-COMMUNIST ACTIVITIES ARE BANNED IN SOUTH KOREA, AND
OFFENDERS FACE TOUGH PENALTIES.
    WHEN NEWS OF PARK'S DEATH BROKE PRESIDENT CHUN DOO HWAN
SACKED HIS INTERIOR MINISTER AND NATIONAL POLICE CHIEF IN A
BID TO DEFUSE PUBLIC ANGER, AND TOLD THE CABINET TO SET UP A
SPECIAL BODY TO PREVENT ANY REPETITION OF THE INCIDENT.
    COURT OFFICIALS SAID TWO POLICEMEN WERE EXPECTED TO GO ON
TRIAL IN MARCH CHARGED WITH KILLING THE SEOUL STUDENT EARLIER
THIS MONTH BY PLUNGING HIS HEAD INTO A BATHTUB DURING
QUESTIONING.
    HUNDREDS OF STUDENTS CHANTING +DOWN WITH DICTATORSHIP+ AND
+STEP DOWN MURDERER REGIME+ HAVE CLASHED WITH RIOT POLICE
DAILY IN THE CAPITAL IN THE PAST WEEK.
    REUTER

번 호 : USW(F)- 89

이 28143 :

수 신 : 장관(미북.정문.해신)

발 신 : 주미대사

제 목 : 학생 데모   (2매)

The New York Times   WEDNESDAY, JANUARY 28, 1987   A

Agence France-Presse

DEATH OF STUDENT PROTESTED: South Korean riot police dragging away a student yesterday during an anti-Government demonstration by more than 300 people at Yonsei University in Seoul.

0196

The Washington Times | PAGE 6C / WEDNESDAY, JANUARY 28,

Korean students clash with police

SEOUL, South Korea — About 500 ents chanting "down with dicta-ip" and "go away murderer re-?" clashed with riot police at d's Presbyterian Yonsei Univer-yesterday, witnesses said.

They said at least two student ers were detained by police.

he students pledged that they ill actively take part next week nationwide protest against tor- to mourn the death of Park

Chong-chol, 21, who died while be-ing questioned by police about anti-government activities. The planned protest was announced yesterday by dissidents Kim Dae-jung and Kim Young-sam.

Church bells will toll, car horns will blare, flags will be hoisted at half mast and pedestrians will be urged to pray in the streets during the protest on Feb. ?. the two dissi-dents told a news conference.

They said almost 10,000 people, including some 1,800 Roman Catholic, Protestant and Buddhist clergymen, had agreed to organize the protest to demand an immediate end to torture in South Korea.

A memorial service also will be held that day at Seoul's largest church, Myongdong Cathedral.

Yesterday the protesters, al-though on a winter vacation, gath-ered at the campus to mourn the death of Mr. Park.

They hurled stones and gasoline bombs at riot police, who retaliated with tear gas shells.

Hundreds of policemen entered the campus to break up the protest after the students tried to march on to the street with their arms linked.

Two policemen face trial on charges of torturing Mr. Park to death earlier this month.

On Monday night, more than 2,000 angry Christians, led by 200 placard-carrying priests, demonstrated at Myongdong Cathedral.

89-2

0197

노안
중계

P.002

번 호 : USW(F)- 92

이 2 9 1 1 4 8

수 신 : 장관 (중남아 미북)
발 신 : 주미대사

제 목 : ANC 지도자 슐츠장관 면담
(2매)

The Washington Post

Shultz, ANC Chief Exchange Views

Meeting With Tambo Symbolizes Change in Policy Toward S. Africa

By David B. Ottaway
Washington Post Staff Writer

Secretary of State George P. Shultz met for nearly an hour yesterday with South African black nationalist leader Oliver Tambo for what both sides later agreed was "a serious and substantive exchange of views" on South Africa.

The meeting, more important for its symbolism than substance, marks the first time any U.S. secretary of state has met with a leader of the African National Congress (ANC), the main black nationalist group in South Africa.

It was widely regarded here and in South Africa as a turning point in U.S.-South African relations, with the Reagan administration now placing equal emphasis on cultivating good relations with militant black nationalists and white South African government leaders.

Conservatives in and out of Congress decried Shultz's meeting with the top leader of what they regard as a "terrorist" organization committed to violence and closely tied to the Communist Party of South Africa. A small group of conservatives protested outside the State Department before and after the meeting, shouting "Tambo Go Home" and "The ANC means the KGB."

Several times, the group of 20 to 30 protesters performed a mock "necklacing," the brutal practice of fatally burning suspected black informers for the South African police by placing a gasoline-soaked tire around their necks and setting it afire. Department officials called in fire trucks before discovering that there was no gasoline in the tires.

After the 50-minute meeting, State Department spokesman Charles E. Redman said Shultz had "laid out our concern" about the degree of Soviet influence in the ANC and its espousal of violence in the struggle to end the apartheid system.

"The secretary made it clear that a policy of violence from any party is not the answer to South Africa's problems and that there are other options. The pursuit of violence will only lead to a catastrophe for all," Redman said.

Asked what other options Shultz had in mind in light of the South African government's refusal to negotiate with black leaders, Redman replied, "negotiations."

Redman said much of the meeting was devoted to discussing ways to initiate negotiations between white and black South African leaders. Shultz called on the ANC to "spell out its vision of the future with more specificity" and expressed U.S. opposition to replacing

학교관차보의아미무뚜아프꼬경경영공의정충충부기
전주주주유두기사무무의여기리기부수
장국국국국국국국보고사실실실실
0198

apartheid with "another form of un-representative government," Red-man said.

Tambo said he had sought to per-suade the Reagan administration to give its full support to the black nationalist struggle. He also said he asked the United States to use its good offices and influence "as the leader" of the West to persuade oth-er Western countries to adopt the same sanctions passed by Congress last October over President Rea-gan's veto.

Tambo also told Shultz that the administration's policy of "construc-tive engagement"—quiet diplomacy in dealing with the white South Af-rican government—had been "un-helpful" in the search for a solution to apartheid.

Tambo said he had found "a large area of agreement" with Shultz on the nature of the apartheid system and the need to abolish it. "We are considering together the best way to achieve it," he told reporters.

He said he hoped that this would not be the last meeting between ANC leaders and the secretary and that the two sides could continue to review the situation together "with a view to bringing about an end to the apartheid system and establish-ing in South Africa a democracy, nonracial."

Redman said Shultz has no im-mediate plans to meet again with Tambo but that the U.S. Embassy in Lusaka, Zambia, where the ANC is based, would remain in contact with the organization.

0199

外務部　情報1課

韓国関係主要外信

1987.1.30(金)　07:40

(第 1 便)

外 信 名	内　　　　　容	페이지
A F P (東京發)	[슐츠]國務長官,　3月中　韓國,中共,日本 訪問　豫定　　　　　　　　　　　）솔	1
A P , Reuter (코펜하겐, 마드리드發)	[盧信永]總理,　덴마크　訪問 - [박종철]　事件에　遺憾　表明　(2)	2
外信綜合 (東京發)	北韓人　11名　亡命　事件 - 亡命意思　명백히　表明,　希望地는　未定 - 日本,　아시아　第3國에　北韓人　亡命接受 　可能性　打診(台灣은　拒否) - 韓國　外交官　1.28,　11名　面談 - 北韓,　11名　送還要求　不應時　스파이 　嫌疑로　北韓抑留　日船員　2名에　報復威脅	5
A P , A F P , U P I (서울發)	國會　人權委　關聯,　新民黨　議員　24시간 籠城後　解散　(2)	18
Reuter (서울發)	87　政局展望　不透明	22
A P (서울發)	[박종철]事件　關聯　示威學生　27名　逮捕 (2)　0200	26

W385

U 31 87 DJ017U

MSG⊕

W386

R XXX

DENMARK-SOUTH KOREAN,0292

PRIME MINISTER ARRIVES IN DENMARK FOR TRADE TALKS

COPENHAGEN, DENMARK (AP) - SOUTH KOREAN PRIME MINISTER SHINYONG LHO ARRIVED HERE WEDNESDAY FOR TALKS WITH DANISH LEADERS ABOUT EXPANDING ECONOMIC TIES WITH THE EUROPEAN ECONOMIC COMMUNITY, A SOUTH KOREAN EMBASSY SPOKESMAN SAID.

HYONG-SEOK KANG, PRESS ATTACHE AT THE SOUTH KOREAN EMBASSY IN COPENHAGEN, SAID LHO'S TALKS ON THURSDAY WITH PRIME MINISTER POUL SCHLUETER WOULD FOCUS ON SOUTH KOREA'S EFFORTS TO BROADEN ITS ECONOMIC AND TRADE TIES WITH THE EEC.

DENMARK TAKES OVER THE REVOLVING PRESIDENCY OF THE EUROPEAN COUNCIL IN JULY.

SINCE PRESIDENT CHUN DOO-HWAN'S TOUR OF BRITAIN, FRANCE, BELGIUM AND WEST GERMANY EARLY LAST YEAR, SOUTH KOREA HAD BEGUN A ''TILT TOWARD EUROPE'' POLICY IN A BID TO DIVERSIFY ITS EXPORT MARKETS AND REDUCE ITS DEPENDENCY ON JAPANESE AND AMERICAN MARKETS, KANG SAID.

LHO AND SCHLUETER WOULD ALSO REVIEW BILATERAL RELATIONS AND TRADE, EXCHANGE VIEWS ON INTERNATIONAL ISSUES AND DISCUSS DETAILS OF DEVELOPMENTS IN RELATIONS BETWEEN SOUTH AND NORTH KOREA, THE ATTACHE SAID.

LHO, WHOSE OFFICIAL EUROPEAN TOUR ALSO INCLUDES STOPS IN THE NETHERLANDS, PORTUGAL, SPAIN AND ITALY, WAS MET AT THE AIRPORT BY THE DANISH PRIME MINISTER, WHO VISITED SEOUL IN OCT. 1985.

HE WAS TO HAVE AN AUDIENCE HT THE ROYAL AMALIENBORG PALACE WITH 18-YEAR OLD CROWN PRINCE FREDERIK, THE ACTING REGENT WHILE QUEEN MARGRETHE IS AWAY ON STATE VISITS TO AUSTRALIA AND NEW ZEALAND.

DURING HIS FOUR-DAY STAY IN DENMARK, LHO AND A GROUP OF KOREAN BUSINESS LEADERS ARE TO VISIT THE FEDERATION OF DANISH INDUSTRIES, THE DANISH SUGAR CORPORATION AND BORUP COOPERATIVE DAIRY.

LHO AND HIS PARTY LEAVE ON SATURDAY FOR ITALY, THE FINAL LEG OF THEIR 16-DAY EEC TOUR.

END

AP-NY-01-28-87 1525GMT

0201

```
ØØ
W447
    R XXX
    DENMARK-SOUTH KOREAN,0260
    PRIME MINSTER SAYS POLICE KILLING OF DISSIDENT A 'TRAGIC
ACCIDENT'
    COPENHAGEN, DENMARK (AP) - SOUTH KOREAN PRIME MINISTER SHINYONG
LHO SAID THURSDAY THAT THE DEATH OF A STUDENT DISSIDENT WHILE UNDER
POLICE INTERROGATION LAST WEEK WAS A ''TRAGIC ACCIDENT.''
    ''I AM VERY SORRY, AND VERY MUCH REGRET SUCH A TRAGIC AND BAD
ACCIDENT, WHICH SHOULD NEVER HAVE HAPPENED IN OUR SOCIETY,'' LHO
TOLD REPORTERS.
    ''A SUSPECT DIED DURING THE COURSE OF INTERROGATION BY THE
POLICE. WE WERE VERY SHOCKED, AND WE MADE A THOROUGH INVESTIGATION
AND CONCLUDED THERE WAS POLICE BRUTALITY,'' HE SAID.
    LHO, ACCOMPANIED BY A DELEGATION OF BUSINESS LEADERS, IS IN
DENMARK ON THE FOURTH LEG OF A FIVE-NATION EUROPEAN TOUR AIMED AT
EXPANDING ECONOMIC TIES BETWEEN SOUTH KOREA AND THE EEC.
    HE SAID HIS COUNTRY WANTED TO EXPAND TRADE WITH DENMARK.
    ''AS A CONCRETE EXAMPLE, WE HAVE INITIALED DURING MY STAY HERE A
MUTUAL INVESTMENT PROTECTION AGREEMENT TO LAY A SOLID FOUNDATION
FOR INVESTMENT IN EACH OTHER'S COUNTRIES,'' LHO SAID.
    EARLIER IN THE DAY, LHO MET WITH HIS DANISH COLLEAGUE, PRIME
MINISTER POUL SCHLUETER, FOR TALKS ON BILATERAL AND INTERNATIONAL
ISSUES.
    SCHLUETER VISITED SOUTH KOREA IN 1985.
    ''OUR BILATERAL COOPERATION IN THE FIELDS OF SCIENCE AND
TECHNOLOGY HAS STEADILY INCREASED. AND IN PARTICULAR, TECHNICAL
EXCHANGE IN SHIPBUILDING AND AGRICULTURE HAVE ALREADY MADE
SUBSTANTIAL PROGRESS,'' LHO SAID.
    LHO AND HIS PARTY ARE SCHEDULED TO MEET WITH DANISH
INDUSTRIALISTS DURING THE REST OF THEIR STAY BEFORE TRAVELING ON TO
ITALY.
    END
AP-NY-01-29-87 1651GMT

                                        3


ØØ
W448
    U
```

NNNN

B YK0376

281806 :AM-LHO
SOUTH KOREAN PRIME MINISTER LEAVES SPAIN FOR COPENHAGEN
MADRID, JAN 28, REUTER - SOUTH KOREAN PRIME MINISTER LHO
SHIN-YONG HEADED FOR COPENHAGEN TODAY AFTER A TWO-DAY VISIT TO
MADRID AIMED AT REINFORCING TRADE TIES BETWEEN BOTH COUNTRIES.
LHO, ON A TOUR OF EUROPEAN CAPITALS, HEADS A DELEGATION OF
BUSINESSMEN WHO WANT TO DIVERSIFY THEIR EXPORT MARKETS,
CURRENTLY HEAVILY DEPENDENT ON THE UNITED STATES.
SOUTH KOREAN EXPORTS TO SPAIN MORE THAN TREBLED LAST YEAR TO
AROUND 350 MILLION DOLLARS, NEARLY FIVE TIMES THE VALUE OF TRADE
IN THE OTHER DIRECTION.
OFFICIALS SAID A SPANISH TRADE OFFICE WOULD BE OPENED SOON
IN SEOUL AND COMMERCIAL BANKING ACTIVITY WOULD ALSO BE INCREASED
TO FOSTER TRADE.
SEOUL'S EXPERIENCE IN ORGANISING THE 1988 SUMMER OLYMPIC
GAMES ALSO FIGURED IN LHO'S TALKS WITH PRIME MINISTER FELIPE
GONZALEZ. BARCELONA HAS BEEN CHOSEN FOR THE 1992 GAMES.
REUTER

0203

W215

R

SOUTH KOREA-POLITICS

RA

NATIONAL ASSEMBLY DEADLOCKED OVER FORMING HUMAN RIGHTS COMMITTEE

SEOUL, SOUTH KOREA (AP) - SOUTH KOREA'S NATIONAL ASSEMBLY, CONVENED TO TAKE UP THE RECENT TORTURE DEATH OF A UNIVERSITY STUDENT, FAILED TO HOLD ITS SCHEDULED SESSION WEDNESDAY BECAUSE OF A SIT-IN BY OPPOSITION LAWMAKERS.

THE ASSEMBLY OPENED A THREE-DAY SPECIAL SESSION MONDAY, BUT THE MAIN OPPOSITION NEW KOREA DEMOCRATIC PARTY BEGAN A SIT-IN PROTEST IN AN ASSEMBLY CHAMBER ON TUESDAY NIGHT.

THE ACTION CAME AFTER THE RULING DEMOCRATIC JUSTICE PARTY REJECTED OPPOSITION DEMANDS THAT A PROPOSED HUMAN RIGHTS COMMITTEE BE EMPOWERED TO MAKE A FULL INVESTIGATION OF TORTURE CASES, LAWMAKERS SAID.

THE TWO OPPOSING CAMPS WERE TO HAVE CONCLUDED THE SPECIAL ASSEMBLY SESSION WEDNESDAY, AFTER INAUGURATING THE HUMAN RIGHTS COMMITTEE.

LEADERS OF THE TWO PARTIES WERE CONTINUING NEGOTIATIONS TO NARROW DIFFERENCES OVER THE FUCTION OF THE PROPOSED COMMITTEE.

THE DEATH OF THE STUDENT TWO WEEKS AGO DURING POLICE INTERROGATION HAS BUILT UP INTO A SERIOUS POLITICAL ISSUE, LEADING TO THE DISMISSAL OF THE HOME MINISTER AND THE DIRECTOR OF THE NATIONAL POLICE.

TWO POLICE OFFICERS ACCUSED IN THE STUDENT'S DEATH HAVE BEEN ARRESTED, AND THREE OTHER SENIOR OFFICERS HAVE BEEN REMOVED FROM THEIR DUTIES.

DEPITE THOSE QUICK STEPS BY GOVERNMENT AUTHORITIES, A PUBLIC OUTCRY OVER THE CASE HAS CONTINUED. A MAJOR RALLY IS SCHEDULED FEB. 7 AT MYUNGDONG CATHEDRAL IN CENTRAL SEOUL AS PART OF PLANS FOR NATIONWIDE MEMORIAL SERVICES BY DISSIDENTS, RELIGIOUS ACTIVISTS AND OPPOSITION POLITICIANS.

END

AP-NY-01-28-87 0758GMT

18

0204

GLGL
EXR0309 3 /AFP-AD20
SKOREA-TORTURE LEAD-1
(REPETITION)
S. KOREAN OPPOSITION MP'S END SIT-IN

SEOUL, JAN 28 (AFP) - OPPOSITION MP'S ENDED A 24-HOUR SIT-IN IN
THE SOUTH KOREAN PARLIAMENT HERE WEDNESDAY AS THE GOVERNMENT
MAJORITY STUCK BY ITS REFUSAL TO EMPOWER A PROPOSED PARLIAMENTARY
COMMITTEE ON HUMAN RIGHTS TO INVESTIGATE THE ADMINISTRATION.
OPPOSITION NEW KOREA DEMOCRATIC PARTY (NKDP) FLOOR LEADER KIM
HYUN-KYU ISSUED A WRITTEN STATEMENT AT THE END OF THE SIT-IN
DENOUNCING PRESIDENT CHUN DOO-HWAN'S RULING DEMOCRATIC JUSTICE
PARTY (DJP) FOR ONCE AGAIN DEMONSTRATING ITS ''SCHEME TO PERPETUATE
ITS POWER.''
THE SIT-IN BY THE NKDP MEMBERS BEGAN AFTER THE TWO RIVAL
PARTIES FAILED TO NARROW THEIR DIFFERENCES OVER THE FORMATION OF
THE PROPOSED PARLIAMENTARY COMMITTEE TO INVESTIGATE INFRINGEMENTS
OF HUMAN RIGHTS.
THE TWO PARTIES AGREED IN PRINCIPLE TO SET UP THE COMMITTEE,
FOLLOWING THE DEATH DURING POLICE TORTURE OF A DISSIDENT STUDENT
TWO WEEKS AGO, BUT A SPECIAL THREE-DAY PARLIAMENTARY SESSION ENDED
WEDNESDAY WITHOUT HAVING DONE SO BECAUSE THE DJP MAJORITY REFUSED
TO GIVE IT POWER TO INVESTIGATE THE ADMINISTRATION.
THE OPPOSITION NOW PLANS TO HOLD PUBLIC RALLIES TO PRESS ITS
ARGUMENT.
MORE PKM/JM
AFP 281519 GMT JAN 87

19

NSNS
EXR0310 3 /AFP-AD28

0205

VOID
AFP 281520 GMT JAN 87

GLGL
EXR0311 3 /AFP-AD08
SKOREA-TORTURE LEAD-2-LAST
    (SEOUL)

    THE OPPOSITION AND DISSIDENTS HAVE ALREADY DECIDED TO HOLD
MEMORIAL SERVICES NATIONWIDE ON FEBRUARY 7 FOR PARK CHONG-CHUL, A
21-YEAR-OLD SEOUL NATIONAL UNIVERSITY STUDENT, THE FIRST MAN
OFFICIALLY CONFIRMED TO HAVE DIED WHILE BEING TORTURED IN SOUTH
KOREA.
    HOWEVER, THE DJP DID DECIDE TO URGE MR. CHUN'S ADMINISTRATION
TO LOOK INTO AND DISCLOSE THE TRUTH ABOUT SOME 50 DISSIDENTS WHO,
THE OPPOSITION ALLEGED, ARE DETAINED INCOMMUNICADO AND POSSIBLY
SUBJECT TO TORTURE.
    AND HOME MINISTER CHUNG HO-YONG TOLD PARLIAMENT TUESDAY HE
WOULD ORDER AN INVESTIGATION INTO AN OPPOSITION ALLEGATION THAT MR.
PARK HAD BEEN SUBJECT TO ELECTRIC-SHOCK TORTURE JUST BEFORE HE DIED.
    MR. PARK SUFFOCATED TO DEATH WHEN POLICE INTERROGATORS TRYING
TO SUBMERGE HIS HEAD IN A TUB OF WATER PUSHED HIS NECK AGAINST THE
EDGE OF THE TUB.
    MR. CHUNG ALSO PROMISED TO REOPEN AN INVESTIGATION INTO WHAT
THE OPPOSITION DESCRIBED AS THE MYSTERIOUS DEATHS OF TWO OTHER
UNIVERSITY STUDENTS IN OCTOBER 1985 AND JUNE 1986, AND THE CASE OF
A LABOR ACTIVIST FOUND DEAD AFTER BEING TAKEN AWAY BY POLICE IN MAY
LAST YEAR.
    (NO PICKUP)
    PKM/JM
AFP 281524 GMT JAN 87   2

0206

ZCZC HKA050 KHA002 NXI
UU HED HUP

R I
    KOREA 1-29
    SEOUL, JAN.29 (UPI) -- MORE THAN 70 OPPOSITION LAWMAKERS THURSDAY
ENDED A 24-HOUR SIT-IN AFTER FAILING TO SET UP A SPECIAL
PARLIAMENTARY COMMITTEE TO INVESTIGATE ALLEGED HUMAN RIGHTS
VIOLATIONS IN SOUTH KOREA.
    THE LAWMAKERS, ALL MEMBERS OF THE MAJOR OPPOSITION NEW KOREA
DEMOCRATIC PARTY (NKDP), CALLED OFF THE SIT-IN AT THE NATIONAL
ASSEMBLY BUT VOWED TO CONTINUE THEIR STRUGGLE.
    THE OPPOSITION SIT-IN MARKED THE END OF A THREE-DAY PARLIAMENTARY
SESSION CALLED MONDAY TO DISCUSS THE RECENT TORTURE DEATH OF A
DISSIDENT COLLEGE STUDENT DURING A POLICE INVESTIGATION.
    THE OPPOSITIONISTS BEGAN THE SIT-IN EARLY WEDNESDAY MORNING,
DEMNDING THAT A SPECIAL COMMITTEE TO BE SET UP IN THE ONE-HOUSE
NATIONAL ASSEMBLY BЫ EMPOWERED TO INVESTIGATE CERTAIN CASES OF
ALLEGED HUMAN RIGHTS VIOLATIONS.
    UNDER A BIPARTISAN AGREEMENT, THE RULING DEMOCRATIC JUSTICE PARTY
(DJP) AGREED ON THE ESTABLISHMENT OF A SPECIAL PARLIAMENTARY
COMMITTEE BUT OBJECTED TO ARMING IT WITH BROAD POWERS TO INVESTIGATE
STATE AFFAIRS.
    THE RULING DJP MAINTAINED THAT THE OPPSOITION DEMAND CAN BE DEALT
WITH ONLY AFTER THE PROPOSED PARLIAMENTARY COMMITTEE IS SET UP.
    NKDP FLOOR LEADER KIM HYUN-KYU SAID, +ANY COMMITTEE WITHOUT POWER
TO INVESTIGATE NATIONL AFFAIRS IS MEANINGLESS. WE WILL CONTINUE TO
FIGHT TO ACHIEVE OUR GOAL.+
    THE SHARP CONFRONATION WILL FURTHER STRAIN KOREA'&S VOLATILE
POLITICAL SCENE CURRENTLY GRAPPLING WITH CONSTITUTIONAL AMENDMENTS.
    THE MAIN OPPOSITION NKDP, ALLIED WITH DISSIDENT GROUPS, IS
PLANNING TO HOLD A NATIONWIDE MEMORIAL SERVICE FOR THE DEAD STUDENT,
PARK CHONG-CHUL, 21, WHO WAS TORTURED TO DEATH DURING A POLICE
INVESTIGATION JAN.14.
    GOVERNMENT OFFICIALS ADMITTED THAT PARK WAS A VICTIM OF POLICE
TORTURE BUT SAID IT WAS +AN ISOLATED CASE.+
    GOVERNMENT CRITICS SAY THAT PARK'&S CASE IS +ONLY A TIP OF AN
ICEBERG+ IN ALLEGED HUMAN RIGHTS VIOLATIONS IN KOREA.
    (UPI) PS
CCCCQQE ZCZ   21
=01290243
NNNN   0207

290541 :PM-KOREA (NEWS ANALYSIS, SCHEDULED)

CRYSTAL BALL CLOUDED AS SOUTH KOREA STARTS NEW YEAR

BY ROGER CRABB, REUTERS

SEOUL, JAN 29, REUTER - KOREANS LOVE CONSULTING FORTUNE TELLERS BUT FEW POLITICAL SEERS IN SEOUL TODAY ARE WILLING TO PREDICT HOW SOUTH KOREA CAN RESOLVE ITS DEEP POLITICAL CRISIS IN THE NEXT 12 MONTHS AND CHOOSE A NATIONALLY ACCEPTABLE LEADER.

BY THE END OF THIS NEW LUNAR YEAR OF THE RABBIT, THE COUNTRY MUST ELECT A SUCCESSOR TO RETIRING PRESIDENT CHUN DOO-HWAN YET PARLIAMENT REMAINS TOTALLY DEADLOCKED ON THE ELECTORAL SYSTEM TO BE USED, AND EVEN ON THE FORM OF GOVERNMENT TO ADOPT.

IN THE WAKE OF THIS MONTH'S REVELATION THAT POLICE TORTURED A YOUNG STUDENT TO DEATH, AND OPPOSITION CLAIMS THAT THE INCIDENT WAS MERELY THE +TIP OF AN ICEBERG+ OF INSTITUTIONALISED BRUTALITY BY THE CHUN GOVERNMENT, POLITICAL LIFE HAS SO SOURED THAT MOST OBSERVERS SEE NO CHANCE OF EARLY PROGRESS TOWARDS A CONSTITUTIONAL COMPROMISE.

FOR THE FACTION-RIDDEN PARLIAMENTARY OPPOSITION, FRUSTRATED AND DEMORALISED JUST TWO WEEKS AGO, THE TORTURE ISSUE HAS BEEN SEIZED AS A HEAVEN-SENT STICK WITH WHICH TO BEAT CHUN, WHOSE LEGITIMACY THEY HAVE ALWAYS CONTESTED.

THE PRESIDENT IS A FORMER GENERAL WHO TOOK POWER IN A MILITARY COUP, REWROTE THE CONSTITUTION AND IN 1981 WON A SEVEN-YEAR MANDATE FROM AN ELECTORAL COLLEGE.

MORE

22

0208

296547 :PH-KOREA =1.2

LEE WAS QUICKLY DISAVOWED BY THE NKDP'S TWO MAIN FACTIONAL
LEADERS, KIM DAE-JUNG AND KIM YOUNG-SAM, AND THE OPPOSITION
BEGAN THE YEAR IN OPEN DISARRAY.

THE TIME LOOKED RIPE FOR THE DJP TO MAKE ITS MOVE IN
PARLIAMENT. PARTY CHAIRMAN ROH TAE-WOO WAS EVEN QUOTED AS
SAYING A NEW CONSTITUTION COULD BE IN FORCE BY MARCH.

THEN CAME THE TORTURE REVELATION WHICH SPARKED WIDESPREAD
PUBLIC ANGER AND POLITICAL UPROAR, FORCING CHUN TO SACK HIS
INTERIOR MINISTER AND SET UP A COMMISSION TO PREVENT HUMAN
RIGHTS ABUSES.

THE NKDP AND KNP JOINED FORCES TO OBLIGE THE GOVERNMENT TO
HOLD A SPECIAL ASSEMBLY SESSION TO DEBATE THE TORTURE ISSUE.
THE DEBATE GOT NOWHERE AND THE PRO-GOVERNMENT KOREA HERALD
TODAY CALLED THE SESSION A TOTAL FIASCO.

GOVERNMENT OFFICIALS NOW CONCEDE IN PRIVATE THAT THE MARCH
DEADLINE FOR CONSTITUTIONAL AMENDMENT IS NO LONGER REALISTIC.
+IN THE PRESENT CLIMATE, AND WITHOUT A SECRET BALLOT, NO
OPPOSITION MEMBER WOULD DARE TO VOTE FOR THE DJP PROJECT,+ ONE
OFFICIAL SAID.

THE OPPOSITION IS NOW PLANNING NATIONWIDE PROTESTS NEXT
WEEK AGAINST THE GOVERNMENT'S ALLEGED WIDESPREAD USE OF
TORTURE AND OTHER HUMAN RIGHTS VIOLATIONS. THE AUTHORITIES
HAVE ALREADY ANNOUNCED THEY WILL NOT ALLOW SUCH DEMONSTRATIONS
TO TAKE PLACE.

MORE

2 o

0209

NNNN

a YK0636

290544 :PM-KOREA =1.1
    CHUN PLEDGED NOT TO SEEK A SECOND TERM. LAST YEAR HE TOLD
THE PARTIES IN THE NATIONAL ASSEMBLY TO HAMMER OUT AN
ELECTORAL SYSTEM THE WHOLE COUNTRY COULD ACCEPT SO HE COULD
ACHIEVE SOUTH KOREA'S FIRST PEACEFUL TRANSFER OF POWER.
    BUT THE DEBATE SOON POLARISED, WITH THE MAIN OPPOSITION
NEW KOREA DEMOCRATIC PARTY (NKDP) DEMANDING PRESIDENTIAL
ELECTION BY UNIVERSAL SUFFRAGE AND CHUN'S DEMOCRATIC JUSTICE
PARTY (DJP) PRESSING FOR ADOPTION OF A PARLIAMENTARY SYSTEM OF
GOVERNMENT LED BY A PRIME MINISTER ARMED WITH MANY OF THE
POWERS CURRENTLY WIELDED BY THE PRESIDENT.
    THE NKDP DISMISSED THE PARLIAMENTARY FORMULA AS A RUSE BY
THE COUNTRY'S RULERS TO STAY IN OFFICE, WHILE THE DJP REJECTED
A DIRECT PRESIDENTIAL ELECTION AS A RECIPE FOR DICTATORSHIP.
    WITH NO SIGN OF COMPROMISE BETWEEN THE TWO HOSTILE CAMPS,
GOVERNMENT OFFICIALS FLOATED THE POSSIBILITY LATE LAST YEAR OF
SUBMITTING THE DJP'S PROPOSAL TO PARLIAMENT ANYWAY. THE
ARGUMENT WENT THAT WITH THE VOTES OF THE MINOR OPPOSITION
KOREA NATIONAL PARTY (KNP) PLUS A FEW DEFECTORS FROM NKDP
RANKS, THE PROJECT WOULD RECEIVE THE TWO-THIRDS MAJORITY
NECESSARY TO CHANGE THE CONSTITUTION.
    IN LATE DECEMBER NKDP PRESIDENT LEE MIN-WOO CAUSED SHOCK
WAVES IN THE OPPOSITION BY SAYING THE PARTY COULD ACCEPT THE
DJP'S PARLIAMENTARY SYSTEM PROPOSAL IF THE GOVERNMENT MADE
CONCESSIONS ON DEMOCRATISATION AND CIVIL RIGHTS.
    MORE

                                        2)

NNNN

0210

NNNN

a YK0688

290549 :PM-KOREA =1.3

SOUTH KOREA'S ONE-MILLION-PLUS STUDENTS ARE STILL ON
WINTER HOLIDAY BUT A FEW VIOLENT CAMPUS PROTESTS IN RECENT
DAYS PRESAGED FURTHER TROUBLE FOR THE WEEKS AHEAD. LAST YEAR
MILITANT STUDENTS STAGED DEMONSTRATIONS ALMOST DAILY AGAINST
WHAT THEY CALL CHUN'S MILITARY DICTATORSHIP.

IN HIS NEW YEAR MESSAGE TO THE NATION IN MID-JANUARY, CHUN
URGED THE FEUDING POLITICIANS TO COMPROMISE ON A NEW
CONSTITUTION, WARNING THAT OTHERWISE HE COULD BE FORCED TO
TAKE A +GRAVE DECISION+.

THE PRESIDENT DID NOT ELABORATE BUT RULING CAMP OFFICIALS
POINT OUT THAT HE HAS THE POWER TO DISSOLVE PARLIAMENT OR EVEN
TO IMPOSE MARTIAL LAW.

THEY ADD THAT THE COUNTRY HAS A VALID CONSTITUTION ALREADY
AND THAT, IF PARLIAMENT CANNOT AGREE HOW TO AMEND IT, THE
PROPOSED DEMOCRATIC REFORM COULD BE PUT ASIDE AND CHUN'S
SUCCESSOR BE CHOSEN INDIRECTLY, AS HE WAS, BY ELECTORAL
COLLEGE.

REUTER   25

0211

W125
    R
    SOUTH KOREA-TORTURE
    RA
    .27 STUDENT DEMONSTRATORS UNDER POLICE DETENTION
    SEOUL, SOUTH KOREA (AP) - POLICE DETAINED 27 STUDENTS WEDNESDAY
NIGHT AFTER BREAKING UP A STREET PROTEST AGAINST THE RECENT TORTURE
DEATH OF A UNIVERSITY STUDENT, IT WAS REPORTED THURSDAY.
    ABOUT 300 STUDENTS GATHERED AT A CROWDED INTERSECTION IN EASTERN
SEOUL AND THEN MARCHED 50LICE, REPOYARDS) ALONG THE STREETS BEFORE
CLASHING WITH RIOT POLICE, REPORTED THE HANKOOK ILBO, A LEADING
SEOUL NEWSPAPER.
    THE STUDENTS, LED BY A PLACARD THAT READ ''CRUSH THE MILITARY
DICETROL BOMBS AT 500 RIN MURDEROUS TORTURE,'' HURLED STONES AND
PETROL BOMBS AT 500 RIOT POLICE DU
    NO CONFIHOUR-LONG STREET
DISTURBANCES, HANKOOK ILBO SAID.
    NO CONFIRMATION OR COMMENT WAS AVAINAL HOLIDAY FOR THEND OTHER
AUTHORITIES THURSDAY DUE TO A NATIONAL HOLIDAY FOR THE LUNAR NEW
YEAR.
    THE DEATH OF A STUDENT TWO WEEKS AGO DURING POLICE INTERROGATION
HAS DEVELOPED INTO A SERSTER AND THEAL ISSUE, LEADING TO THE
DISMISSAL OF THE HOME MINISTER AND THE DIRECTOR OF THE NATI HAVE
BEICE. TWO POLICE OFFICERS ACCUSED IN THE STUDENT'S DEATH HAVE
BEEN ARRESTED, AND THREE OTHER SENIOR OFFICERS HAVE BEEN REMOVED
FROM THEIR DUTIES.
    DESPITE SUCH QUICK STEPS BY GOVERNMENT AUTHORITIES, A PUBLIC
OUTCRY OVER THE CASE AND TORTURE IN GENERAL HAS CONTINUED, RANGING
FRORIGHTS GR AND MEMORIAL SERVICES BY OPPOSITION FORCES AND HUMAN
RIGHTS GROUPS TO VIOLENT DEMONSTRATIONS ON CAMPUS.
    A SPECIAL NATIONAL ASSEMBLY SESSION CONVENED TO TAKE UP THE CASE
ENDED MIDNIGHT WEDNESDAY WITH NO PROGRESS AFTER RIVAL PARTIES
FAILED TO NARROW DIFFERENCES OVER THE FUNCTION OF A PROPOSED HUMAN
RIGHTS COMMITTEE.
    THE ASSEMBLY OPENED A THREE-DAY SITTING MONDAY BUT STALLED
TUESDAY NIGHT WHEN THE MAIN OPPOSITION NEW KOREA DEMOCRATIC PARTY
BEGAN A SIT-IN TO PROTESTHAT THE COMMITTEE BE LING DEMOCRATIC
JUSTICE PARTY TO DEMANDS THAT THE COMMITTEE BE EMPOWERED T-TK-01-29
FULL INVESTIGATION OF TORTURE CASES.
    END
AP-NY-01-29-87 0432GMT   25

긴급보고사항 (외신)

1987. 2. 2.

정 보 1 과

제　목 : 뉴욕 타임즈紙, 韓國의 政治 不安 가능성 경고

@ YK0585

020603 :PM-KOREA-TIMES
NEW YORK TIMES WARNS OF +DISORDER+ IN SOUTH KOREA
　　NEW YORK, FEB 2, REUTER - SOUTH KOREA COULD FACE +DISORDER
AND WORSE+ UNLESS OPPOSITION LEADERS AGREE WITH THE GOVERNMENT
ON DEMOCRATIC CHANGE, THE NEW YORK TIMES SAID TODAY.
　　AN EDITORIAL SAID PRESIDENT CHUN DOO HWAN'S DESIRE TO
PROJECT A SUCCESSFUL IMAGE FOR THE SEOUL OLYMPICS AND
PRESIDENTIAL ELECTIONS IN 1988 GAVE THE OPPOSITION REAL
LEVERAGE TO REACH SUCH AN ACCORD.
　　+IF A SOLUTION IS NOT WORKED OUT THIS YEAR IN TIME FOR
ORDERLY ELECTIONS, 1988 COULD BRING DISORDER AND WORSE ... A
DISTINCT POSSIBLITY THAT MODERATES ON BOTH SIDES SHOULD NOW BE
DOING THEIR UTMOST TO AVOID,+ IT SAID.
　　IT SAID A RECENT PROPOSAL BY OPPOSITION LEADER LEE MIN WOO
THAT SOFTENED OPPOSITION DEMANDS FOR DIRECT BALLOTING IN THE
ELECTIONS AS AN EXAMPLE OF THE ACCOMODATION APPROACH.
　　+HIS PLAN FOCUSES PROPERLY ON THE SUBSTANCE OF
DEMOCRATISATION, FREEDOMS AND FAIR ELECTIONS, RATHER THAN THE
FORM OF GOVERNMENT,+ THE NEWSPAPER SAID.
　　INSTEAD OF UNIVERSAL SUFFRAGE, THE PRESIDENT'S DEMOCRATIC
JUSTICE PARTY WANTS A PARLIAMENTARY SYSTEM OF GOVERNMENT LED
BY A PRIME MINISTER ARMED WITH MANY OF THE POWERS CURRENTLY
WIELDED BY THE PREIDENT.
　　REUTER

0213

번 호 : USE(F)- 109

수 신 : 장관 (미북.정문.해기)   발 신 : 주미대사

제 목 : 아국정국(87.2.2자 NYT 사설)   /매

The New York Times

MONDAY, FEBRUARY 2, 1987   A16

Take a Chance in South Korea

President Chun Doo Hwan's repressive South Korean Government doesn't deserve much benefit of doubt. But Mr. Chun has cause now to be more reasonable. He desperately seeks success for the Olympics in his country next year and the legitimacy the games will confer. This gives the democratic opposition real leverage. There could be an opportunity here for opposition leaders to find an accommodation, to establish democracy without a mutually destructive showdown.

The obstacles loom large. Compromise does not figure prominently in the Korean political tradition. The winner-take-all attitude seems ingrained. Yet on both sides, some leaders privately profess flexibility. Public flexibility is constrained on the right by the military and on the left by the students. To suggest compromise is to risk loss of power, as one opposition leader recently discovered. Trust remains the critical missing ingredient.

Recently the atmosphere has become even more difficult because of the death, under police torture, of a young political detainee. But under pressure, the Government took the highly unusual steps of accepting responsibility for the tragedy and dismissing the Interior Minister and the national police chief for their roles.

The central political debate is over the vastly different proposals for restructuring the Constitution before President Chun steps down in 1988. The President wants an indirect parliamentary system; the opposition wants a continued presidential system but with direct elections. In theory, there is room here for advancing democracy by compromise, but so far that has not happened.

Power is at stake as well as philosophy. Articulate and well-known opposition leaders like Kim Dae Jung and Kim Young Sam would fare well in a direct democratic presidential election. The ruling party, with no equally appealing personalities, figures its best bet is an indirect parliamentary system that maximizes the advantages of organization and incumbency. The Government could force its plan through, but hesitates for fear of tainting the credibility of the resulting regime both in South Korea and in the United States.

Lee Min Woo, an opposition leader, recently proposed a middle ground. The opposition would consider parliamentary rule in exchange for guarantees of broader political freedoms and truly free elections. His own party quickly repudiated him. Nonetheless, his plan focuses properly on the substance of democratization, freedoms and fair elections, rather than the form of government. Perhaps the opposition could reformulate this in some way that would test the Chun Government's real intentions.

If a solution is not worked out this year, in time for orderly elections, 1988 could bring disorder and worse. That is a distinct possibility that moderates on both sides should now be doing their utmost to avoid. Let them find courage and take a chance.

주 로 론 토 총 영 사 관

토론토 (정)764-*147*   1987. 3. 5.

수신 : 장관

참조 : 정보문화국장, 미주국장

제목 : 박종철 49제

                대 : AM-0060

                연 : TRW-0120

　카나다 전국일간지 *Globe & Mail* 및 최대 지방일간지
Toronto Star 는 '87.3.4자 동지에 "Police Stifle Seoul
Protest rally" 및 "50,000 Police fight protesters on Seoul
march" 제하에 대호관련 기사를 서울발 Reuter 및 AP 통신을 인용
현장 사진과함께 게재하였기 이를 발췌 별첨 송부합니다.

첨부 : 동 발췌기사 2부. 끝.

주   로   론   토   총   영   사

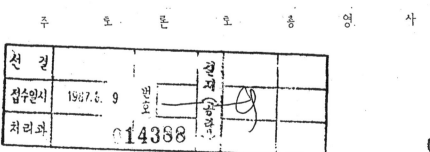

0215

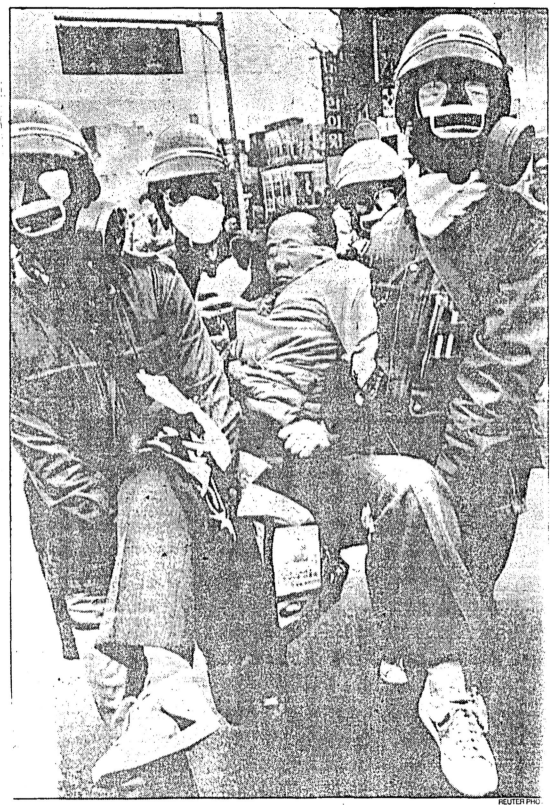

REUTER PHO

Gassed marcher: South Korean riot police in gas masks carry away a demonstrator yesterday afte tear-gassing him during clashes in Seoul. Police said a total of 20 people were injured in violence seven cities, marking the death 49 days ago of a student being tortured by police.

0216

50,000 police fight protesters on Seoul march

SEOUL (AP) — Demonstrators fought for hours against almost 50,000 South Korean riot police in hit-and-run clashes yesterday on the streets of Seoul during a day of remembrance for a student who died during police torture.

Violent confrontations also were reported in six other cities. Police said 20 people were hurt in all, two seriously, and 395 were detained.

At least four opposition lawmakers were injured, one seriously, as they led protesters against police firing tear gas and using shields and truncheons.

The "Grand Peace Marches for Anti-Torture and Democratization" were called by the main opposition New Korea Democratic party and 47 dissident and church groups to mark the 49th day after the death of Park Chong-chul, 21.

Park, a dissident student from Seoul National University, died Jan. 14 while being questioned by police using water torture.

The 49th-day rite is a Buddhist practice to mark the entry of the deceased person's soul into another world.

National police chief Lee Yong-chang said 20 people were put under house arrest. But Dong-A Ilbo, the nation's biggest independent national daily newspaper, and Yonhap News Agency said at least 72 people, including top dissident leaders Kim Young-sam and Kim Dae-jung, were confined to their homes.

When the students and dissidents marching in their thousands toward Pagoda Park in central Seoul met police in key areas, they split up into groups of 10 to 30, fighting police.

0217

Reuter

New Korea Democratic Party members wear masks against police tear gas in Seoul.

Police stifle Seoul protest rally

Reuter and Associated Press

SEOUL

The sixth anniversary of President Chun Doo-hwan's inauguration was marked yesterday with a show of overwhelming police force stifling opposition attempts to stage a nation-wide "grand march for democracy."

In Seoul, where most of the opposition's efforts were concentrated, more than 30,000 riot police and plainclothes officers confronted a few thousand demonstrators, preventing any of them from reaching the park where the rally was to be held, witnesses said.

There were isolated clashes in the capital between rock-throwing students and police, who quickly dis-persed them with tear gas. One police post was set on fire by a Molotov cocktail. Police sources said more than 600 arrests were made.

Violent confrontations also were reported in six other cities. Police said 20 people were hurt.

At least four opposition legislators were injured, one seriously, in leading protesters against police, who fired tear gas and used shields and truncheons.

The over-all results represented the third humiliation in three months for the anti-Government street campaign led by dissident leaders Kim Dae-jung and Kim Young-sam.

However, the protests overshadowed the customary tributes marking the start of the seventh year of Mr. Chun's term in office.

0218

The New York Times

WEDNESDAY, FEBRUARY 4, 1987　　A9

SEOUL BARS RALLY FOR DEAD STUDENT

But Opposition Vows to Hold Memorial at a Cathedral for Victim of Torture

By NICHOLAS D. KRISTOF
Special to The New York Times

SEOUL, South Korea, Feb. 3 — The Government said today that it would block a major rally planned here Saturday to mourn the torture and killing of a student protester in police custody.

Opposition leaders said that nonetheless they would attempt to hold the rally at Myongdong Cathedral in central Seoul, setting the stage for a confrontation on the snowy hillock and narrow streets around the cathedral.

While such confrontations have sometimes turned violent, the last one, on Nov. 29, fizzled in the face of an enormous show of force by the authorities. Opposition leaders were put under house arrest and some 70,000 police officers were mobilized in the streets.

The rally Saturday is scheduled as a memorial service for Park Jong Chul, a 21-year-old linguistics student who died as police interrogators repeatedly submerged his head in a tub of water. Police officials said Mr. Park was suffocated when his throat was crushed against the rim of the tub.

Family and Religious Leaders

"What they have in mind is not to organize a memorial service, but to organize a violent demonstration," Ku Chang Rim, the assistant Minister of Information, said of the coalition of dissident groups organizing the rally. As a result, he said in an interview, the authorities decided to permit only Mr. Park's family and religious leaders into the cathedral for the service. The police will turn everyone else away, he said.

Dissident leaders said they would go ahead with the rally, the first since the abortive demonstration last November. "We lose nothing if the Government blocks the memorial service by force," Kim Young Sam, an opposition leader, said in an interview.

Mr. Kim said he would like to go to the rally but expected to be placed under house arrest.

Disbanded a Group

Kim Dae Jung, another opposition leader, said in an interview: "We have no intention of exploiting this prayer meeting. The Government should not intervene; if it does, it must take responsibility for whatever happens."

In an another announcement today, the Government said it had disbanded a large revolutionary group that had distributed 200,000 leaflets and organized more than 30 demonstrations last year. The Seoul District Prosecutor's Office said the group had raised more than $115,000 through contributions and through business operations that included a restaurant, a funeral parlor and a publishing company.

Officials said 32 people had been arrested over the last five months, and that 28 more were wanted in connection with the group.

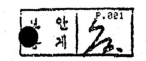
번 호 : USW(F)- 118

수 신 : 장관 (미북정문.해신)

제 목 : 인권보호기구 설치

발신 : 두미대사

02050950

1매

Chicago Tribune   Thursday, February 5, 1987   4   Section 1

Special S. Korea agency to target rights abuses

Chun

SEOUL—South Korea will set up a special agency this month to help stop torture and protect human rights, a government spokesman said Wednesday. He told a press conference the move, following the death of a student activist under police questioning last month, reflected President Chun Doo Hwan's "unswerving determination to safeguard and develop the liberal democratic system and enhance freedom and basic rights of the citizens." The new agency, the Special Commission for the Protection of Human Rights, will have about 30 members who will recommend ways to protect human rights better and improve the operation of other government agencies involved, the spokesman said.

己2 (趙, 白)

ᅡ

外務部 情報1課

韓国関係主要外信

1987.2.6(金) 07:30

(第 1 便)

外 信 名	内　　　　　　容	페이지
AFP,UPI Reuter (서울發)	2.7 追悼會 關聯, 政局緊張 高潮 [金聖基]法務長官 談話發表, 追悼會 不許方針 强力 表明	1
AP (東京發)	亡命 北韓人, 亡命希望地 意見一致	9
AFP. (台北發)	自由中國, 亡命北韓人 接受計劃 否認	10
AFP,UPI (로마發)	[盧信永]總理, 이태리 訪問 終了	11
UPI (서울發)	學生等 7名 新民黨 종로地區黨舍 占據 籠城 - 對政府 强硬 鬪爭 主張	13
AP.AFP (카트만두發)	韓國등반대, 에베레스트 등정 포기 - 네팔人 셸파 1名 추락사	14

0221

GLGL

EXR0142 3 /AFP-AJ12

SKOREA-TORTURE SCHED-1

TENSIONS MOUNT AS GOVERNMENT BANS MEMORIAL SERVICE FOR TORTURE
VICTIM

BY PATRICK MINN

SEOUL, FEB 5 (AFP) - TENSIONS MOUNTED IN SOUTH KOREA THURSDAY
AS THE GOVERNMENT FORMALLY BANNED A NATIONAL MEMORIAL SERVICE FOR A
POLICE TORTURE VICTIM WHICH OPPOSITION AND DISSIDENT FORCES
RESOLVED TO HOLD SATURDAY.
JUSTICE MINISTER KIM SUNG-KY ISSUED A PUBLIC STATEMENT
DECLARING THE PLANNED GATHERING AT SEOUL'S MYONGDONG ROMAN CATHOLIC
CATHDRAL ILLEGAL.
HE SAID PRESIDENT CHUN DOO-HWAN'S GOVERNMENT WOULD MOVE TO
''COUNTERACT ANY SINISTER MOVES TO USE PARK CHONG-CHUL'S DEATH FOR
POLITICAL DEMOGAGUERY.''
THE GOVERNMENT ADMITTED THAT THE 21-YEAR-OLD SEOUL NATIONAL
UNIVERSITY STUDENT DIED LAST MONTH DURING POLICE INTERROGATION.
MR. PARK'S DEATH TRIGGERED A PUBLIC FURORE OVER POLICE TORTURE
IN SOUTH KOREA AS IT WAS THE FIRST TIME THE AUTHORITIES HAD
ADMITTED USING TORTURE ON A DETAINEE.
MR. KIM SAID OPPOSITION AND DISSIDENT FORCES WERE HOPING TO
ATTRACT A HUGE CROWD TO THE BUSY DOWNTOWN AREA, WHERE THE
2,000-SEAT CATHEDRAL IS LOCATED, WITH THE ''ULTIMATE AIM OF
TRIGGERING VIOLENT DISTURBANCES AND OF OVERTHROWING BOTH THE
GOVERNMENT AND THE PRESENT POLITICAL SYSTEM THROUGH VIOLENCE.''
SOME 30,000 POLICE ARE TO BE MOBILIZED TO COMPLETELY SEAL OFF
THE CATHEDRAL IN AN EFFORT TO PREVENT OPPOSITION POLITICIANS,
DISSIDENTS AND RADICAL STUDENTS FROM ATTENDING THE SERVICE
SCHEDULED TO START THERE AT 2 P.M. SATURDAY, POLICE SOURCES SAID.
MORE/PKM/KH
AFP   050729 GMT FEB 87   I

0222

GLGL
EXR0143 3 /RFP-RJ13
SKOREA-TORTURE 2
    (SEOUL)

    MOST OF THE SPONSORS OF THE MEMORIAL SERVICE -- INCLUDING
OPPOSITION LEADERS KIM DAE-JUNG AND KIM YOUNG-SAM, AND DISSIDENT
LEADER KYE HOON-JAE -- WOULD BE PLACED UNDER HOUSE ARREST ON THAT
DAY, POLICE SAID.
    THE MEMORIAL SERVICE PREPARATORY COMMITTEE, MEETING THURSDAY AT
THE HEADQUARTERS OF THE NATIONAL COUNCIL OF CHURCHES, DENOUNCED THE
GOVERNMENT'S BAN ON THE GATHERING PLANNED FOR SATURDAY.
    THE COMMITTEE SAID IN A STATEMENT THAT IF SATURDAY'S SERVICE
WAS OBSTRUCTED BY THE AUTHORITIES, IT WOULD CONTINUE ATTEMPTS TO
HOLD SUCH A GATHERING.
    IT SAID THAT 62,301 PEOPLE HAD SIGNED UP AS COMMITTEE MEMBERS,
INCLUDING MANY ROMAN CATHOLIC AND PROTESTANT CLERGY, UNIVERSITY
PROFESSORS AND STUDENTS.
    THE COMMITTEE SAID CARDINAL STEPHAN KIM, PRESBYTERIAN REVERAND
PARK HYUNG-KYU, AND BUDDHIST ABBOT CHI-SUN WOULD OFFICIATE IN TURN
AT THE SERVICE.
    POLICE ARE TO BE DEPLOYED AT ALL CHURCHES AND TEMPLES TO THWART
THE COMMITTEE'S PLAN TO HAVE BELLS AND GONGS RUNG AT 2 P.M.
    POLICE ALSO SAID THEY WOULD ARREST ANYONE WEARING BLACK RIBBONS
OR HONKING THEIR CAR HORNS AT THAT TIME IN A GESTURE OF SUPPORT FOR
THE MEMORIAL SERVICE ASKED FOR BY THE COMMITTEE.
    THE MAIN OPPOSITION NEW KOREA DEMOCRATIC PARTY (NKDP) ISSUED A
STATEMENT DENOUNCING THE GOVERNMENT'S ATTEMPTS TO PREVENT THE
MEMORIAL SERVICE AND ASKED THOSE PLANNING TO ATTEND TO REFRAIN FROM
VIOLENCE.
    MORE/PKM
RFP   050733 GMT FEB 87

                            2

                        0223

GLGL
EXR0144 3 /AFP-AJ14
SKOREA-TORTURE 3-LAST
     (SEOUL)

THE STATEMENT BY NKDP SPOKESMAN KIM TAE-RYONG SAID THE SERVICE
WOULD BE HELD IN A PEACEFUL AND ORDERLY MANNER, AND THAT THE
OPPOSITION PARTY HAD NO INTENTION OF EXPLOITING IT FOR POLITICAL
PURPOSES.
     THE OPPOSITION PARTY WARNED AGAINST DISTURBANCES WHICH MIGHT BE
DELIBERATELY CREATED BY THE AUTHORITIES, AS IT SAID HAD HAPPENED IN
INCHON, WEST OF SEOUL, IN MAY LAST YEAR.
     THE GOVERNMENT SAID THE INCHON RIOT WAS TRIGGERED BY RADICAL
STUDENTS AND PRO-COMMUNIST ACTIVISTS INTENT ON OVERTHROWING THE
GOVERNMENT BY FORCE.
     MEANWHILE, A GROUP OF SEVEN DISSIDENT STUDENTS STORMED INTO THE
OFFICE OF NKDP CHAIRMAN LEE MIN-WOO THURSDAY AND BEGAN A SIT-IN BY
LOCKING THEMSELVES INSIDE THE OFFICE. THEY DISTRIBUTED TRACTS
DENOUNCING ''THE DICTATORSHIP PERPETRATING TORTURE.''
     THE LEADER OF THE GROUPS OF STUDENTS, LEE KANG-RYUN, 23, TOLD
REPORTERS THEY BELONGED TO THE DISSIDENT NATIONWIDE DEMOCRATIC
STUDENT FEDERATION, WHICH OBSERVERS SAID HAD ORGANIZED
ANTI-GOVERNMENT CAMPUS PROTESTS LAST YEAR.
     PKM/KH
AFP   050736 GMT FEB 87   3

0224

ZCZC HKA155 KHA005 NXI
UU HED HUP

R I
    KOREA 2-5
    SEOUL, FEB.5 (UPI) -- JUSTICE MINISTER KIM SUNG-KY SAID THURSDAY
HIS GOVERNMENT WILL MOVE RESOLUTELY TO FOIL NATIONWIDE MEMORIAL
SERVICES SCHEDULED FOR SATURDAY THROUGHOUT THE COUNTRY TO MOURN A
STUDENT ACTIVIST KILLED UNDER POLICE TORTURE LAST MONTH.
    +IT IS THE POLICY OF THE GOVERNMENT TO RESOLUTELY COUNTERACT THE
SINISTER MOVES TO ABUSE PARK'&S DEATH FOR POLITICAL DEMOGOGUERY,+
KIM SAID IN A HARSHLY WORDED STATEMENT.
    REFLECTING THE RULING CAMP'&S HARDLINE POLICY, KIM BRANDED
SATURDAY'&S MEMORIAL SERVICES AS +AN UNLAWFUL SUBVERSIVE POLITICAL
ASSEMBLY WITH THE ULTIMATE AIM OF OVETHROWING BOTH THE GOVERNMENT
AND THE PRESENT POLITICAL SYSTEM THROUGH VIOLENCE.+
    KIM REGRETTED THE DEATH OF THE STUDENT, PARK CHONG-CHUL, BUT SAID
HIS DEATH IS BEING USED BY ANTI-GOVERNMENT FORCES FOR AN +IMPURE+
POLITICAL OFFENSIVE.
    PARK, 21, A LINGUISTICS JUNIOR AT THE STATE-RUN SEOUL NATIONAL
UNIVERSITY, WAS THE FIRST POLITICAL DISSIDENT WHO GOVERNMENT
AUTHORITIES ACKNOWLEDGED WAS KILLED BY TORTURE.
    GOVERNMENT OFFICIALS TEND TO DISMISS PARK'&S DEATH AS +AN
ISOLATED CASE+ BUT CRITICS ARGUE THAT TORTURE IS WIDESPREAD AND
SYSTEMATIC.
    SATURDAY'&S MEMORIAL SERVICES IN SEOUL AND OTHER PARTS OF THE
COUNTRY ARE BEING ORGANIZED BY 47 DISSIDENT GROUPS ALLIED WITH THE
MAIN OPPOSITION NEW KOREA DEMOCRATIC PARTY (NKDP).
    ORGANIZERS SAID AS MANY AS 62,301 PEOPLE REPRESENTING VARIOUS
WALKS OF LIFE HAVE VOLUNTEERED TO SPONSOR SATURDAY'&S SERVICES.
    IN A NATIONWIDE CAMPAIGN TO MUSTER PUBLIC SUPPORT, THE ORGANIZERS
ARE ASKING 25,000 CHURHES IN THE COUNTRY TO TOLL THEIR BELLS
SIMULTANEOUSLY AT THE START OF THE MEMORIAL SERVICES AT 2 P.M. (0500
GMT).
    ALL CARS ARE ASKED TO HONK AND CITIZENS ARE URGED TO WEAR BLACK
MOURNING RIBBONS ON THEIR JACKETS.
    POLICE COUNTER WITH A WARNING THAT SUCH ACTS ARE ILLEGAL AND
PUNISHABLE BY LAW.
    MORE
CCCCQQE ZCZ   4
=02050718
NNNN

0225

ZCZC HKA164 KHA007 NXI
UU HED HUP

R I
    KOREA-1STADD-SEOUL 2-5
X X X PUNISHED.
    GOVERNMENT OFFICIALS SAID THE NATION'&S 120,000 POLICE FORCES
WILL BE PUT ON FULL ALERT FROM FRIDAY THROUGH SUNDAY TO THWART THE
MEMORIAL SERVICES.
    IN SEOUL, 25,000 RIOT POLICE WILL BE MOBILIZED TO BLOCK A
MEMORIAL SERVICE AT THE MYUNGDONG CATHEDRAL, THE HEADQUARTERS OF
KOREA'&S 2.3 MILLION CATHOLICS WHERE MORE THAN 20,000 QEOPLE ARE
EXPECTED TO GATHER, THE OFFICIALS SAID.
    ALL ACCESS TO THE CATHEDRAL IN DOWNTOWN SEOUL WILL BE SEALED OFF
AND ONLY AUTHORITIES CATHOLIC PRIESTS, NUNS AND BEREAVED FAMILY
MEMBERS WILL BE ALLOWED IN, THE OFFICIALS SAID.
    SOME 260 KEY ORGANIZERS OF THE SEOUL GATHERING WILL BE PUT UNDER
TEMPORARY HOUSE ARREST IN A PREVENTIVE POLICE ACTION, THE OFFICIALS
SAID.
    ORGANIZERS SAID THE MEMORIAL SERVICES WILL BE PEACEFUL AND
ORDERLY. BUT GOVERNMENT AUTHORITIES DISCREDIT THE PROMISE, SAYING
THAT SUCH LARGE-SCALE MEMORIAL SERIVICES WOULD CERTAINLY TURN INTO A
VIOLENT STREET RALLY.
    THEY CITED AS AN EXAMPLE AN OPPOSITION RALLY IN THE WESTERN PORT
CITY OF INCHON MAY 3, 1986, IN WHICH THOUSANDS OF YOUTHS RIOTED,
ATTACKING A GOVERNMENT PARTY BUILDING AND BURNED POLICE CARS.
    PARK'&S DEATH AND VIOLENT PROTESTS THAT ENSUE ARE A NEW TWIST IN
KOREA'&S COMPLEX POLITICAL SCENE GRAPPLING WITH CONSTITUTIONAL
AMENDMENTS.
    THE NATION'&S RIVAL POLITICAL GROUPS HAVE YET TO ADOPT A NEW
CONSTITUTION THAT WOULD BE EFFECTED BEFORE PRESIDENT CHUN DOO HWAN
STEPS DOWN AT THE END OF HIS PRESENT SEVEN-YEAR TERM FEB.24 NEXT
YEAR.
    THE RULING GROUP FAVORS A CABINET SYSTEM OF GOVERNMENT BUT THE
OPPOSITION SUPPORTS A DIRECT ELECTION OF THE PRESIDENT INSTEAD OF
THE CURRENT ELECTORAL COLLEGE SYSTEM.
    PARK'&S TORTURE-DEATH FURTHER DIMMED HOPE FOR THE NATION'&S TWO
RIVAL GROUPS TO COME TO TERMS ON THE CONSTITUTIONAL ISSUE.
    (UPI) PS
CCCCQQE ZCZ
=02050741
NNNN

5

0226

051050 :AM-KOREA (SCHEDULED)

POLICE ON TOP ALERT TO THWART TORTURE PROTEST RALLIES

BY OH ILSON, REUTERS

SEOUL, FEB 5, REUTER - SOUTH KOREA'S 120,000 POLICE GO ON TOP ALERT TOMORROW AS AUTHORITIES SEEK TO FOIL PLANNED ANTI-TORTURE PROTESTS ACROSS THE COUNTRY ON SATURDAY.

DENOUNCING RALLY ORGANISERS FOR THEIR DECISION TO DEFY AN OFFICIAL BAN, THE GOVERNMENT SAID TODAY IT WOULD MOBILISE 30,000 POLICE IN THE CAPITAL ALONE TO GUARD AGAINST VIOLENCE.

POLICE WARNED TOP DISSIDENTS AND RADICAL LEADERS THEY WOULD BE PLACED UNDER HOUSE ARREST.

THE RALLIES ARE INTENDED TO COMMEMORATE SEOUL STUDENT PARK CHONG-CHOL, WHO DIED ON JANUARY 14 UNDER QUESTIONING BY TWO MEMBERS OF AN ANTI-COMMUNIST POLICE UNIT.

IN AN UNPRECEDENTED ADMISSION, THE GOVERNMENT SAID PARK WAS KILLED WHEN THE POLICEMEN TRIED TO FORCE HIS HEAD INTO A BATH FULL OF WATER AND THROTTLED HIM. IT ALSO SET UP A PANEL TO GUARD AGAINST FURTHER POLICE USE OF TORTURE.

IT DID HOWEVER DENOUNCE ANGRILY WHAT IT SAW AS EFFORTS BY THE OPPOSITION NEW KOREA DEMOCRATIC PARTY (NKDP), BACKED BY DISSIDENTS KIM DAE-JUNG AND KIM YOUNG-SAM, TO USE PARK'S DEATH TO PROVOKE AN UPRISING TO OVERTHROW PRESIDENT CHUN DOO HWAN.

IN A STATEMENT TODAY, JUSTICE MINISTER KIM SEUNG-KEY CALLED THE RALLIES +AN ILLEGAL, IMPURE ATTEMPT TO ABUSE (THE PARK TRAGEDY) FOR POLITICAL DEMAGOGUERY, FAR FROM ANY PURE HUMAN RIGHTS PURPOSES.+

MORE

G

0227

NNNN

¤ YK0303

051053 :AM-KOREA =1.1
        KIM ADDED: +THE GOVERNMENT HAS ALREADY MADE CLEAR THAT ALL
ITS AGENCIES HAVE MADE AN EXTRAORDINARY PLEDGE AND RESOLVE ...
TO ERADICATE ATROCITIES DURING CRIMINAL INVESTIGATIONS,
DRAWING A GOOD LESSON FROM THIS INCIDENT.+
        DESPITE THE PROMPT OFFICIAL ADMISSION, ORGANISERS SAID
TODAY MORE THAN 62,000 PEOPLE HAVE NOW VOLUNTEERED TO HELP
STAGE SATURDAY'S PROTEST RALLIES. THEY INCLUDED CHRISTIAN
CLERGY AND LAY PEOPLE, BUDDHISTS, PROFESSORS, STUDENTS,
WORKERS, ARTISTS AND JOURNALISTS.
        THERE HAVE BEEN NUMEROUS ALLEGATIONS, AT HOME AND ABROAD,
THAT SOUTH KOREA TORTURES POLITICAL OPPONENTS. THE GOVERNMENT
HABITUALLY DENIES THIS.
        THE OPPOSITION ACCUSES THE RULING CAMP OF OPPRESSING A
DEMOCRATIC MOVEMENT TO JUSTIFY AND PROLONG MILITARY
DICTATORSHIP.
        THE RIVAL CAMPS ARE LOCKED IN CONFRONTATION OVER THE
ELECTORAL SYSTEM TO ADOPT FOR CHOOSING A SUCCESSOR TO CHUN,
WHO IS DUE TO STAND DOWN IN 1988.
        HUNDREDS OF PEOPLE WERE ARRESTED LAST YEAR WHEN THE NKDP
CAMPAIGNED NATIONWIDE FOR SIGNATURES ON A PETITION CALLING FOR
DIRECT PRESIDENTIAL ELECTIONS SO THAT SOUTH KOREANS COULD
+CHOOSE THEIR GOVERNMENT WITH THEIR OWN HANDS.+ AT PRESENT THE
PRESIDENT IS ELECTED BY A 5,300-STRONG ELECTORAL COLLEGE.
    MORE

                                                7

                                    0228

NNNN
¤ YK0304

051055 :AM-KOREA =1.2
     LAST NOVEMBER AUTHORITIES DEPLOYED MORE THAN 60,000 POLICE
TO THWART OPPOSITION ATTEMPTS TO STAGE SOUTH KOREA'S BIGGEST
ANTI-GOVERNMENT RALLY IN A SEOUL PARK. POLICE MADE 2,200
ARRESTS THOUGH MOST WERE LATER RELEASED.
     THE GOVERNMENT SAYS MANY POLITICAL MILITANTS ARE IMBUED
WITH COMMUNIST IDEOLOGY AND AIM TO SUBVERT CAPITALIST SOUTH
KOREA IN FAVOUR OF THE COMMUNIST NORTH. THE KOREAS HAVE
REMAINED ARCH FOES SINCE THEIR THREE-YEAR WAR IN THE 1950S,
AND PRO-COMMUNIST ACTIVITIES ARE PUNISHABLE HERE BY DEATH.
     DESPITE THE RALLY BAN, AUTHORITIES SAY THEY WILL ALLOW A
SCHEDULED MEMORIAL SERVICE FOR PARK AT SEOUL'S CATHOLIC
CATHEDRAL TO GO AHEAD ON SATURDAY. POLICE SAID THEY WOULD BAN
ALL BUT GENUINE WORSHIPPERS.
     PROTEST ORGANISERS HAVE APPEALED TO CHURCHES TO TOLL THEIR
BELLS, DRIVERS TO HONK THEIR HORNS, AND CITIZENS TO WEAR BLACK
RIBBONS IN MEMORY OF PARK.
     THE INFLUENTIAL DONG-A ILBO NEWSPAPER, IN AN EDITORIAL
ENTITLED +DO THEY REALLY HAVE TO BLOCK MEMORIAL GATHERINGS FOR
PARK?,+ ADVISED THE AUTHORITIES NOT TO OVER-REACT TO THE
PLANNED PROTEST.
     IT SAID: +FRANKLY ... WE CANNOT UNDERSTAND THE GOVERNMENT'S
EXAGGERATION, MAKING IT SOUND AS THOUGH THE FATE OF THE WHOLE
REGIME WERE AT STAKE OVER THE PROPOSED MEMORIAL FUNCTIONS.
  MORE

NNNN
¤ YK0305

051058 :AM-KOREA =1.3
     +ALLOWING PEOPLE TO WEEP WHEN THEY FEEL SORROWFUL CAN BE
THERAPEUTIC.+
  REUTER   5   0229

R I
     KOREA-STUDENT-1STLD-WRITHRU 2-5
     SEOUL, FEB.5 (UPI) -- SEVEN DISSIDENT YOUTHS, ARMED WITH
+PETROLEUM BOMBS AND STEEL PIPES,+ THURSDAY OCCUPIED AN OPPOSITION
PARTY OFFICE IN SEOUL, DEMANDING A MORE VIGOROUS ANTI-GOVERNMENT
STRUGGLE, WITNESSES SAID.
     THE YOUTHS, INCLUDING FOUR COLLEGE STUDENTS AND THREE LABOR
ACTIVISTS, STORMED INTO THE THE CHONGRO BRANCH OFFICE OF THE MAIN
OPPOSITION NEW KOREA DEMOCRATIC PARTY (NKDP) AND BARRICADED
THEMSELVES BEHIND TABLES, CHAIRS AND FURNITURE, THE WITNESSES SAID.
     THE NKDP'＊S CHONGRO BRANCH IS HEADED BY PARTY LEADER LEE MIN-WOO.
     IMMEDIATELY AFTER THE SIEGE AT 10:30 A.M. (0130 GMT), THE YOUTHS
DISTRIBUTED 50 LEAFLETS PRODING THE NKDP INTO A MORE SPIRITED
ANTI-GOVERNMENT FIGHT AND A MEETING WITH THE NATION'＊S TWO
BEST-KNOWN DISSIDENTS, KIM YOUNG-SAM AND KIM DAE-JUNG, THE WITNESSES
SAID.
     +WE WILL NOT GIVE UP THE STRUGGLE UNTIL OUR DEMAND IS MET,+ THE
WITNESSES QUOTED ONE OF THE YOUTHS AS SHOUTING OUT OF A SECOND-STORY
WINDOW.
     THE YOUTHS THREATENED TO SET THE OFFICE ON FIRE IF 200 RIOT
POLICE STANDING BY TRY TO STOP THE SIEGE, THE WITNESSES SAID.
     THE YOUTHS, ONE OF THEM BELIEVED TO BE A COED, HUNG DOWN A
PLACARD READING:+NO COMPROMISE WITH MILITARY DICTATORSHIP+ AND
+NKDP, STRIVE TO GET CONSTITUENT ASSEMBLY TO BE FORMED IMMEDIATELY,+
THE WITNSSES SAID.
     THE WITNESSES ALSO SAID THE DISSIDENT YOUTHS DEMANDED THAT
SATURDAY'＊S MEMORIAL SERVICES FOR A COLLEGE STUDENT KILLED BY POLICE
TORTURE LAST MONTH BE HELD AS A POLITICAL RALLY TO +CRUSH MILITARY
DICTATORSHIP.+
     RADICAL STUDENTS ARE DEMANDING THAT A +CONSTITUENT ASSEMBLY+ BE
SET UP TO DRAFT A NEW CONSTITUTION THAT WILL REPLACE THE CURRENT
+DICTATORIAL+ GOVERNMENT WITH A REGIME THE GENUINE INTEREST OF THE
GRASS-ROOT PEOPLE.
     OPPOSITION-SPONSORED NATIONWIDE MEMORIAL SERVICES ARE SCHEDULED
FOR 2 P.M. (0500 GMT) THROUGHOUT THE COUNTRY TO MOURN PARK
CHONG-CHUL, 21, A SEOUL COLLEGE STUDENT WHO WAS TORTURED TO DEATH
DURING POLICE INTERROGATION JAN.14.
     THE GOVERNMENT HAS OUTLAWED THE MEMORIAL SERVICES, PLEDGING TO
FOIL IT WITH MASSIVE POLICE FORCES.
     (INCLUDES PREVIOUS)
     (UPI) PS
CCCCQQE ZCZ   13
=02051250   0230
NNNN

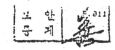
The Washington Times | FRIDAY, FEBRUARY 6, 1987 / PAGE 5D

Rallies banned in S. Korea

SEOUL (Reuters) — South Korea banned rallies marking the death of a student at the hands of the police and placed 120,000 policemen on alert to prevent demonstrations tomorrow.

Denouncing rally organizers for their decision to defy an official ban, the government said it would mobilize 50,000 police in the capital alone to guard against violence.

Police warned dissident and radical leaders they would be placed under house arrest.

The rallies were intended to commemorate Seoul student Park Chong-chol, who died Jan. 14 during interrogation by two members of a police unit.

In an unprecedented admission, the government said Mr. Park was killed when the policemen tried to force his head into a bath full of water and choked him. It also set up a panel to guard against further police use of torture.

However, the government denounced what it saw as efforts by the opposition New Korea Democratic Party, backed by dissidents Kim Dae-jung and Kim Young-sam, to use Mr. Park's death to provoke riots

Students shout yesterday from the Seoul, South Korea, office of opposition New Korea Democratic Party leader Lee Min-Woo.

against President Chun Doo Hwan.

In banning the protests, Justice Minister Kim Seung-key issued a statement calling the effort "an illegal, impure attempt to abuse [the Park tragedy] for political demagoguery, far from any pure human rights purposes."

Last November, authorities deployed more than 60,000 police to thwart opposition attempts to stage South Korea's biggest anti-

government rally in a Seoul park. Police made 2,200 arrests.

The government says many political militants are ideologists who aim to subvert capitalist South Korea in favor of the communist North.

Despite the rally ban, authorities said they will allow a memorial service scheduled tomorrow for Mr. Park at Seoul's Catholic cathedral. Police said they would ban all but genuine worshipers.

4A · FRIDAY, FEBRUARY 6 1987 · USA TODAY

SPANNING THE GLOBE: South Korean authorities banned a rally set for this weekend in Seoul to protest last month's torture-death of a student by police. ... A Chi-

韓国關係主要外信

1987. 2. 6(金) 15:30

(第 2 便)

外 信 名	内 容	페이지
AP, AFP Reuter (서울發)	2.7 追悼會 關聯, 政局緊張 高潮 - 警察, 不法集會 저지 對策에 부심 - [金大中] 等 10여명 家宅 保護 措置	1
AFP (서울發)	新安 앞바다 遺物 도굴조직 檢擧 - 第2의 遺物船 存在 可能性 대두	9

0232

GLGL
EXR0075 3 /AFP-AM86
SKOREA-RALLY 1
    KIM DAE-JUNG PLACED UNDER HOUSE ARREST, POLICE PUT ON ALERT

    SEOUL, FEB 6 (AFP) - SOUTH KOREA PUT KIM DAE-JUNG AND OTHER
OPPOSITION LEADERS UNDER HOUSE ARREST FRIDAY ON THE EVE OF A
PLANNED MEMORIAL GATHERING FOR A COLLEGE STUDENT WHO DIED UNDER
POLICE TORTURE THREE WEEKS AGO.
    POLICE MEANWHILE WERE PUT ON ALERT ACROSS THE COUNTRY.
    AIDES TO MR. KIM SAID HE HAD BEEN PLACED UNDER WHAT THE
AUTHORITIES CALLED ''HOUSE PROTECTION,'' WITH HUNDREDS OF POLICE
OFFICERS SURROUNDING HIS HOME IN WESTERN SEOUL.
    ALSO CONFINED TO THEIR HOUSES WERE CHOI HYUNG-WOO AND YANG
SUN-JIK, BOTH VICE-PRESIDENTS OF THE OPPOSITION NEW KOREA
DEMOCRATIC PARTY (NKDP), AMONG OTHER DISSIDENT LEADERS, THE AIDES
SAID.
    POLICE SAID THEY WERE PUT ON A 48-HOUR ALERT FRIDAY MORNING AND
THEY HAD ROUNDED UP 2,374 PEOPLE DURING AN EXTENSIVE
CHECK-AND-SEARCH OPERATION BY 41,000 OFFICERS IN SEOUL.
    ABOUT 330 WERE CHARGED, THEY SAID, INCLUDING THREE PEOPLE WHO
WERE CARRYING LEAFLETS ANNOUNCING THE RALLY AT THE MYUNDONG ROMAN
CATHOLIC CATHEDRAL IN DOWNTOWN SEOUL.
    SOUTH KOREA HAS SAID THAT DISSIDENT STUDENT PARK CHONG CHOL,
ENROLLED AT SEOUL NATIONAL UNIVERSITY, DIED DURING POLICE TORTURE
IN JANUARY.
    THE REVELATION LED TO THE RESIGNATION OF HOME AFFAIRS MINISTER
KIM CHONG HOH AND POLICE CHIEF KANG MIN CHANG, WHILE THE TWO
ALLEGED POLICE INTERROGATORS FACE LIFE IMPRISONMENT IF CONVICTED
FOR HOMICIDE.
    MORE/CKP/ROM
AFP 060405 GMT FEB 87   1

0233

GLGL
EXR0076 3 /AFP-RM87
SKOREA-RALLY 2-LAST
   (SEOUL)

PRESIDENT CHUN DOO-HWAN'S GOVERNMENT HAS BRANDED SATURDAY'S
PLANNED MEMORIAL RALLY AN ''ILLEGAL POLITICAL GATHERING.''
   JUSTICE MINISTER KIM SUNG-KY HAS SAID THAT SPONSORS OF SEVERAL
VIOLENT DEMONSTRATIONS IN THE PAST ARE AMONG ITS ORGANIZERS.
   IN A STATEMENT THURSDAY, HE SAID ORGANIZERS WERE TRYING TO
CREATE A DEMAGOGIC ATMOSPHERE BY CALLING ON DRIVERS, CHURCHES AND
BUDDHIST TEMPLES TO HONK HORNS AND RING BELLS AT 2 P.M. (0500 GMT)
AS THE RALLY TAKES PLACE.
   ''THE RALLY MUST BE STOPPED ... AS LAW-BREAKING ACTIVITIES
WHICH ARE LIKELY TO FOLLOW WILL CREATE SOCIAL CONFUSION,'' HE SAID.
   THE NKDP CRITICIZED THE GOVERNMENT FOR TRYING TO BLOCK THE
RALLY, WHICH THEY SAID WILL BE HELD ''IN A PEACEFUL AND ORDERLY
MANNER.''
   NKDP SPOKESMAN KIM TAE-RYONG WARNED THAT USE OF FORCE TO STOP
THE RALLY MIGHT CAUSE BLOODSHED.
   NATIONAL POLICE CHIEF LEE YOUNG-CHANG SAID THOSE WHO SPEARHEAD
ILLEGAL RALLIES AND DISTURBANCES SATURDAY WILL BE PUNISHED BY LAW
''REGARDLESS OF THEIR RANKS AND POSITIONS.''
   ''IF UNEXPECTED CONTINGENCIES SHOULD DEVELOP, THE ORGANIZERS OF
THE MEMORIAL EVENT MUST BEAR FULL RESPONSIBILITY,'' HE SAID IN A
STATEMENT RELEASED LATE THURSDAY.
   CKP/ROM
AFP   060408 GMT FEB 87   2

                                                0234

B B
W040

    U
SOUTH KOREA-RALLY
RA
POLICE BEGIN ANTI-RALLY MEASURES; KIM DAE-JUNG RESTRICTED
    SEOUL, SOUTH KOREA (AP) - SOUTH KOREAN AUTHORITIES EARLY FRIDAY
BEGAN CARRYING OUT EXTENSIVE MEASURES AIMED AT THWARTING
OPPOSITION-SPONSORED RALLIES MARKING THE DEATH OF A UNIVERSITY
STUDENT AT THE HANDS OF POLICE INTERROGATORS.
    THE GOVERNMENT OF PRESIDENT CHUN DOO-HWAN CHARGES THE HOLDING OF
THE MEETINGS SATURDAY IN SEOUL AND PROVINCIAL AREAS WOULD
CONSTITUTE ILLEGAL POLITICAL ACTS AND WILL NOT BE PERMITTED. THE
OPPOSITION CLAIMS THEY WILL BE PEACEFUL MEMORIALS FOR THE DEAD
STUDENT.
    AIDES TO KIM DAE-JUNG, THIS COUNTRY'S BEST KNOWN DISSIDENT
LEADER, SAID HE WAS PLACED UNDER HOUSE ARREST AT 9 A.M. (2400 GMT),
MORE THAN 24 HOURS BEFORE THE MAJOR OPPOSITION RALLY SET FOR
SATURDAY AFTERNOON AT MYUNGDONG CATHEDRAL IN DOWNTOWN SEOUL. THE
AIDES SAID TWO BUSLOADS OF POLICE WERE DEPLOYED AROUND KIM'S HOME,
BUT THAT HE HAD REFUSED TO TALK WITH POLICE OFFICIALS WHO CARRIED
THE WORD OF HIS RESTRICTION AND TERMED THEIR MOVE ILLEGAL AND
UNCONSTITUTIONAL.
    KIM, WHO RETURNED FROM A TWO-YEAR EXILE IN THE UNITED STATES IN
FEBRUARY 1985, HAS BEEN PLACED UNDER SIMILAR RESTRICTIONS ON
NUMEROUS OCCASIONS TO KEEP HIM FROM TAKING PART IN POLITICAL
MEETINGS OR OTHER ACTIVITIES. HE STILL IS UNDER A SUSPENDED 20-YEAR
PRISON SENTENCE ON A SEDITION CONVICTION THAT TOOK AWAY HIS CIVIL
RIGHTS.
    DISSIDENT SOURCES SAID THE ANTI-RALLY POLICE ACTION BEGAN
THURSDAY NIGHT AND THAT BY EARLY FRIDAY AT LEAST A HALF DOZEN
PEOPLE HAD BEEN PLACED UNDER HOUSE ARREST RESTRICTIONS. THERE
EARLIER WERE REPORTS THAT SUCH ACTION WOULD BE TAKEN AGAINST ABOUT
30 OPPOSITION AND DISSIDENT LEADERS.
    THERE WAS NO CONFIRMATION FROM POLICE OR OTHER AUTHORITIES, BUT
THE SOURCES SAID WIDESPREAD POLICE PATROLS AND RANDOM CHECKS OF
POSSIBLE TROUBLE SITES WERE BEING CARRIED OUT IN THE SOUTH KOREAN
CAPITAL AND OTHER AREAS.
    MORE
AP-NY-02-06-87 0201GMT

3

0235

B B
W044

DD

W052

U

SEOUL - SOUTH KOREA-RALLY 2

RA

THE YONHAP NEWS AGENCY REPORTED 42,000 POLICE HAD BEEN DEPLOYED OVERNIGHT AND HAD DETAINED 2,373 PEOPLE SAID TO HAVE BEEN CARRYING ILLEGAL LEAFLETS OR DESCRIBED AS OTHER ''SECURITY-RELATED OFFENDERS.'' THE REPORT SAID 1,003 WERE RELEASED AFTER WARNINGS, 1,041 WERE REFERRED TO SUMMARY COURTS WHILE THE REMAINDER WERE BEING BOOKED.

ON THE STREETS OF SEOUL, EVER-PRESENT PLAINCLOTHES POLICE WERE OBSERVED FRIDAY MAKING EVEN CLOSER CHECKS ON THE MOVEMENT OF YOUNG PEOPLE, APPARENTLY IN EFFORTS TO PREVENT STUDENT ACTIVISTS FROM LINKING UP IN ADVANCE OF THE SATURDAY RALLIES. SCHOOL BAGS AND IDENTIFICATION WERE BEING CAREFULLY EXAMINED.

POLICE REINFORCEMENTS WERE BEING BROUGHT INTO SEOUL FROM PROVINCIAL AREAS. THE FIRST GROUP OF 20 COMPANIES OF COMBAT FORCES WERE SAID TO HAVE REACHED THE CITY THURSDAY NIGHT. PUBLISHED REPORTS HAVE SAID ABOUT 20,000 POLICE WILL BE DEPLOYED AROUND MYUNGDONG CATHEDRAL, THE MAIN ROMAN CATHOLIC CENTER IN THE COUNTRY, TO SEAL OFF ALL ENTRY SATURDAY EXCEPT BY MEMBERS OF THE CLERGY. IT WAS EXPECTED THAT THOUSANDS OF OTHER POLICE WOULD BE POSITIONED AT OTHER STRATEGIC LOCATIONS THROUGHOUT THE CITY.

LEE YOUNG-CHANG, DIRECTOR GENERAL OF THE NATIONAL POLICE, SAID THURSDAY NIGHT THAT THE MEMORIAL RALLIES WOULD BE CONSIDERED ILLEGAL AND THAT THOSE TAKING LEADING ROLES IN THEM WOULD BE PUNISHED ''REGARDLESS OF THEIR RANK OR POSITION.''

THE TOP POLICE OFFICER SENT A LETTER TO LEE MIN-WOO, PRESIDENT OF THE MAJOR OPPOSITION NEW KOREA DEMOCRATIC PARTY, TELLING HIM THE RALLY WAS BANNED, BUT SOURCES SAID PARTY LEADERS REFUSED TO ACCEPT THE COMMUNICATION. SIMILAR LETTERS WERE REPORTED TO HAVE BEEN SENT BY POLICE TO OTHER DISSIDENT AND HUMAN RIGHTS GROUPS SPONSORING THE RALLIES.

MORE

AP-NY-02-06-87 0226GMT

4

DD

W053

U

QQ

W063

U
SEOUL - SOUTH KOREA-RALLY 3
RA

THE DEATH ON JAN. 14 OF 21-YEAR-OLD PARK CHONG-CHUL, A LANGUAGE STUDENT AT SEOUL NATIONAL UNIVERSITY, BROUGHT A SENSITIVE NEW ISSUE TO THE ALREADY TURBULENT SOUTH KOREAN POLITICAL SCENE. BY OFFICIAL ACCOUNTS, HE SUFFOCATED WHEN TWO POLICE OFFICERS FORCED HIS THROAT AGAINST THE EDGE OF A BATHTUB DURING A WATER TORTURE SESSION.

THE TWO POLICEMEN BELIEVED INVOLVED HAVE BEEN ARRESTED, OTHER POLICE OFFICERS HAVE BEEN TRANSFERRED AND THE HOME MINISTER AND NATIONAL POLICE DIRECTOR FIRED IN THE AFTERMATH OF THE STUDENT DEATH.

PRESIDENT CHUN AND HIGHEST RANKING OFFICIALS IN HIS GOVERNMENT AND RULING PARTY HAVE ISSUED SOLEMN STATEMENTS OF REGRET AND VOWS AGAINST THE RECURRENCE OF SUCH INCIDENTS.

DESPITE THESE MOVES, WIDESPREAD PUBLIC REACTION FOLLOWED THE DISCLOSURE OF THE STUDENT'S DEATH WHILE THE POLITICAL OPPOSITION, DISSIDENTS AND HUMAN RIGHTS ACTIVISTS HAVE SEIZED ON THE ISSUE AS WHAT THEY CHARGE IS AN EXAMPLE OF HARSH, REPRESSIVE RULE.

THE GOVERNMENT AND OPPOSITION ALREADY WERE DIVIDED SHARPLY OVER PROPOSALS TO REVISE THE CONSTITUTION PRIOR TO THE END OF CHUN'S PRESIDENTIAL TERM IN FEBRUARY 1988. THE MAJOR OPPOSITION IS DEMANDING CHANGES TO BRING ABOUT THE DIRECT, POPULAR ELECTION OF THE COUNTRY'S PRESIDENT, AND RULING AUTHORITIES NOW ARE PUSHING FOR A PARLIAMENTARY FORM OF GOVERNMENT UNDER A STRONG PRIME MINISTER.

NO AGREEMENT WAS IN SIGHT EVEN BEFORE THE STUDENT TORTURE DEATH, AND THE CONTROVERSY OVER IT APPEARED TO HAVE DISRUPTED ANY TIMETABLE EVEN MORE.

END

5

AP-NY-02-06-87 0247GMT

QQ
W064

0237

CK 060533 NNNN

B YK0725

060539 :PM-KOREA (SCHEDULED,EXPECT PIX SE0001)
   POLICE SWOOP, DISSIDENTS HELD, ON EVE OF TORTURE PROTEST DAY
     BY MOON IHLWAN, REUTERS
     SEOUL, FEB 6, REUTER - SOUTH KOREAN POLICE ROUNDED UP MORE
THAN 2,000 PEOPLE OVERNIGHT AND DISSIDENTS SAID 10 OF THEIR
LEADERS WERE UNDER 48-HOUR HOUSE ARREST AS OFFICIALS SOUGHT TO
DEFUSE NATIONWIDE ANTI-TORTURE PROTESTS PLANNED FOR TOMORROW.
     THE COUNTRY'S 120,000 POLICE WENT ON HIGH ALERT IN
PREPARATION FOR THE RALLIES, SCHEDULED FOR 22 CITIES ACROSS
SOUTH KOREA TOMORROW TO MOURN THE DEATH OF STUDENT ACTIVIST
PARK CHONG-CHOL IN POLICE CUSTODY.
     +WE ROUNDED UP A TOTAL OF 2,373 CRIMINAL SUSPECTS IN A
PRECAUTIONARY OVERNIGHT SWOOP AGAINST TOMORROW'S RALLIES AND
SENT 1,041 OF THEM TO SUMMARY COURTS,+ A POLICE SPOKESMAN TOLD
REPORTERS.
     HE SAID THE REMAINDER WERE STILL BEING QUESTIONED OR HAD
BEEN RELEASED AFTER WARNINGS.
     THOSE SENT TO SUMMARY COURTS COULD FACE UP TO 29 DAYS IN
JAIL. POLICE SAID SOME WERE ACCUSED OF ANTI-GOVERNMENT
ACTIVITIES AND VIOLENCE WHILE OTHERS WERE COMMON PICKPOCKETS
AND HOODLUMS BUT COULD GIVE NO DETAILS OF THE CHARGES.
     DISSIDENTS SAID AT LEAST 10 OF THEIR LEADERS, INCLUDING
FORMER PRESIDENTIAL CANDIDATE KIM DAE-JUNG, WERE PLACED UNDER
48-HOUR HOUSE ARREST TO PREVENT THEM FROM ATTENDING THE
RALLIES.
  MORE
                            6

0238

NNNN

@ YK0726

060541 :PM-KOREA =1.1

THE POLICE CRACKDOWN WAS MADE AFTER MORE THAN 60,000
PEOPLE, INCLUDING ROMAN CATHOLIC, PROTESTANT AND BUDDHIST
CLERGYMEN, VOWED TO DEFY AN OFFICIAL BAN ON THE RALLIES, WHICH
THE AUTHORITIES SAID COULD DEGENERATE INTO RIOTING AND
BLOODSHED.

POLICE CHIEF LEE YONG-CHANG TOLD REPORTERS THAT ALL
POLITICIANS, DISSIDENTS AND RADICAL LEADERS WOULD BE BARRED
FROM ATTENDING THE RALLIES AS +THEY WOULD TRY TO TURN (THE
RALLIES) INTO POLITICAL ASSEMBLIES.+

LEE SAID PRIESTS AND RELATIVES OF PARK WOULD BE ALLOWED TO
HOLD A MEMORIAL SERVICE ALONG WITH +PURE LAYPEOPLE+, BUT
POLICE WOULD MAKE EVERY EFFORT TO PREVENT ILLEGAL
DEMONSTRATIONS.

KIM DAE-JUNG, A CHRISTIAN, HAD PLANNED TO ATTEND THE
SERVICE AT SEOUL'S CATHOLIC CATHEDRAL. HE IS BANNED FROM ALL
POLITICAL ACTIVITY BECAUSE OF A CONVICTION FOR SEDITION.

STUDENT PARK, 21, DIED ON JANUARY 14 WHILE BEING
INTERROGATED BY MEN OF A SPECIAL ANTI-COMMUNIST POLICE UNIT ON
THE WHEREABOUTS OF A FUGITIVE ACTIVIST.

TWO POLICEMEN FACE TRIAL AFTER ADMITTING FORCING PARK'S
HEAD INTO A TUB OF WATER AND SUFFOCATING HIM DURING
QUESTIONING.

THE GOVERNMENT HAS ACKNOWLEDGED THAT PARK WAS TORTURED BUT
SAYS IT WAS AN ISOLATED INCIDENT AND ACCUSES THE OPPOSITION
NEW KOREA DEMOCRATIC PARTY (NKDP) AND DISSIDENTS OF TRYING TO
EXPLOIT PARK'S DEATH TO SPARK AN UPRISING TO OVERTHROW
PRESIDENT CHUN DOO HWAN.

MORE   7

0239

NNNN
B YK0727

060544 :PM-KOREA =1.2
    NKDP SPOKESMAN KIM TAE-RYONG WARNED THAT IF EFFORTS TO
HOLD THE SERVICES WERE FOILED, +DREADFUL BLOODSHED+ MIGHT
RESULT. HE ADDED: +WE URGE THE GOVERNMENT TO IMMEDIATELY STOP
MANOEUVRES TO HAMPER THE SERVICES.+
    JUSTICE MINISTER KIM SEUNG-KEY ISSUED A STATEMENT
YESTERDAY SAYING ALL GOVERNMENT AGENCIES HAD PLEDGED TO
ERADICATE BRUTALITY DURING CRIMINAL INVERSTIGATIONS.
    LAST NOVEMBER, MORE THAN 60,000 POLICE WERE DEPLOYED ON
THE STREETS OF SEOUL TO THWART OPPOSITION ATTEMPTS TO STAGE A
HUGE ANTI-GOVERNMENT RALLY IN A CITY PARK. POLICE MADE 2,200
ARRESTS BUT MOST WERE LATER RELEASED.
    REUTER

8

0240

外務部　情報1課

韓国関係主要外信

1987. 2. 9(月)　07:10

(第　1　便)

外 信 名	内　　　容	페이지
AFP , Reuter (서울發)	亡命　北韓人　11名，서울　到着	1
UPI , AFP Reuter (東京發)	北韓，　日政府의　亡命　北韓人　台灣 出國　措置　關聯　韓 . 日　兩國　非難	6
AFP , Reuter (서울發)	警察，　〔朴鍾哲〕君　追悼　大會 關聯　示威者　740名　拘束	11
AP (서울發)	韓國　政局　展望　關聯　AP通信　記事	15

0241

080430 :PM-KOREA (SCHEDULED)

SOUTH KOREAN POLICE QUESTION 740 ARRESTED AFTER PROTEST DAY

BY MOON IHLWAN, REUTERS

SEOUL, FEB 8, REUTER - SOUTH KOREAN POLICE SAID TODAY THEY WERE QUESTIONING 740 PEOPLE ARRESTED DURING NATIONWIDE DEMONSTRATIONS YESTERDAY BUT DISSIDENTS WERE FREED FROM HOUSE ARREST AND 120,000 POLICE TAKEN OFF ALERT.

A POLICE SPOKESMAN TOLD REPORTERS 799 PEOPLE HAD BEEN HELD AFTER ABOUT 10,000 PEOPLE IN SEVERAL CITIES DEFIED A GOVERNMENT BAN ON RALLIES CALLED AFTER THE DEATH OF STUDENT ACTIVIST PARK CHONG-CHOL IN POLICE CUSTODY LAST MONTH.

+A GROUP OF 59 HAVE BEEN RELEASED AFTER WARNINGS AND MANY MORE MIGHT BE RELEASED LATER BUT RADICALS WHO SET POLICE VANS ON FIRE OR ATTACKED GOVERNMENT OFFICES WITH STONES AND PETROL BOMBS WILL FACE TOUGH PENALTIES,+ HE ADDED.

SCORES OF POLICE WHO HAD SURROUNDED THE HOMES OF DISSIDENT LEADERS KIM DAE-JUNG AND KIM YOUNG-SAM TO PREVENT THEM LEADING THE RALLIES WITHDREW DURING THE NIGHT, THE POLITICIANS' AIDES SAID. DOZENS OF OTHER DISSIDENTS WERE ALSO FREED FROM SIMILAR MEASURES.

MORE THAN 70,000 PEOPLE, INCLUDING PROFESSORS, LAWYERS AND ROMAN CATHOLIC, PROTESTANT AND BUDDHIST CLERGYMEN, HAD VOLUNTEERED TO ORGANISE DEMONSTRATIONS AT 65 PLACES ACROSS SOUTH KOREA TO MARK PARK'S DEATH BUT MOST OF THE RALLIES WERE THWARTED BY A MASSIVE SHOW OF POLICE FORCE YESTERDAY.

MORE

11

0242

NNNN

080432 :PM-KOREA =1.1
      THE GOVERNMENT OF PRESIDENT CHUN DOO HWAN HAD BANNED THE
RALLIES, ACCUSING THE OPPOSITION OF TRYING TO SPARK AN
UPRISING IN A BID TO TOPPLE THE PRESIDENT. TENS OF THOUSANDS
OF POLICE WERE MOBILISED WITH ORDERS TO FIRE TEAR GAS.
      BUT ABOUT 10,000 PEOPLE IN SEOUL, KWANGJU, PUSAN AND TAEGU
BRAVED THE TEAR GAS TO DENOUNCE THE GOVERNMENT AND POLICE SAID
3,200 OF THEM FOUGHT A RUNNING BATTLE WITH RIOT POLICE IN THE
CAPITAL.
      A POLICE SPOKESMAN SAID TWO POLICE VANS AND FOUR
GOVERNMENT OFFICES WERE WRECKED BY THE PROTESTERS WHILE
WITNESSES SAID MORE THAN 50 DEMONSTRATORS AND POLICEMEN WERE
INJURED.
      THE TWO KIMS TODAY ISSUED STATEMENTS DESCRIBING
YESTERDAY'S PROTESTS AS A SUCCESS AMID +BARBAROUS ACTS BY THE
DICTATORIAL REGIME+ AND PLEDGED THEY WOULD STEP UP THEIR
STRUGGLE AGAINST THE CHUN GOVERNMENT.
      KIM YOUNG-SAM SAID YESTERDAY'S PROTESTS +SATISFACTORILY
DEMONSTRATED TO THE WORLD OUR PEOPLE'S WILL TO EXPEL TORTURE
... AND DETERMINATION NOT TO TOLERATE A DICTATORIAL REGIME ANY
LONGER+.
      THE GOVERNMENT DENIES OPPOSITION ALLEGATIONS THAT POLICE
REGULARLY USE TORTURE AGAINST DISSIDENTS. BUT IT ACKNOWLEDGED
THAT PARK SUFFOCATED WHEN TWO POLICEMEN FORCED HIS HEAD INTO A
BATHTUB WHILE QUESTIONING HIM ABOUT THE WHEREABOUTS OF A
FUIGITIVE ACTIVIST.
      MORE

      NNNN
      ¤ YK0567

080435 :PM-KOREA =1.2
      A GOVERNMENT SPOKESMAN SAID ALL GOVERNMENT AGENCIES`HAD
PLEDGED TO ERADICATE BRUTALITY DURING CRIMINAL INVESTIGATIONS.
HE ACCUSED THE OPPOSITION OF TRYING TO EXPLOIT PARK'S DEATH TO
CREATE SOCIAL UNREST TO OVERTHROW THE GOVERNMENT.
      REUTER

12   0243

EXR0073 3 /AFP-AI83
SKOREA-DEMO 1
  CALM RETURNS TO SOUTH KOREA AFTER SATURDAY RIOTS

    SEOUL, FEB 8 (AFP) - CALM RETURNED TO SOUTH KOREA ON SUNDAY
AFTER TUMULTUOUS ANTI-GOVERNMENT DEMONSTRATIONS IN SIX CITIES TO
PROTEST THE DEATH OF A DISSIDENT STUDENT WHO WAS TORTURED BY POLICE
LAST MONTH.
    POLICE SAID 799 DEMONSTRATORS WERE ARRESTED, 475 OF THEM IN
SEOUL, IN CLASHES WITH RIOT POLICE SATURDAY. FIFTY-NINE WERE FREED
EARLY SUNDAY AND MANY OF THE REST WERE TO BE RELEASED LATER SUNDAY,
THEY SAID.
    ONLY THE LEADERS OF THE DEMONSTRATIONS AND THOSE WHO TOOK PART
IN BURNING POLICE SUB-STATIONS AND ONE POLICE BUS WILL BE
PROSECUTED, POLICE SOURCES SAID.
    FOURTY-SEVEN RIOT POLICE WERE INJURED IN THE VIOLENCE.
    MORE THAN 20,000 DEMONSTRATORS, ACCORDING TO NEWSPAPER
ESTIMATES, TOOK TO THE STREETS OF DOWNTOWN SEOUL AFTER POLICE
BLOCKADES BARRED THEM FROM GATHERING AT MYONGDONG CATHEDRAL FOR A
BANNED MEMORIAL SERVICE IN MEMORY OF SEOUL NATIONAL UNIVERSITY
STUDENT PARK CHONG-CHUL.
    NATIONAL POLICE DIRECTOR LEE YOUNG-CHANG, HOWEVER, SAID THE
TURNOUT IN SEOUL WAS ONLY 2,000.
    THE GOVERNMENT HAS ACKNOWLEDGED THAT MR. PARK, 21, DIED WHILE
BEING TORTURED BY POLICE INTERROGATORS. TWO POLICE OFFICERS HAVE
BEEN CHARGED WITH HOMICIDE AND PRESIDENT CHUN DOO-HWAN'S HOME
MINISTER AND A RANKING POLICE OFFICIAL WERE FORCED TO RESIGN.
    MORE/PKM/ROM
AFP 080458 GMT FEB 87   13

                                        0244

GLGL
EXR0074 3 /AFP-AI84
SKOREA-DEMO 2-LAST
    (SEOUL)

    MR. CHUN'S RULING DEMOCRATIC JUSTICE PARTY (DJP) SAID IN A
STATEMENT THAT MOST SOUTH KOREANS DISPLAYED ''POLITICAL MATURITY BY
NOT BEING DRAWN INTO THE OPPOSITION-INSTIGATED ILLEGAL GATHERINGS,
ALTHOUGH SOME IMPURE FORCES STAGED SPORADIC DEMONSTRATIONS.''
    IT SAID MOST CITIZENS DID NOT RESPOND TO AN OPPOSITION'S CALL
TO HONK THEIR CAR HORNS IN A GESTURE OF ANTI-GOVERNMENT PROTEST AT
2 P.M. SATURDAY TO COINCIDE WITH THE MEMORIAL SERVICE.
    BUT PROMINENT OPPOSITION FIGURE KIM DAE-JUNG, WHO HAD BEEN
PLACED UNDER HOUSE ARREST BY POLICE FOR THE LAST TWO DAYS, SAID HE
WAS ENCOURAGED BY SATURDAY'S ANTI-GOVERNMENT GATHERINGS WHICH HE
TERMED ''A SUCCESS.''
    MR. KIM, 61, HAD BEEN LEADING A CAMPAIGN CALLING FOR GREATER
DEMOCRACY IN SOUTH KOREA SINCE HE RETURNED HOME TWO YEARS AGO FROM
SELF-EXILE IN THE UNITED STATES.
    PKM/RON   14
AFP   080500 GMT FEB 87

0245

R 233

SOUTH KOREA-POLITICS,0295

SOUTH KOREAN POLITICS: NO COMPROMISE IN SIGHT

AN AP NEWS ANALYSIS

BY EDWIN Q. WHITE

ASSOCIATED PRESS WRITER

SEOUL, SOUTH KOREA (AP) - LEE MIN-WOO, THE 71-YEAR-OLD PRESIDENT OF SOUTH KOREA'S MAJOR OPPOSITION PARTY, SAT IN A RESTAURANT IN DOWNTOWN SEOUL, WAITING, AS AIDES TORE OFF STRIPS OF PLASTIC KITCHEN WRAP AND HANDED THEM OUT.

THE STRIPS WERE TO SERVE AS MAKESHIFT GAS MASKS, PROTECTION FOR EYES AND NOSES. THEY WERE NEEDED WHEN LEE'S ENTOURAGE LEFT THE RESTAURANT TO WALK TOWARD A MEMORIAL RALLY FOR A STUDENT TORTURED TO DEATH BY POLICE LAST MONTH.

THE GOVERNMENT HAD DECLARED THE RALLY ILLEGAL AND RIOT POLICE MOVED IN QUICKLY, FIRING TEAR GAS TO BREAK UP THE MARCH OF THE ELDERLY POLITICIAN AND HIS FOLLOWERS.

THE CONFRONTATION -- REPEATED DOZENS OF TIMES SATURDAY -- ILLUSTRATES THE BITTER DIVISIONS IN SOUTH KOREAN POLITICS AND INDICATES TIME MAY BE RUNNING OUT FOR AN ORDERLY TRANSFER OF POWER WHEN PRESIDENT CHUN DOO-HWAN STEPS DOWN IN 1988.

THROUGHOUT ITS RELATIVELY SHORT MODERN POLITICAL HISTORY, SOUTH KOREA HAS SEEN ATTEMPTS TO DEVELOP DEMOCRACY MIRED DOWN IN FACTIONAL FIGHTING THAT LED TO AUTHORITARIAN RULE, OFTEN WITH MILITARY BACKING.

LEE'S NEW KOREA DEMOCRATIC PARTY WAS FORMED BEFORE THE NATIONAL ASSEMBLY ELECTIONS IN FEBRUARY 1985, AND RAN A STRONG SECOND TO THE GOVERNING DEMOCRACTIC JUSTICE PARTY, PRESENTING CHUN WITH HIS FIRST CHALLENGE SINCE HE TOOK POWER IN 1980.

SINCE THEN, THE GOVERNMENT AND THE OPPOSITION HAVE BEEN LOCKED IN A BITTER AND OFTEN-VIOLENT CONFRONTATION THAT HAS NOT PERMITTED COMPROMISE.

THE NEW KOREA DEMOCRATIC PARTY QUESTIONS THE LEGITIMACY OF THE GOVERNMENT, SAYING IT DOES NOT HAVE POPULAR BACKING AND IS IN POWER ONLY BECAUSE OF MILITARY SUPPORT.

.MORE

15   0246

AP-NY-02-08-87 1831GMT

W254

R 233

SEOUL - SOUTH KOREA-POLITICS 2,0275

THE GOVERNMENT COUNTERS THAT MOST SOUTH KOREANS FAVOR ITS PROGRAMS AND POLICIES -- OFTEN CITING SOUTH KOREA'S ''ECONOMIC MIRACLE'' -- AND MAINTAINS THAT IT IS MOVING CAUTIOUSLY TOWARD MORE DEMOCRACY.

IT ALSO CHARGES THAT MEMBERS OF THE OPPOSITION HAVE COME UNDER RADICAL INFLUENCE THAT VERGES ON A COMMUNIST OR PRO-COMMUNIST LINE AND COULD ONLY SERVE TO BENEFIT NORTH KOREA AND ITS IDEOLOGICAL ALLIES.

AS POSITIONS KEEP HARDENING, BOTH SIDES CONCEDE THAT TIME IS RUNNING OUT FOR WHAT COULD BE SOUTH KOREA'S FIRST ORDERLY TRANSFER OF POWER. CHUN HAS SAID HE WOULD STEP DOWN WHEN HIS TERM EXPIRES IN FEBRUARY 1988.

THE GOVERNMENT HAS IN PRINCIPLE AGREED TO AN OPPOSITION DEMAND FOR CONSTITUTIONAL REFORM, BUT THE TWO SIDES REMAIN FAR APART ON ISSUES.

THE OPPOSITION IS PUSHING FOR A DIRECT, POPULAR PRESIDENTIAL VOTE TO REPLACE THE PRESENT ELECTORAL COLLEGE SYSTEM. THE GOVERNMENT WANTS A SYSTEM WITH A STRONG PRIME MINISTER AND A LARGELY SYMBOLIC PRESIDENCY.

THE OPPOSITION HAS DENOUNCED BOTH THE PRESENT SYSTEM AND THE GOVERNMENT PROPOSAL, SAYING BOTH SYSTEMS FAVOR THOSE ALREADY IN POWER.

ATTEMPTS IN THE NATIONAL ASSEMBLY TO RESOLVE DIFFERENCES HAVE BROKEN DOWN BEFORE THEY COULD GET STARTED.

A CONSTITUTIONAL CHANGE REQUIRES TWO-THIRDS APPROVAL IN THE ASSEMBLY AND IN A NATIONAL REFERENDUM. IF THE NEW CONSTITUTION CALLS FOR A DIFFERENT FORM OF GOVERNMENT, NEW ELECTIONS HAVE TO BE HELD.

HOW ALL THAT COULD BE ACCOMPLISHED WITH ANY DEGREE OF EQUANIMITY IN THE TIME LEFT IS DIFFICULT TO IMAGINE.

SATURDAY'S CLASHES SHOWED THAT INSTEAD, THE OPPOSING FACTIONS MAY BE EVEN LESS INCLINED TO SEARCH FOR A COMPROMISE.

END

16   0247

AP-NY-02-08-87 1834GMT

Seoul Police Fire Tear Gas To Halt Rally

By John Burgess
Washington Post Foreign Service

SEOUL, Feb. 7 (Saturday)— South Korean riot police in central Seoul today began firing tear gas and arresting people who turned out for a banned memorial service for a student who died during police torture.

On a busy avenue near Seoul's Myongdong Cathedral, where the memorial was scheduled, people were hustled into waiting police vans. A group of women in black held flowers and a portrait of the dead student and listened as one woman read a memorial statement for him.

With more protesters set to arrive and thousands of riot police standing at the ready on street corners and squares around the city's central area, a confrontation seemed imminent between government and dissidents.

Rows of riot police with shields, helmets and tear gas were sealing all streets leading to the cathedral, which is seat of the archdiocese for South Korea's 2 million Catholics. The rally has officially been banned.

Police had picked up close to 2,300 people believed to be involved in organizing the memorial during sweeps around the city Thursday night, government television reported yesterday.

The government maintained that dissidents are "politically abusing" the student's death.

"The planned rally is designed as an unlawful subversive political assembly with the ultimate aim of overthrowing both the government and the present political system through violence," Justice Minister Kim Sung Ky said in a statement.

The police said they will allow a small service to proceed inside the cathedral. But only priests affiliated with the church and genuine members of the congregation will be allowed to enter.

Dissident groups said they will

See KOREA, A18, Col 1

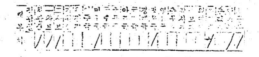

0248

Seoul Police Fire Tear Gas To Halt Rally

KOREA, From A1

not initiate violence and only want to honor the student, Park Chong Chul, 21, who studied linguistics at the elite Seoul National University and was active in antigovernment protests.

"We would like to express the people's desire that this kind of torture should never happen again," said Suh Chui Yung, a spokesman for the Committee for Promotion of Democracy, one of the gathering's sponsors.

In recent days, dissidents turned aside government requests to cancel their plans and both sides yesterday stepped up preparations for a confrontation.

Authorities raided campuses and offices of dissident organizations and confiscated thousands of leaflets, placards, bottles they said could be used for gasoline bombs and a few mock coffins.

Kim Dae Jung and Kim Young Sam, the two unofficial leaders of the opposition New Korea Democratic Party, were placed under house arrest. Estimates of the total number of government opponents placed under house arrest ranged from a dozen to more than 30.

Lawmakers from the opposition party yesterday passed out leaflets in Seoul shopping areas urging people to attend the gathering at the cathedral. Police at the scene attempted to confiscate the leaflets, according to press reports.

About 100 professors at Park's university reportedly marked the student's death by remaining in their offices late Thursday night.

Smaller memorials are also planned around the country at 2 p.m. today. Organizers are asking people to ring church and Buddhist temple bells, honk car horns and engage in a minute's silent meditation. Police have been instructed to stop these actions.

Park's death in a police interrogation center in Seoul on Jan. 14 quickly became the focus of campaigning against the government when officials acknowledged five days later that it had occurred during torture.

It threw the government on the defensive at a time when it had appeared to be gaining the upper hand against its opponents through political maneuvering and a series of crackdowns.

The government formally apologized for the death and took steps that included the arrest and indictment of two police officers and replacement of the national police chief and home affairs minister. The opposition, however, charging that torture is widespread in South Korea, demanded more measures to end abuses.

In November, the New Korea Democratic Party tried to stage a mass rally in Seoul to break a deadlock in negotiations with the government for constitutional change.

The gathering was crushed quickly and decisively by a show of police power on the city's streets and mass arrests. Emotions quickly settled down, as is often the case in South Korea when politics seems to be heading toward the boiling point.

The government hopes to block today's with similar efficiency. There are some differences in circumstances this time, however. The student's death appears to have angered large numbers of South Koreans and given the opposition a valuable new organizing issue.

November's attempted rally was sponsored only by the party. Today's was organized by close to 50 church, labor, student and dissident groups, as well as the political party.

As of several days ago, 22,000 people had signed up to be on the memorial's organizing committee. Among them are Roman Catholic Cardinal Kim Sou Hwan, also known as Stephen Kim, and major Protestant leaders.

NEW YORK TIMES International News SATURDAY, FEBRUARY 7, 1987

2,400 Seized in South Korea On Eve of Protests in Death

SEOUL, South Korea, Feb. 6 (Reuters) — President Chun Doo Hwan issued a warning today against rioting on the eve of planned national demonstrations over the torture death of a student while in police custody.

According to the authorities the police rounded up nearly 2,400 people overnight and placed about a dozen leading dissidents, including a former Presidential candidate, Kim Dae Jung, under house arrest.

The national police also tightened security to head off the rallies planned to protest the death of the student, Park Chong Chol, during police questioning last month.

126-2

0249

反制者들● 拷問 폭로하겠다고

(AFP, 서울, 2.18, 1테이크)

　　韓國의 두 지도적인 반정부지도자는 18일 다음 주에 있을 예정인 人權集會에서 정부의 여러 拷問事件을 폭로하겠다고 말했다.

　　반체제기구인 民推協의 공동의장 김대중과 김영삼 양씨는 오는 25일 서울에 있는 민추협 본부에서 있을 집회에서 고문을 폭로하겠다고 말했다.

　　이 집회에서는 또 지난 1월 경찰의 조사를 받다가 사망한 21세의 대학생 박종철군의 고문치사에 대한 비난발언도 있을 것이다. 박군의 사망은 정부가 시인한 유일한 경찰의 拷問死亡事件이다.

　　한편 고 박종철군 범국민추도회 준비위원회는 오는 3월3일 서울에서 "民主化와 고문근절을 위한 범국민 평화행진"을 벌이겠다고 말했다. 3월3일은 49일간의 불교애도기간이 끝나는 날이다.

　　反體制人士들과 종교지도자들을 포함하고 있는 이 준비위원회는 또 지난 2월7일 반정부 가두시위중 서울에서 연행된 34명의 정부당국은 석방하라고 말했다.

　　지난 2월7일 서울명동성당에서 추도대회를 열려던 추도회 준비위원회의 노력은 경찰의 봉쇄로 좌절되었다. 성당에 접근하려던 약 2만명은 경찰과 격렬한 대결을 벌였다.

I-6

0250

1987年2月20日　金曜日

「朴군 49齋」비상

경찰 事前봉쇄령

在野 종교계 集會기미에
油類판매 소등 체크

경찰, 民言協수색

新民과 朴鍾哲군사건 報告書발표

0251

박종철 서울대생 고문치사 사건, 1987　653

東亞日報

3·3大行進「강행」「저지」맞서

警察 22,000명 동원 계획

주동자 가택보호 街頭통제

京仁9곳 정오에 침묵 행진

当局 主催측

28일밤 17개大學 일제 수색

佛教 5개단체는 조계사서 49명 예정

政治이용말고 院內복귀를 民正

民主의 지 있다면 沮止말라 新民

0252

3일大行進 철저봉쇄

鄭內務담화 뚜렷한 不法… 관련자 엄중措置

鄭鎬溶내무부장관은 28일 담화문을 발표 「3월 정치권과 재야단체 연합계획」등이 오는3월3일 釜山에서 발표한 담화문을 통해 「사회불순세력들의 군중행사 등을 빙자, 오는 3월 3일 불법가두시위를 통해 평화대행진」이란는 정치적 수도서울의 기능마비를 초래시키려는 것으로 확신한 다고 말했다.

鄭장관은 지방순시중 이날 부산에서 발표한 담화문을 통해 「사회불순세력들이 이른바 「국제정치투쟁」으로 연계 국정으로 또다시 기도하고 있다고 지적했다.

鄭장관은 「정부는 박군의 전을 계기로 인권보호와 기본권신장을위해 최선을 다할 것을 다시한번 다짐한다」고 말하고 「국민들은 극소수 안의 정치악용의 목적으로 개재돼있는 것으로 확신한 다고 말했다.

鄭장관은 「그러나 법으로 허용된 정치광장에서 제기되 는 정부는 이를 수렴하여 정 책수립에 최대한 반영할것이 며 합법적정치집회 순수한 종교행사 건전한 학생및 노 동활동에의 차원에서 최대한 허용하고 보호할 방침」이라 고 밝혔다.

지난40년간 피땀흘려 이룩해놓 은 모든것을 포기하려것」이 라고 말했다.

鄭장관은 「근동안 시국의 흐름과 사회동향을 지켜본 결과 우리정치 사회 경제의 지속적인 발전을 위해 절대 다수의 국민들이 국가사회의 안정을 희구하고 있다는 사 실과 일부 극소수의 운동좌 경화운동과 급진주의자들의 작 태에 혐오감을 느끼고 있다 고 밝히고 「반드시가정의 반 사회적인 국가질서파괴행위 가 발복되는것을 더이상 방 관하지 않고 고위력을 총동 원, 단호히 대처하고 관련자 를 엄중조치하겠다」고 말 했다.

2감 로써야ㅂ.

정부 人権特委 발족

어제 첫 会議 위원장 李英燮씨…위원 28명 위촉

◇李英燮위원장

정부는 25일 국무총리직속기구인 인권보호특별위원회위원장에 李英燮전대법원장을 위촉하는등 모두 28명의 위원을 위촉하고 人権保護特委 제1차회의를 이날오후 국무총리대접견실에서 열었다. 〈관련기사 3면〉

인권보호특위는 올해 상반기중에 ▲임의동행제도 보호실제도등 인권침해가 가능성이있는 제도의 남용방지대책 ▲피의자조사과정에서의 인권침해방지등 수사구조개선 ▲수사공무원의 교육감독 강화등 단기적과제를 연구심의키로 했다.

또 하반기중에는 ▲형사소송법·特加法·경범죄 처벌법등 관련법규의 타당성및 실효성검토 ▲인권보호 관련기구의 운영강화 ▲국민의 인권의식 提高 ▲외국인권제도의 조사분석등을 연구심의키로 했다. 부위원장 및 위원은 다음과 같다.

▲부위원장 金道昶(한양大교협의부이사장) 朴金淎(한국부인회협의회장) 朴相熙(내무차관) 李種南(법무차관)朴鈗炘(법제처차장)李揆成(총리실행정조정실장)

▲위원 金泰淸 金斗鉉 朴承緒 崔光律(이상·변호사)裵載湜(서울大법대학장) 孫海睦(東国大교수)曺斗欽(한국일보주필) 崔鍾律(中央日報주필)李浩浩(朝鮮日報주필) 申東浩(서울신문논설주간)李斗洙(京郷新聞주필) 尹相哲(민족통일중앙협의회회장)池學淳(가톨릭慶州교구장)洪性徹(勞総위원장)徐義玄(불교조계종총무원장)金東仁(國際펜클럽한국지부부회장)田淑禧(文洪淑子(여성단체協부이사장)趙炳華(국제

THE CHRISTIAN SCIENCE MONITOR   MONDAY, FEBRUARY 9, 1987   8

Torture issue aids S. Korea opposition

By Maggie Ford
Special to The Christian Science Monitor

Seoul

South Korea's political opposition is gaining strong support from the nation's influential Christian church, along with academic, student, and human rights groups, for its stand against government use of torture.

Continuing public anger over the death of a student last month by police torture also appears to be hindering government efforts to achieve a consensus with the opposition over the type of elections that are to be held later this year.

Sunday night some 400 worshippers and 20 priests held a demonstration after a memorial service at Seoul's Anglican cathedral. The service was held in memory of Park Jong Chul, the student who died three weeks ago after police interrogators repeatedly forced his head into a tub of water.

There were no arrests or violence Sunday, unlike the day before when efforts were made to hold a similar service at the Roman Catholic cathedral. On Saturday, police detained some 800 people in clashes in the nation's four main cities. In Seoul, some 30,000 po-

lice were brought in to prevent mourners from reaching the cathedral. About 600 people attended the service, which was organized by a cross-section of political, religious, human rights, and student groups. After the mass, a resolution was adopted, calling on rulers to reveal all facts about the student's death, to release all political prisoners, and to hold direct presidential elections. The government favors parliamentary elections.

South Korea's main dissident leaders, Kim Dae Jung and Kim Young Sam, said the protest was successful, because thousands of people defied government warnings against participation.

Kim Dae Jung, who was placed under house arrest Sunday, said that the torture issue is having a strong effect on the growing middle class: "Even though he was not suspected of radicalism, this student was tortured and killed by the police," Kim said. "People think it could happen to their own sons and daughters."

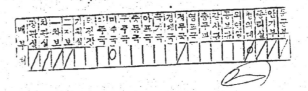

4A · MONDAY, FEBRUARY 9, 1987 · USA TODAY

S. KOREA DETAINS PROTESTERS:
South Korean police questioned 799 people held after anti-government protests in Seoul, Pusan and Kwangju over the weekend. By Sunday, house arrest restrictions were lifted for dozens of dissident leaders but continued for Kim Dae Jung, the best-known dissident.

The Washington Times | MONDAY, FEBRUARY 9, 1987 / PAGE 7A

S. Korea detains 700 protesters

FROM COMBINED DISPATCHES

SEOUL — South Korean authorities said yesterday they were questioning more than 700 people detained in a second round of violent anti-government demonstrations over the death of a student during police interrogation.

A police spokesman said most of the protesters, "except those found involved in extremely radical actions," would be freed today.

In police custody were 455 people in Seoul, 181 in the nation's second-largest city of Pusan and 102 in Kwangju, the scene of the bloody nine-day armed anti-government rioting in 1980.

Calm returned to the streets of Seoul, where clouds of tear gas hung in the air for hours Saturday after battles between demonstrators and riot police.

Violence broke out when police, in a massive show of force, blocked the roads to rallies that foes of President Chun Doo Hwan's government organized to protest the government ban on memorial rallies for Park Jong-chul, 21, a Seoul National University student, who died during police questioning.

According to an official investigation, Mr. Park died Jan. 14 after his throat was pressed against a bathtub during questioning by police about anti-government activities. Police had pushed his head under water twice.

Riots followed the first report of his death last month, and on Saturday demonstrators again hurled rocks and fire bombs at police, who fired back tear gas.

Estimates of the number of demonstrators involved varied from a few thousand to as many as 20,000 in Seoul alone. Reports said 70,000 police were mobilized across the country, and about 37,000 were deployed in Seoul.

By official count, 34 police were injured. There were no estimates on how many demonstrators were hurt.

By yesterday morning, house arrest restrictions that kept dozens of dissident leaders at home had been lifted. But Kim Dae-jung, South Korea's best-known opposition politician, was confined at home for the second time in two days.

Aides said the action was to prevent him from attending a memorial service at a downtown Anglican church building.

THE WALL STREET JOURNAL MONDAY, FEBRUARY 9, 1987 1

South Korean authorities placed opposition leader Kim Dae Jung under house arrest to prevent him from attending a prayer service for a student who died last month during a police interrogation. Officials in Seoul also began questioning nearly 800 people detained Saturday in violent anti-government rallies over the student's death.

USW(F)-131

3-2

0256

Chicago Tribune   Monday, February 9, 1987   Section 1   5

Agence France Presse photo

'The heavens weep' for slain student

Anglican church members carry a banner   Seoul Sunday to protest the death last month
reading "The heavens weep, the earth cries" in   of a student in police custody. Story, Page 5.

S. Korean dissenter corralled

From Chicago Tribune wires

SEOUL—South Korea's leading dissident, Kim Dae Jung, was placed under house arrest Sunday to stop him from attending a prayer meeting for a student who died during police questioning, his aides said.

Hundreds of police surrounded Kim's home to bar him from the meeting at a church in Seoul for Park Jong Chul, whose death last month brought widespread calls for an end to police use of torture.

Authorities, meanwhile, said they were questioning almost 800 people detained in violent antigovernment protests Saturday in Seoul as well as in Pusan and Kwangju. A dissident leader called the rallies a success, despite "barbarous" behavior by police.

Violence broke out in the capital when police blocked the roads to rallies that foes of President Chun Doo Hwan's government organized to protest Park's death. Demonstrators hurled rocks and fire bombs at police, who fired back barrages of tear gas.

Estimates of the number of demonstrators involved varied from a few thousand to as many as 20,000 in Seoul alone. Reports said 70,000 police were mobilized across the country, with about 37,000 of them deployed in Seoul.

Police said 799 demonstrators were detained across the country. They said Sunday that 34 had been released, with many others due to be freed.

The house detention of Kim was the 45th such move against him since he returned home from two years of self-imposed exile in the United States shortly before general elections in 1985. Kim's New Korea Democratic Party [NKDP] emerged as the main opposition group in that poll.

Kim, 61, a former presidential candidate. still is barred from politics because of a suspended 20-year jail term for sedition, but he controls the NKDP behind the scenes.

About 500 demonstrators marched Sunday night shouting antigovernment slogans after a mass for Park, a 21-year-old student who died Jan. 14while being questioned by two members of an anticommunist police unit.

The two policemen have been formally charged with torturing him to death.

USW-131
3-3

0257

보안
공제

편 호 : USW(F)- 221   0303 09)0

수 신 : 장관 (미북,정문,해신)   발신 : 주미대사

제 목 : 박종철군 49재   오대

The Washington Post
TUESDAY, MARCH 3, 1987 **A17**

Seoul Police Tear-Gas Marching Monks

■ SEOUL—Riot police fired tear gas at a dozen Buddhist monks today as they headed toward an opposition-sponsored memorial service for a student tortured to death while in police custody.

Organizers asked participants to meet at 15 locations around the city and march toward Pagoda Park for the traditional Buddhist 49th-day memorial rite for Park Chong Cul, 21, who authorities say was suffocated by police while held on suspicion of anti-government activities.

The government forbade the memorial ceremony, and police sources said 20,000 police were mobilized across the capital to break up any groups participating in the opposition-sponsored "peace marches" toward the park.

As a dozen Buddhist monks marched out of the Chogyesa Temple carrying a photograph of Park, riot police rushed the group, blocked their way and pushed them with their shields. The monks pushed back and police fired tear-gas bombs to disperse the marchers. About three monks were taken away by police, a witness said. There were no reports of injuries.

THE CHRISTIAN SCIENCE MONITOR   TUESDAY, MARCH 3, 1987   2

Police in South Korea go on alert for protests

Seoul

South Korea's 120,000 police went on highest alert Monday and dissident leader Kim Dae Jung was placed under house arrest as the authorities moved to foil opposition plans for nationwide protests scheduled for today.

The dissident-backed New Korea Democratic Party and rally organizers have vowed to defy an official ban on the demonstrations, called to protest alleged police torture and human rights abuses and to demand full democracy.

0258

S. Korea to use police to foil demonstrators

SEOUL (Reuters) — South Korean officials expressed confidence that a huge turnout of police would thwart opposition plans today for nationwide street demonstrations against President Chun Doo Hwan's government.

Officials of Mr Chun's Democratic Justice Party said they were less worried about what might happen today than at more distant prospects for dangerous confrontations over political reform.

"The government's official power should be able, as before, to deter the so-called grand peace marches without bloodshed," one DJP official said.

The showdown is due to take place three days before a scheduled visit here by U.S. Secretary of State George Shultz.

Authorities have accused the opposition of trying to use the marches, called to protest alleged police torture and human rights abuses, to create a mass uprising to overthrow the government.

The opposition charges that the government prohibits rallies to stifle democracy.

South Korea's 120,000 police were on alert to foil street protests planned in Seoul, Pusan, Taegu, Kwangju and other cities.

Nearly half of the police force will be mobilized to physically block all attempts at street protests and the rest will be on standby. In Seoul alone, some 30,000 policemen will be deployed, police said.

The government said purely religious indoor gatherings would be exempted from a general government ban.

The main opposition New Korea Democratic Party and rally organizers, who include Buddhist and Christian clergymen, said they would defy the injunction against the marches.

The rallies are also intended as memorials to Park Chong-chol, a student the government has admitted was tortured to death by police last month.

Police once again placed Kim Dae-jung, South Korea's best known dissident, and several of his colleagues under house arrest in Seoul to prevent them from taking part in the protests.

KOREAN POLICE GAS MONKS: South Korean police fired tear gas at a dozen Buddhist monks heading for an opposition-sponsored memorial service in Seoul early today. Police deployed 20,000 officers to block the service for a student tortured to death by police. Dissident leaders Kim Dae Jung and Kim Young Sam were put under house arrest to prevent their attendance.

221-2

0259

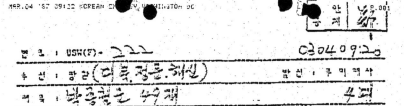 
The Washington Post

WEDNESDAY, MARCH 4, 1987 A25

Seoul Police Foil Rallies Commemorating Student

Protests Quashed Throughout South Korea

By John Burgess
Washington Post Foreign Service

TOKYO, March 3—Thousands of South Korean riot police, some of them firing tear gas grenades, today broke up by force another attempt by dissidents to stage a mass demonstration in Seoul, according to reports from the South Korean capital.

More than 1,000 students held simultaneous rallies at six campuses around the huge city, it was reported, but were unable to enter the streets due to blockades formed by rows of police and plainclothesmen.

The protests were called to mark the death of Park Chong Chul, a 21-year-old university student who died during police torture in January. Today was the 49th day since his death, an interval that is commemorated with special rites under the Buddhist religion.

Today's events were largely a replay of foiled rallies in November and February. The government banned those gatherings in advance and mobilized thousands of police who dispersed or arrested demonstrators before they could gather in significant numbers.

Today, opposition protests were also blocked by police in six other cities, including Pusan, Taegu and Kwangju. Police reported 395 arrests, 171 of them in Seoul, and 20 injuries, two classified as serious.

In Seoul, dissidents had planned a large march to a central square known as Pagoda Park. But the police blocked off the park and, in about two and a half hours of sporadic clashes, dispersed everyone who attempted to reach it.

At about 10 points around central Seoul, demonstrators succeeded in gathering in small groups. Some sang the national anthem and chanted slogans, including "End torture" and "Down with dictatorship," before being dispersed or arrested.

There was no reliable count of the demonstrators but observers said at least several thousand seemed to have taken part. Little violence from the demonstrators was reported and police were said to have used a lower level of force than is often the case.

At the headquarters of the opposition New Korea Democratic Party, meanwhile, rows of policemen physically prevented party president Lee Min Woo and associates from going out to join in the demonstration.

Dissident leaders Kim Dae Jung and Kim Young Sam were put under house arrest to prevent them from participating. Aides to Kim Dae Jung said it was his 49th house arrest since he returned to Seoul from exile two years ago. According to the Chosun Ilbo newspaper, house arrests today totaled about 70.

Dissidents said that the march was intended as a peaceful salute to the dead student. However, the government maintained the real purpose was violence. "They are trying to mobilize people and foster social unrest in Seoul," said National Police Director Lee Yong Chang, with the aim of "instigating a popular uprising to overthrow the government."

THE WALL STREET JOURNAL WEDNESDAY, MARCH 4, 1987

Demonstrators in Seoul clashed with almost 30,000 South Korean riot police during rallies to protest the Jan. 14 death of a student during police interrogation. Violent confrontations, which coincided with the sixth anniversary of President Chun's inauguration, also were reported in six other cities throughout South Korea.

The New York Times WEDNESDAY, MARCH, 1987 A3

Protesters in Seoul Routed by Tear Gas

By DAVID E. PITT
Special to The New York Times

SEOUL, South Korea, March 3 — Tens of thousands of riot police officers blocked an anti-Government march today before it could start, scattering protesters and passers-by with volleys of tear gas.

For days the Government had warned that Communists might try to turn what it called "this attempt to foster unrest" into an insurrection.

Today there were two reported incidents of gasoline bombs being thrown at the police — one in the capital, the other in the southern city of Kwangju. But most of the demonstrators in downtown Seoul were nonviolent, confining themselves to chanting anti-Government slogans, waving tiny Korean flags and occasionally showering the sidewalks with leaflets.

The attempted "grand march against torture and for democratization" was called by opposition and religious groups in memory of a university student who died in police custody Jan. 14. The authorities said he suffocated after his throat was crushed as he was held over the edge of a tub of water; the opposition New Korea Democratic Party has asserted that the cause of death was torture by electroshock.

Estimates of the number of demonstrators in Seoul ranged from the police figure of 1,500 to the opposition's of 30,000. The actual figure seemed in the neighborhood of 10,000. The police said 257 people had been detained in disturbances in the capital, as well as in the cities of Taegu and Kwangju.

In any event, the police far outnumbered the protesters, with 35,000 riot and tactical officers deployed in Seoul alone, and another 25,000 nationwide. There was a similarly vast show of force Feb. 7, when thousands of demonstrators rallied in Seoul and three other cities to mourn the torture death of the student, Park Jong Chul.

Today's march was called to mark the 49th day since the death of Mr. Park, a Buddhist. In Buddhism it is the point at which the soul is supposed to enter the next world. By coincidence, today also marked the beginning of President Chun Doo Hwan's seventh year in office.

The police, wearing Darth Vader-style helmets and carrying shields, confronted demonstrators who included college students, graying opposition politicians, Buddhist monks and businessmen on their lunch hour.

Chants of "Down with Chun!" and "Restore human rights!" were met with charges by the police and clouds of stinging tear gas. Passers-by caught between skirmish line dashed for safety, handkerchiefs clutched to their faces. Many blamed the authorities.

"You know we hate this military Government," an elderly man in a dark suit said through his handkerchief in English as he hurried by.

Anti-Government March Blocked in Korea (서울/뉴)

Lee Min Woo, left foreground, head of the opposition New Korea Democratic Party, at rally in Seoul. Riot police officers blocked the path of the march and scattered demonstrators with tear gas. Page A3.

Shopkeepers, many of whom had shuttered their windows for the day, also seemed outraged by the disruption. "Idiots, idiots," one muttered as he sought to sweep a white stain, caused by the explosion of a tear gas canister, from the pavement in front of his variety store.

The organizers of the rally, who included members of the opposition New Korea Democratic Party, seemed pleased by the results.

"We intended to have a peaceful rally and we did," said Kim Dae Jung, who is among 20 opposition leaders placed under house arrest Monday to keep them from attending the march.

"Last time, on Feb. 7, even though most people kept a peaceful attitude, some students' attitudes were radical," Mr. Kim said. "But now I think our moderate and nonviolent attitude has taken root. I am confident that in the future we can have a peaceful rally to get support, especially middle-class support."

Although Government officials had promised that indoor religious commemorations would be permitted, witnesses said the police had tear-gassed a column of 50 Buddhist monks and their followers as the group tried to enter their temple for 49th Day ceremonies. When the monks regrouped and tried to hold the rites outdoors, the police moved in again. Ten monks and students were reported detained.

Sixteen policemen were injured, two or three seriously, according to the national police chief, Lee Chung Chang. He said four civilians, apparently all opposition legislators, were slightly hurt.

222-2

0261

The Washington Times | WEDNESDAY, MARCH 4, 1987 / PAGE 9

Korean protesters fight police

SEOUL, South Korea (AP) — Demonstrators fought against nearly 50,000 riot police in hit-and-run clashes yesterday on the streets of Seoul during a day of remembrance for a student who died during police torture.

Confrontations also were reported in six other cities. Police said 20 people were hurt in all, two seriously, and 395 were detained.

At least four opposition lawmakers were injured, one seriously, in leading protesters against police, who fired tear gas and used shields and truncheons to fend off demonstrators.

The "Grand Peace Marches for Anti-Torture and Democratization" were called by the main opposition New Korea Democratic Party and 47 dissident and church groups to mark the 49th day of the death of dissident student Park Chong-chul, 21. A 49th-day rite is a Buddhist practice to mark the entry of the deceased person's soul into another world.

Mr. Park, a Seoul National University student, died Jan. 14 while being questioned by police using water torture.

National Police Director Lee Yong-chang said 20 people were put under house arrest.

Mr. Lee said 123 students were among those detained. He said 171 people were held in Seoul and 25 in Pusan.

THE CHRISTIAN SCIENCE MONITOR   WEDNESDAY, MARCH 4, 1987   2

Protesters battle police in Seoul demonstrations

Seoul

Demonstrators fought for hours against nearly 50,000 riot police in clashes yesterday on the streets of Seoul during a day of remembrance for a student who was killed during police torture. Violent confrontations were also reported in six other cities. Police said 20 people were hurt in all and 395 were detained.

222-3

0262

THE SUN

WEDNESDAY, MARCH 4, 1987

Confrontation in South Korea

Gas-masked riot police in Seoul, the South Korean capital, seized anti-government demonstrators yesterday during "Day of Remembrance" for a student who died while he was being questioned in January. Police said 20 people were injured and 395 were detained.

ASSOCIATED PRESS

0263

ﾛﾛ

W081

R

SOUTH KOREA-DISSIDENTS
(OUT OF ORDER)
RA

DEMONSTRATORS DETAINED FOR QUESTIONING AFTER RALLIES

SEOUL, SOUTH KOREA (AP) - SOME 439 PEOPLE WERE UNDER POLICE DETENTION WEDNESDAY FOLLOWING NATIONWIDE RALLIES WHICH DREW NEARLY 30,000 TO THE STREETS TO REMEMBER A STUDENT DISSIDENT WHO DIED UNDER POLICE TORTURE.

POLICE ALSO REPORTED 36 PEOPLE WERE INJURED, INCLUDING FIVE SERIOUSLY, WHEN DEMONSTRATORS CLASHED WITH RIOT POLICE TUESDAY IN SEOUL AND SIX OTHER CITIES. OPPOSITION GROUPS CLAIMED DOZENS WERE INJURED BUT GAVE NO SPECIFIC FIGURES.

BY NIGHTFALL, CALM HAD RETURNED TO SEOUL, WHERE REPORTS SAID 7,000 DEMONSTRATED IN 25 LOCATIONS THROUGHOUT THE DAY, BUT PROTESTS WERE REPORTED TO HAVE CONTINUED AFTER DARK FOR SEVERAL HOURS IN TWO MAJOR PROVINCIAL CITIES -- PUSAN, 400 KILOMETERS (250 MILES) SOUTHEAST OF SEOUL, AND KWANGJU, 320 KILOMETERS (200 MILES) SOUTHWEST OF SEOUL.

IN PUSAN, THE COUNTRY'S SECOND LARGEST CITY, THE NEWSPAPER CHOSUN ILBO SAID ABOUT 10,000 CITIZENS OCCUPIED DOWNTOWN STREETS AT ONE POINT BRIEFLY UNTIL THEY WERE BROKEN UP BY RIOT POLICE.

POLICE ALSO REPORTED THAT TUESDAY NEARLY 8,000 STUDENTS TOOK PART IN SEPARATE DEMONSTRATIONS AT 62 UNIVERSITIES AND COLLEGES ACROSS THE COUNTRY.

''WE SUCCEEDED IN ESTABLISHING A COMMON GROUND WITH THE GENERAL PUBLIC, ALTHOUGH OUR PEACEFUL MARCHES HAVE BEEN BLOCKED BY POLICE,'' SAID LEE MIN-WOO, PRESIDENT OF THE MAIN OPPOSITION NEW KOREA DEMOCRATIC PARTY, WHICH, ALONG WITH 47 DISSIDENT AND CHURCH GROUPS, HAD CALLED THE ''GRAND PEACE MARCHES FOR ANTI-TORTURE AND DEMOCRATIZATION.''

MORE
AP-NY-03-04-87 0319GMT

4

ﾑﾑ

0264

MSGⴺ
W065

R

SEOUL - SOUTH KOREA-DISSIDENTS 2

RA

THE RALLIES WERE CALLED TO MARK THE 49TH DAY AFTER THE DEATH OF PARK JONG-CHUL, A 21-YEAR-OLD STUDENT AT SEOUL NATIONAL UNIVERSITY, WHO DIED JAN. 14. A 49TH-DAY RITE IS A BUDDHIST PRACTICE MARKING THE ENTRY OF A DECEASED PERSON'S SOUL INTO ANOTHER WORLD.

THE NKDP AND DISSIDENT GROUPS CLAIMED ''DOZENS OF CIVILIANS'' WERE INJURED. ONE NKDP LAWMAKER, KIM BONG-UK, SUFFERED BURNS AROUND HIS LEFT EYE WHEN HE WAS HIT BY A TEAR GAS GRENADE. HE WAS TAKEN TO A HOSPITAL FOR TREATMENT.

BY WEDNESDAY MORNING, HOUSE ARREST RESTRICTIONS THAT KEPT DOZENS OF DISSIDENT LEADERS, INCLUDING OPPOSITION LEADERS KIM DAE-JUNG AND KIM YONG-SAM, AT HOME DURING THE RALLIES, HAD BEEN LIFTED.

THE GOVERNMENT WAS REPORTED TO HAVE MOBILIZED ABOUT 60,000 POLICE TO BLOCK THE OPPOSITION PROTESTS AFTER ALLEGING THAT THEY WERE ''BENT ON STIRRING EXTREME SOCIAL CONFUSION SEEKING TO OVERTHROW THE ESTABLISHED POLITICAL SYSTEM.''

IN SEOUL, ABOUT 50,000 POLICE WERE DEPLOYED IN KEY AREAS TO BLOCK DEMONSTRATORS FROM MARCHING TO A DOWNTOWN PARK WHERE ORGANIZERS HAD SCHEDULED A MEMORIAL RALLY.

TUESDAY ALSO MARKED THE START OF PRESIDENT CHUN DOO-HWAN'S SEVENTH AND LAST YEAR IN OFFICE. CHUN HAS SAID REPEATEDLY HE WILL STEP DOWN NEXT FEBRUARY WHEN HIS SEVEN-YEAR TERM ENDS. UNDER THE PRESENT CONSTITUTION, ONLY A SINGLE TERM IS ALLOWED.

END

AP-NY-03-04-87 0240GMT

5

0265

GLGL
EXR0111 3 /AFP-AM60
SKOREA-DEMO

POLICE ROUND UP 439 ANTI-GOVERNMENT DEMONSTRATORS

SEOUL, MARCH 4 (AFP) - AT LEAST 41 POLICEMEN WERE INJURED, FIVE OF THEM SERIOUSLY, IN VIOLENT CLASHES THROUGHOUT SOUTH KOREA WITH DEMONSTRATORS CALLING FOR MORE DEMOCRACY AND AN END TO TORTURE, POLICE SAID HERE WEDNESDAY.

THEY SAID THE POLICEMEN WERE INJURED TUESDAY DURING NATIONWIDE DEMONSTRATIONS CALLED BY THE OPPOSITION TO MARK THE END OF A 49-DAY MOURNING PERIOD FOR DISSIDENT STUDENT PARK CHONG-CHUL, WHO DIED UNDER POLICE TORTURE IN JANUARY.

LOCAL NEWSPAPERS SAID THAT ABOUT 11 CIVILIANS HAD BEEN INJURED IN CLASHES WITH POLICE TUESDAY, INCLUDING AN OPPOSITION MP AND TWO JOURNALISTS.

THE MOST SERIOUS PROTEST ERUPTED IN THE SOUTHWESTERN CITY OF KWANGJU WHERE STUDENTS ATTACKED A POLICE SUB-STATION WITH PETROL BOMBS. TWO POLICEMEN WERE TAKEN TO HOSPITAL SUFFERING FROM BURNS, REPORTS SAID.

POLICE HERE SAID THAT 439 PEOPLE, INCLUDING 293 STUDENTS, HAD BEEN DETAINED NATIONWIDE FOLLOWING TUESDAY'S DEMONSTRATIONS.

THEY SAID 193 DEMONSTRATORS HAD BEEN ARRESTED HERE TUESDAY, DURING A PROTEST MARCH BY SOME 7,000 PEOPLE CALLING FOR MORE DEMOCRACY AND AN END TO TORTURE.

PROSECUTION SOURCES SAID THAT ABOUT 20 OF THE 439 PEOPLE DETAINED WOULD BE FORMALLY ARRESTED AND CHARGED. THE REST WOULD EITHER BE RELEASED OR TRIED BEFORE A SUMMARY COURT IN A DAY OR TWO.

OPPOSITION AND DISSIDENT RELIGIOUS LEADERS WEDNESDAY ISSUED A STATEMENT DEMANDING THE IMMEDIATE RELEASE OF ALL THOSE DETAINED DURING TUESDAY'S MARCHES.

IT ADDED THAT THE 37-MEMBER ORGANIZING COMMITTEE OF TUESDAY'S DEMONSTRATIONS WOULD STAGE A 24-HOUR SIT-IN PROTEST AT THE NATIONAL COUNCIL OF CHURCHES HEADQUARTERS HERE IF POLICE REFUSED THEIR DEMAND BY 5 PM (0800 GMT) WEDNESDAY.

PKM/LD
AFP 040529 GMT MAR 87

6

0266

ZCZC HKA030 KHA003 NXI
UU HED HUP

R I
    KOREA 3-4
    SEOUL, MARCH 4 (UPI) -- POLICE HELD AND QUESTIONED 439 PEOPLE
WEDNESDY FOR INVOLVEMENT IN SPORADIC DEMONSTRATIONS IN SEOUL AND
OTHER CITIES PROTESTING THE DEATH OF A COLLEGE STUDENT AT THE HANDS
OF POLICE INVESTIGATORS.
    THOSE UNDER CUSTODY INCLUDED 293 STUDENTS WHO CLASHED WITH
POLICE TUESDAY WHILE TRYING TO STAGE +PEACE MARCHES+ IN MEMORY OF
PARK CHONG-CHUL, A 21-YEAR-OLD SEOUL NATIONAL UNIVERSITY STUDENT WHO
DIED WHILE UNDER POLICE INTERROGATION FOR DISSIDENT ACTIVITY.
    A LATEST REPORT SAID A TOTAL OF 8,300 STUDENTS STAGED RALLIES AND
DEMONSTRATIONS TUESDAY AT 62 UNIVERSITIES ACROSS THE COUNTRY AND PART
OF THEM TOOK TO THE STREET.
    IN SEOUL OPPOSITION POLITICIANS, DISSIDENTS, CHURCH CIRCLES AND
BUDDHIST MONKS TRIED TO STAGE MARCHES TO MARK THE 49TH DAY OF PARK'S
DEATH BUT THOUSANDS OF POLICE BLOCKED THE ATTEMPTS. YOUTHS CLASHED
WITH POLICE WHO FIRED TEAR GAS TO DISPERSE PROTESTORS.
    THOUGH A 49TH-DAY MEMORIAL RITE IS A BUDDHIST PRACTICE, A NUMBER
OF CHRISTIAN GROUPS JOINED IN THE ATTEMPTED MARCHES TO HONOR THE DEAD
STUDENT.
    IN PUSAN, SOUTH KOREA'S SECOND LARGEST CITY AND PARK'S HOMETOWN,
ABOUT 500 PEOPLE STAGED DEMONSTRATIONS OFF AND ON UNTIL LATE AT
NIGHT, POLICE SAID.
    POLICE SAID 41 POLICEMEN WERE INJURED DURING THE DAY, FIVE OF
THEM SERIOUSLY.
    MOST OF THOSE UNDER QUESTIONING WILL BE FREED WITH ADMONITION,
POLICE SAID, BUT THOSE WHO PLAYED LEADING ROLES IN THE +ILLEGAL+
DEMONSTRATIONS WILL FACE FORMAL CHARGES.
    PARK DIED ON JAN. 14 WHEN POLICE INVESTIGATORS FORCED HIS HEAD
INTO A TUB OF WATER CRUSHING HIS NECK ON THE RIM OF THE TUB. TWO
POLICE OFFICERS WERE ARRESTED AND INDICTED FOR MURDER THROUGH ACTS
OF ATROCITY.
UPI JK   7
CCCCQQE ZCZ
=03040141
NNNN

Los Angeles Times   Wednesday, March 4, 1987/Part I   5

S. Korean Demonstrators and Police Clash; 20 Hurt

SEOUL, South Korea (P)—Demonstrators fought for hours Tuesday against nearly 50,000 riot police in hit-and-run clashes on the streets of Seoul during a day of remembrance for a student who died during police torture.

Violent confrontations were also reported in six other cities. Police said that 20 people were hurt in all—two seriously—and that 395 were detained.

At least four opposition lawmakers were injured, one seriously, in leading protesters against police, who fired tear gas and used shields and truncheons to fend off demonstrators.

Tuesday's "Grand Peace Marches for Anti-Torture and Democratization" were called by the main opposition New Korea Democratic Party and 47 dissident and church groups to mark the 49th day after the death of Park Jong Chul, 21. The 49th-day rite is a Buddhist practice to mark the entry of the deceased person's soul into another world.

49 Days After Death

Park, a dissident student from Seoul National University, died Jan. 14 while being questioned by police using water torture. An official investigation found that Park died after his throat was pressed against a bathtub during police interrogation. President Chun Doo Hwan dismissed his home minister and the national police chief as a result. The government arrested two police officers in the case and promised steps to prevent any recurrence, but it accused the opposition of exploiting Park's death.

National Police Director Lee Yong Chang said Tuesday that 20 people were put under house arrest. But Dong-A Ilbo, the nation's biggest independent national daily newspaper, and Yonhap News Agency said at least 72 people, including top dissident leaders Kim Young Sam and Kim Dae Jung, were confined to their homes.

Lee said 123 students were among those detained. He said 171 people were held in Seoul and 25 in Pusan, the nation's second largest city, 205 miles southeast of the capital. Other arrests were made in Taegu, Kwangju and Taejon.

Demonstrations also were reported in Chonju, 120 miles south of Seoul, and Chongju, 70 miles south-southeast of the capital.

Despite the violence, police were largely in control of Tuesday's street actions, through which critics of the government sought to point up their demands for greater democracy and protection of human rights in South Korea.

The number of marchers obviously fell short of organizers' expectations. Many students chose to hold their own rallies on campus.

Chun's Seventh Year

The opposition protests clouded the start Tuesday of President Chun's seventh year in office. The usual tributes accorded Chun on such an occasion were buried in coverage of street clashes.

The South Korean constitution limits a president to seven years in office. Chun, a former general, has said several times he will step down in 1988 when his time is up.

Thousands of students and dissidents began marching from 15 different locations at noon, heading toward Pagoda Park in central Seoul.

3. 국제 사회 반응.

0269

관리
번호 87/280

김종훈
(총리서리쪽)
검위
UN과

주 영 대 사 관

영국(정) 723-//　　　　　　　　　　　　　1987. 1. 23.

수신 : 장관

참조 : 구주국장

제목 : 박종철 사망사건

　　　　연 : UKW-0136

　　　　연호 노신영 총리앞 Telex 및 본직앞 서한의 사본을　별첨과
같이 송부합니다.

　　　　첨부 : Telex 및 서한 사본 각 1부.　끝.

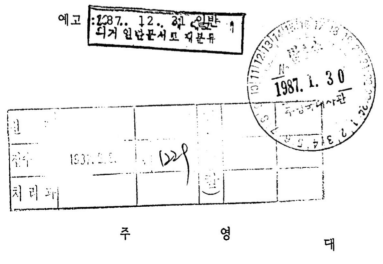

예고 : 1987.. 12.. 31 일반
되거 일반문서로 재분류

1987. 1. 30
주영국대사관

주　　　　　영　　　　　대

0270

87-01-19 18:15
007
EA085 18.16*
28502 AMNSTY G
KEY+80124651+
WOIMUBU K24651
28502 AMNSTY G
3237 87-01-19 18:16

PLEASE FORWARD TO HIS EXCELLENCY PRIME MINISTER LHO SHIN-YONG
REPUBLIC OF KOREA

REF.: 837/TG ASA/25/87.1
DATE: 19 JANUARY 1987

YOUR EXCELLENCY,

AMNESTY INTERNATIONAL IS DEEPLY CONCERNED AT REPORTS THAT PARK
CHONG-CHOL DIED ON 14 JANUARY IN CUSTODY OF THE ANTI-COMMUNIST BUREAU
OF THE NATIONAL POLICE IN NAMYOUNG-DONG, SEOUL AS A RESULT OF
TORTURE. AS YOU KNOW, AMNESTY INTERNATIONAL HAS BEEN CONCERNED ABOUT
FREQUENT REPORTS OF TORTURE AND ILL-TREATMENT AND OF SEVERAL DEATHS
IN CUSTODY, AT THE HANDS OF OFFICERS OF THE ANTI-COMMUNIST BUREAU OF
THE NATIONAL POLICE, THE ARMY SECURITY COMMAND AND THE AGENCY
FOR NATIONAL SECURITY PLANNING, OCCURING OVER THE LAST YEAR.

WHILE WELCOMING THE PROSECUTION AUTHORITIES' DECISION TO INVESTIGATE,
IN THIS INSTANCE, THE DEATH OF PARK CHONG-CHOL AND TO PROSECUTE TWO
POLICEMEN FOR TORTURING HIM TO DEATH, AMNESTY INTERNATIONAL URGES
YOUR EXCELLENCY'S GOVERNMENT TO ISSUE FIRM PUBLIC DIRECTIVES THAT
TORTURE AND ILL-TREATMENT OF DETAINEES IS PROHIBITED IN ALL CASES AND
THAT ITS USE WILL INVARIABLY LEAD TO PROSECUTIONS. AMNESTY
INTERNATIONAL ALSO RECOMMENDS THAT SPECIFIC INSTRUCTIONS BE GIVEN TO
ALL LAW ENFORCEMENT AGENCIES NOT TO RESORT TO SUCH PRACTICES. AMNESTY
INTERNATIONAL NOTES ANNOUNCEMENTS MADE TODAY BY THE HEAD OF THE
NATIONAL POLICE AND THE MINISTER OF HOME AFFAIRS THAT MEASURES WILL
BE TAKEN BY THE POLICE TO PREVENT THE TORTURE OF DETAINEES. AMNESTY
INTERNATIONAL WOULD APPRECIATE TO BE INFORMED OF THOSE MEASURES AND
WHETHER THEY INCLUDE AN EXPRESS PROHIBITION OF INCOMMUNICADO
DETENTION AND THE END OF DETENTION OF SUSPECTS IN PLACES OTHER THAN
REGULAR POLICE STATIONS, MEASURES WHICH WERE AMONG THE
RECOMMENDATIONS IN THE MEMORANDUM AMNESTY INTERNATIONAL SUBMITTED TO
YOUR EXCELLENCY'S GOVERNMENT IN AUGUST 1985.

YOURS SINCERELY AND RESPECTFULLY

IAN MARTIN
SECRETARY GENERAL

++++
+
WOIMUBU K24651
28502 AMNSTY G

0271

amnesty international

INTERNATIONAL SECRETARIAT
1 Easton Street London WC1X 8DJ
United Kingdom

Our reference:
TG ASA/25/87.2
Direct line:

His Excellency
Mr. Young Choo Kim
Ambassador Extraordinary and Plenipotentiary
Embassy of the Republic of Korea
4 Palace Gate
London W8 5NF

20 January 1987

Your Excellency,

I have the honour to enclose for Your Excellency's information a copy of a telex which the Secretary General of Amnesty International sent yesterday to His Excellency Prime Minister Lho Shin-yong. As Your Excellency will observe, this expresses Amnesty International's concern about the death of Mr. Park Chong-chol in police custody on 14 January 1987, reportedly as a result of torture. It also urges that the authorities of the Republic of Korea should make public their determination to prevent the torture of detainees and to prosecute all officials found to have committed such abuses, and to take concrete measures to prevent the torture and ill-treatment of detainees in the future.

I would be grateful if Your Excellency could arrange for Amnesty International to receive details of the legal proceedings against the police officers said to have tortured Mr. Park Chong-chol, as well as information on the measures Your Excellency's Government is taking to prevent the recurrence of torture in South Korea.

Yours sincerely and respectfully,

Larry Cox
for the Secretary General

Encl.

☎ 01-833 1771 Telegrams: Amnesty London WC1 Telex: 28502   0272

Amnesty International is an independent worldwide movement working impartially for the release of all prisoners of conscience, fair and prompt trials for political prisoners and an end to torture and executions. It is funded by donations from its members and supporters throughout the world. It has formal relations with the United Nations, Unesco, the Council of Europe, the Organization of African Unity and the Organization of American States

발 신 전 보

번 호: _WFR-0146_   일 시: _201231800_   전보종별: _____

수 신: 주불   대사·총영사

발 신: 장   관 (국연)

제 목: 인권 관련 자료 요청

　　　관계부처의 요청이니 주재국 인권성 (secretaire d'Etat
aupres du Premier ministre, chare des droite de
l'homme) 에 관한 아래자료를 조사, 지급보고 바람.

　　　가. 설치연혁

　　　나. 구성 - 기구 및 인원

　　　다. 임무, 기능, 업무등 (법무성및 내무성과의 업무협조 관계 포함)

　　　라. 업무실적

　　　마. 기타 참고자료   끝· (국장 -신기복)

예고 19 87. 12. 31. 일반문서로 재분류

보통문서로 재분류(8

검토필 (198 7. 6. 30.   보안
통제

		기안자	과 장	국 장	차 관	장 관	0273
앙고재	87년 1월 일	76경복		전결			외신과 접수자 통제

외 무 부 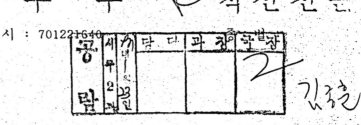 착신전보

번 호 : UKW-0136　　　일 시 : 701221640

수 신 : 장관(구일)

발 신 : 주 영 대사

제 목 : 박종철 사망사건

1. 당지 AMNESTY INTERNATIONAL 은 박종철 사망사건 관련, 동 단체가 아국정부
의 노신영 총리앞으로 보낸 TELEX 사본과 함께 상기 사건과 관련된 경찰 관리들에
대한 재판절차 및 아국정부가 고문 재발을 방지하기 위해 취하고 있는 조치에 대한
정보를 제공하여 줄것을 요청하는 서한을 본직에게 87.1.20. 보내왔음.

2. 동 단체는 상기 노신영 총리앞 TELEX 에서 고문에 의해 박종철이 사망한 것
에 대해 우려를 표명 하면서 아국정부 당국이 고문방지, 관련자 처벌등 구체적 조치
를 취할것을 요구하고 있음.

3. 노신영 총리앞 TELEX 및 본직앞 서한 사본 금주 파편 송부예정임.

(대사 김영주-국장)

예고 : 87. 6.30. 일반

구주국　차관실　1차보　정문국　청와대　총리실　안기

박종철사건 관련 국제사면위원회 사무총장 전보 처리
----

1. 전보 주요 내용

   o 박종철 사건보도에 깊은 관심을 표명

      - 국제사면위는 작년도에 치안본부, 보안사 및 안기부
        직원들에 의한 구금중 고문, 가혹행위 및 사망에 대한
        보고에 관심을 가졌음.

   o 금번사건에 대한 검찰의 수사 및 관련 경찰관의 기소등의
      조치를 환영하며, 수감자에 대한 고문 및 가혹행위가
      근절되도록 한국정부가 확고한 지침을 발표할 것을 요청함.

   o 국제사면위는 고문방지를 위한 조치를 경찰이 마련할 것이라는
      내무부장관 및 치안본부장의 발표에 유의하고, 상기조치의 내용이
      통보되기를 기대함.

0275

2. 대응조치

　○ 국제사면위 사무총장으로부터의 전보 인점을 감안、
　　금번사건과 관련하여 정부가 취한일련의 조치를 통보토록함·

　○ 다만、전보로 접수되었고、또한 국무총리앞 전보 발송 사례가
　　점증하는 실정에 비추어 총리 명의서한 발송 대신、주영대사가
　　국제사면위측에 금번 전보의 접수 사실을 확인하고 아국정부의
　　조치내용을 구두로 설명토록 함·

0276

WOIMUBU K24651
28502 AMNSTY G
3237 87-01-19 18:16

PLEASE FORWARD TO HIS EXCELLENCY PRIME MINISTER LHO SHIN-YONG
REPUBLIC OF KOREA

REF.: 837/TG ASA/25/87.1
DATE: 19 JANUARY 1987

YOUR EXCELLENCY,

AMNESTY INTERNATIONAL IS DEEPLY CONCERNED AT REPORTS THAT PARK
CHONG-CHOL DIED ON 14 JANUARY IN CUSTODY OF THE ANTI-COMMUNIST BUREAU
OF THE NATIONAL POLICE IN NAMYOUNG-DONG, SEOUL AS A RESULT OF
TORTURE. AS YOU KNOW, AMNESTY INTERNATIONAL HAS BEEN CONCERNED ABOUT
FREQUENT REPORTS OF TORTURE AND ILL-TREATMENT AND OF SEVERAL DEATHS
IN CUSTODY, AT THE HANDS OF OFFICERS OF THE ANTI-COMMUNIST BUREAU OF
THE NATIONAL POLICE, THE ARMY SECURITY COMMAND AND THE AGENCY
FOR NATIONAL SECURITY PLANNING, OCCURING OVER THE LAST YEAR.

WHILE WELCOMING THE PROSECUTION AUTHORITIES' DECISION TO INVESTIGATE,
IN THIS INSTANCE, THE DEATH OF PARK CHONG-CHOL AND TO PROSECUTE TWO
POLICEMEN FOR TORTURING HIM TO DEATH, AMNESTY INTERNATIONAL URGES
YOUR EXCELLENCY'S GOVERNMENT TO ISSUE FIRM PUBLIC DIRECTIVES THAT
TORTURE AND ILL-TREATMENT OF DETAINEES IS PROHIBITED IN ALL CASES AND
THAT ITS USE WILL INVARIABLY LEAD TO PROSECUTIONS. AMNESTY
INTERNATIONAL ALSO RECOMMENDS THAT SPECIFIC INSTRUCTIONS BE GIVEN TO
ALL LAW ENFORCEMENT AGENCIES NOT TO RESORT TO SUCH PRACTICES. AMNESTY
INTERNATIONAL NOTES ANNOUNCEMENTS MADE TODAY BY THE HEAD OF THE
NATIONAL POLICE AND THE MINISTER OF HOME AFFAIRS THAT MEASURES WILL
BE TAKEN BY THE POLICE TO PREVENT THE TORTURE OF DETAINEES. AMNESTY
INTERNATIONAL WOULD APPRECIATE TO BE INFORMED OF THOSE MEASURES AND
WHETHER THEY INCLUDE AN EXPRESS PROHIBITION OF INCOMMUNICADO
DETENTION AND THE END OF DETENTION OF SUSPECTS IN PLACES OTHER THAN
REGULAR POLICE STATIONS, MEASURES WHICH WERE AMONG THE
RECOMMENDATIONS IN THE MEMORANDUM AMNESTY INTERNATIONAL SUBMITTED TO
YOUR EXCELLENCY'S GOVERNMENT IN AUGUST 1985.

YOURS SINCERELY AND RESPECTFULLY

IAN MARTIN
SECRETARY GENERAL

++++

WOIMUBU K24651
28502 AMNSTY G

0277

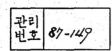

관리
번호 87-149

외 무 부   착 신 전 문

번 호 : FRW-0238   일 시 : 701290900   종 별 :

수 신 : 장관(국연,구일)

발 신 : 주불대사

제 목 : 인권관련 자료

대 : WFR-0146

대호, 당관 문하영서기관이 1.28(수) 주재국 인권성 국제문제 담당관   M.DE RAYMO
ND   과 면담, 파악한 내용을 하기 보고함

1. 설치연혁

가. 86.3.신임 쉬락행 정부의 출범과 함께 수상직속으로 인권담당 국무상직을 신설
함

나. 한편 전임 사회당 행정부하에는 인권 자문위원회(COMMISSION CONSULTATIVE DES
DROIT DE L'HOMME) 가 있었는바 동위원회도 계속 활동하고 있으며 현   CLAUDE MALH
URET   인권담당 국무상이 위원장을 겸직하고 있음

2. 구성

가. 동 인권성은 인권담당 국무상 밑에 비서실장,국제문제담당 보좌관 및 담당관,
국내문제담당 보좌관 및 담당관, 대의회관계 보좌관, 법률문제 보좌관, 공보관등 총 8
명의 주요요원과 기타 약간명의 실무급 행정요원, 비서등으로 구성되어 있는 매우 소
규모 조직임

나. 한편 인권자문위원회는 정부 각 관련부처 대표 1명 및 국내 인권 관계 단체장,
각계 저명인사등 총 40여명으로 구성되어 있으며 매달 1번 씩 정기회합을 개최하고
인권관계에 관한 각종문제 토의 및 자문을 하고 있음

3. 임무 및 기능

가. 인권담당 국무상의 임무는 86.4.17.공포된 법령 86-710호에 근거하고 있음. 국
내적으로 불란서에는 외국인이 다수 거주하므로 인종차별문제,피난민 보호문제가 주

국기국   구주국   1차년   정보국   청와대   안기부

PAGE 1   87.01.30 09:05
            외신 2과 통제관

0278

임무이고 이외 이혼가정의 자녀보호 및 양육문제,민간인의 서한에 따른 민원문제도 다루고 있음

나. 또한 인권성은 상기문제와 관련 주재국 내무성,법무성,보건성등이 입법을 할때 입법논의과정 부터 참여하여 협의 및 조언을 하고있으며 현재는 인권관계 법령도 직접 발안하여 각부처와 협의,성안중에 있음

다. 국제적으로는 인권관련 각정 정부간,비정부간 기구와 관련을 맺고 있으며 필요시 보조금을 지원하기도함. 또한 인권관계 국제협약 가입문제등을 외무성의 주관하 상호 사전협의를 하고있음

라. 또한 외무성을 통해 인권문제가 있다고 생각되는 각국의 현지공관을 통해 해외 인권사태에 대하여도 정기보를 받고 주의깊게 관찰하고 있음. 그리고 필요하다고 생각할 경우 특정 해외인권 탄압 사태를 비난하고 시정을 촉구하는 성명을 발표하고 있으며 몇몇 국가에게는 외교챈널을 통해 조용히 인권개선을 촉구하기도 하고있음

마. 결국 인권성은 국내외적으로 각종 인권사태에 대하여 필요시 조사하고 관계부처와 협의하고 있으므로 업무의 정형이나 현계는 없다고 보아야 할것임. 예를들어 인권성앞의 국제 및 국내 민원 서한은 하루 수천통에 다 할때가 많음

4. 타부처와의 업무협조 관게

가. 내무성은 피난민문제를 주관하고 있는바 동 피난민의 국제법상 난민자격 부여문제를 많이 협의하고 있음. 기타 공권력에 의한 인권탄압 사례 발생시에는 내무성에 인권담당 국무상의 명의로 설명을 요구하고 진상을 파악하고 있으나 이에대한 구체적 강제규정은 없으며 법령 86-710호에 의거한 일반적권한에 근거하고 있음

나. 법무성과는 인권관계 법령입안시 초기부터 수시로 의견교환 및 협의를 하고있음. 또한 외무성과는 국제인권사태 발생시 수시로 업무 협의하고 있음. 인권성은 모든 관련부처와 늘 업무협의를 하고 보고를 받고 있으며 따라서 담당관은 하루종일 전화에 매달리고 있는 경우가 많음

5. 기타

가. 그간 업무실적은 국제적으로 태국국경 근처 난민지원 및 아프간 난민지원등을 들수 있으며 국내적으로는 각종 입법협조,민원해결등 여러건 있음

PAGE 2

나. 그러나 타부커와 업무협조가 순조롭지 못할때도 솔직히 있으며 이경우 수상실 직속으로 소속되어 있는것이 도움될때가 많음

다. 미국과 알젠틴에 유사한 인권담당부서가 있는것으로 알고있는바 동국에 알아보는것이 참고가 될것임

6. 인권성 설치령(법령 86-710호)은 차주파편 송부함. 끝.

(대사 윤억섭-국장)

예고 :987. 12. 31. 일반녀고
외거 일반문서로 ㅈ

UN

김종훈

주　불　대　사　관

불정 760-115   1987. 2. 4

수신 장관

참조 국제기구국장

제목 주재국 인권성 관련자료 송부

　　　대 : WFR-0146

　　　연 : FRW-0238

　　　연호, 주재국 인권성 설치령 (법령 86-710호) 1부를 별첨 송부합니다.

　　　첨부 : 동 설치령 1부. 끝.

주　　　불　　　대

선 결		결		
접수일시	1987. 2. 7	재(공란)		
처리과	^07613			

Décret n° 86-710 du 17 avril 1986 relatif aux attributions du secrétaire d'Etat auprès du Premier ministre, chargé des droits de l'homme

Le Président de la République,

Sur le rapport du Premier ministre,

Vu le décret n° 47-233 du 23 janvier 1947 modifié autorisant les ministres à déléguer, par arrêté, leur signature ;

Vu le décret n° 84-72 du 30 janvier 1984 relatif à la commission consultative des droits de l'homme ;

Vu le décret du 20 mars 1986 portant nomination du Premier ministre ;

Vu le décret du 20 mars 1986 portant nomination des membres du Gouvernement,

Décrète :

Art. 1er. - M. Claude Malhuret, secrétaire d'Etat auprès du Premier ministre, chargé des droits de l'homme, anime et coordonne, sous l'autorité du Premier ministre et en liaison étroite avec les autres ministres concernés, la politique en matière de droits de l'homme en France.

Il est associé par le ministre des affaires étrangères à la définition et à la mise en œuvre de la politique française en cette matière dans les organisations intergouvernementales ainsi qu'à la négociation des conventions internationales sur ce sujet.

Il se tient en rapport avec les organisations non gouvernementales qui agissent en faveur du respect des droits de l'homme.

Art. 2. - Par délégation du ministre des affaires étrangères, il exerce les attributions conférées au ministre des relations extérieures par les articles 3 à 5 du décret du 30 janvier 1984 susvisé.

Art. 3. - La délégation interministérielle aux réfugiés est mise à la disposition du secrétaire d'Etat pour l'exercice de ses attributions.

Art. 4. - Le secrétaire d'Etat auprès du Premier ministre, chargé des droits de l'homme, fait appel en tant que de besoin aux services compétents des départements ministériels, notamment du ministère de la justice, du ministère de la culture et de la communication, du ministère des affaires étrangères, du ministère de l'intérieur, du ministère de l'éducation nationale, du ministère des affaires sociales et de l'emploi et du ministère de la coopération.

Art. 5. - M. Claude Malhuret reçoit délégation du Premier ministre pour signer en son nom tous actes, arrêtés et décisions dans la limite des attributions mentionnées ci-dessus. Il contresigne les décrets relatifs aux mêmes attributions. Il est autorisé à déléguer sa signature dans les conditions prévues par le décret du 23 janvier 1947 susvisé.

Art. 6. - Le Premier ministre, le garde des sceaux, ministre de la justice, le ministre de la culture et de la communication, le ministre des affaires étrangères, le ministre de l'intérieur, le ministre de l'éducation nationale, le ministre des affaires sociales et de l'emploi et le ministre de la coopération sont chargés, chacun en ce qui le concerne, de l'exécution du présent décret, qui sera publié au *Journal officiel* de la République française.

Fait à Paris, le 17 avril 1986.

FRANÇOIS MITTERRAND

Par le Président de la République :

Le Premier ministre,
JACQUES CHIRAC

Le garde des sceaux, ministre de la justice,
ALBIN CHALANDON

Le ministre de la culture et de la communication,
FRANÇOIS LÉOTARD

Le ministre des affaires étrangères,
JEAN-BERNARD RAIMOND

Le ministre de l'intérieur,
CHARLES PASQUA

Le ministre de l'éducation nationale,
RENÉ MONORY

Le ministre des affaires sociales et de l'emploi,
PHILIPPE SÉGUIN

Le ministre de la coopération,
MICHEL AURILLAC

0282

발 신 전 보

번 호 : UNK-0319   일 시 : 703031230   전보종별 : _____

수 신 : 주 영   대사·총영사

발 신 : 장   관 (국연)

제 목 : 박종철 사망 사건

대 : UNW-0136

대호 관련、본부는   Ian Martin   국제사면위 (AI)

사무총장 방한 문제를 기본적으로 동인의 방한에 협조한다는

자세에서 관계부처와 협의중인 바、동 사무총장의 방한 실현시

대호 1항 요청 정보를 제공 예정임을 귀관 참고로 함. (국기국장 - 김세택)

필요시 이를 AI 측에 통보 바람.

예고 : 87. 6. 30. 일반

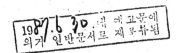

0283

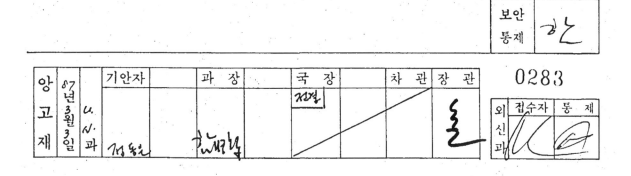

앙 고 재	87 년 3 월 3 일	U. N. 과	기안자	과 장	국 장	차 관	장 관	외 신 과	접수자	통제

주 　제　 내 　바 　대 　표 　부

제네(정) 2032　　〔발송〕　　　　　　　　1987. 4. 7.

〔1987. 4. 3〕

수신 : 장관

참조 : 국제기구조 약국장, 정보 문화국 장

제목 : 세계 기독교 협의회 (WCC)아국 관련 기사 보고

　　　연 : 제네(정) 20322-228 (87.3.20)

　　　당지 WCC 발간　　Ecumenical Press Service
제 8호 및 제 11호에 박종철 사건 관련기사가 게재된바, 동 기사를
별첨 송부 합니다.

　　　첨부 : 기사 2부.　끝.

　　　　주 　제 　내 　바 　대

선 결			결재 (공람)		
접수일시	1987.4. 7	번호			
처리과	020956				

0284

ECUMENICAL PRESS SERVICE

Box 66 CH-1211 Geneva 20.   Telephone (022) 91 61 42   Telex 23 423 OIK CH   Cable Oikoumene Geneva.   Editor Tom Dorris.

1-10 March 1987   year 54 / issue 08

0285

Ecumenical Press
Service <u>87.03.03</u>

SEOUL - Moderator Chang Dong Jin of the Presbyterian Church of Korea and Cho
Nam Ki, who chairs its human rights committee, have protested the death of
student Park Jong Ch'ol, who "died under torture" at national police
headquarters in mid-January. "We are deeply shocked and greatly incensed",
say the Presbyterian leaders. They called the death, and continuing torture
by police, a "disgrace to our society" which "must stop immediately". Because
of these and other reasons, "it is difficult to recognize" the current
government as "the government of the people", say Chang and Cho, urging those
in office to "turn now and repent of their sins".

Other South Korean church leaders have also spoken out in reaction to the
death, as have such US bodies as the Presbyterian Church (USA) and the
32-denomination National Council of Churches.

The government reportedly made major efforts to limit attendance at a memorial
service for Park, in the Roman Catholic cathedral here (7 February). Buses
and trains were not allowed to stop within a mile of the cathedral, and an
estimated 30,000 riot police kept student and worker activists and political
opposition groups away. About 1000 people attended.

The committee organising the memorial service included opposition political
leaders, Quaker pacifist Hahm Sok-hoon, Stephen Kim Sou-hwan (the Roman
Catholic cardinal archbishop here), and other Christian and Buddhist figures.
In all, 27 memorial gatherings were planned throughout the country during the
week. Two policemen have been charged with Ch'ol's death. [EPS]

**US: CHURCH UNION UNIT
CONSIDERS 'MARKETING'**

Ecumenical Press
Service <u>87.03.04</u>

This item is based on material from Religious News Service.

PRINCETON (New Jersey) - The Consultation on Church Union, a 25-year-old
effort to unite nine US denominations, is now turning its attention to the
best ways to encourage leaders and members of the nine to move forward with
COCU proposals for visible unity.

David Taylor, a Presbyterian minister who was named last year to direct COCU
strategy and interpretation, says it is important to identify "what our
product is, who our market is, what motives we can appeal to, and what
resources we have." He said decision-making bodies of COCU members would
approve COCU proposals "only if you tap into their perceived self-interest".

Some members of the existing denominations fear the size of the proposed
united denomination (more than 20 million members), or that it would mean
unacceptable changes in theology and/or church order, or that it would reduce
contacts with members of their tradition in other parts of the world.

One part of the marketing could be a new videotape, "Being One Can Be Fun".
The consultation's next plenary, at the end of 1988 in New Orleans, is
considered a "window of opportunity" for their proposals - a theological
consensus (on ministry, worship, sacraments, and doctrine), a covenanting
proposal, and liturgies for initiating the new relationships.

COCU includes four Methodist denominations (UMC, CMC, AME, AMEZ), the
[Anglican] Episcopal Church, Christian Church (Disciples of Christ), United
Church of Christ, International Council of Community Churches, and
Presbyterian Churh (USA). [EPS]

0286

ECUMENICAL PRESS SERVICE

Box 66 CH-1211 Geneva 20.   Telephone (022) 91 61 42.   Telex 23 423 OIK CH.   Cable Oikoumene Geneva.   Editor Tom Dorris.

26-31 March 1987   year 54 / issue 11

Ecumenical Press Service provides news and information about the ecumenical movement. Its material may be freely reproduced with acknowledgement. EPS is a service of the World Council of Churches in partnership with the World Student Christian Federation, the World Alliance of YMCAs, and the World YWCA. Opinions expressed are not necessarily those of the WCC or the partners.

0287

PNG: Church campaigns against 'cultural alcoholism'   EPS 87.03.99

LAE - The Evangelical Lutheran Church of Papua New Guinea has launched an extensive campaign to combat "cultural alcholism" in the country. Until the country gained its independence from Australia (1967), alcohol consumption was prohibited. Once the ban was lifted, drinking became widespread, since alcohol was associated with the power, knowledge, and money of the former colonial rulers. The consumption of beer in particular has become a strong tradition, playing an important part in the exchange of gifts, and putting would-be abstainers under intense peer pressure. The church campaign includes an alcohol-education project in its three seminaries, where young theologians are trained to deal with cultural alcoholism in their future ministries. The seminarians also go out to show movies or slides, hold group discussions, and distribute papers on the effects of alcoholism. [EPS]

Creole Bibles for Mauritius/Seychelles   EPS 87.03.100

PORT LOUIS (Mauritius) - With Bible Society, Roman Catholic, Anglican, and Reformed (Presbyterian) support, a project has been launched to translate the scriptures into the Creole language used in these two Indian Ocean island nations. There is currently little official church use of Creole, which is spoken by nearly everyone. [EPS]

US: NCC denies charges of interference in Philippines   EPS 87.03.101

NEW YORK - The 32-denomination [US] National Council of Churches has denied claims by the Institute for Religion and Democracy that US church groups, particularly the United Methodist Church, are seeking to undermine the government of Philippine President Corazon Aquino by supporting communist rebels. Responding to the IRD charges, NCC General Secretary Arie Brouwer said, "Political distortion under the guise of religion...is a severe threat to the freedom of the people of both the Philippines and the United States, as well as to the integrity of the church." [EPS]

Philippines: women religious call for removal of US base   EPS 87.03.102

OLONGAPO CITY - An association of members of Roman Catholic religious orders for women in Zambales (AWRIZ) have criticized the Columban Fathers, a group of priests, who work in the area of Subic Bay, because, the women say, the priests are not concerned about the serious problems caused by the US naval base there. The women mention "sexual exploitation of women and children, drug addiction of the youth, steady increase of orphaned Amerasian children, disintegration of family values ... the moral degradation of our people", and call for removal of the base. Among Olongapo's population of 230,000, there are about 16,000 prostitutes and 500 night clubs, many of which are owned by city politicians. Olongapo is one of the two Philippine towns in which the disease Aids has been discovered. The other one is Angeles, situated just outside a US air base. [EPS]

South Korea: unrest over torture death continues   EPS 87.03.103

SEOUL - Following a public outcry against the death of a 21-year-old student who was in police custody [EPS 87.03.03], the Christian Broadcast System aired a two-hour live programme entitled "Torture Should be Eradicated Once and for All". The programme was cut short without explanation. Since public memorial services for the student, Park Chong Chol, were curtailed by police, the major opposition party and other groups organized a national day of mourning, and the National Council of Churches of Korea (NCCK) declared the following Sunday as "Anti-Torture Sunday". The student's death was first announced as "due to shock", but, under pressure, the government investigated and later announced that the death was due to water torture. Opposition groups have demanded an independent investigation, charging that the victim's wounds indicated electric-shock torture as well. While officials say the case is an isolated incident, opposition leaders and dissidents claim that it is "the tip of the iceberg". [EPS]

0288

외교문서 비밀해제: 한국 인권문제 16

한국 인권문제 민주화 관련 기타 자료 1

초판인쇄 2024년 03월 15일
초판발행 2024년 03월 15일

지은이 한국학술정보(주)
펴낸이 채종준
펴낸곳 한국학술정보(주)
주 소 경기도 파주시 회동길 230(문발동)
전 화 031-908-3181(대표)
팩 스 031-908-3189
홈페이지 http://ebook.kstudy.com
E-mail 출판사업부 publish@kstudy.com
등 록 제일산-115호(2000. 6. 19)

ISBN   979-11-7217-070-7 94340
       979-11-7217-054-7 94340 (set)